Middle School 3-1
중간고사 완벽대비

적중 100

영어 기출 문제집

중3

천재 | 이재영

Best Collection

구성과 특징

교과서의 주요 학습 내용을 중심으로 학습 영역별 특성에 맞춰 단계별로 다양한 학습 기회를 제공하여
단원별 학습능력 평가는 물론 중간 및 기말고사 시험 등에 완벽하게 대비할 수 있도록 내용을 구성

Words & Expressions

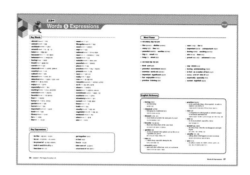

Step1 Key Words 단원별 핵심 단어 설명 및 풀이
       Key Expression 단원별 핵심 숙어 및 관용어 설명
       Word Power 반대 또는 비슷한 뜻 단어 배우기
       English Dictionary 영어로 배우는 영어 단어

Step2 실력평가 단원별 수시평가 대비 주관식, 객관식 문제풀이

Step3 서술형 대비 학업성취도 및 수행능력평가 대비 서술형 문제풀이

Conversation

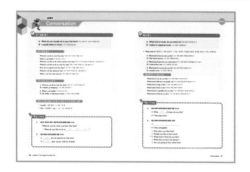

Step1 핵심 의사소통 소통에 필요한 주요 표현 방법 요약
       핵심 Check 기본적인 표현 방법 및 활용능력 확인

Step2 대화문 익히기 교과서 대화문 심층 분석 및 확인

Step3 교과서 확인학습 빈칸 채우기를 통한 문장 완성 능력 확인

Step4 기본평가 시험대비 기초 학습 능력 평가

Step5 실력평가 단원별 수시평가 대비 주관식, 객관식 문제풀이

Step6 서술형 대비 학업성취도 및 수행능력평가 대비 서술형 문제풀이

Grammar

Step1 주요 문법 단원별 주요 문법 사항과 예문을 알기 쉽게 설명
       핵심 Check 기본 문법사항에 대한 이해 여부 확인

Step2 기본평가 시험대비 기초 학습 능력 평가

Step3 실력평가 단원별 수시평가 대비 주관식, 객관식 문제풀이

Step4 서술형 대비 학업성취도 및 수행능력평가 대비 서술형 문제풀이

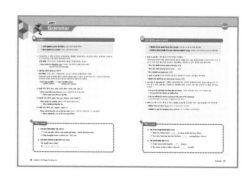

Reading

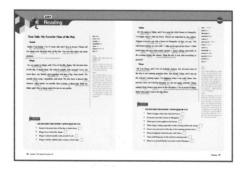

Step1 구문 분석 단원별로 제시된 문장에 대한 구문별 분석과 내용 설명
       확인문제 문장에 대한 기본적인 이해와 인지능력 확인

Step2 확인학습A 빈칸 채우기를 통한 문장 완성 능력 확인

Step3 확인학습B 제시된 우리말을 영어로 완성하여 작문 능력 키우기

Step4 실력평가 단원별 수시평가 대비 주관식, 객관식 문제풀이

Step5 서술형 대비 학업성취도 및 수행능력평가 대비 서술형 문제풀이
       교과서 구석구석 교과서에 나오는 기타 문장까지 완벽 학습

Composition

|영역별 핵심문제|

단어 및 어휘, 대화문, 문법, 독해 등 각 영역별 기출문제의 출제 유형을 분석하여 실전에 대비하고 연습할 수 있도록 문제를 배열

|단원별 예상문제|

기출문제를 분석한 후 새로운 시험 출제 경향을 더하여 새롭게 출제될 수 있는 문제를 포함하여 시험에 완벽하게 대비할 수 있도록 준비

|서술형 실전 및 창의사고력 문제|

학교 시험에서 점차 늘어나는 서술형 시험에 집중 대비하고 고득점을 취득하는데 만전을 기하기 위한 학습 코너

|단원별 모의고사|

영역별, 단계별 학습을 모두 마친 후 실전 연습을 위한 모의고사

교과서 파헤치기

- **단어Test1~3** 영어 단어 우리말 쓰기, 우리말을 영어 단어로 쓰기, 영영풀이에 해당하는 단어와 우리말 쓰기
- **대화문Test1~2** 대화문 빈칸 완성 및 전체 대화문 쓰기
- **본문Test1~5** 빈칸 완성, 우리말 쓰기, 문장 배열연습, 영어 작문하기 복습 등 단계별 반복 학습을 통해 교과서 지문에 대한 완벽한 습득
- **구석구석지문Test1~2** 지문 빈칸 완성 및 전문 영어로 쓰기

Contents

Lesson 1

What Matters to You?

🔧 의사소통 기능

- 감정 표현하기
  A: It's going to rain all day long.
  B: Really? I'm glad I can wear my new raincoat.

- 동의하기
  A: I think the most boring day of the week is Monday.
  B: You can say that again.

🔧 언어 형식

- 관계대명사 what
  They didn't tell me **what** I wanted to know.

- 지각동사+목적어+동사원형
  I **saw** Mom **come** into my room.

Words & Expressions

Key Words

- **allowance** [əláuəns] 몡 용돈
- **amazing** [əméiziŋ] 혱 놀라운
- **animation** [ænəméiʃən] 몡 애니메이션, 만화 영화
- **appear** [əpíər] 동 나타나다
- **boring** [bɔ́ːriŋ] 혱 지루한
- **chase** [tʃeis] 동 추적하다
- **chest** [tʃest] 몡 상자, 가슴
- **chew** [tʃuː] 동 씹다
- **delighted** [diláitid] 혱 기쁜
- **faraway** [fáːrəwèi] 혱 멀리 떨어진
- **goods** [ɡudz] 몡 상품
- **greatly** [ɡréitli] 뷰 매우
- **hurry** [hɔ́ːri] 동 서두르다
- **include** [inklúːd] 동 포함하다
- **invention** [invénʃən] 몡 발명, 발명품
- **jealous** [dʒéləs] 혱 질투하는
- **jewel** [dʒúːəl] 몡 보물
- **kitten** [kítn] 몡 새끼 고양이
- **merchant** [mɔ́ːrtʃənt] 몡 상인
- **pack** [pæk] 동 짐을 꾸리다, 가득 채우다
- **palace** [pǽlis] 몡 궁전
- **pleased** [pliːzd] 혱 기쁜
- **prepare** [pripɛ́ər] 동 준비하다
- **present** [prizént] 동 주다, 선사하다
- **priceless** [práislis] 혱 소중한
- **puzzled** [pʌ́zld] 혱 당황스러운
- **raincoat** [réinkòut] 몡 비옷
- **rat** [ræt] 몡 쥐
- **realize** [ríːəlàiz] 동 깨닫다
- **relax** [rilǽks] 동 쉬다
- **repay** [ripéi] 동 갚다
- **servant** [sɔ́ːrvənt] 몡 하인
- **serve** [səːrv] 동 음식을 날라 주다
- **speechless** [spíːtʃlis] 혱 말문이 막힌
- **spice** [spais] 몡 향료
- **subject** [sʌ́bdʒikt] 몡 과목
- **tool** [tuːl] 몡 도구, 연장
- **trade** [treid] 동 무역하다, 교역하다
- **valuable** [vǽljuəbl] 혱 소중한
- **whisper** [hwíspər] 동 속삭이다
- **wonder** [wʌ́ndər] 동 놀라워하다
- **worthless** [wɔ́ːrθlis] 혱 가치 없는

Key Expressions

- **a walking dictionary** 살아 있는 사전, 만물박사
- **after a while** 잠시 후에
- **all day long** 하루 종일
- **be sure that** ~ ~을 확신하다
- **Break a leg!** 행운을 빌어!
- **chase A away** A를 쫓아내다
- **get a chance to** ~ ~할 기회를 얻다
- **get over** 극복하다
- **Good for you.** 잘했다.
- **have two left feet** 동작이 어색하다
- **in history** 역사적으로
- **student card** 학생증
- **support ~ by trading** 무역으로 ~을 부양하다
- **take a picture** 사진을 찍다
- **take care of** ~ ~을 돌보다
- **take ~ hard** ~을 심각하게 받아들이다
- **tell the time** 시간을 알아보다
- **thanks to** ~ ~ 덕택에
- **weather report** 일기예보
- **What a surprise!** 정말 놀랍구나!
- **You can say that again.** 네 말이 맞아.

Word Power

※ 서로 비슷한 뜻을 가진 어휘

- □ **amazing** 놀라운 : **surprising** 놀라운
- □ **chase** 추적하다 : **follow** 뒤따르다
- □ **delighted** 기쁜 : **pleased** 기쁜
- □ **jealous** 질투하는 : **envious** 부러워하는
- □ **merchant** 상인 : **dealer** 상인
- □ **play** 연극 : **drama** 연극
- □ **present** 주다, 선사하다 : **give** 주다
- □ **puzzled** 당황스러운 : **embarrassed** 당황한
- □ **tool** 도구, 연장 : **device** 기구

- □ **boring** 지루한 : **dull** 지루한
- □ **chest** 상자 : **box** 상자
- □ **goods** 상품 : **product** 상품
- □ **jewel** 보물 : **treasure** 보물
- □ **pack** 가득 채우다 : **fill** 채우다
- □ **pleased** 기쁜 : **glad** 기쁜
- □ **priceless** 소중한 : **valuable** 소중한
- □ **relax** 휴식을 취하다 : **rest** 쉬다
- □ **worthless** 가치 없는 : **valueless** 가치 없는

※ 서로 반대의 뜻을 가진 어휘

- □ **appear** 나타나다 ↔ **disappear** 사라지다
- □ **delighted** 기쁜 ↔ **sorrowful** 슬퍼하는
- □ **include** 포함하다 ↔ **exclude** 제외하다
- □ **happy** 행복한 ↔ **unhappy** 불행한
- □ **priceless** 소중한 ↔ **worthless** 가치 없는

- □ **boring** 지루한 ↔ **exciting** 흥미진진한
- □ **glad** 기쁜 ↔ **sad** 슬픈
- □ **pack** 짐을 꾸리다 ↔ **unpack** 짐을 풀다
- □ **popular** 인기 있는 ↔ **unpopular** 인기 없는

English Dictionary

□ **allowance** 용돈
→ an amount of money that you are given regularly or for a special purpose
규칙적으로 또는 특별한 목적을 위하여 주어지는 상당한 양의 돈

□ **animation** 만화 영화
→ a film, television programme, computer game, etc that has pictures, clay models, etc that seem to be really moving
실제로 움직이는 듯한 그림, 점토 모형 등을 가진 영화, TV 프로그램, 컴퓨터 게임 등

□ **chase** 추적하다
→ to quickly follow someone or something in order to catch them
붙잡기 위하여 어떤 사람 또는 무엇인가를 빠르게 쫓아가다

□ **chest** 상자
→ a large strong box that you use to store things in or to move your personal possessions from one place to another
물건을 옮기거나 보관하기 위하여 사용하는 크고 튼튼한 상자

□ **include** 포함하다
→ to make someone or something part of a larger group
무엇인가를 더 큰 집단의 한 부분으로 만들다

□ **merchant** 상인
→ someone who buys and sells goods in large quantities
대량으로 물건을 사고파는 사람

□ **pack** 짐을 꾸리다
→ to put things into cases, bags, etc ready for a trip somewhere
어딘가로 여행할 준비로 물건을 상자, 가방 등에 넣다

□ **servant** 하인
→ someone, especially in the past, who was paid to clean someone's house, cook for them, answer the door, etc
집을 청소하기, 요리하기, 손님맞이 등을 위하여 고용된 사람

[01~02] 다음 대화의 빈칸에 들어갈 말을 고르시오.

01

A: It's going to rain all day long.
B: Really? I'm glad I can _____ my new raincoat.

① wash   ② choose
③ repay   ④ wear
⑤ wonder

02

A: I think the most boring day of the week is Monday.
B: You can _____ that again.

① speak   ② say
③ talk   ④ hear
⑤ wonder

[03~04] 다음 빈칸에 들어갈 말로 적절한 것을 고르시오.

03

The merchant went to different places to _____ his family by trading.

① support   ② call
③ move   ④ communicate
⑤ visit

04

One day, the merchant filled his ship with _____ and visited a faraway island.

① consumers   ② values
③ goods   ④ lists
⑤ areas

05 다음 중 밑줄 친 부분의 뜻풀이가 바르지 않은 것은?

① It's going to rain all day long. (비가 내리다)
② I think the most boring day of the week is Monday. (지루한)
③ The food looks so delicious. (맛있는)
④ I don't agree with you on that issue. (동의하다)
⑤ I didn't know you didn't like the plan. (~같은)

06 다음 빈칸에 알맞은 말이 바르게 짝지어진 것은?

• Some servants chased rats _____ with sticks.
• Rix got a rabbit from a friend and did his best to take good care _____ it.

① on – for   ② along – in
③ back – with   ④ off – on
⑤ away – of

07 다음 영영풀이에 해당하는 단어를 고르시오.

to bite food several times before swallowing it

① punch   ② chase
③ chew   ④ trade
⑤ present

서답형

08 다음 주어진 단어를 이용해 빈칸을 완성하시오.

There are many great _____ around us.

➡ _____ (invent)

01 다음 짝지어진 단어의 관계가 같도록 빈칸에 알맞은 말을 쓰시오. (주어진 철자로 시작할 것)

amazing : s_____ = boring : dull

02 다음 영어 풀이에 해당하는 단어를 주어진 철자로 시작하여 쓰시오.

an amount of money that you are given regularly or for a special purpose

➡ a_____

03 다음 짝지어진 단어의 관계가 같도록 빈칸에 알맞은 말을 쓰시오. (주어진 철자로 시작할 것)

appear : disappear = b_____ : exciting

[04~05] 다음 대화의 빈칸에 들어가기에 적절한 단어를 주어진 철자로 시작하여 쓰시오.

04

Many people will agree that paper is the greatest invention. T_____ _____ paper, we all can read books and write things down.

05

- I need some time to relax. We all need to do something to g_____ _____ stress.
- I will g_____ _____ this difficulty by myself.
- He will help you to g_____ _____ your broken heart.

[06~07] 내용상 다음 주어진 빈칸에 들어가기에 적절한 단어를 쓰시오. (주어진 철자로 시작할 것)

06

Antonio asked, "Are there no cats on this island?" The queen looked p_____. "What is a cat?" she asked.

07

After a while, the servant returned with a box, and the queen p_____ it to Luigi. When Luigi opened the box, he was speechless.

08 다음 밑줄 친 단어와 의미가 같은 단어를 쓰시오. (주어진 철자로 시작할 것)

You can say that again! Mom would love it as a birthday <u>present</u>.

➡ g_____

09 다음 우리말에 맞게 빈칸에 알맞은 말을 쓰시오.

(1) 우리는 목요일에 어려운 과목이 모두 있어.
  ➡ We have all the difficult _____ on Thursday.
(2) 너는 서둘러서 돌아가야 해.
  ➡ You must _____ to go back.
(3) 너는 어떤 종류의 학교를 염두에 두고 있니?
  ➡ What kind of school do you have in _____?

Conversation

① 감정 표현하기

> • I'm glad I can wear my new raincoat. 새로 산 비옷을 입게 되어 기뻐.

- 'I'm glad I can wear my new raincoat.'는 자신의 감정 상태를 나타내는 표현이다. 'I'm 감정 형용사 ~'로 표현하며 'I feel 감정 형용사 ~'로 나타낼 수도 있다.

- '~에 대해 …하다'의 뜻으로 'I'm 감정 형용사 ~' 또는 'I feel 감정 형용사 ~'에서 감정 형용사는 glad, delighted, pleased, worried 등을 쓴다.

- 감정을 표현할 때 'I'm glad 감정 형용사 ~' 또는 'I feel 감정 형용사 ~'에서 사용하는 감정 형용사 뒤에는 접속사 that과 함께 '주어+동사~'가 이어져서 감정의 원인을 나타낸다. 여기에 사용되는 접속사 that은 보통 생략한다.

감정 표현하기

- I'm glad ~. ~하게 되어 기뻐.
  = I feel glad ~.
- I'm worried ~. ~하게 되어 걱정이야.
  = I feel worried ~.

- I'm pleased ~. ~하게 되어 기뻐.
  = I feel pleased ~.
- I'm delighted ~. ~하게 되어 기뻐.
  = I feel delighted ~.

감정 표현에 대한 응답

- Good for you. 잘 됐구나.
- Don't worry. 걱정하지 마.

- Don't take it so hard. 너무 심각하게 생각하지 마.

핵심 Check

1. 다음 우리말과 일치하도록 빈칸에 알맞은 말을 쓰시오.

   A: It's going to rain all day long. (하루 종일 비가 올 거야.)

   B: Really? I'm _____ I can wear my new raincoat.

   (정말? 나는 새로 산 비옷을 입을 수 있어 기뻐.)

2. 다음 대화의 순서를 바르게 배열하시오.

   (A) Good for you

   (B) Yes. It's going to rain all day long.

   (C) Really? I'm glad I can use my new umbrella.

   (D) Did you hear the weather report?

   ➡ _____

② 동의하기

> • You can say that again. 네 말이 맞아.

■ 상대방의 말이나 의견에 동의할 때는 'You can say that again.'이라고 한다. 'I agree with you.'라고 할 수도 있다. 상대방의 말에 동의하지 않을 때는 'I don't agree.'라고 한다.

■ 상대방의 표현에 동의할 때는 '나도 그래.'의 의미로 'Me, too.' 또는 'So+동사+주어.'의 형태를 쓴다. 이때 사용하는 동사는 be동사, do, does, did를 포함하는 조동사들이다. 부정문에 이어지는 경우에는 so 대신 neither를 사용하여 'Neither+동사+주어.'라고 하거나 'Me neither.'라고 할 수 있다.

동의하기

• You can say that again. 네 말이 맞아.

• I agree with you. 동의해.

• So am/do I. 나도 마찬가지야.

• Neither am/do I. 나도 그래.

• Me, too./Me, neither. 나도 그래.

반대하기

• I don't agree with you. 나는 동의하지 않아.

• I have a different idea. 나는 생각이 달라.

• I don't think so. 나는 그렇게 생각하지 않아.

핵심 Check

3. 다음 우리말과 일치하도록 빈칸에 알맞은 말을 쓰시오.

(1) A: That man looks just like Ben. (저 사람은 꼭 Ben처럼 보여.)

　　B: You can _____ that again. (네 말이 맞아.)

(2) A: I think I have time to eat a snack. (나는 간식 먹을 시간이 있다고 생각해.)

　　B: I don't _____. You must hurry to go back. (그렇지 않아. 너는 서둘러 돌아가야 해.)

4. 다음 주어진 문장을 자연스러운 대화가 되도록 배열하시오.

G: Hey, Minjun. What a surprise!

B: Hi, Sora. I'm glad we're in the same class.

(A) I'm a little worried that there'll be more schoolwork.

(B) I'm thinking of an animation high school. I love painting.

(C) I am, too. We're now in our last year in middle school. How do you feel?

(D) Me, too. We also have to think about our high school.

(E) Which kind of school do you have in mind?

➡ _____

Listen – Listen & Answer Dialog 1

> **G:** Hey, Minjun. ❶What a surprise!
>
> **B:** Hi, Sora. ❷I'm glad we're in the same class.
>
> **G:** ❸I am, too. We're now in our last year in middle school. How do you feel?
>
> **B:** I'm a little worried ❹that there'll be more schoolwork.
>
> **G:** Me, too. We also have to think about our high school.
>
> **B:** ❺Which kind of school do you ❻have in mind?
>
> **G:** I'm thinking of an animation high school. I love painting.

G: 야, 민준아. 정말 놀랍다!
B: 안녕, 소라야. 우리가 같은 반에 있어서 기뻐.
G: 나도 그래. 우리 이제 중학교의 마지막 학년이야. 기분이 어떠니?
B: 공부할 게 더 많을 것 같아서 조금 걱정이야.
G: 나도 그래. 고등학교에 대해서도 생각해야 하지.
B: 너는 어떤 학교를 마음에 두고 있니?
G: 나는 애니메이션 고등학교를 생각하고 있어. 내가 그림 그리는 걸 좋아하거든.

❶ 'What a surprise!'는 감탄문으로 '주어+동사'가 생략되었다.
❷ 'I am glad'는 감정을 나타내는 표현으로 감정 형용사 뒤에는 감정의 이유를 나타내는 종속절을 유도하는 접속사 that이 생략되었다.
❸ 'I am, too.'는 동의하는 표현으로 am 뒤에는 앞 문장에 있었던 glad가 생략되었다. 동의를 나타내는 표현은 'I agree.' 또는 'Me, too.'를 쓸 수도 있다.
❹ that은 접속사로 쓰여서 감정을 나타내는 worried의 원인을 유도하고 있다.
❺ 'Which kind of school'이 문장의 목적어 역할을 한다.
❻ have A in mind: A를 염두에 두다

Check(√) True or False

(1) Minjun and Sora are in the same class.　　　　　T ☐　F ☐

(2) Minjun is thinking of an animation high school.　　T ☐　F ☐

 Listen – Listen & Answer Dialog 2

> **G:** Oliver, what club are you going to join?
>
> **B:** I'm not sure. ❶How about you, Sora?
>
> **G:** I want to join the school dance club.
>
> **B:** Really? But I heard you're preparing for an animation high school.
>
> **G:** Right, but I need some time to relax. We all need to do something to get over stress.
>
> **B:** You can say that again.
>
> **G:** Why don't you join me? It'll be fun.
>
> **B:** No, thanks. Dancing is not for me. I ❷have two left feet.

G: Oliver, 넌 어느 동아리에 들어갈 거니?
B: 잘 모르겠어. 소라, 너는?
G: 난 학교 춤 동아리에 가입하고 싶어.
B: 정말? 하지만 네가 애니메이션 고등학교를 준비하고 있다고 들었는데.
G: 그렇긴 한데, 좀 쉴 시간이 필요해. 우리 모두 스트레스를 극복하려면 뭔가를 할 필요가 있잖아.
B: 전적으로 동의해.
G: 너 나랑 함께하는 게 어때? 재미있을 거야.
B: 고맙지만 사양할게. 춤은 내게 맞지 않아. 난 몸치야.

❶ 'How about ~?'는 상대에게 제안하는 표현으로 'What about ~?'라고 할 수도 있다.
❷ 'have two left feet'은 '동작이 서툴다'는 의미이다.

Check(√) True or False

(3) Sora is preparing for an animation high school.　T ☐　F ☐

(4) Oliver will join the dance club.　　　　　　　　T ☐　F ☐

(5) Sora thinks she has two left feet.　　　　　　　T ☐　F ☐

Listen More – Listen and say

B: Jimin, look! That red phone case ❶looks nice!

G: You can say that again! Mom would love it ❷ as a birthday present.

B: I wonder how much it costs.

G: Let me see. It costs 40,000 won.

B: Really? That's so expensive!

G: I don't agree. Look! It works as a wallet, too.

B: Oh, I didn't see that. Then let's buy it for Mom.

G: Okay. I'm delighted to buy something special for Mom.

B: ❸So am I.

❶ 자동사 look은 주격보어 형용사가 필요하다.
❷ as는 전치사로 쓰였다.
❸ 'So am I.'는 동의하는 표현이다.

Speak – Talk in pairs.

A: Did you hear ❶the weather report?

B: Yes. It's going to rain all day long.

A: Really? I'm ❷glad I can wear my new raincoat.

B: Good for you.

❶ 'the weather report'는 '일기예보'이다.
❷ glad 뒤에는 접속사 that이 생략되었다.

Speak – Rap Time

A: I'm really worried I can't find my ❶student card.

B: You can make another one. ❷Don't take it so hard.

❶ student card: 학생증
❷ 동사 take는 '받아들이다, 생각하다'의 의미로 'Don't take it so hard.'는 '심각하게 생각하지 마.'에 해당한다.

Speak – Talk in groups.

A: I think the most ❶boring day of the week is Monday.

B: ❷You can say that again.

C: I don't think so. Thursday is the most boring.

D: I agree. We have all the difficult subjects on Thursday.

❶ boring은 '사람을 지루하게 하는'의 뜻으로 분사형용사이다.
❷ 'You can say that again.'은 상대의 말에 동의한다는 의미이다.

My Speaking Portfolio.

1. B1: What do you do in your free time? I listen to music. I think it's the greatest invention. I can't ❶live without it.

2. G: I think chocolate is the greatest invention. It makes me feel good. It also helps me focus better when I study.

3. B2: Many people will agree that paper is the greatest invention. ❸Thanks to paper, we all can read books and write things down.

❶ live without: ~ 없이 살다
❷ thanks to ~: ~ 덕택에

Wrap Up – Listen & Speaking ❺

B: You ❶look so serious. What's going on?

G: Oh, I'm just practicing for the school play tomorrow.

B: How do you feel about it?

G: I'm worried ❷I may make a mistake.

B: I'm sure you'll do well. ❸Break a leg!

G: Thanks.

❶ 자동사 look의 보어는 형용사이다.
❷ 접속사 that이 생략되었다.
❸ 'Break a leg!'는 상대에게 행운을 빌어주는 표현이다.

Wrap Up – Listen & Speaking ❻

G: ❶Have you heard about Mr. Oh?

B: No. What about him?

G: He ❷won first prize in the TV quiz show.

B: It's not surprising. He ❸seems to know about everything.

G: You can say that again! He's ❹a walking dictionary.

❶ 경험의 의미를 가지는 현재완료이다.
❷ win의 과거 won은 '(상을) 받았다'의 의미로 쓰였다.
❸ seem은 보어로 to부정사를 가진다.
❹ 'a walking dictionary'는 '걸어 다니는 사전, 박식한 사람, 살아 있는 사전'이라는 의미이다.

● 다음 우리말과 일치하도록 빈칸에 알맞은 말을 쓰시오.

Listen – Listen and Answer – Dialog 1

G: Hey, Minjun. _____ a _____!

B: Hi, Sora. I'm _____ we're in the _____ class.

G: I _____, too. We're now in our _____ year in middle school. _____ do you feel?

B: I'm a little _____ that there'll be more schoolwork.

G: Me, too. We also _____ _____ think about our _____ school.

B: _____ kind of school do you _____ in _____?

G: I'm _____ of an animation high school. I love _____.

G: 야, 민준아. 정말 놀랍다!
B: 안녕, 소라야. 우리가 같은 반에 있어서 기뻐.
G: 나도 그래. 우리 이제 중학교의 마지막 학년이야. 기분이 어때니?
B: 공부할 게 더 많을 것 같아서 조금 걱정이야.
G: 나도 그래. 고등학교에 대해서도 생각해야 하지.
B: 너는 어떤 학교를 마음에 두고 있니?
G: 나는 애니메이션 고등학교를 생각하고 있어. 내가 그림 그리는 걸 좋아하거든.

Listen – Listen and Answer – Dialog 2

G: Oliver, _____ club are you _____ to _____?

B: I'm not _____. How _____ you, Sora?

G: I want to _____ the school dance club.

B: Really? But I _____ you're _____ for an animation high school.

G: Right, but I _____ some time to _____. We all _____ to do something to _____ _____ stress.

B: _____ _____ _____ that again.

G: _____ _____ you join me? It'll be fun.

B: No, thanks. Dancing is not _____ _____. I have _____ _____ feet.

G: Oliver, 넌 어느 동아리에 들어갈 거니?
B: 잘 모르겠어. 소라, 너는?
G: 난 학교 춤 동아리에 가입하고 싶어.
B: 정말? 하지만 네가 애니메이션 고등학교를 준비하고 있다고 들었는데.
G: 그렇긴 한데, 좀 쉴 시간이 필요해. 우리 모두 스트레스를 극복하려면 뭔가를 할 필요가 있잖아.
B: 전적으로 동의해.
G: 너 나랑 함께하는 게 어때? 재미있을 거야.
B: 고맙지만 사양할게. 춤은 내게 맞지 않아. 난 몸치야.

Listen More – Listen and say

B: Jimin, look! That red phone _____ _____ nice!

G: You can _____ _____ again! Mom would love it _____ a birthday present.

B: I _____ _____ _____ it costs.

G: _____ me see. It _____ 40,000 won.

B: Really? That's so _____.

G: I don't _____. Look! It _____ _____ a wallet, too.

B: Oh, I didn't see that. Then let's _____ it for Mom.

G: Okay. I'm _____ to buy something _____ for Mom.

B: _____ _____ I.

B: 지민아, 봐! 저 빨간 전화기 케이스 멋지다!
G: 정말 그렇다! 생신 선물로 어머니께서 좋아하실 거야.
B: 난 가격이 얼마인지 궁금해.
G: 어디 보자. 가격은 40,000원이야.
B: 정말? 그거 너무 비싸다!
G: 난 동의하지 않아. 봐! 이건 지갑 역할도 해.
B: 아, 그건 못 봤어. 그럼 어머니를 위해 그걸 사자.
G: 알았어. 어머니께 뭔가 특별한 것을 사 드리게 되어 기뻐.
B: 나도 그래.

Speak – Talk in pairs.

A: Did you hear the _____ _____?

B: Yes. It's _____ _____ all day long.

A: Really? I'm _____ I can _____ my new raincoat.

B: _____ for you.

Speak – Talk in groups.

A: I think the most _____ day of the _____ is Monday.

B: You _____ _____ that again.

C: I _____ _____ so. Thursday is the most boring.

D: I _____. We have all the _____ _____ on Thursday.

My Speaking Portfolio.

1. B1: _____ do you do in your _____ time? I _____ to music.
I think it's the _____ _____. I can't _____ without it.

2. G: I think chocolate is the _____ _____. It makes me _____
_____. It also helps me _____ better when I study.

3. B2: Many people will _____ that paper is the greatest invention.
_____ _____ paper, we all can _____ books and
_____ things down.

Wrap Up - Listening & Speaking ❺

B: You look so _____. What's _____ on?

G: Oh, I'm just _____ for the school play tomorrow.

B: How do you _____ _____ it?

G: I'm _____ I may _____ a mistake.

B: I'm _____ you'll do well. _____ a _____!

G: Thanks.

Wrap Up - Listening & Speaking ❻

G: Have you _____ about Mr. Oh?

B: No. _____ about him?

G: He _____ first _____ in the TV quiz show.

B: It's not _____. He _____ to know about everything.

G: You can say that again! He's a _____ dictionary.

Conversation 시험대비 기본평가

[01~02] 다음 대화의 빈칸에 들어갈 말로 알맞은 것은?

01

> A: It's going to rain all day long.
> B: Really? I'm _____ I can wear my new raincoat.

① glad   ② surprised   ③ tired

④ worried   ⑤ missed

02

> A: I'm glad I can go to the zoo.
> B: You're going to the zoo? _____ for you.

① Good   ② Well   ③ Rather

④ Yet   ⑤ Sad

03 다음 주어진 단어를 이용하여 우리말에 해당하는 영어 문장을 쓰시오.

> B: I heard you're preparing for an animation high school.
> G: Right, but I want to join the school dance club to have some time to relax. We all need to do something to get over stress.
> B: 전적으로 동의해. (say, again)
> G: Why don't you join me? It'll be fun.

➡ _____

04 다음 대화의 순서가 바르게 배열된 것을 고르시오.

> B: You look so serious. What's going on?
> G: Oh, I'm just practicing for the school play tomorrow.
> (A) Thanks.
> (B) How do you feel about it?
> (C) I'm worried I may make a mistake.
> (D) I'm sure you'll do well. Break a leg!

① (A) – (C) – (D) – (B)   ② (D) – (B) – (A) – (C)

③ (B) – (C) – (D) – (A)   ④ (C) – (A) – (B) – (D)

⑤ (C) – (B) – (D) – (A)

[01~02] 다음 대화를 읽고 물음에 답하시오.

B: Jimin, look! That red phone case looks nice!

G: _____(A)_____ Mom would love it as a birthday present.

B: I wonder how much it costs.

G: Let me see. It costs 40,000 won.

B: Really? That's so expensive.

G: I don't agree. Look! It works as a wallet, too.

B: Oh, I didn't see that. Then let's buy it for Mom.

G: Okay. I'm delighted to buy something special for Mom.

B: So am I.

01 위 대화의 빈칸 (A)에 들어가기에 적절하지 <u>않은</u> 것은?

① I think so, too!

② You can say that again!

③ Me, neither!

④ I agree with you!

⑤ Me, too!

02 According to the dialogue, which one is NOT true?

① Jimin thinks her mom will love the phone case.

② The boy didn't know the phone case works as a wallet, too.

③ Jimin thinks the phone case is too expensive.

④ The boy agrees to buy the phone case as a birthday present for his mother.

⑤ The boy is delighted to buy something special for his mom.

[03~04] 다음 대화를 읽고 물음에 답하시오.

G: Hey, Minjun. What a surprise!

B: Hi, Sora. I'm ___(A)___ we're in the same class.

G: I am, too. We're now in our last year in middle school. How do you feel?

B: I'm a little worried that there'll be more schoolwork.

G: ___(B)___, too. We also have to think about our high school.

B: Which kind of school do you have in mind?

G: I'm thinking of an animation high school. I love painting.

03 빈칸 (A)에 들어갈 가장 알맞은 말을 고르시오.

① worried　　② glad　　③ tired

④ nervous　　⑤ sad

04 빈칸 (B)에 알맞은 말을 쓰시오.

➡ _____

05 다음 대화의 빈칸에 들어갈 말로 알맞은 것은?

A: I'm really worried I can't find my student card.

B: You can make another one. Don't _____ it so hard.

① leave　　② play　　③ take

④ wear　　⑤ enjoy

06 다음 대화의 빈칸에 들어갈 말로 알맞은 것은?

> G: I'm worried I may make a mistake.
>
> B: I'm sure you'll do well. Break a _____!
>
> G: Thanks.

① stick　　② leg　　③ dish
④ waist　　⑤ chair

[07~08] 다음 대화의 순서가 바르게 배열된 것을 고르시오.

07

> A: Did you hear the weather report?
>
> (A) Yes. It's going to rain all day long.
>
> (B) Good for you.
>
> (C) Really? I'm glad I can wear my new raincoat.

① (A) – (C) – (B)　　② (B) – (A) – (C)
③ (B) – (C) – (A)　　④ (C) – (A) – (B)
⑤ (C) – (B) – (A)

> B: Hi, Sora. I'm glad we're in the same class.
>
> G: I am, too. We're now in our last year in middle school. How do you feel?
>
> B: I'm a little worried that there'll be more schoolwork.
>
> (A) Which kind of school do you have in mind?
>
> (B) Me, too. We also have to think about our high school.
>
> (C) I'm thinking of an animation high school. I love painting.

① (A) – (C) – (B)　　② (B) – (A) – (C)
③ (B) – (C) – (A)　　④ (C) – (A) – (B)
⑤ (C) – (B) – (A)

 다음 짝지어진 대화가 어색한 것을 고르시오.

> ① A: I love cheese pizza.
>   B: Me, too.
> ② A: I think history is an interesting subject.
>   B: I think so, too.
> ③ A: That man looks just like Ben.
>   B: You can say that again.
> ④ A: What is the greatest invention in history?
>   B: I'd say the clock. We can't tell the time without it.
> ⑤ A: Did you hear the weather report?
>   B: No. It's going to rain all day long.

서답형

10 다음 대화의 빈칸에 들어갈 말을 〈보기〉에서 골라 순서대로 배열하시오.

> G: Oliver, what club are you going to join?
>
> B: I'm not sure. How about you, Sora?
>
> G: I want to join the school dance club.
>
> B: _____
>
> G: _____
>
> B: _____
>
> G: _____
>
> B: _____

┤ 보기 ├

> (A) Why don't you join me? It'll be fun.
> (B) No, thanks. Dancing is not for me. I have two left feet.
> (C) Really? But I heard you're preparing for an animation high school.
> (D) You can say that again.
> (E) Right, but I need some time to relax. We all need to do something to get over stress.

➡ _____

[01~02] 다음 대화의 빈칸에 들어갈 말로 알맞은 말을 한 단어로 쓰시오.

01

> A: I think I have _____ to eat a snack.
>
> B: I don't agree. You must hurry to go back.

➡ _____

02

> B: Hi, Sora. I'm glad we're in the same class.
>
> G: I am, too. We're now in our last year in middle school. How do you feel?
>
> B: I'm a little _____ that there'll be more schoolwork.
>
> G: Me, too. We also have to think about our high school.

➡ _____

[03~05] 다음 대화를 읽고 물음에 답하시오.

> B: You look so serious. ___(A)___'s going on?
>
> G: Oh, I'm just practicing for the school play tomorrow.
>
> B: How do you feel about it?
>
> G: I'm worried I may make a ___(B)___.
>
> B: I'm sure you'll do well. (C)행운을 빌어!
>
> G: Thanks.

03 빈칸 (A)에 알맞은 의문사를 쓰시오.

➡ _____

04 내용상 빈칸 (B)에 들어가기에 적절한 한 단어를 주어진 철자로 시작하여 쓰시오.

➡ m_____

05 밑줄 친 (C)의 우리말을 괄호 안의 단어를 포함하여 영작하시오.

➡ _____ (leg)

[06~07] 다음 대화를 읽고 물음에 답하시오.

> G: Have you heard about Mr. Oh?
>
> B: No. What about him?
>
> G: He ___(A)___ first prize in the TV quiz show.
>
> B: It's not surprising. He seems to know about everything.
>
> G: You can say that again! (B)그는 만물박사야.

06 내용상 위 대화의 (A)에 들어가기에 적절한 한 단어를 쓰시오.

➡ _____

07 위 대화의 밑줄 친 (B)의 우리말에 어울리는 영어 문장을 완성하시오. (dictionary 포함)

➡ _____

08 다음 밑줄 친 우리말을 영작하시오. (don't really 포함)

> A: What is the greatest invention in history?
>
> B: I'd say the clock. We can't tell the time without it.
>
> C: 나는 동의할 수 없어. I think the cell phone is the greatest invention.

➡ _____

Grammar

① 관계대명사 what

> • They didn't tell me **what** she wanted to know.
> 그들은 그녀가 알기를 원하는 것을 내게 말하지 않았다.

- 형태: what+주어+동사

  의미: ~하는 것

- 관계대명사 what은 선행사를 포함한 관계대명사로 형용사절이 아니라 명사절을 유도한다. 선행사가 별도로 없기 때문에 해석할 때는 '~하는 것' 등으로 해석한다.

  - what I saw 내가 본 것
  - what she heard 그녀가 들은 것
  - I want to read **what** she wrote. (what she wrote는 동사 read의 목적어)
  - She told me **what** she had heard at the meeting. (what she had heard ~는 동사 told의 직접목적어)

- 명사절을 유도하는 관계대명사 what은 명사절 속에서 주어나 목적어 역할을 한다.

  - He picked up **what** was on the table. (관계대명사 what은 동사 was의 주어 역할을 하는 주격이다.)
  - He doesn't like **what** she sent to him. (관계대명사 what은 동사 sent의 목적어 역할을 하는 목적격이다.)

관계대명사 what이 포함된 관용적인 표현

- what one has (사람이) 가진 것, 그의 재산
- what one is 현재의 그 사람 (사람 됨됨이, 인격)
- what one was 과거의 그 사람
- what is better 더욱 좋은 것은
- what is worse 더욱 나쁜 것은

핵심 Check

1. 다음 주어진 문장에서 적절한 것을 고르시오.

(1) He didn't show me (that / what) she had brought.

(2) I don't understand (that / what) he said.

(3) (That / What) he had painted made us surprised.

(4) He didn't read the message (that / what) she had sent to him.

(5) Did you see (that / what) he had put on the table?

② 지각동사의 목적격보어 – 원형부정사

> • **I saw** Mom **come** into my room. 나는 엄마가 방에 들어오시는 것을 보았다.

■ 형태: 지각동사+목적어+동사원형

　의미: ~가 …하는 것을 보다/듣다/느끼다

■ allow, ask, cause 등의 동사 뒤에서 목적어의 행위를 설명하는 목적격보어를 쓸 때는 to부정사를 쓰지만, see, watch, notice, hear, listen to, feel 등의 지각동사는 목적어의 행위를 나타내는 목적격보어로 부정사를 쓸 때는 to가 없는 원형부정사를 쓴다.

  • We **saw** him **move** the table. 우리는 그가 테이블을 옮기는 것을 보았다.

  • She **heard** the baby **cry** in the room. 그녀는 아기가 방에서 우는 것을 들었다.

  • He **felt** someone **touch** his shoulder. 그는 누군가가 그의 어깨를 만지는 것을 느꼈다.

  • She **listened to** someone **open** the door. 그녀는 누가 문을 여는 것을 들었다.

  cf. She **allowed** us **to watch** TV. 그녀는 우리가 TV를 보는 것을 허락했다.

■ 지각동사의 목적격보어로 원형부정사를 쓰지만, 목적어의 행위가 진행 중임을 강조할 때는 현재분사를 쓰기도 한다.

  • I **saw** them **playing** on the ground. 나는 그들이 운동장에서 놀고 있는 것을 보았다.

  • We **heard** her **singing** in the room. 우리는 그녀가 방에서 노래하고 있는 것을 들었다.

  • I **noticed** him **turning** on the TV. 나는 그가 TV를 켜는 것을 보았다.

핵심 Check

2. 다음 주어진 문장에 어울리는 것을 고르시오.

　(1) Mary watched the artist (to draw / draw) a picture.

　(2) They watched the sun (to set / set) in the west.

　(3) He saw the sun (to rise / rising) in the east.

　(4) She felt a drop of water (to fall / falling) on the head.

　(5) I watched her (to make / making) some food.

　(6) She allowed us (to go / going) out for a walk.

　(7) He advised them (to take / take) some rest.

　(8) I saw the dog (to run / running) in the garden.

　(9) She was listening to the rain (to fall / falling) on the roof.

　(10) Mary heard him (to fall / fall) on the stairs.

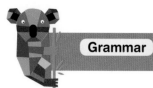
01 다음 빈칸에 들어갈 알맞은 것은?

> Did you tell him _____ you had heard?

① that   ② which   ③ what
④ about what   ⑤ who

02 다음 중 밑줄 친 부분의 쓰임이 <u>어색한</u> 것을 고르시오.

① I asked him <u>move</u> the bag.
② She heard him <u>call</u> her name.
③ I didn't allow him <u>to go</u> out.
④ He saw the dog <u>run</u> out of the room.
⑤ I felt him <u>touch</u> my back.

03 다음 우리말에 맞게 괄호 안에 주어진 어휘를 바르게 배열하시오. (필요하면 어형을 바꿀 것)

(1) 그는 시장에서 많은 사람들이 소리 지르는 것을 들었다. (many people, at the market, hear, shout, he)

➡ _____

(2) 유나는 그들이 운동장에서 놀고 있는 것을 보았다. (Yuna, on the ground, see, play, they)

➡ _____

04 다음 빈칸에 들어갈 말로 알맞은 것은?

> When I opened the door, I found _____ he had sent to me.

① that   ② which   ③ what
④ about what   ⑤ who

05 다음 빈칸에 들어가기에 적절한 것으로 짝지어진 것은?

> She listened to them _____ the violin.

① to play – play   ② to play – playing
③ play – playing   ④ playing – played
⑤ have played – to play

01 다음 중 밑줄 친 부분의 쓰임이 나머지 넷과 <u>다른</u> 것은?

① I saw them <u>climb</u> the tree to catch a bird.
② I can't allow you <u>to behave</u> like that.
③ I went to the place <u>to meet</u> my friends.
④ We heard him <u>get</u> out of the room to catch the bus.
⑤ He felt her <u>push</u> his back in the crowded bus.

02 다음 주어진 문장의 빈칸에 들어가기에 <u>어색한</u> 것은?

> He _____ her to come early after the class.

① told
② asked
③ saw
④ expected
⑤ wanted

03 빈칸에 들어갈 말을 순서대로 바르게 연결한 것은?

> • She told them _____ quiet in the class.
> • They advised him _____ some rest after the work.
> • We saw him _____ some rest after he finished the work.

① be – take – take
② be – to take – take
③ to be – to take – take
④ to be – take – to take
⑤ be – to take – to take

04 다음 빈칸에 들어갈 알맞은 것은?

> Did you hear anyone _____ you?

① to call
② called
③ call
④ have called
⑤ being called

05 다음 중 밑줄 친 부분의 쓰임이 <u>어색한</u> 것을 고르시오.

① I found <u>what</u> he had lost.
② She knew <u>what</u> he wanted to buy.
③ She knew <u>that</u> he was busy.
④ She told me <u>that</u> she wanted.
⑤ We understand <u>what</u> he said.

06 다음 빈칸에 들어갈 말이 바르게 짝지어진 것은?

> • John heard a man _____ about the picture.
> • I saw John _____ in the living room.

① talking – dancing
② to talk – dancing
③ talked – danced
④ talking – to dance
⑤ talk – to dance

07 다음 중 어법상 <u>어색한</u> 문장을 고르시오.

① We expect him to send the letter on his way to school.
② His mother told him to study law at the college.
③ He saw them to walk on the street this afternoon.
④ I heard the phone ringing in the room.
⑤ They watched us play after the class.

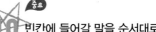

08 다음 괄호 안에서 알맞은 말을 고르시오.

(1) He doesn't like the gift (that / what) she gave him.

(2) She was pleased with (that / what) he had given her.

(3) (That / What) made me pleased was his kindness.

(4) We heard him (to play / play) the piano.

(5) They saw the students (to run / running) across the road.

09 다음 우리말에 맞게 괄호 안에 주어진 어휘를 바르게 배열하시오.

(1) 그는 내가 설명하는 것을 이해하지 못했다. (didn't, what, he, understand, explained, I)

➡ _____

(2) 그녀는 내가 그녀에게 사준 것을 좋아하지 않았다. (didn't, like, had bought, I, for her, what, she)

➡ _____

(3) 그는 그가 그린 것을 나에게 보여주었다. (he, he, me, showed, had painted, what)

➡ _____

(4) 나는 그녀가 방에서 우는 것을 들었다. (I, her, in the room, cry, heard)

➡ _____

(5) 우리는 그가 제시간에 오기를 기대한다. (we, him, to, expect, come, on time)

➡ _____

10 빈칸에 들어갈 말을 순서대로 바르게 연결한 것은?

- They are constructing the building _____ is the tallest in the city.
- He is now trying to make _____ I asked him to make for my brother's birthday party.

① that – that
② that – which
③ that – what
④ what – that
⑤ what – which

11 다음 중 어법상 <u>틀린</u> 문장을 <u>모두</u> 고르면? (정답 3개)

① He watched some people live in tents.
② Can you smell something burning?
③ She felt someone touches her arm.
④ I saw your sister takes the subway.
⑤ I could hear her to sing her favorite song.

12 다음 우리말을 영어로 바르게 옮긴 것은?

중요한 것은 너의 계획이다.

① What is important is you planned.
② That is important is your plan.
③ What is important is your plan.
④ Your plan is that is important
⑤ Your plan is the thing what is important.

13 빈칸에 들어갈 말을 순서대로 바르게 연결한 것은?

> • His father listened to him _____ on the phone.
> • The teacher told him _____ to school on time.

① to talk – to come
② talk – to come
③ talking – come
④ talking – came
⑤ talk – coming

14 다음 우리말을 영어로 바르게 옮긴 것은?

> 나는 그가 말하는 것을 이해했다.

① I understood that he said.
② I understood what he said.
③ I understood which he was saying.
④ I understood what he said it.
⑤ I understood the thing what he said.

15 다음 중 밑줄 친 부분의 쓰임이 <u>어색한</u> 것을 고르시오.

① We expect the weather <u>to be</u> fine.
② He saw her <u>prepare</u> dinner.
③ I heard him <u>open</u> the case.
④ He told her <u>to send</u> the letter.
⑤ She ordered them <u>get</u> up early.

16 다음 중 어법상 <u>어색한</u> 문장을 고르시오.

① I saw the car that he was driving.
② She knew the boy that I was talking about.
③ That is the most important is your choice.
④ He is reading the book that I gave him.
⑤ Jenny lives in the house that her grandfather built.

17 다음 빈칸에 들어갈 수 있는 말이 <u>다른</u> 것을 <u>두 개</u> 고르시오.

① I cannot find _____ he gave me.
② She showed me the photos _____ she had taken.
③ We need to pay attention to _____ she is saying.
④ She read the message _____ he had sent to her.
⑤ I have something _____ I want to tell you.

서답형

18 주어진 어휘를 이용하여 다음 우리말을 영어로 쓰시오.

> 우리는 인사동에서 우리가 즐길 수 있는 것을 발견했다. (find, enjoy)

➡ _____ in Insa-dong

19 다음 중 밑줄 친 부분의 쓰임이 <u>어색한</u> 것을 고르시오.

① He allowed them <u>to play</u> in the room.
② She asked me <u>to leave</u> the room.
③ She saw them <u>enter</u> the room.
④ I heard him <u>to sing</u> a song.
⑤ He felt her <u>touch</u> his hand.

20 다음 빈칸에 들어갈 말로 알맞은 것은?

> She won't tell me _____ you talked about the accident.

① what
② which
③ who
④ that
⑤ how

01 다음 우리말에 맞게 괄호 안에 주어진 어휘를 바르게 배열하시오. (필요한 어휘 변형 및 추가 가능)

(1) 나를 놀라게 한 것은 그의 불친절한 대답이었다. (I, he, answer, rude, be, what, surprised)

　➡ _____

(2) 그는 학교에서 들은 것을 나에게 말했다. (told, had heard, he, I, what, at school)

　➡ _____

(3) 너는 네가 말하는 것에 책임을 져야 한다. (you, you, have to, are saying, responsible for, what)

　➡ _____

(4) 우리는 지난여름에 그가 집을 짓는 것을 보았다. (we, he, saw, the house, build, last summer)

　➡ _____

(5) 그녀는 나에게 문을 열어 달라고 요청했다. (she, me, asked, open the door)

　➡ _____

(6) 그녀는 우리가 집 밖으로 나가는 소리를 들었다. (hear, go, she, out of the house, us)

　➡ _____

(7) 우리는 그가 우리에게 가지고 온 것을 너에게 줄 것이다. (will give, bring, what, we, you, to us)

　➡ _____

02 다음 문장에서 잘못된 부분을 바르게 고쳐, 전체 문장을 다시 쓰시오.

(1) I heard him to talk on the phone.

　➡ _____

(2) She felt the man to pull her by the hand.

　➡ _____

(3) They expected him being quiet during the class.

　➡ _____
　_____

(4) That is important is to finish the work before dinner.

　➡ _____
　_____

03 다음 중 어법상 어색한 문장 2개를 골라 번호를 쓰고, 올바른 형태로 고쳐서 다시 쓰시오.

ⓐ I can hear the bell ring.
ⓑ I feel my body getting cold.
ⓒ She heard the child cries.
ⓓ He hears the students laughing.
ⓔ They saw he wearing that hat.

　　　번호　　　　올바르게 고친 문장
(1) _____ ➡ _____
(2) _____ ➡ _____

04 다음 우리말을 관계대명사 what과 함께 괄호 안에 주어진 단어를 사용하여 영작하시오.

그는 나에게 내가 가진 것에 만족하라고 조언했다.
(advise / be satisfied with)

➡ He _____.

05 다음 우리말과 같은 의미가 되도록 괄호 안의 단어를 이용하여 5단어로 영작하시오.

그녀는 그들이 축구하고 있는 것을 보았다.
(watch)

➡ _____

06 다음 〈보기〉에서 빈칸에 들어가기에 적절한 말을 골라 쓰시오. (필요한 경우 단어 추가)

> 보기
> what   that   exercise   walk   drawing

(1) Mary watched the artist _____ the picture.

(2) What do you think about _____ she said?

(3) Will you move the bag _____ is on the chair?

(4) Did you advise him _____ every day?

(5) Who heard the boy _____ up the stairs?

07 〈보기〉를 참고하여 주어진 두 문장을 부정사를 이용하여 한 문장으로 연결하여 쓰시오.

> 보기
> • My sister sang a song at the party.
> • I heard her.
> ➡ I heard my sister sing a song at the party.

(1) • He stopped at the traffic light.
 • I watched it.
 ➡ _____

(2) • He was swimming in the pool.
 • When I turned my head, I saw it.
 ➡ When I turned my head, _____
 _____.

(3) • He laughed loudly at the table.
 • My mother heard him.
 ➡ _____

(4) • She pushed me on the back.
 • I felt it.
 ➡ _____

(5) • He was pulling my hand.
 • I felt it.
 ➡ _____

08 다음 주어진 단어를 적절하게 배열하여 주어진 문장을 완성하시오.

(1) Mary _____ in the kitchen. (her brother / cook / watched)

(2) He wants to _____. (she / eat / what / cooked)

(3) James _____. (his mother / open / heard / the window)

(4) He told me to _____.
 (what / had sent / read / she / to me)

09 다음 문장에 공통으로 들어가기에 적절한 한 단어를 쓰시오.

> • Would you tell me _____ you have in mind?
> • She showed me _____ she had bought.

➡ _____

A Priceless Gift

Long ago, an honest merchant lived in Genoa, Italy. His name
좁은 장소+넓은 장소

was Antonio, and he went to different places to support his family
부사적 용법(목적)

by trading. One day, he filled his ship with goods and visited a faraway
by ~ing(전치사+동명사): ~함으로써   fill A with B: A를 B로 채우다   상품

island. There he traded tools for spices and books for nuts. Thanks to
trade A for B: A와 B를 교환하다   ~ 덕분에(= because of. owing to. due to)

Antonio, the islanders could get what they needed.
= the things which

One night, Antonio had dinner with the island's queen at her
had a dinner(×)

palace. When dinner was served, rats appeared, and some servants
served(×)   were appeared(×): appear는 수동태로 쓸 수 없다.

chased them away with sticks.
chased away them(×): 이어동사에서 목적어가 인칭대명사일 때는 목적어를 동사와 부사 사이에 써야 함.

Antonio was greatly surprised that there were rats in the palace.
형용사 surprised 수식   이유를 나타내는 부사절을 이끄는 접속사

He asked, "Are there no cats on this island?" The queen looked
look+형용사: ~하게 보이다

puzzled. "What is a cat?" she asked.
감정을 나타내는 동사는 사람을 수식할 때 보통 과거분사를 사용

honest 정직한

merchant 상인

different 다른

support 부양하다. 지원하다

trade 교역. 교역하다

faraway 멀리 떨어진

tool 도구. 공구

spice 향신료

islander 섬사람

appear 나타나다

servant 하인

stick 막대기

puzzled 당황한. 어리둥절한

 **확인문제**

● 다음 문장이 본문의 내용과 일치하면 T, 일치하지 않으면 F를 쓰시오.

1 Antonio was an honest merchant who lived in Genoa, Italy. ☐

2 Antonio traded tools for spices and books for nuts in his village. ☐

3 Thanks to Antonio, the islanders could get what they needed. ☐

4 When Antonio had dinner with some servants, rats appeared. ☐

5 Antonio was surprised that there were rats in the palace. ☐

6 The queen knew what a cat was. ☐

The merchant said to himself, "What the islanders here need is
주어와 목적어가 같을 때는 재귀대명사를 쓴다.

not tools or books, but cats." He brought two cats from his ship and
└ not A but B: A가 아니라 B ┘

let them run free. "What amazing animals!" cried the queen when she
사역동사 let+목적어+원형부정사   = How amazing the animals are!

saw all the rats run away. She gave Antonio a chest that was filled with
지각동사 saw+목적어+원형부정사(running도 가능함)   주격 관계대명사   be filled with = be full of:
                                                              ~로 가득 차다

jewels.

Back in Italy, Antonio told his friends about his good fortune.
= (When he came) Back in Italy

Luigi, the richest merchant in Genoa, heard the story and was jealous.
└ 동격 ┘   = envious

"Cats are worthless," Luigi thought. "I'll bring the queen what is really
    = valueless   = the thing which

valuable. I'm sure that the queen will give me more jewels."
                  = It is certain

Luigi packed his ship with wonderful paintings and other works of
    pack A with B: A를 B로 가득 채우다   (문학 · 예술 따위의) 작품, 저작물, 제작품

art. He took the gifts to the island. To get a chance to meet the queen,
                            부사적 용법(목적)   형용사적 용법

he told the islanders a lie that he was a good friend of Antonio's. When
                      동격의 접속사   한정사(관사/소유격/지시형용사)끼리 중복해서 쓸 수 없으므로
                                              이중소유격(of+소유대명사/~'s) 사용

the queen heard about Luigi, she invited him to her palace for dinner.

Before sitting down at the table, Luigi presented the queen with all his
= Before he sat   present+사람+with+사물= present+사물+to+사람

gifts, and the queen thanked him again and again. "I'll repay you with
                                    = over and over

a priceless gift," said the queen.
    값진

---

run free 마음대로 돌아다니다

run away 달아나다

chest 상자

jewel 보석

fortune 행운, 재산

jealous 질투하는, 시샘하는

worthless 가치 없는, 쓸모없는

valuable 가치 있는, 귀중한, 소중한

pack 짐을 싸다

gift 선물

present 주다, 제시하다

again and again 여러 번, 반복하여

reply 보답하다, (돈을) 갚다

📎 **확인문제**

● 다음 문장이 본문의 내용과 일치하면 T, 일치하지 않으면 F를 쓰시오.

1   The islanders didn't need tools or books. ☐

2   The queen gave Antonio a chest that was filled with jewels. ☐

3   Luigi was the richest merchant in Genoa. ☐

4   Luigi thought that cats were priceless. ☐

5   Luigi packed his ship with wonderful paintings and other works of art. ☐

6   Luigi was a good friend of Antonio's. ☐

Luigi watched the queen whisper in a servant's ear. He became
지각동사 watched+목적어+원형부정사(whispering도 가능함)

excited and hopeful. He was sure that he would receive more jewels
감정을 나타내는 동사는 사람을 수식할 때 보통 과거분사를 사용

than Antonio.

After a while, the servant returned with a box, and the queen
잠시 후에

presented it to Luigi. When Luigi opened the box, he was speechless.
present+사물+to+사람 = present+사람+with+사물   speechless: (특히 너무 화가 나거나 놀라서) 말을 못하는

There was a kitten in the box. "Antonio gave us the priceless
→ (3형식) Antonio gave the priceless cats to us

cats, and we now have some kittens," said the queen. "In return
in return for: ~의 답례로

for the wonderful gifts you gave us, we want to give you what is
= that you gave us   the thing which

most valuable to us."
valuable의 최상급

Luigi realized that, in the queen's mind, the kitten was worth

far more than all the jewels in the world. He tried to look pleased with
= much, even, still, a lot: 비교급 강조(훨씬)   감정을 나타내는 동사는 사람을 수식할 때 보통 과거분사를 사용

the gift. He knew that was the right thing to do.
           to look pleased with the gift   형용사적 용법

Luigi did not return home a richer man. But he was surely a wiser
= When Luigi returned home, he was not a richer man.

one.
= man

어휘	
whisper 속삭이다, 귓속말을 하다	
hopeful 희망에 찬	
receive 받다	
speechless 말이 안 나오는, 말을 못 하는	
kitten 새끼 고양이	
worth ~의 가치가 있는	
pleased 기뻐하는, 만족한	
valuable 귀중한	
right 옳은	
surely 확실히, 분명히	

📎 **확인문제**

● 다음 문장이 본문의 내용과 일치하면 T, 일치하지 <u>않으면</u> F를 쓰시오.

1 Luigi was sure that he would receive more jewels than Antonio. ☐

2 When Luigi opened the box that the queen presented to him, he was satisfied. ☐

3 There was the gift that Luigi expected to receive in the box. ☐

4 Luigi realized that, in the queen's mind, the kitten was worth far more than all the
   jewels in the world. ☐

5 Luigi tried to look pleased with the gift. ☐

6 Luigi did not become a wise man. ☐

● 우리말을 참고하여 빈칸에 알맞은 말을 쓰시오.

1 A _____ Gift

2 Long ago, _____ _____ _____ lived in Genoa, Italy.

3 His name was Antonio, and he went to different places _____ _____ _____ _____ by trading.

4 One day, he _____ his ship _____ goods and visited a faraway island.

5 There he _____ tools _____ spices and books _____ nuts.

6 _____ _____ Antonio, the islanders could get _____ they needed.

7 One night, Antonio _____ _____ _____ _____ the island's queen at her palace.

8 When dinner _____ _____, rats _____, and some servants _____ _____ _____ with sticks.

9 Antonio was _____ _____ that there were rats in the palace.

10 He asked, "_____ _____ _____ _____ on this island?"

11 The queen _____ _____.

12 "What is a cat?" _____ _____.

13 The merchant _____ _____ _____, "_____ the islanders here need is _____ tools or books, _____ cats."

14 He _____ two cats _____ his ship and _____ _____ _____ free.

15 "_____ amazing animals!" cried the queen when she saw all the rats _____ away.

16 She gave Antonio a chest that _____ _____ _____ jewels.

17 _____ in Italy, Antonio told his friends about his _____ _____.

18 Luigi, _____ _____ _____ in Genoa, heard the story and was _____.

19 "Cats are _____," Luigi thought.

20 "I'll bring the queen _____ is really valuable.

21 _____ _____ that the queen will give me more jewels."

22 Luigi _____ his ship _____ wonderful paintings and other _____ of art.

23 He _____ the gifts _____ the island.

24 To get a chance to meet the queen, he told the islanders a lie that he was _____ _____ _____ _____ _____.

25 When the queen heard about Luigi, she _____ him _____ her palace for dinner.

26 Before _____ down at the table, Luigi _____ the queen _____ all his gifts, and the queen thanked him _____ _____ _____.

27 "I'll _____ you _____ a priceless gift," said the queen.

28 Luigi watched the queen _____ in a servant's ear.

29 He became _____ and _____.

30 He was sure that he would receive _____ _____ _____ Antonio.

31 After a while, the servant returned with a box, and the queen _____ it _____ Luigi.

32 When Luigi opened the box, he was _____.

33 There was a _____ in the box.

34 "Antonio gave us the _____ cats, and we now have some kittens," said the queen.

35 "_____ _____ _____ the wonderful gifts you gave us, we want to give you _____ _____ _____ _____ to us."

36 Luigi realized that, in the queen's mind, the kitten was worth _____ _____ _____ all the jewels in the world.

37 He tried to _____ _____ with the gift.

38 He knew that was the _____ _____ _____ _____.

39 Luigi did not return home a _____ man.

40 But he was surely _____ _____ _____.

21 틀림없이 여왕이 내게 더 많은 보석을 줄 거야."

22 Luigi는 멋진 그림들과 다른 예술 작품을 배에 실었다.

23 그는 선물을 섬으로 가지고 갔다.

24 여왕을 만날 기회를 얻기 위해서, 그는 자신이 Antonio의 친한 친구라고 섬사람에게 거짓말을 했다.

25 Luigi에 관해 듣고, 여왕은 그를 궁전으로 저녁 식사에 초대했다.

26 식탁에 앉기 전에 Luigi는 여왕에게 자신이 가져온 온갖 선물을 전했고, 여왕은 그에게 여러 차례 감사하다고 했다.

27 "당신께 값진 선물로 보답하겠습니다."라고 여왕이 말했다.

28 Luigi는 여왕이 하인의 귀에 대고 속삭이는 것을 지켜보았다.

29 그는 흥분되고 기대에 부풀었다.

30 그는 Antonio보다 많은 보석을 받게 될 거라고 확신했다.

31 잠시 후에 하인이 상자 하나를 가지고 돌아왔고, 여왕은 그것을 Luigi에게 주었다.

32 상자를 열어본 Luigi는 말문이 막혔다.

33 상자 안에는 새끼 고양이 한 마리가 들어 있었다.

34 "Antonio가 우리에게 매우 귀한 고양이들을 줬는데, 이제 새끼 고양이 몇 마리가 생겼어요."라고 여왕이 말했다.

35 "당신이 우리에게 준 멋진 선물에 보답하는 뜻에서, 우리에게 가장 값진 것을 당신에게 드리고 싶어요."

36 여왕의 생각에는 세상의 온갖 보석보다 새끼 고양이가 훨씬 더 가치 있다는 것을 Luigi는 깨달았다.

37 그는 선물에 대해 기뻐하는 표정을 지으려고 애썼다.

38 그게 올바른 행동이라는 것을 그는 알았다.

39 Luigi는 더 부유한 사람이 되어 집으로 돌아오지는 않았다.

40 하지만 그는 분명히 더 현명한 사람이 되었다.

● 우리말을 참고하여 본문을 영작하시오.

1 소중한 선물
➡ _____

2 먼 옛날 이탈리아 제노바에 정직한 상인 한 명이 살았다.
➡ _____

3 그의 이름은 Antonio로, 그는 교역으로 가족을 부양하기 위해 여러 곳을 다녔다.
➡ _____

4 어느 날 그는 배에 상품을 가득 싣고 머나먼 섬으로 갔다.
➡ _____

5 거기서 그는 공구를 향신료와 바꾸었고, 책을 견과류와 바꾸었다.
➡ _____

6 Antonio 덕에 섬사람들은 필요한 것을 얻을 수 있었다.
➡ _____

7 어느 날 밤, Antonio는 궁전에서 그 섬의 여왕과 저녁 식사를 했다.
➡ _____

8 식사가 나왔을 때 쥐들이 나타났고, 하인 몇 명이 막대기로 쥐를 쫓아내었다.
➡ _____

9 Antonio는 궁전에 쥐가 있다는 사실에 무척 놀랐다.
➡ _____

10 그는 "이 섬에는 고양이가 없습니까?"라고 물었다.
➡ _____

11 여왕은 어리둥절한 것처럼 보였다.
➡ _____

12 "고양이가 뭔가요?"라고 그녀가 물었다.
➡ _____

13 상인은 "여기 섬사람들이 필요로 하는 것은 공구나 책이 아니라 고양이야."라고 혼자 중얼거렸다.
➡ _____

14 그는 배에서 고양이 두 마리를 데리고 와서, 자유롭게 돌아다니도록 풀어놓았다.
➡ _____

15 "정말 놀라운 동물이네요!" 쥐가 모두 도망가는 것을 보자 여왕이 감탄하였다.
➡ _____

16 그녀는 Antonio에게 보석이 가득한 상자를 주었다.
➡ _____

17 이탈리아로 돌아와서, Antonio는 자신에게 일어난 행운을 친구들에게 이야기했다.
➡ _____

18 제노바에서 가장 부유한 상인인 Luigi는 그 이야기를 듣고 시샘이 일었다.
➡ _____

19 "고양이는 쓸모없어." Luigi가 생각했다.
➡ _____

20 "난 여왕에게 정말로 귀중한 것을 가지고 갈 거야.
➡ _____

21 틀림없이 여왕이 내게 더 많은 보석을 줄 거야."
➡ _____

22 Luigi는 멋진 그림들과 다른 예술 작품을 배에 실었다.
➡ _____

23 그는 선물을 섬으로 가지고 갔다.
➡ _____

24 여왕을 만날 기회를 얻기 위해서, 그는 자신이 Antonio의 친한 친구라고 섬사람들에게 거짓말을 했다.
➡ _____

25 Luigi에 관해 듣고, 여왕은 그를 궁전으로 저녁 식사에 초대했다.
➡ _____

26 식탁에 앉기 전에 Luigi는 여왕에게 자신이 가져온 온갖 선물을 전했고, 여왕은 그에게 여러 차례 감사하다고 했다.
➡ _____

27 "당신께 값진 선물로 보답하겠습니다."라고 여왕이 말했다.
➡ _____

28 Luigi는 여왕이 하인의 귀에 대고 속삭이는 것을 지켜보았다.
➡ _____

29 그는 흥분되고 기대에 부풀었다.
➡ _____

30 그는 Antonio보다 많은 보석을 받게 될 거라고 확신했다.
➡ _____

31 잠시 후에 하인이 상자 하나를 가지고 돌아왔고, 여왕은 그것을 Luigi에게 주었다.
➡ _____

32 상자를 열어본 Luigi는 말문이 막혔다.
➡ _____

33 상자 안에는 새끼 고양이 한 마리가 들어 있었다.
➡ _____

34 "Antonio가 우리에게 매우 귀한 고양이들을 줬는데, 이제 새끼 고양이 몇 마리가 생겼어요."라고 여왕이 말했다.
➡ _____

35 "당신이 우리에게 준 멋진 선물에 보답하는 뜻에서, 우리에게 가장 값진 것을 당신에게 드리고 싶어요."
➡ _____

36 여왕의 생각에는 세상의 온갖 보석보다 새끼 고양이가 훨씬 더 가치 있다는 것을 Luigi는 깨달았다.
➡ _____

37 그는 선물에 대해 기뻐하는 표정을 지으려고 애썼다.
➡ _____

38 그게 올바른 행동이라는 것을 그는 알았다.
➡ _____

39 Luigi는 더 부유한 사람이 되어 집으로 돌아오지는 않았다.
➡ _____

40 하지만 그는 분명히 더 현명한 사람이 되었다.
➡ _____

[01~03] 다음 글을 읽고 물음에 답하시오.

Long ago, an honest merchant lived in Genoa, Italy. His name was Antonio, and he went to different places (A)to support his family by trading. One day, he filled his ship ____ⓐ____ goods and visited a faraway island. There he traded tools ____ⓑ____ spices and books ____ⓑ____ nuts. Thanks to Antonio, the islanders could get what they needed.

One night, Antonio had dinner with the island's queen at her palace. When dinner was served, rats appeared, and some servants chased them away with sticks.

01 위 글의 빈칸 ⓐ와 ⓑ에 들어갈 전치사가 바르게 짝지어진 것은?

① of – from
② with – to
③ with – for
④ for – to
⑤ of – for

02 아래 〈보기〉에서 위 글의 밑줄 친 (A)to support와 to부정사의 용법이 같은 것의 개수를 고르시오.

┤ 보기 ├
① English is difficult to learn.
② He had the fortune to be born with a silver spoon in his mouth.
③ My ultimate goal is to become a great scientist.
④ He promised me to be here at ten o'clock.
⑤ This plan leaves nothing to be desired.

① 1개   ② 2개   ③ 3개   ④ 4개   ⑤ 5개

03 According to the passage, which is NOT true?

① Antonio was an honest merchant who lived in Genoa, Italy.
② Antonio supported his family by trading goods.
③ Antonio traded tools for spices and books for nuts.
④ Antonio had dinner with the island's queen at his ship.
⑤ Some servants chased rats away with sticks.

[04~05] 다음 글을 읽고 물음에 답하시오.

Antonio was greatly surprised that there were rats in the palace. He asked, "Are there no cats on this island?" The queen looked puzzled. "What is a cat?" she asked.

The merchant said to himself, "____ⓐ____ the islanders here need is not tools or books, but cats." He brought two cats from his ship and let them run free. "____ⓑ____ amazing animals!" cried the queen when she saw all the rats run away. She gave Antonio a chest that was filled with jewels.

서답형

04 위 글의 빈칸 ⓐ와 ⓑ에 공통으로 들어갈 알맞은 말을 쓰시오.

➡ _____

05 위 글의 제목으로 알맞은 것을 고르시오.

① How Many Cats Do You Have?
② Rats in the Palace? How Wonderful!
③ How Lovely the Cats Are!
④ What They Really Need Are Cats!
⑤ The Queen Gave Antonio Jewels.

[06~08] 다음 글을 읽고 물음에 답하시오.

Back in Italy, Antonio told ①his friends about his good fortune. Luigi, the richest merchant in Genoa, heard the story and was jealous. "Cats are ⓐworthless," Luigi thought. "I'll bring the queen what is really valuable. I'm sure that the queen will give ② me more jewels."

Luigi packed his ship with wonderful paintings and other works of art. He took the gifts to the island. To get a chance to meet the queen, ③he told the islanders a lie that he was ⓑAntonio의 친한 친구. When the queen heard about Luigi, she invited ④him to her palace for dinner. Before sitting down at the table, Luigi presented the queen with all his gifts, and the queen thanked him again and again. "I'll repay ⑤you with a priceless gift," said the queen.

06 위 글의 밑줄 친 ①~⑤ 중에서 가리키는 대상이 나머지 넷과 다른 것은?

①   ②   ③   ④   ⑤

07 위 글의 밑줄 친 ⓐworthless와 바꿔 쓸 수 있는 말을 고르시오.

① priceless   ② invaluable
③ precious   ④ valuable
⑤ valueless

08 위 글의 밑줄 친 ⓑ의 우리말에 맞게 5단어로 영작하시오.

➡ _____

[09~11] 다음 글을 읽고 물음에 답하시오.

Luigi watched the queen whisper in a servant's ear. He became excited and hopeful. He was sure that he would receive more jewels than Antonio.

After a while, the servant returned with a box, and the queen presented it ⓐ Luigi. When Luigi opened the box, he was speechless.

There was a kitten in the box. "Antonio gave us the priceless cats, and we now have some kittens," said the queen. "In return for the wonderful gifts you gave us, we want to give you ⓑ우리에게 가장 값진 것."

09 위 글의 빈칸 ⓐ에 알맞은 것은?

① on   ② for   ③ to
④ at   ⑤ with

10 위 글의 밑줄 친 ⓑ의 우리말에 맞게 6단어로 영작하시오.

➡ _____

11 위 글을 읽고 알 수 없는 것을 고르시오.

① What present did Luigi expect?
② What present did the queen give to Luigi?
③ How did Luigi react when he saw the queen's present?
④ How many cats did Antonio give to the queen?
⑤ Why did the queen give such a present to Luigi?

[12~14] 다음 글을 읽고 물음에 답하시오.

Back in Italy, Antonio told his friends about his good fortune. Luigi, the richest merchant in Genoa, heard the story and was ①jealous. "Cats are worthless," Luigi thought. "I'll bring the queen (A)[who / what] is really valuable. I'm sure that the queen will give me more jewels."

Luigi ②packed his ship with wonderful paintings and (B)[other / another] works of art. He took the gifts to the island. To get ③a chance to meet the queen, he told the islanders a lie that he was a good friend of (C)[Antonio / Antonio's]. When the queen heard about Luigi, she ④invited him to her palace for dinner. Before sitting down at the table, Luigi presented the queen with all his gifts, and the queen thanked him ⑤again and again. "I'll repay you with a priceless gift," said the queen.

12 위 글의 괄호 (A)~(C)에서 어법상 알맞은 낱말을 골라 쓰시오.

➡ (A) _____ (B) _____ (C) _____

13 위 글의 밑줄 친 ①~⑤와 바꿔 쓸 수 있는 말로 옳지 않은 것을 고르시오.

① envious   ② filled

③ an opportunity   ④ visited

⑤ over and over

14 According to the passage, which is NOT true?

① Luigi was the richest merchant in Genoa.

② Luigi thought that cats were valueless.

③ Luigi was Antonio's good friend.

④ The queen invited Luigi to her palace for dinner.

⑤ Luigi presented all his gifts to the queen.

[15~17] 다음 글을 읽고 물음에 답하시오.

Luigi watched the queen whisper in a servant's ear. He became ___ⓐ___ and ___ⓑ___ . He was sure that he would receive more jewels than Antonio.

After a while, the servant returned with a box, and the queen presented it to Luigi. When Luigi opened the box, he was speechless.

There was a kitten in the box. "Antonio gave us the priceless cats, and we now have some kittens," said the queen. "ⓒIn spite of the wonderful gifts you gave us, we want to give you what is most valuable to us."

15 위 글의 빈칸 ⓐ와 ⓑ에 들어갈 알맞은 말을 고르시오.

① nervous – upset

② excited – hopeful

③ excited – hopeless

④ upset – bored

⑤ disappointed – surprised

16 다음 질문에 대한 알맞은 대답을 주어진 단어로 시작하여 빈칸에 쓰시오. (7단어)

> Q: Why was Luigi speechless when he opened the box?
> A: Because _____
> instead of more jewels than Antonio had received.

17 위 글의 밑줄 친 ⓒ에서 흐름상 어색한 부분을 찾아 고치시오.

_____ ➡ _____

[18~20] 다음 글을 읽고 물음에 답하시오.

> There was a kitten in the box. "Antonio gave us the priceless cats, and we now have some kittens," said the queen. "In return for the wonderful gifts you gave us, we want to give you (A)[that / what] is most valuable to us."
> Luigi realized that, in the queen's mind, the kitten was worth far (B)[more / less] than all the jewels in the world. He tried to look (C)[pleasing / pleased] with the gift. He knew that was the right thing to do.
> Luigi did not return home a richer man. But he was surely a wiser ⓐ .

18 위 글의 빈칸 ⓐ에 들어갈 알맞은 대명사를 쓰시오.

➡ _____

19 위 글의 괄호 (A)~(C)에서 문맥이나 어법상 알맞은 낱말을 골라 쓰시오.

➡ (A) _____ (B) _____ (C) _____

20 Luigi에 대한 묘사로 가장 알맞은 것은?

① rude   ② thoughtful
③ brave   ④ lonely
⑤ humorous

[21~23] 다음 글을 읽고 물음에 답하시오.

> Long ago, an honest merchant lived in Genoa, Italy. (①) His name was Antonio, and he went to different places to support his family by trading. (②) One day, he filled his ship with goods and visited a faraway island. (③) There he traded tools for spices and books for nuts. (④)
> One night, Antonio had dinner with the island's queen at her palace. (⑤) When dinner ___ⓐ___ , rats appeared, and some servants chased ⓑthem away with sticks.

21 위 글의 빈칸 ⓐ에 serve를 알맞은 형태로 쓰시오.

➡ _____

22 위 글의 흐름으로 보아, 주어진 문장이 들어가기에 가장 적절한 곳은?

> Thanks to Antonio, the islanders could get what they needed.

①   ②   ③   ④   ⑤

23 위 글의 밑줄 친 ⓑthem이 가리키는 것을 본문에서 찾아 쓰시오.

➡ _____

[24~26] 다음 글을 읽고 물음에 답하시오.

Antonio was greatly surprised that there were rats in the palace. He asked, "Are there no cats on this island?" The queen looked puzzled. "(A)What is a cat?" she asked.

The merchant said to himself, "(B)What the islanders here need is ⓐ tools or books, ⓑ cats." He brought two cats from his ship and let them run free. "(C)What amazing animals!" cried the queen when she saw all the rats run away. (D)She gave Antonio a chest that was filled with jewels.

24 위 글의 빈칸 ⓐ와 ⓑ에 들어갈 알맞은 말을 고르시오.

① either – or 　② neither – nor

③ not – but 　④ both – and

⑤ at once – and

25 위 글의 밑줄 친 (A)~(C)의 What과 문법적 쓰임이 같은 것을 <u>모두</u> 골라 쓰시오.

① That's not what I meant to say.

② What a fool you are!

③ What can I do for you?

④ What I said is true.

⑤ What a charming girl she is!

➡ (A)와 쓰임이 같은 것: _____ ,

(B)와 쓰임이 같은 것: _____ ,

(C)와 쓰임이 같은 것: _____

26 위 글의 밑줄 친 문장 (D)에서 생략할 수 있는 부분을 생략하고 문장을 다시 쓰시오.

➡ _____

[27~29] 다음 글을 읽고 물음에 답하시오.

There was a kitten in the box. "Antonio gave us the priceless cats, and we now have some kittens," said the queen. "In return for the wonderful gifts you gave us, we want to give you what is most valuable to us."

Luigi realized that, in the queen's mind, the kitten was worth (A)far more than all the jewels in the world. He tried to look pleased with the gift. He knew that was the right thing (B)to do.

Luigi did not return home a ⓐ man. But he was surely a ⓑ one.

27 위 글의 빈칸 ⓐ와 ⓑ에 들어갈 알맞은 말을 고르시오.

① richer – more foolish

② poorer – wiser

③ wiser – poorer

④ richer – wiser

⑤ poorer – more foolish

28 위 글의 밑줄 친 (A)far와 바꿔 쓸 수 <u>없는</u> 말을 고르시오.

① much 　② even 　③ very

④ still 　⑤ a lot

29 아래 <보기>에서 위 글의 밑줄 친 (B)to do와 문법적 쓰임이 같은 것의 개수를 고르시오.

┌─ 보기 ┤

① I got up early to catch the train.

② There was not a moment to lose.

③ It is difficult to know oneself.

④ He was kind enough to lend me the money.

⑤ He has many children to look after.

└──────

① 1개 　② 2개 　③ 3개 　④ 4개 　⑤ 5개

[01~03] 다음 글을 읽고 물음에 답하시오.

Long ago, an honest merchant lived in Genoa, Italy. His name was Antonio, and he went to different places to support his family by trading. One day, he filled his ship with goods and visited a faraway island. There he traded tools for spices and books for nuts. ⓐThanks to Antonio, the islanders could get what they needed.

One night, Antonio had dinner with the island's queen at her palace. ⓑWhen dinner was served, rats were appeared, and some servants chased them away with sticks.

01 위 글의 밑줄 친 ⓐ를 enable을 사용하여 고칠 때, 빈칸에 들어갈 알맞은 말을 쓰시오.

➡ Antonio enabled the islanders _____ what they needed.

02 위 글의 밑줄 친 ⓑ에서 어법상 틀린 부분을 찾아 고치시오.

_____ ➡ _____

03 다음 빈칸 (A)와 (B)에 알맞은 단어를 넣어 섬사람들이 필요한 물건을 구한 방법을 완성하시오.

> The islanders could get what they needed such as tools and books by trading __(A)__ for tools and __(B)__ for books with Antonio.

➡ (A) _____ (B) _____

[04~06] 다음 글을 읽고 물음에 답하시오.

Back in Italy, Antonio told his friends about his good fortune. Luigi, the richest merchant in Genoa, heard the story and was jealous. "Cats are worthless," Luigi thought. "ⓐI'll bring the queen what is really valuable. I'm sure that ⓑthe queen will give me more jewels."

Luigi packed his ship with wonderful paintings and other works of art. He took the gifts to the island. To get a chance to meet the queen, he told the islanders ⓒa lie that he was a good friend of Antonio's. When the queen heard about Luigi, she invited him to her palace for dinner. ⓓBefore sitting down at the table, Luigi presented the queen with all his gifts, and the queen thanked him again and again. "I'll repay you with a priceless gift," said the queen.

04 위 글의 밑줄 친 ⓐ와 ⓑ를 3형식 문장으로 고치시오.

➡ ⓐ _____
ⓑ _____

05 위 글의 밑줄 친 ⓒa lie의 내용을 본문에서 찾아 쓰시오.

➡ _____

06 위 글의 밑줄 친 ⓓ를 다음과 같이 바꿔 쓸 때 빈칸에 들어갈 알맞은 말을 두 단어로 쓰시오.

➡ Before _____ down at the table,

[07~10] 다음 글을 읽고 물음에 답하시오.

Antonio was (A)[great / greatly] surprised that there were rats in the palace. He asked, "Are there no cats on this island?" The queen looked (B)[puzzling / puzzled]. "What is a cat?" she asked.

The merchant said to (C)[him / himself], "ⓐ여기 섬사람들이 필요로 하는 것은 공구나 책이 아니라 고양이야." He brought two cats from his ship and let them run free. "ⓑWhat amazing animals!" cried the queen when she saw all the rats run away. ⓒShe gave Antonio a chest that was filled with jewels.

07 위 글의 괄호 (A)~(C)에서 어법상 알맞은 낱말을 골라 쓰시오.

➡ (A) _____ (B) _____ (C) _____

08 위 글의 밑줄 친 ⓐ의 우리말에 맞게 한 단어를 보충하여, 주어진 어휘를 알맞게 배열하시오.

> but / need / tools or books / is / cats / here / not / the islanders / ,

➡ _____

09 위 글의 밑줄 친 ⓑ를 다음과 같이 바꿔 쓸 때 빈칸에 들어갈 알맞은 말을 쓰시오.

➡ _____ amazing the animals are!

10 위 글의 밑줄 친 ⓒ를 다음과 같이 바꿔 쓸 때 빈칸에 들어갈 알맞은 말을 쓰시오.

➡ She gave Antonio a chest that _____ _____ jewels.

[11~14] 다음 글을 읽고 물음에 답하시오.

Luigi watched the queen whisper in a servant's ear. He became excited and hopeful. He was sure that he would receive more jewels than Antonio.

After a while, the servant returned with a box, and ⓐthe queen presented it to Luigi. When Luigi opened the box, he was speechless.

There was a kitten in the box. "ⓑAntonio gave us the worthless cats, and we now have some kittens," said the queen. "In return for the wonderful gifts you gave us, we want to give you ⓒwhat is most valuable to us."

11 위 글의 밑줄 친 ⓐ를 다음과 같이 바꿔 쓸 때 빈칸에 들어갈 알맞은 말을 쓰시오.

➡ the queen presented Luigi _____ _____.

12 위 글의 밑줄 친 ⓑ에서 흐름상 어색한 부분을 찾아 고치시오.

_____ ➡ _____

13 위 글의 밑줄 친 ⓒ가 가리키는 것을 본문에서 찾아 쓰시오.

➡ _____

14 본문의 내용과 일치하도록 다음 빈칸 (A)와 (B)에 알맞은 단어를 쓰시오.

> Luigi gave the queen (A)_____ _____ and he was sure that he would receive more jewels than Antonio, but the queen presented a kitten to Luigi in return because a kitten was (B)_____ _____ to them.

My Speaking Portfolio

A: What is the greatest invention in history?
최상급에 the가 쓰였다.

B: I'd say the clock. We can't tell the time without it.
= I would say   시간을 알다

C: I don't really agree with you. I think the cell phone is the greatest invention.
동사 think 다음에 접속사 that 생략

D: You can say that again.

구문해설 · You can say that again. 네 말이 맞아.

해석

A: 무엇이 역사상 가장 위대한 발명품이니?

B: 나는 시계라고 말하겠어. 그것이 없으면 시간을 알 수 없어.

C: 나는 동의하지 않아. 나는 휴대전화가 가장 위대한 발명품이라고 생각해.

D: 네 말이 맞아.

All Ears

M: 1. I don't agree with you on that issue.

2. I didn't know you didn't like the plan.
동사 know의 목적어가 되는 명사절을 이끄는 접속사 that 생략

A: I'm glad I can go to the zoo.

B: You're going to the zoo? Good for you.
평서문의 형태이지만 의미상 질문을 나타낸다.

A: I think I have time to eat a snack.
형용사적 용법의 부정사

B: I don't agree. You must hurry to go back.

구문해설 · Good for you. 좋겠다. 잘되었구나.　· hurry 서두르다

M: 1. 나는 그 문제에 대하여 너에게 동의하지 않아.

2. 나는 네가 그 계획을 좋아하지 않는다는 것을 알지 못했어.

A: 나는 동물원에 갈 수 있어서 기뻐.

B: 동물원에 가니? 좋겠구나.

A: 나는 간식을 먹을 시간이 있다고 생각해.

B: 나는 동의하지 않아. 너는 서둘러 돌아가야 해.

Wrap Up – Reading

Isabel lives in a small village near Kakamega, Kenya. In the past, she had to walk a long distance every day to get clean water. She sometimes got
must의 과거   부사적 용법(목적)
sick because of the dirty water she drank. Three months ago, she received a
because of+명사구   dirty water (that) she drank
valuable gift from a volunteer worker. It looks like a thick straw. Dirty water
= precious   looks like+명사
goes into the straw, and clean water comes out of it. Isabel carries the straw
= the straw
everywhere. Now, she does not get sick anymore. She can go to school every
더 이상 ~ 아닌
day. So, the straw is what is most valuable to Isabel.
the thing which

구문해설 · village: 마을 · past: 과거 · distance: 거리 · receive: ~을 받다
· volunteer: 자원 봉사자 · straw: 빨대

Isabel은 케냐의 Kakamega 인근 마을에 살고 있다. 예전에 그녀는 깨끗한 물을 구하기 위해 매일 먼 거리를 걸어야 했다. 그녀는 가끔 그녀가 마신 더러운 물로 인해 병에 걸리기도 했다. 석달 전 그녀는 자원봉사자 한 명에게서 귀한 선물을 받았다. 그것은 두꺼운 빨대처럼 생겼다. 더러운 물이 빨대로 들어가면 깨끗한 물이 나온다. Isabel은 그것을 어디나 가지고 다닌다. 이제 그녀는 더 이상 병에 걸리지 않는다. 매일 학교에 갈 수 있다. 그래서 그 빨대는 Isabel에게 가장 귀중한 것이다.

Words & Expressions

01 다음 영영풀이에 해당하는 단어를 고르시오.

> to quickly follow someone or something in order to catch them

① drive   ② chase   ③ order
④ walk   ⑤ look after

02 다음 문장의 빈칸에 들어가기에 적절한 것은?

> A: We're now in our last year in middle school. Which kind of school do you _____?
> B: I'm thinking of an animation high school.

① want to visit   ② take care of
③ want to draw   ④ appear to get
⑤ have in mind

03 다음 빈칸에 들어가기에 적절한 것을 고르시오.

> There the merchant _____ tools for spices and books for nuts. Thanks to Antonio, the islanders could get what they needed.

① supported   ② visited   ③ got
④ invited   ⑤ traded

04 다음 밑줄 친 단어와 의미가 같은 단어를 고르시오.

> We can't <u>tell</u> the time without the clock.

① know   ② repay   ③ set
④ talk   ⑤ present

Conversation

05 다음 대화의 빈칸에 들어가기에 알맞은 말은?

> A: I think the most boring day of the week is Monday.
> B: You can say that again.
> C: I don't _____ so. Thursday is the most boring.
> D: I agree. We have all the difficult subjects on Thursday.

① think   ② agree   ③ say
④ tell   ⑤ intend

06 다음 대화의 순서가 바르게 배열된 것을 고르시오.

> A: Did you hear the weather report?
> (A) Really? I'm glad I can wear my new raincoat.
> (B) Yes. It's going to rain all day long.
> (C) Good for you.

① (A) – (C) – (B)   ② (B) – (A) – (C)
③ (B) – (C) – (A)   ④ (C) – (A) – (B)
⑤ (C) – (B) – (A)

07 다음 대화의 빈칸에 들어갈 말로 알맞은 것은?

> G: Have you heard about Mr. Oh? He won first prize in the TV quiz show.
> B: It's not surprising. He seems to know about everything.
> G: You can say that again! He's a _____ dictionary.

① walking   ② useful   ③ surprising
④ wise   ⑤ large

08 다음 짝지어진 대화가 어색한 것을 고르시오.

① A: I think I have time to eat a snack.
B: I don't agree. You must hurry to go back.

② A: I think the most boring day of the week is Monday.
B: You can say that again.

③ A: I think the cell phone is the greatest invention.
B: You can say that again.

④ A: It's going to rain all day long.
B: Really? I'm sad I can wear my new raincoat.

⑤ A: Did you hear the weather report?
B: Yes. It's going to rain all day long.

[09~11] 다음 대화를 읽고 물음에 답하시오.

B: Jimin, look! That red phone case looks nice!
G: You can say that again! Mom would love it as a birthday present.
B: I ___(A)___ how much it costs.
G: Let me see. It costs 40,000 won.
B: Really? That's so expensive.
G: I don't agree. Look! It works as a wallet, too.
B: Oh, I didn't see that. Then let's buy it for Mom.
G: Okay. I'm delighted to buy something special for Mom.
B: (B)나도 마찬가지야.

09 빈칸 (A)에 들어갈 가장 알맞은 말을 고르시오.

① wonder   ② know
③ tell   ④ recognize
⑤ think

10 밑줄 친 (B)의 우리말을 영작하시오. (so를 포함하시오.)

➡ _____ (3단어)

11 위 대화를 읽고 대답할 수 없는 것은?

① What would they like to buy?
② Who thinks the red phone case is too expensive?
③ What are they going to buy?
④ What does their mother want as a birthday present?
⑤ Does the boy agree to buy the red phone case?

Grammar

12 다음 우리말을 영어로 바르게 옮긴 것은?

> 그녀는 자기가 만든 것을 나에게 주었다.

① She made what I had given to her.
② She gave me what I had made for her.
③ I gave her what I had made.
④ I gave her what she had made.
⑤ She gave me what she had made.

13 빈칸에 들어갈 말을 순서대로 바르게 연결한 것은?

> • Can you imagine _____ he describes?
> • I saw the boy _____ along the street yesterday.

① that – walk
② that – to walk
③ what – walk
④ what – to walk
⑤ that – walking

14 다음 중 밑줄 친 부분의 쓰임이 어색한 것을 고르시오.

① I don't know <u>what</u> she bought.

② We saw <u>what</u> she had put on the table.

③ She learned <u>what</u> he had some time to rest.

④ We should know <u>what</u> is the most important.

⑤ I don't understand <u>what</u> he told me.

15 다음 중 밑줄 친 부분의 쓰임이 어색한 것을 고르시오.

① I expect him <u>to win</u> the match.

② He told them <u>to come</u> early.

③ She asked him <u>to move</u> the bag.

④ He saw her <u>to take</u> the book.

⑤ They allowed him <u>to swim</u> there.

16 다음 중 어법상 어색한 문장을 고르시오.

① I asked him to be quiet during dinner.

② She told him to clean the room.

③ He listened to her to explain the situation.

④ We allowed them to go to the beach.

⑤ They expected him to be quiet.

17 다음 빈칸에 들어갈 말로 알맞은 것은?

Jack told me _____ early after the school was over.

① coming   ② come

③ to come   ④ comes

⑤ came

18 다음 괄호 안에서 알맞은 말을 고르시오.

(1) He was reading (that / what) she had sent to him.

(2) We saw them (to swim / swimming) across the river.

(3) You should carefully listen to (that / what) the teacher is saying.

(4) His mother asked him (to take / take) the waste out.

(5) Mary's mother saw her (to study / study) for the exam.

19 다음 중 밑줄 친 부분의 쓰임이 어색한 것을 고르시오.

① She heard him <u>to break</u> the window.

② He asked us <u>to take</u> some rest.

③ She expected him <u>to call</u> her.

④ She told him <u>to get</u> up early.

⑤ He advised us <u>to exercise</u> every day.

20 빈칸에 들어갈 말을 순서대로 바르게 연결한 것은?

• She told me _____ she had heard at the library.

• Did she tell you _____ she had in mind?

① that – that

② that – what

③ what – which

④ what – what

⑤ what – that

Reading

[21~23] 다음 글을 읽고 물음에 답하시오.

Long ago, an honest merchant lived in Genoa, Italy. His name was Antonio, and he went to different places to support his family by ⓐtrading. One day, he filled his ship with goods and visited a faraway island. There he traded tools for spices and books for nuts. ⓑThanks to Antonio, the islanders could get ⓒwhat they needed.

21 위 글의 밑줄 친 ⓐtrading과 문법적 쓰임이 같은 것을 모두 고르시오.

① He is collecting stamps.
② My hobby is swimming.
③ I heard him playing the piano.
④ We enjoy watching action movies.
⑤ Keeping a diary every day is not easy.

22 위 글의 밑줄 친 ⓑThanks to와 바꿔 쓸 수 없는 말을 모두 고르시오.

① Because of   ② Instead of
③ Owing to   ④ Due to
⑤ In spite of

23 위 글의 밑줄 친 ⓒwhat을 선행사와 관계대명사로 나눠 세 단어로 바꿔 쓰시오.

➡ _____

[24~26] 다음 글을 읽고 물음에 답하시오.

Antonio was greatly surprised (A)that there were rats in the palace. He asked, "Are there no cats on this island?" The queen looked puzzled. "What is a cat?" she asked.

The merchant said to himself, "What the islanders here need is not tools or books, but cats." He brought two cats from his ship and let them ___ⓐ___ free. "What amazing animals!" cried the queen when she saw all the rats ___ⓑ___ away. She gave Antonio a chest (B)that was filled with jewels.

24 위 글의 빈칸 ⓐ와 ⓑ에 공통으로 들어갈 알맞은 말을 고르시오.

① run   ② ran
③ to run   ④ running
⑤ were running

25 위 글의 밑줄 친 (A)와 (B)의 that과 문법적 쓰임이 같은 것을 각각 아래 〈보기〉에서 모두 골라 쓰시오.

┌─── 보기 ───┐
① He is the greatest novelist that has ever lived.
② He was the first man that came here.
③ I'm glad that you like it.
④ We will discuss all that matters.
⑤ I am sorry that he is gone.
└───────────┘

➡ (A)의 that과 쓰임이 같은 것: _____
  (B)의 that과 쓰임이 같은 것: _____

26 According to the passage, which is NOT true?

① Antonio asked the queen if there were no cats on that island.
② At first, the queen didn't know what a cat was.
③ The islanders didn't need tools or books.
④ Antonio brought two cats from his ship and let them run free.
⑤ The queen gave Antonio a chest full of jewels.

[27~28] 다음 글을 읽고 물음에 답하시오.

Luigi packed his ship with wonderful paintings and other ⓐworks of art. He took the gifts to the island. To get a chance ⓑto meet the queen, he told the islanders a lie that he was a good friend of Antonio's. When the queen heard about Luigi, she invited him to her palace for dinner. Before sitting down at the table, Luigi presented the queen with all his gifts, and the queen thanked him again and again. "I'll repay you with a priceless gift," said the queen.

27 위 글의 밑줄 친 ⓐworks와 같은 의미로 쓰인 것을 고르시오.

① Look at the works of a clock.

② I like the works of Picasso.

③ He works 40 hours a week.

④ The ice works aren't closed even in winter.

⑤ This pill works on you.

28 위 글의 밑줄 친 ⓑto meet과 to부정사의 용법이 같은 것을 모두 고르시오.

① He has no money to buy the book with.

② He is the last man to tell a lie.

③ It is not easy to write good English.

④ I went to the airport to see him off.

⑤ I don't know what to do next.

[29~30] 다음 글을 읽고 물음에 답하시오.

Dear future Jihun,

How are you doing? You are now a writer, ⓐ_____ _____?

I have included two things in the time capsule for you. The first thing is a pair of basketball shoes. They helped me make many friends in the basketball club. The other thing is my favorite book. I wanted to become a writer after I read it.

I hope these things will bring back happy memories of your middle school days.

Jihun

29 위 글의 빈칸 ⓐ에 들어갈 알맞은 부가의문문을 쓰시오.

➡ _____

30 Fill in the blanks (A) and (B) with the suitable words.

In the time capsule, Jihun has included a pair of (A)_____ _____ because they helped him make many friends in the basketball club, and his favorite book because it gave him a dream to become (B)_____ _____.

31 주어진 글 다음에 이어질 글의 순서로 가장 적절한 것은?

One night, Antonio had dinner with the island's queen at her palace.

(A) Antonio was greatly surprised that there were rats in the palace. He asked, "Are there no cats on this island?"

(B) The queen looked puzzled. "What is a cat?" she asked.

(C) When dinner was served, rats appeared, and some servants chased them away with sticks.

① (A) – (C) – (B)　　② (B) – (A) – (C)

③ (B) – (C) – (A)　　④ (C) – (A) – (B)

⑤ (C) – (B) – (A)

[01~02] 다음 빈칸에 들어갈 말로 적절한 것을 고르시오.

출제율 90%

01

I have _____ two things in the time capsule for you.

① found   ② included
③ repayed   ④ realized
⑤ counted

출제율 95%

02

Rix got a rabbit from a friend and did his best to take good _____ of it.

① help   ② look
③ fun   ④ care
⑤ delight

[03~04] 다음 영영풀이에 해당하는 단어를 쓰시오. (주어진 철자로 시작할 것)

출제율 90%

03

a large strong box that you use to store things in or to move your personal possessions from one place to another

➡ c_____

출제율 85%

04

things that are produced in order to be sold

➡ g_____

[05~06] 다음 빈칸에 들어갈 말로 적절한 것을 고르시오.

출제율 95%

05

A: Did you hear the _____ report?
B: Yes. It's going to rain all day long.

① advice   ② weather
③ school   ④ homework
⑤ cloud

출제율 95%

06

A: I'm really _____ I can't find my student card.
B: You can make another one. Don't take it so hard.

① worried   ② delighted   ③ glad
④ surprised   ⑤ pleased

출제율 90%

07 짝지어진 단어의 관계가 같도록 빈칸에 알맞은 말을 쓰시오.

delighted : pleased = p_____ : valuable

출제율 90%

08 다음 대화의 빈칸에 알맞은 것을 고르시오.

I heard you will join the school dance club but I don't want to join you because I have _____. Dancing is not for me.

① right hands   ② too much work
③ a good eye   ④ no friends there
⑤ too left feet

출제율 95%

09 다음 대화의 순서가 바르게 배열된 것을 고르시오.

G: Have you heard about Mr. Oh?
B: No. What about him?
(A) You can say that again! He's a walking dictionary.
(B) He won first prize in the TV quiz show.
(C) It's not surprising. He seems to know about everything.

① (A) – (C) – (B)   ② (B) – (A) – (C)
③ (B) – (C) – (A)   ④ (C) – (A) – (B)
⑤ (C) – (B) – (A)

> G: Oliver, what club are you going to join?
> B: I'm not sure. How ___(A)___ you, Sora?
> G: I want to join the school dance club.
> B: Really? But I heard you're preparing for an animation high school.
> G: Right, but I need some time to relax. We all need to do something to get over stress.
> B: You can say that again.
> G: Why don't you join me? It'll be fun,
> B: No, thanks. (B)춤은 나와 맞지 않아. I am really poor at dancing.

✏️ 출제율 95%

10 위 대화의 빈칸 (A)에 들어가기에 적절한 것은?

① for
② with
③ from
④ about
⑤ against

✏️ 출제율 90%

11 밑줄 친 (B)의 우리말을 영작하시오. (dancing, for를 포함할 것)

➡ _____ (5단어)

✏️ 출제율 95%

12 위 대화의 내용과 일치하지 <u>않는</u> 것은?

① Oliver is going to join the school dance club.
② Sora is preparing for an animation high school.
③ Sora wants to do something to get over stress.
④ Sora wants Oliver to join her.
⑤ Oliver thinks he has two left feet.

✏️ 출제율 90%

13 다음 빈칸에 들어갈 말로 알맞은 것은?

> I was listening to the rain _____ on the ground.

① to fall
② falling
③ falls
④ fell
⑤ fallen

✏️ 출제율 100%

14 빈칸에 들어갈 말을 순서대로 바르게 연결한 것은?

> • We will discuss the plan _____ he suggested.
> • She didn't like _____ I had given her.

① what – what
② what – that
③ what – which
④ that – that
⑤ that – what

✏️ 출제율 90%

15 다음 우리말을 영어로 바르게 옮긴 것은?

> 나는 그가 담을 넘는 것을 보았다.

① He saw me to cross the fence.
② He saw me crossing the fence
③ I saw him crossed the fence.
④ I saw him to cross the fence.
⑤ I saw him cross the fence.

✏️ 출제율 95%

16 다음 빈칸에 들어갈 말로 알맞은 것은?

> She was pleased with _____ he had heard from me.

① that
② what
③ which
④ from which
⑤ in which

17 다음 중 밑줄 친 부분의 쓰임이 어색한 것을 고르시오. 출제율 95%

① She asked him to turn on the TV.

② He advised them to study hard.

③ I saw him to drive the car.

④ He expected her to tell the truth.

⑤ I told him to go home early.

[18~20] 다음 글을 읽고 물음에 답하시오.

Long ago, an honest merchant lived in Genoa, Italy. His name was Antonio, and he went to different places to support his family by trading. One day, he (A)filled his ship with goods and visited a faraway island. There he traded tools for spices and books for nuts. Thanks to Antonio, the islanders could get (B)what they needed.

One night, Antonio had dinner with the island's queen at her palace. When dinner was served, rats appeared, and some servants ____ⓐ____ them away with sticks.

18 주어진 영영풀이를 참고하여 빈칸 ⓐ에 철자 c로 시작하는 단어를 쓰시오. (어법에 맞게 어형 변화를 할 것) 출제율 90%

to run after something or follow it quickly in order to catch or reach it

➡ _____

19 위 글의 밑줄 친 (A)filled와 바꿔 쓸 수 있는 단어를 고르시오. 출제율 95%

① full   ② packed

③ picked   ④ gathered

⑤ chose

20 위 글의 밑줄 친 (B)what they needed가 가리키는 것을 본문에서 찾아 쓰시오. (두 개) 출제율 90%

➡ _____, _____

[21~23] 다음 글을 읽고 물음에 답하시오.

Antonio was greatly surprised that there were rats in the palace. He asked, "Are there no cats on this island?" The queen looked puzzled. "What is a cat?" she asked.

The merchant said to himself, "What the islanders here need is not tools or books, but cats." He brought two cats from his ship and let ⓐthem run free. "What amazing animals!" cried the queen when she saw all the rats run away. She gave Antonio a chest that was filled with jewels.

21 위 글을 읽고 고양이에 대한 여왕의 심경 변화로 가장 알맞은 것을 고르시오. 출제율 100%

① bored   → surprised

② nervous   → pleased

③ confused → nervous

④ satisfied → confused

⑤ puzzled   → amazed

22 위 글의 밑줄 친 ⓐthem이 가리키는 것을 본문에서 찾아 쓰시오. 출제율 90%

➡ _____

23 본문의 내용과 일치하도록 다음 빈칸 (A)와 (B)에 알맞은 단어를 쓰시오. 출제율 90%

When the queen saw two cats that Antonio had brought from his ship run free and all (A)_____ _____ run away, she gave Antonio a chest that was filled with (B)_____ in return for his help.

[24~26] 다음 글을 읽고 물음에 답하시오.

Luigi watched the queen ____ⓐ____ in a servant's ear. He became excited and hopeful. He was sure that he would receive more jewels than Antonio.

After a while, the servant returned with a box, and the queen presented it to Luigi. When Luigi opened the box, he was speechless.

There was a kitten in the box. "Antonio gave us the priceless cats, and we now have some kittens," said the queen. "In return for the wonderful gifts you gave us, we want to give you what is most valuable to us."

출제율 90%

24 위 글의 빈칸 ⓐ에 들어갈 알맞은 말을 모두 고르시오.

① to whisper   ② would whisper
③ whispering   ④ whispered
⑤ whisper

출제율 100%

25 위 글의 제목으로 알맞은 것을 고르시오.

① Wow! I'll Surely Receive More Jewels!
② Poor Luigi's Unrealized Expectation
③ It Turned Out as Expected
④ A Kitten, a Perfect Present
⑤ How to Give Wonderful Gifts

출제율 95%

26 Which question canNOT be answered after reading the passage?

① When did Luigi become excited and hopeful?
② Did Luigi receive what he wanted as gifts?
③ When Luigi opened the box, was he satisfied with what was in the box?

④ When did Antonio give the queen the priceless cats?
⑤ What was most valuable to the queen?

[27~28] 다음 글을 읽고 물음에 답하시오.

Isabel lives in a small village near Kakamega, Kenya. In the past, she had to walk a long distance every day to get clean water. She sometimes got sick ⓐbecause of the dirty water she drank. Three months ago, she received ⓑa valuable gift from a volunteer worker. It looks like a thick straw. Dirty water goes into the straw, and clean water comes out of it. Isabel carries the straw everywhere. Now, she does not get sick anymore. She can go to school every day. So, the straw is what is most valuable to Isabel.

출제율 90%

27 위 글의 밑줄 친 ⓐ를 다음과 같이 바꿔 쓸 때 빈칸에 들어갈 알맞은 말을 쓰시오.

➡ _____ she drank dirty water

출제율 100%

28 위 글의 ⓑa valuable gift에 관한 내용으로 적절하지 않은 것은?

① 자원봉사자가 3개월 전에 Isabel에게 주었다.
② 두꺼운 빨대처럼 생겼다.
③ 더러운 물이 빨대 속으로 들어가면, 깨끗한 물이 그 밖으로 나온다.
④ Isabel은 그것을 집에 소중하게 간직해 두었다.
⑤ 그것은 Isabel에게 가장 귀중한 것이다.

01 다음 우리말에 맞게 빈칸에 알맞은 말을 쓰시오.

(1) 춤은 나와 어울리지 않아. 나는 동작이 서툴러.

➡ Dancing is not for me. I have two _____ feet.

(2) 그는 무역으로 가족을 부양하기 위하여 여기저기 다녔다.

➡ He went to different places to _____ his family by trading.

(3) Antonio 덕택에 그 섬사람들은 그들이 원하는 것을 얻을 수 있었다.

➡ _____ to Antonio, the islanders could get what they needed.

(4) 몇몇 하인들이 막대기로 쥐를 쫓아냈다.

➡ Some _____ chased the rats away with sticks.

02 다음 영영풀이에 해당하는 단어를 쓰시오. (주어진 철자로 시작할 것)

someone, especially in the past, who was paid to clean someone's house, cook for them, answer the door, etc

➡ s_____

[03~04] 다음 대화를 읽고 물음에 답하시오.

G: Hey, Minjun. What a surprise!

B: Hi, Sora. I'm glad we're in the same class.

G: I am, too. We're now in our last year in middle school. How do you feel?

B: (A)나는 학교 공부가 더 많을 것 같아서 좀 걱정이 돼.

G: (B)Me, too. We also have to think about our high school.

B: Which kind of school do you have in mind?

G: I'm thinking of an animation high school. I love painting.

03 밑줄 친 (A)의 우리말을 영어로 옮기시오.

필수 어휘: a little, that, there, schoolwork

➡ _____

_____

04 밑줄 친 (B)와 같은 의미가 되도록 다음 빈칸을 채우시오.

➡ _____ _____ _____.

05 다음 우리말에 맞게 괄호 안에 주어진 어휘를 바르게 배열하시오. (어형 변화 가능 / 필요한 어휘 추가)

(1) 나는 비가 창문에 떨어지는 것을 들었다. (I, the rain, fall, hear, on the window)

➡ _____

(2) 우리는 그가 운동장에서 공을 차고 있는 것을 보았다. (we, he, kicking, saw, the ball, on the ground)

➡ _____

(3) 그녀는 내가 말한 것을 이해할 수 없었다. (I, her, she, told, understand, what, couldn't)

➡ _____

06 다음 대화의 빈칸에 들어갈 말을 고르시오. (주어진 철자로 시작할 것)

A: I think I have time to eat a snack.

B: I don't agree. You must _____ to go back.

➡ h_____

Back in Italy, Antonio told his friends about his good fortune. Luigi, the richest merchant in Genoa, heard the story and was jealous. "Cats are worthless," Luigi thought. "I'll bring the queen what is really valuable. ⓐI'm sure that the queen will give me more jewels."

Luigi packed his ship with wonderful paintings and other works of art. He took the gifts to the island. To get a chance to meet the queen, he told the islanders a lie that he was a good friend of Antonio's. When the queen heard about Luigi, she invited him to her palace for dinner. Before sitting down at the table, ⓑLuigi presented the queen with all his gifts, and the queen thanked him again and again. "I'll repay you with a priceless gift," said the queen.

07 위 글의 밑줄 친 ⓐ를 다음과 같이 바꿔 쓸 때 빈칸에 들어갈 알맞은 말을 쓰시오.

➡ It is _____ that the queen will give me more jewels. = The queen will _____ give me more jewels.

08 위 글의 밑줄 친 ⓑ를 다음과 같이 바꿔 쓸 때 빈칸에 들어갈 알맞은 말을 쓰시오.

➡ Luigi presented all his gifts _____ _____ _____.

Long ago, an honest (A)[consumer / merchant] lived in Genoa, Italy. His name was Antonio, and he went to different places (B)[to support / supporting] his family by trading. One day, he filled his ship with (C)[good / goods] and visited a faraway island. There he traded tools for spices and books for nuts. ⓐAntonio 덕에 섬사람들은 필요한 것을 얻을 수 있었다.

One night, Antonio had dinner with the island's queen at her palace. ⓑWhen dinner was served, rats appeared, and some servants chased away them with sticks.

09 위 글의 괄호 (A)~(C)에서 문맥이나 어법상 알맞은 낱말을 골라 쓰시오.

➡ (A) _____ (B) _____ (C) _____

10 위 글의 밑줄 친 ⓐ의 우리말에 맞게 주어진 어휘를 이용하여 10 단어로 영작하시오.

Thanks to, the islanders

➡ _____
_____

11 위 글의 밑줄 친 ⓑ에서 어법상 틀린 부분을 찾아 고치시오.

_____ ➡ _____

01 빈칸에 알맞은 말을 넣어 Antonio와 Luigi의 이야기를 정리해 봅시다.

> Antonio visited an island for trading. → He gave _____ to the queen, so the rats ran away. → The queen gave him _____. → Luigi heard about Antonio's good fortune. → He gave expensive gifts to the _____. → The queen _____.

02 빈칸에 알맞은 표현을 넣어 〈보기〉처럼 자신의 생각을 말해 봅시다.

> — 보기 —
> What I want to do the most is to take a trip to Africa.

(1) What I want to eat now is _____.

(2) _____ is what I usually do in my free time.

(3) I will never forget what _____.

03 다음 내용을 바탕으로 지훈이가 타임 캡슐에 넣을 편지를 쓰시오.

> 미래의 나에게 궁금한 점: You are now a writer, aren't you?
> 타임 캡슐에 넣을 물건: • a pair of basketball shoes   • my favorite book
> 이유: • helped me make many friends in the basketball club
>   • gave me a dream to become a writer

> Dear future Jihun,
> How are you doing? You are now (A)_____, aren't you?
> I have included two things in the time capsule for you. The first thing is a pair of (B)_____. They helped me make (C)_____ in the basketball club.
> The other thing is my (D)_____. I wanted to become (E)_____ after I read it.
> I hope these things will bring back happy memories of your middle school days.
>
> *Jihun*

단원별 모의고사

[01~02] 다음 짝지어진 두 단어의 관계가 같도록 빈칸에 알맞은 말을 쓰시오. (주어진 철자로 시작할 것)

01 tool : device = amazing : s_____

02 delighted : sorrowful = include : e_____

03 다음 우리말에 맞게 빈칸에 알맞은 말을 쓰시오. (주어진 철자로 시작할 것)

(1) 상인은 "이곳 섬사람들이 필요한 것은 고양이들이야."라고 혼잣말을 했다.
➡ The merchant said to _____, "What the islanders here need is cats."

(2) 그녀는 Antonio에게 보물로 가득 찬 상자를 주었다.
➡ She gave Antonio a c_____ that was filled with jewels.

(3) Luigi는 그의 배를 훌륭한 그림으로 가득 채웠다.
➡ Luigi p_____ his ship with wonderful paintings.

04 다음 중 밑줄 친 부분의 뜻풀이가 바르지 <u>않은</u> 것은?

① Did you hear the <u>weather report</u>? (일기예보)
② I'm glad I can <u>wear</u> my new raincoat. (입다)
③ It's all right. Don't <u>take</u> it so hard. (가지고 가다)
④ We have all the difficult <u>subjects</u> on Thursday. (과목들)
⑤ That man looks just <u>like</u> Ben. (~ 같은)

05 다음 영영풀이에 해당하는 단어를 쓰시오. (주어진 철자로 시작할 것.)

someone who buys and sells goods in large quantities

➡ m_____

06 다음 밑줄 친 단어와 의미가 같은 단어를 고르시오.

I'll bring the queen what is really <u>valuable</u>.

① priceless   ② valueless
③ worthless   ④ expensive
⑤ terrible

07 다음 대화의 순서가 바르게 배열된 것을 고르시오.

B: Jimin, look! That red phone case looks nice!
G: You can say that again! Mom would love it as a birthday present.
B: I wonder how much it costs.
G: Let me see. It costs 40,000 won.
B: Really? That's so expensive.

(A) Okay. I'm delighted to buy something special for Mom.
(B) I don't agree. Look! It works as a wallet, too.
(C) Oh, I didn't see that. Then let's buy it for Mom.

B: So am I.

① (A) – (C) – (B)   ② (B) – (A) – (C)
③ (B) – (C) – (A)   ④ (C) – (A) – (B)
⑤ (C) – (B) – (A)

[08~10] 다음 대화를 읽고 물음에 답하시오.

G: Oliver, what club are you going to join?

B: I'm not sure. How about you, Sora?

G: I want to join the school dance club.

B: Really? But I heard you're preparing for an animation high school.

G: Right, but I need some time to relax. We all need to do something to ___(A)___ over stress.

B: You can say that again.

G: Why don't you join me? It'll be fun.

B: No, thanks. Dancing is not for me. I have two left ___(B)___.

08 빈칸 (A)에 들어갈 가장 알맞은 말을 고르시오.

① take   ② get   ③ make
④ turn   ⑤ grow

09 빈칸 (B)에 알맞은 말을 쓰시오.

➡ _____

10 위 대화를 읽고, 대답할 수 <u>없는</u> 질문은?

① What does Sora want to do to get over stress?
② What kind of high school is Sora preparing for?
③ What club is Oliver going to join?
④ Why doesn't Oliver agree to join the dance club?
⑤ Does Oliver think Sora needs some time to relax?

[11~13] 다음 대화를 읽고 물음에 답하시오.

B: Jimin, look! That red phone case looks nice!

G: You can say that again! Mom would love it as a birthday present.

B: I ___(A)___ how much it costs.

G: Let me see. It costs 40,000 won.

B: Really? That's so expensive.

G: I don't agree. Look! It works as a wallet, too.

B: Oh, I didn't see that. Then let's buy it for Mom.

G: Okay. I'm delighted to buy something special for Mom.

B: ___(B)___ am I.

11 빈칸 (A)에 들어갈 가장 알맞은 말을 고르시오.

① guess   ② know   ③ ask
④ say   ⑤ wonder

12 빈칸 (B)에 알맞은 말을 쓰시오.

➡ _____

13 위 대화의 내용과 일치하는 것은?

① Jimin doesn't agree that the red phone case looks nice.
② They are looking for a cheap phone case.
③ Jimin doesn't think the red phone case is too expensive.
④ The boy doesn't want Jimin to buy the phone case.
⑤ The boy isn't delighted to buy the phone case.

14 다음 빈칸에 들어갈 말로 알맞은 것은?

> He told me _____ he had in mind.

① what   ② which   ③ that
④ how   ⑤ who

15 다음 빈칸에 들어갈 말로 알맞은 것은?

He likes the picture _____ he took during the holiday.

① that
② what
③ in which
④ in that
⑤ with which

16 다음 중 밑줄 친 부분의 쓰임이 <u>어색한</u> 것을 고르시오.

① I heard him <u>talk</u> on the phone.
② She saw them <u>sit</u> on the bench.
③ They listened to him <u>sing</u> a song.
④ She expects them <u>arrive</u> on time.
⑤ He felt her <u>touch</u> his hand.

17 다음 우리말을 영어로 바르게 옮긴 것은?

우리는 그가 그 사건을 설명하는 것을 들었다.

① We heard him explain the accident.
② He explained what we heard about the accident.
③ We heard his explain the accident.
④ We heard him to explain the accident.
⑤ He heard us explain the accident.

18 다음 중 어법상 <u>어색한</u> 문장을 고르시오.

① My father told me to do my homework.
② I heard him play the violin in the yard.
③ She didn't read the letter what he had sent to her.
④ He liked the painting that she had given to her.
⑤ He knew what he had to buy on his way home.

19 다음 괄호 안에서 알맞은 말을 고르시오.

(1) He took pictures of (that / what) he saw during the travel.
(2) I couldn't find the money (that / what) he had put on the table.
(3) He heard the children (to talk / talk) about the animation.
(4) He noticed the players (to take / taking) a rest.

[20~21] 다음 글을 읽고 물음에 답하시오.

Long ago, an honest merchant lived in Genoa, Italy. His name was Antonio, and he went to different places to support his family by trading. One day, he filled his ship with goods and visited a faraway island. There he traded tools for spices and books for nuts. Thanks to Antonio, the islanders could get ⓐ they needed.
One night, Antonio had dinner with the island's queen at her palace. When dinner was served, rats appeared, and some servants chased them away with sticks.

20 위 글의 빈칸 ⓐ에 들어갈 알맞은 말을 고르시오.

① which
② what
③ that
④ when
⑤ where

21 Which question canNOT be answered after reading the passage?

① Where did Antonio live?
② How did Antonio support his family?
③ How long did it take for Antonio to reach a faraway island?
④ What did Antonio trade on the island?
⑤ When did rats appear?

[22~23] 다음 글을 읽고 물음에 답하시오.

Antonio was greatly surprised that there were rats in the palace. He asked, "Are there no cats on this island?" The queen looked puzzled. (①) "What is a cat?" she asked. (②)

The merchant said to himself, "What the islanders here need is not tools or books, but cats." (③) "What amazing animals!" cried the queen when she saw all the rats run away. (④) She gave Antonio a chest that was filled with jewels. (⑤)

22 위 글의 흐름으로 보아, 주어진 문장이 들어가기에 가장 적절한 곳은?

> He brought two cats from his ship and let them run free.

①   ②   ③   ④   ⑤

23 주어진 영영풀이에 해당하는 단어를 본문에서 찾아 쓰시오.

> a large, heavy box used for storing things

➡ _____

[24~26] 다음 글을 읽고 물음에 답하시오.

Back in Italy, Antonio told his friends about his good fortune. Luigi, the richest merchant in Genoa, heard the story and was jealous. "Cats are (A)[priceless / worthless]," Luigi thought. "I'll bring the queen what is really (B)[valuable / valueless]. I'm sure that the queen will give me more jewels."

Luigi packed his ship with wonderful paintings and other works of art. He took the gifts to the island. ⓐTo get a chance to meet the queen, he told the islanders a lie ⓑthat he was a good friend of Antonio's. When the queen heard about Luigi, she invited him to her palace for dinner. Before sitting down at the table, Luigi presented the queen with all his gifts, and the queen thanked him again and again. "I'll repay you with a (C)[priceless / worthless] gift," said the queen.

24 위 글의 괄호 (A)~(C)에서 문맥상 알맞은 낱말을 골라 쓰시오.

➡ (A) _____ (B) _____ (C) _____

25 위 글의 밑줄 친 ⓐTo get과 to부정사의 용법이 다른 것을 모두 고르시오.

① You will find it difficult to read the novel.
② I am sorry to hear that.
③ He grew up to be a great doctor.
④ There was nothing to be seen.
⑤ He must be foolish to believe such a thing.

26 위 글의 밑줄 친 ⓑthat과 문법적 쓰임이 같은 것을 모두 고르시오.

① This is the dress that she bought yesterday.
② No one can deny the fact that you are guilty.
③ My arm doesn't reach that far.
④ The climate of this country is like that of Italy.
⑤ There was no hope that she would recover her health.

Lesson 2

Animals, Big and Small

🎙 의사소통 기능

- 선호 묻고 답하기
  A: Which do you like better, dogs or cats?
  B: I like dogs better.

- 설명 요청하기
  A: It's an animal.
  B: Can you tell me more about it?

🎙 언어 형식

- 명사를 뒤에서 꾸미는 분사
  Look at the sun **rising** over the sea.

- 접속사 since
  Since it rained heavily, the station was closed.

Words & Expressions

Key Words

- **appear** [əpíər] 동 나타나다, (글 속에) 나오다
- **Arctic** [á:rktik] 형 북극의 cf. **Antarctic** 남극의
- **beehive** [bí:hàiv] 명 벌집
- **billion** [bíljən] 명 십억
- **breathe** [bri:ð] 동 호흡하다
- **chemical** [kémikəl] 명 화학물질
- **chestnut** [tʃésnʌt] 명 밤
- **choose** [tʃu:z] 동 고르다, 정하다 (= **pick, select**)
- **colony** [káləni] 명 군락, 군집
- **defend** [difénd] 동 방어하다
- **endangered** [indéindʒərd] 형 위험에 처한, 멸종 위기의
- **entire** [intáiər] 형 전체의
- **except** [iksépt] 전 ~을 제외하고
- **exchange** [ikstʃéindʒ] 명 교환 동 교환하다
- **extremely** [ikstrí:mli] 부 극심하게
- **faraway** [fá:rəwèi] 형 멀리 떨어진
- **female** [fí:meil] 형 여성의, 암컷의
- **flesh** [fleʃ] 명 살, 고기
- **insect** [ínsekt] 명 곤충
- **hardly** [há:rdli] 부 거의 ~ 않다
- **hold** [hould] 동 수용하다, 지니다
- **including** [inklú:diŋ] 전 ~을 포함하여
- **last** [læst] 동 지속되다

- **lung** [lʌŋ] 명 폐
- **male** [meil] 형 남성의, 수컷의
- **million** [míljən] 명 백만
- **nap** [næp] 명 낮잠
- **offer** [ɔ́:fər] 동 제공하다
- **polar bear** 북극곰
- **prefer** [prifə́:r] 동 선호하다
- **produce** [prədjú:s] 동 생산하다, 만들어 내다
- **protect** [prətékt] 동 보호하다
- **resident** [rézədnt] 명 거주자
- **rub** [rʌb] 동 문지르다, 비비다
- **scary** [skɛ́əri] 형 무서운
- **sensitive** [sénsətiv] 형 ~에 민감한, 예민한
- **share** [ʃɛər] 동 공유하다
- **skinny** [skíni] 형 여윈, 두께가 얇은
- **social** [sóuʃəl] 형 사회적인, 사교적인
- **stripe** [straip] 명 줄무늬
- **talent show** 장기 자랑
- **unbelievable** [ʌnbəlívəbəl] 형 믿을 수 없는
- **underwater** [ʌndərwɔ́tər] 형 수중의, 물속의
- **watermelon** [wɔ́tərmelən] 명 수박
- **weigh** [wei] 동 무게가 나가다
- **wild** [waild] 형 야생의, 자연 그대로의

Key Expressions

- **a big fan of** ~ ~의 열렬한 지지자
- **as of** ~ 현재, ~일자로
- **be all ears** 경청하다
- **by the way** 그런데
- **cost an arm and a leg** 비싼 값을 치르다
- **decide on** ~을 결정하다
- **have a hard time** 어려움을 겪다
- **have a long face** 표정이 우울하다
- **have fun** 재미있게 보내다
- **keep an eye on** ~을 지켜보다, ~을 감시하다

- **lay eggs** 알을 낳다
- **learn by heart** 암기하다
- **look after** ~을 돌보다
- **one another** 서로
- **out of nowhere** 어디선지 모르게, 느닷없이
- **pass on** 전달하다
- **seem to** ~인 것 같다
- **take a look at** ~을 보다
- **turn one's nose up at** ~을 거절하다
- **What is/are ~ for?** ~의 용도는 무엇이니?

Word Power

※ 서로 비슷한 뜻을 가진 어휘

□ **hold** 수용하다, 지니다 : **contain** 포함하다

□ **choose** 고르다 : **select** 선택하다

□ **offer** 제공하다 : **provide** 제공하다

□ **protect** 보호하다 : **defend** 방어하다

□ **appear** 나타나다 : **show up** 나타나다

□ **hardly** 거의 ~ 않다 : **scarcely** 거의 ~ 않다

□ **entire** 전체의 : **whole** 전체의

□ **exchange** 교환하다 : **trade** 교환하다

□ **difference** 차이점 : **variety** 다양함

□ **prefer** 선호하다 : **like** 좋아하다

□ **social** 사회적인, 사교적인 : **sociable** 사교적인

□ **extremely** 극심하게 : **highly** 매우

□ **resident** 거주자 : **dweller** 거주자

□ **unbelievable** 믿을 수 없는 : **incredible** 믿을 수 없는

※ 서로 반대의 뜻을 가진 어휘

□ **wild** 야생의 ↔ **tamed** 길들여진

□ **difference** 차이점 ↔ **similarity** 닮은 점

□ **sensitive** 예민한 ↔ **insensitive** 둔한

□ **social** 사교적인 ↔ **unsociable** 사회성이 없는

□ **resident** 거주자 ↔ **nonresident** 비거주자

□ **defend** 방어하다 ↔ **attack** 공격하다

□ **unbelievable** 믿을 수 없는 ↔ **credible** 믿을 만한

□ **Arctic** 북극의 ↔ **Antarctic** 남극의

□ **prefer** 선호하다 ↔ **dislike** 싫어하다

□ **faraway** 멀리 떨어진 ↔ **near** 가까운

□ **appear** 나타나다 ↔ **disappear** 사라지다

□ **male** 남성의, 수컷의 ↔ **female** 여성의, 암컷의

□ **regularly** 규칙적으로 ↔ **irregularly** 불규칙하게

English Dictionary

□ **beehive** 벌집
→ a structure where bees are kept for producing honey
꿀 생산을 위해 벌이 길러지는 구조물

□ **choose** 고르다
→ to decide which one of a number of things or people you want
많은 사람이나 사물 중에서 어느 것을 원하는지 정하다

□ **Arctic** 북극의
→ relating to the most northern part of the world
지구의 가장 북쪽과 관련된

□ **prefer** 선호하다
→ to like someone or something more than someone or something else
다른 어떤 사람이나 어떤 것보다 어떤 사람이나 어떤 것을 더 좋아하다

□ **watermelon** 수박
→ a large round fruit with hard green skin, red flesh, and black seeds
초록 껍질, 빨간 과육, 검정 씨앗을 가진 둥근 과일

□ **insect** 곤충
→ a small creature such as a fly or ant, that has six legs, and sometimes wings
여섯 개의 다리와 때로는 날개를 가진 파리나 개미 같은 작은 생물

□ **colony** 군락, 군집
→ a group of animals or plants of the same type that are living or growing together
함께 살거나 자라는 같은 종류의 동물 또는 식물의 집단

□ **resident** 거주자
→ someone who lives or stays in a particular place
특정한 장소에 살거나 머무르는 사람

□ **exchange** 교환
→ the act of giving someone something and receiving something else from them
무엇인가를 다른 사람에게 주거나 그들로부터 받는 행위

□ **nap** 낮잠
→ a short sleep, especially during the day
낮 동안 짧게 자는 잠

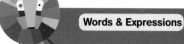

01 다음 영영풀이에 해당하는 단어를 고르시오.

> a structure where bees are kept for producing honey

① flower   ② cave
③ chestnut   ④ beehive
⑤ camp

[02~03] 다음 대화의 빈칸에 들어갈 말을 고르시오.

02

> A: Can you tell me about your dream?
> B: _____ My dream is to make a fantastic team.

① No way.   ② Don't mention it.
③ Not at all.   ④ Really?
⑤ Sure.

03 중요

> B: Mike, how do you like the camp?
> G: It's great. I'm having a lot of _____.

① trouble   ② fun
③ time   ④ difficulty
⑤ problem

[04~05] 다음 빈칸에 들어갈 말로 적절한 것을 고르시오.

04

> People come to the woods and _____ the forest. Many of my friends have lost their homes.

① destroy   ② keep
③ cross   ④ grow
⑤ visit

05

> I get scared whenever I have to cross a big street. This morning I was almost hit. I don't understand why people are in such a _____.

① danger   ② house
③ hurry   ④ plan
⑤ camp

06 중요
다음 주어진 우리말에 어울리는 문장으로 빈칸에 가장 적절한 것은?

> 우리는 종종 개미가 느닷없이 나타나는 것을 본다.
> ➡ We often see ants come _____.

① from time to time
② somewhere near
③ without noticing
④ out of nowhere
⑤ off the corner

07 다음 밑줄 친 단어와 의미가 가장 가까운 단어를 고르시오.

> Can you guess how many bees live there?

① estimate   ② count
③ measure   ④ weigh
⑤ tell

서답형

08 다음 주어진 단어를 이용해 빈칸을 완성하시오.

> Can you tell me about their _____?

➡ _____s (differ)

01 다음 짝지어진 단어의 관계가 같도록 빈칸에 알맞은 말을 쓰시오. (주어진 철자로 시작할 것)

defend : attack – r_____ : irregularly

02 다음 밑줄 친 단어와 의미가 같은 단어를 쓰시오. (주어진 철자로 시작할 것)

The beehive can <u>hold</u> over 50,000 bees.

➡ c_____

03 다음 영영풀이에 해당하는 단어를 쓰시오. (주어진 철자로 시작할 것)

relating to the most northern part of the world

➡ A_____

04 다음 우리말에 맞게 빈칸에 알맞은 말을 쓰시오. (주어진 철자가 있는 경우에는 주어진 철자로 시작할 것)

(1) 나는 배가 몹시 아파요.
➡ I have a t_____ stomachache.

(2) 때때로 나는 너무 어두워서가 아니라 너무 밝아서 길을 잃어요.
➡ Sometimes I get _____ not because it's too dark but because it's too bright.

(3) 불빛이 너무 밝으면 나는 어디로 날아가야 할지 분간할 수 없어요.
➡ When lights are too bright, I can't t_____ which way to fly.

(4) 우리는 종종 느닷없이 개미가 나오는 것을 본다.
➡ We often see ants come out of n_____.

05 다음 문장의 빈칸에 〈보기〉에 있는 단어를 넣어 자연스러운 문장을 만드시오.

┤ 보기 ├
after   breathe   shy   common

(1) The air was so fresh, and the hikers started to _____ slowly.

(2) I had few friends in elementary school since I was extremely _____.

(3) Mother Teresa spent her entire life looking _____ the poor.

(4) A washing machine is a _____ machine that you can see at home.

06 다음 우리말을 영어로 옮길 때 주어진 철자로 시작하여 빈칸에 적절한 말을 완성하시오.

(1) 네가 없는 동안 내가 개를 지켜볼 것이다.
➡ I will k_____ an e_____ o_____ your dog while you are away.

(2) Mike는 오늘 표정이 우울하다.
➡ Mike h_____ a l_____ f_____ today.

07 다음 문장의 빈칸에 들어가기에 적절한 단어를 주어진 철자로 시작하여 쓰시오.

Dogs are more s_____ to smells than humans are.

교과서

Conversation

1 선호 묻고 답하기

> **A** Which do you like better, dogs or cats?
> **B** I like dogs better.

- 선호를 물어보는 표현은 '더 좋아하다'에 해당하는 'like better'를 사용하여 'Which do you like better, A or B?' 또는 'Which one do you like, A or B?'의 형태로 나타낸다.

- 제한된 범위 안에서 '어느 것을 더 좋아하니?'라고 할 때는 의문사 which 또는 which one을 쓴다. '더 좋아하다'의 의미인 'like better'는 동사 'prefer = 선호하다'를 써서 'Which (one) do you prefer, A or B?'라고 할 수 있다.

- 대답할 때는 'like A better than B' 또는 'prefer A to B'라고 한다.

선호 묻기

- Which do you like better, fish or birds? 물고기와 새 중에서 어느 것을 더 좋아하니?
- Which do you prefer, fish or birds?

선호 답하기

- I like fish better than birds. = I prefer fish to birds. 나는 새보다 물고기를 더 좋아한다.

핵심 Check

1. 다음 우리말과 일치하도록 빈칸에 알맞은 말을 쓰시오.
   (1) **A:** _____ do you like better, ice cream or milk?
      (아이스크림과 우유 중에서 어느 것을 더 좋아하니?)
      B: Ice cream is more delicious, I think.
   (2) **A:** Which do you _____ to take, the bus or the subway?
      (버스와 지하철 중에서 어느 것을 타는 것을 선호하니?)
      B: I _____ to take the subway every weekday. (나는 주중에는 지하철 타는 것을 선호해.)

2. 다음 대화의 순서를 바르게 배열하시오.
   (A) Me, too.
   (B) Which do you like better, hot weather or cold weather?
   (C) I like hot weather better. I like going swimming in the sea.
   (D) I like cold weather better. I'm sensitive to hot temperatures. How about you?
   ➡ _____

② 설명 요청하기

> **A** It's an animal. 그것은 동물이야.
>
> **B** Can you tell me more about it? 그것에 대해 더 말해 줄 수 있니?

■ 상대방의 말을 듣고 추가로 더 설명해 달라고 할 때는 'Can you tell me more about it?'이라고 한다. 좀 더 공손하게 표현하여 Can 대신에 Could나 Would를 사용할 수도 있다. tell 대신에 explain을 써서 'Can you explain that more, please?'라고 할 수 있다.

■ 상대방의 말을 잘 알아듣지 못해서 다시 물어볼 때는 'What do you mean (by that)?'이라고 한다. '잘 이해하지 못했습니다.'의 의미로 'I don't get it.' 또는 'I'm not following you.'라고 할 수도 있다.

설명 요청하기

- Can you tell me more about it? 그것에 대해 더 설명해 주시겠습니까?
- Could/Would you tell me more about it?
- Can you explain it more, please?

다시 설명 요청하기

- I don't get it. 잘 이해하지 못했습니다.
- I'm not following you. 이해를 못했어요.

핵심 Check

3. 다음 우리말과 일치하도록 빈칸에 공통으로 알맞은 말을 쓰시오.

  A: Can you _____ me about your plan? (너의 계획에 대해 말해 줄 수 있니?)

  B: Okay. I'll _____ you as soon as I can. (알았어. 가능한 한 빨리 말해 줄게.)

4. 다음 주어진 문장을 자연스러운 대화가 되도록 배열하시오.

  (A) That's too bad. Is there anything we can do to help them?

  (B) Those are good points. I think it's time to get serious about protecting birds.

  (C) I heard birds are having a hard time these days. Can you tell us more?

  (D) Sure. The cities are too bright at night. Many birds lose their way.

  (E) Yes. First, we should turn off unnecessary lights at night. Also we should hold the Earth Hour campaign regularly.

  ➡ _____

Listen – Listen & Answer Dialog 1

B: Amber, how do you like the camp?

G: It's great. I'm ❶having a lot of fun.

B: Me, too. The ❷talent show last night was really great.

G: Yeah. ❸By the way, did you decide on the afternoon program?

B: No, I haven't ❹yet. Which ❺do you think is better, hiking or swimming?

G: I'll go hiking because we can see wild birds and insects in the woods.

B: I'll join you. I like birds and insects.

G: Great. I heard we'll have a hiking guide.

B: Sounds good.

B: Amber, 캠프 어때?

G: 좋아. 아주 재미있어.

B: 나도 그래. 어젯밤 장기 자랑은 정말 멋졌어.

G: 맞아. 그런데 너는 오후 프로그램 결정했니?

B: 아니, 아직 못했어. 너는 산행과 수영 중에 뭐가 낫다고 생각해?

G: 숲에서 야생 조류와 곤충을 볼 수 있으니까 난 산행을 할 거야.

B: 나도 같이할게. 나는 새와 곤충을 좋아하거든.

G: 좋아. 산행 가이드가 있을 거라고 들었어.

B: 잘됐다.

---

❶ have a lot of fun = 매우 재미있게 보내다

❷ talent show = 장기 자랑

❸ 'by the way'는 대화의 화제를 바꾸어 이야기할 때 '그건 그렇고, 그런데' 등의 의미로 사용한다.

❹ 부정문에 쓰인 yet은 '아직'의 의미이다.

❺ 'do you think'에 이어지는 간접의문문이 의문사로 시작할 때는 의문사를 문장 첫 자리에 써야 한다.

Check(√) True or False

(1) The girl didn't decide on the afternoon program.   T ☐ F ☐

(2) The boy will go hiking.   T ☐ F ☐

Listen – Listen & Answer Dialog 2

W: Everyone, look at this chestnut tree. This is the oldest tree in these woods.

B: Can you tell me ❶how old it is?

W: It's about 150 years old.

B: Wow! It's ten ❷times my age.

G: Ms. Oh, is that a beehive up in the tree?

W: Yes. Can you guess how many bees live there?

G: 500 bees?

W: Good guess, but it's big enough to hold over 50,000 bees.

B, G: Unbelievable!

W: 여러분, 이 밤나무를 보세요. 이것은 이 숲에서 가장 오래된 나무랍니다.

B: 그 나무가 몇 살인지 알려 주실 수 있나요?

W: 150살쯤 되었어요.

B: 와! 제 나이의 열 배군요.

G: 오 선생님, 나무 위에 있는 저것은 벌집인가요?

W: 맞아요. 벌이 저곳에서 몇 마리나 사는지 짐작할 수 있겠어요?

G: 500마리요?

W: 좋은 추측입니다. 하지만 저것은 5만 마리 이상을 수용할 만큼 커요.

B, G: 믿을 수 없어요!

---

❶ 'how old it is'는 의문사로 시작하는 간접의문문이다. 간접의문문은 "의문사+주어+동사"의 어순이다.

❷ times는 횟수와 배수를 나타낸다. 여기에서는 배수로 쓰여서 'ten times'는 '열 배'이다.

Check(√) True or False

(3) The tree is ten times older than the boy.   T ☐ F ☐

(4) The tree is 500 years old.   T ☐ F ☐

(5) We can't guess how many bees live in a beehive.   T ☐ F ☐

Listen More – Listen and choose.

B: Sora, can you ❶take a look at these pictures?

G: ❷What are these for?

B: I'm ❸trying to choose a picture for my story in the school newspaper.

G: What's your story about?

B: Nature's future.

G: ❹Can you tell me more about it?

B: It's about ❺endangered animals in the Arctic areas.

G: That sounds interesting.

B: ❻Which picture do you think is better?

G: I like the one showing a skinny polar bear.

❶ take a look at ~ = ~을 보다
❷ What ~ for? = 무슨 용도로 ~?
❸ try to ~ = ~하려고 노력하다
❹ 'Can you tell me more about it?'은 상대방에게 더 많은 설명을 요청하는 말이다.
❺ endangered = 멸종 위기에 처한
❻ Which ~는 정해진 범위 안에서 '어느 것 ~'이라고 물어보는 것이다.

Speak – Talk in groups.

A: Which do ❶like better, dogs or cats?

B: I like dogs better. They are more friendly. ❷ How about you?

C: I like cats better.

D: ❸Me, too. Cats are much cleaner than dogs.

❶ like better = prefer 더 좋아하다, 선호하다
❷ 'How about you?'는 상대의 의견을 물어보거나 권유 또는 제안을 하는 표현이다.
❸ 'Me, too.'는 동의하는 표현으로 'So+동사+주어'의 형태로 나타내기도 한다.

Speak – Talk in pairs.

A: What ❶are you drawing?

B: An elephant.

A: What's an elephant?

B: It's an animal.

A: ❷Can you tell me more about it?

B: It's a big animal that has a long nose and big ears.

❶ 현재진행 시제로 현재 진행되고 있는 동작에 대한 질문이다.
❷ 'Can tell me more about it?'은 추가적인 설명을 요청하는 것으로 tell 대신 explain을 쓸 수도 있다.

My Speaking Portfolio Step 3

A: I heard whales are ❶having a hard time these days. Can you tell me more?

B: Sure. There's lots of trash in the sea. Many whales eat it and ❷get sick.

A: That's too bad. Is there anything we can do ❸ to help them?

B: Yes. First, we should try to clean up the sea. Also, ...

❶ 'have a hard time'은 '어려움이 있다'는 표현으로 'have a difficult time' 'have trouble'이라고 할 수 있다.
❷ 'get sick'은 '병에 걸리다'의 의미로 get은 '~하게 되다'의 의미이다.
❸ 'to help them'은 목적을 나타내는 to부정사로 '돕기 위하여'에 해당하는 의미이다.

Wrap Up – Listening & Speaking ❺

G: What do you do in your free time?

B: I listen to music ❶like EDM or hip-hop.

G: Which do you like better?

B: I prefer hip-hop.

G: Why?

B: Well, it ❷sounds more exciting.

❶ like는 '~처럼'의 의미로 사례를 덧붙일 때 사용한다.
❷ sound는 형용사 보어를 사용하여 'sound+형용사'이다.

Wrap Up – Listening & Speaking ❺

G: Guess what I'm talking about.

B: Okay. ❶Go ahead.

G: It's a common machine ❷that you can see at home.

B: Well, can you tell me more?

G: It helps you wash clothes.

B: Now I know what it is.

❶ 'Go ahead.'는 '계속해.'라는 의미이다.
❷ that은 목적격 관계대명사로 선행사는 a common machine이다.

● 다음 우리말과 일치하도록 빈칸에 알맞은 말을 쓰시오.

Listen – Listen and Answer – Dialog 1

B: Amber, _____ do you like the camp?

G: It's _____. I'm _____ a lot of fun.

B: _____, too. The talent _____ last night was really _____.

G: Yeah. _____ the way, did you _____ on the afternoon program?

B: No, I haven't _____. _____ do you _____ is _____, hiking or swimming?

G: I'll go _____ because we can _____ _____ birds and _____ in the woods.

B: I'll _____ you. I like _____ and insects.

G: Great. I _____ we'll have a hiking _____.

B: Sounds good.

B: Amber, 캠프 어때?
G: 좋아. 아주 재미있어.
B: 나도 그래. 어젯밤 장기 자랑은 정말 멋졌어.
G: 맞아. 그런데 너는 오후 프로그램 결정했니?
B: 아니, 아직 못했어. 너는 산행과 수영 중에 뭐가 낫다고 생각해?
G: 숲에서 야생 조류와 곤충을 볼 수 있으니까 난 산행을 할 거야.
B: 나도 같이할게. 나는 새와 곤충을 좋아하거든.
G: 좋아. 산행 가이드가 있을 거라고 들었어.
B: 잘됐다.

Listen – Listen and Answer – Dialog 2

W: Everyone, _____ at this _____ tree. This is the oldest tree in these _____.

B: Can you _____ me _____ _____ it is?

W: It's _____ 150 years old.

B: Wow! It's _____ _____ my age.

G: Ms. Oh, is that a _____ _____ in the tree?

W: Yes. Can you _____ how many _____ _____ there?

G: 500 bees?

W: Good _____, but it's _____ _____ to _____ over 50,000 bees.

B, G: _____!

W: 여러분, 이 밤나무를 보세요. 이것은 이 숲에서 가장 오래된 나무랍니다.
B: 그 나무가 몇 살인지 알려 주실 수 있나요?
W: 150살쯤 되었어요.
B: 와! 제 나이의 열 배군요.
G: 오 선생님, 나무 위에 있는 저것은 벌집인가요?
W: 맞아요. 벌이 저곳에서 몇 마리나 사는지 짐작할 수 있겠어요?
G: 500마리요?
W: 좋은 추측입니다. 하지만 저것은 5만 마리 이상을 수용할 만큼 커요.
B, G: 믿을 수 없어요!

Listen More - Listen and choose.

B: Sora, can you _____ a _____ at these pictures?

G: _____ are these _____?

B: I'm _____ to _____ a picture for my _____ in the school newspaper.

G: _____ your story _____?

B: Nature's future.

G: Can you _____ me _____ it?

B: It's about _____ _____ in the _____ areas.

G: That _____ interesting.

B: _____ _____ do you think is better?

G: I like the one _____ a _____ polar bear.

B: 소라야, 이 사진들을 한번 봐 줄래?
G: 어디에 쓸 건데?
B: 학교 신문에 실을 내 이야기에 넣을 사진을 고르고 있어.
G: 네 이야기가 무엇에 관한 건데?
B: 자연의 미래.
G: 그것에 대해 더 말해 줄 수 있니?
B: 북극 지역에 사는 멸종 위기의 동물들에 관한 거야.
G: 흥미롭다.
B: 네 생각에는 어느 사진이 더 낫니?
G: 나는 여윈 북극곰을 보여 주는 사진이 마음에 들어.

Speak – Talk in groups.

A: Which do _____ _____, dogs or cats?

B: I _____ dogs better. They are more _____. _____ _____ you?

C: I like cats better.

D: _____, too. Cats are _____ _____ than dogs.

Speak – Talk in pairs.

A: What are you _____?

B: An _____.

A: What's an elephant?

B: It's an _____.

A: Can you _____ _____ _____ about it?

B: It's a _____ animal _____ _____ a long nose and big ears.

My Speaking Portfolio Step 1

1. People _____ to the _____ and _____ the forest. Many of my friends have _____ their homes. I don't know _____ to go.

2. I get _____ _____ I have to _____ a big street. This morning I was _____ hit. I don't _____ _____ people are in _____ a hurry.

3. I have a _____ _____. I _____ something strange. I think it's _____ someone _____ into the sea.

4. Sometimes I _____ _____ not because it's _____ _____ but because it's _____ _____. When lights are too bright, I can't tell which way to fly.

Wrap Up - Listening & Speaking ❺

G: What do you _____ in your _____ _____?

B: I _____ to music _____ EDM or hip-hop.

G: _____ do you _____ _____?

B: I _____ hip-hop.

G: Why?

B: Well, it _____ more _____.

A: 개와 고양이 중에 어느 것을 더 좋아하니?

B: 개를 더 좋아해. 그들이 더 친절해. 너는 어떠니?

C: 나는 고양이를 더 좋아해.

D: 나도 그래. 고양이가 개보다 훨씬 더 깨끗해.

A: 너는 무엇을 그리고 있니?

B: 코끼리.

A: 코끼리가 뭐니?

B: 그것은 동물이야.

A: 그것에 대하여 더 말해 줄 수 있니?

B: 그것은 긴 코와 큰 귀를 가진 덩치 큰 동물이야.

1. 사람들이 숲에 와서 삼림을 파괴해요. 내 친구들 중 많은 수가 집을 잃었어요. 나는 어디로 가야 할지 모르겠어요.

2. 나는 큰 길을 건너야 할 때마다 겁이 나요. 오늘 아침 나는 차에 치일 뻔했다고요. 사람들이 왜 그리 급한지 이해가 안 돼요.

3. 나는 배가 몹시 아파요. 나는 이상한 것을 먹었어요. 내 생각에 그것은 누군가 바다에 버린 것 같아요.

4. 때때로 나는 너무 어두워서가 아니라 너무 밝아서 길을 잃어요. 불빛이 너무 밝으면 나는 어디로 날아가야 할지 분간할 수 없어요.

여: 너는 한가한 시간에 뭘 하니?

남: 나는 EDM이나 힙합 같은 음악을 들어.

여: 어떤 것을 더 좋아하는데?

남: 나는 힙합을 더 좋아해.

여: 왜?

남: 글쎄. 그게 더 신나거든.

[01~02] 다음 대화의 빈칸에 들어갈 말을 고르시오.

01

B: Amber, how do you like the camp?

G: It's great. I'm having a lot of fun.

B: Me, too. The talent show last night was really _____.

① terrible   ② worrying   ③ disappointing

④ great   ⑤ sorry

02

W: Everyone, look at this chestnut tree. This is the oldest tree in these woods.

B: _____ how old it is?

W: It's about 150 years old.

① Did you ask   ② When did you say

③ Can you tell me   ④ Would you ask

⑤ Can I tell you

[03~04] 다음 대화를 읽고 물음에 답하시오.

A: Which do like better, dogs or cats?

B: I like dogs better. They are more friendly. _____(A)_____ you?

C: I like cats better.

D: Me, too. _____(B)_____

03 빈칸 (A)에 들어갈 가장 알맞은 말을 고르시오.

① How about   ② Why are   ③ Which are

④ Which do   ⑤ Why don't

04 다음 중 빈칸 (B)에 들어가기에 가장 적절한 것은?

① Cats are more difficult to grow.

② Cats are much cleaner than dogs.

③ Dogs are more active and cute.

④ Dogs are more cute than cats.

⑤ Cats and dogs are all scary.

[01~02] 다음 대화의 빈칸에 들어갈 말로 알맞은 것은?

01

B: Sora, can you take a look at these pictures?

G: What are these _____?

B: I'm trying to choose a picture for my story in the school newspaper.

G: What's your story about?

B: Nature's future.

① for
② about
③ with
④ by
⑤ in

02

A: Which do like better, dogs or cats?

B: I like dogs better. They are more friendly. How about you?

C: I like cats better.

D: _____ Cats are much cleaner than dogs.

① Why don't you like them?
② How about you?
③ Why not?
④ Neither am I.
⑤ Me, too.

03 다음 빈칸에 들어갈 말이 순서대로 바르게 짝지어진 것은?

G: What do you do in your free time?

B: I listen to music __(A)__ EDM or hip-hop.

G: Which do you like better?

B: I __(B)__ hip-hop.

G: Why?

B: Well, it sounds more __(C)__.

	(A)	(B)	(C)
①	like	prefer	boring
②	like	prefer	exciting
③	about	dislike	boring
④	about	dislike	exciting
⑤	with	listen	boring

[04~05] 다음 대화의 순서가 바르게 배열된 것을 고르시오.

04

A: What are you drawing?

B: Sunglasses.

(A) Can you tell me more about them?

(B) They are things that you wear on your face.

(C) What are sunglasses?

B: They are a pair of lenses that protect your eyes from strong sunlight.

① (A) – (C) – (B)
② (B) – (A) – (C)
③ (B) – (C) – (A)
④ (C) – (A) – (B)
⑤ (C) – (B) – (A)

05

G: Guess what I'm talking about.

B: Okay. Go ahead.

G: It's a common machine that you can see at home.

(A) Now I know what it is.

(B) Well, can you tell me more?

(C) It helps you wash clothes.

① (A) – (C) – (B)
② (B) – (A) – (C)
③ (B) – (C) – (A)
④ (C) – (A) – (B)
⑤ (C) – (B) – (A)

[06~09] 다음 대화를 읽고 물음에 답하시오.

B: Amber, how do you like the camp?

G: It's great. I'm ___(A)___ a lot of fun.

B: (B)Me, too. The talent show last night was really great.

G: Yeah. (C)그런데 넌 오후 프로그램을 결정했니?

B: No, I haven't yet. Which do you think is better, hiking or swimming?

G: I'll go hiking because we can see wild birds and insects in the woods.

B: I'll join you. I like birds and insects.

G: Great. I heard we'll have a hiking guide.

B: Sounds good.

06 빈칸 (A)에 들어갈 가장 알맞은 말을 고르시오.

① giving ② having

③ going ④ thinking

⑤ wondering

07 밑줄 친 (B)와 바꿔 쓸 수 있는 것을 고르시오.

① Neither am I.

② Nor do I.

③ So am I.

④ So do I.

⑤ Neither do I.

08 아래 주어진 단어를 포함하여 밑줄 친 (C)에 어울리는 영어 문장을 완성하시오.

> on, by, decide, did, way

➡ _____

_____

09 위 대화의 내용과 일치하지 <u>않는</u> 것은?

① Amber is satisfied with the camp program.

② Amber likes hiking better than swimming.

③ The boy didn't decide on the afternoon program.

④ Amber wants to join the boy.

⑤ The afternoon program will have a hiking guide.

10 다음 대화를 읽고, 대답할 수 <u>없는</u> 질문은?

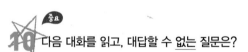

G: Which do you like better, hot weather or cold weather?

B: I like cold weather better. I'm sensitive to hot temperatures. How about you?

G: I like hot weather better. I like going swimming in the sea.

W: Me, too.

G = Girl, B = Boy W = Woman

① Which does the girl like better, hot weather or cold weather?

② Why does the boy like cold weather?

③ Does the woman like hot weather?

④ Which does the boy like better, hot weather or cold weather?

⑤ Does the boy like going swimming?

[01~02] 다음 대화를 읽고 물음에 답하시오.

> B: Sora, can you take a look at these pictures?
> G: What are these for?
> B: I'm trying to choose a picture for my story in the school newspaper.
> G: What's your story about?
> B: Nature's future.
> G: Can you tell me more about it?
> B: It's about endangered animals in the Arctic areas.
> G: That sounds interesting.
> B: Which picture do you think is better?
> G: I like the one showing a skinny polar bear.

01 Why does the boy want to choose a picture? Complete the sentence.

➡ He _____

_____ .

02 What is the boy's story about? Complete the sentence.

➡ It is about _____ .

03 주어진 단어를 사용하여 밑줄 친 우리말에 해당하는 영어 문장을 완성하시오.

> I get scared whenever I have to cross a big street. This morning I was almost hit. 사람들이 왜 그토록 급한지 이해가 안 돼요.

> such, why, understand, in, people, a, hurry

➡ _____

_____

04 다음 대화의 문맥상 또는 어법상 어색한 것을 찾아 고치시오.

> A: What do you prefer, pizza or fried chicken?
> B: I like pizza better. I can choose the toppings I like. How about you?
> A: I like fried chicken better.
> C: Me, too. I'm a meat lover.

➡ _____

[05~06] 다음 대화를 읽고 물음에 답하시오.

> W: Everyone, look at this chestnut tree. This is the oldest tree in these woods.
> B: Can you tell me how old it is?
> W: It's about 150 years old.
> B: Wow! It's ten times my __(A)__ .
> G: Ms. Oh, is that a beehive up in the tree?
> W: Yes. Can you guess how many bees live there?
> G: 500 bees?
> W: Good guess, but (B)그것은 5만 마리 이상을 수용할 만큼 커요. (hold, enough, over, big)
> B: G: Unbelievable!

05 빈칸 (A)에 들어가기에 적절한 단어를 쓰시오.

➡ _____

06 주어진 단어를 포함하여 밑줄 친 (B)의 우리말을 영작하시오.

➡ _____

Grammar

1 명사를 뒤에서 꾸미는 분사

> • Look at the sun **rising over the sea.** 바다 위로 떠오르는 해를 봐.

■ 형태: 명사+현재분사[과거분사]+수식어구

의미: ~하는 … / ~된 …

■ 분사는 현재분사와 과거분사가 있다. 분사는 문장 안에서 형용사 역할을 하여 명사를 수식할 수 있다. 분사가 수식어구와 함께 사용될 때는 명사 뒤에서 수식한다. '명사+분사'는 '명사+주격 관계대명사+ be동사+분사'에서 '주격 관계대명사+be동사'가 생략된 것이라고 볼 수 있다.

• Look at the boy **dancing on the stage**. 무대 위에서 춤을 추는 소년을 보아라.

• Look at the picture **painted by a parrot**. 앵무새에 의해서 그려진 그림을 보아라.

■ 분사가 명사를 수식할 때 현재분사는 능동이나 진행의 의미를 가져서 '~하는, ~하고 있는'의 의미가 된다. 과거분사는 수동이나 완료의 의미를 나타내어 '~해진, ~하게 된'의 의미가 된다.

• Do you know the child **crying at the door**? 문에서 울고 있는 아이를 아니?

• Look at the man **climbing the tall building**. 높은 건물을 올라가고 있는 사람을 봐.

• I like every food **cooked by my grandmother**. 나는 할머니에 의해서 요리된 모든 음식을 좋아해.

• He is carrying a basket **filled with cherries**. 그는 체리로 가득 채워진 바구니를 운반하고 있다.

핵심 Check

1. 다음 주어진 문장에서 적절한 것을 고르시오.

   (1) He visited the doctor (was working / working) at the hospital.

   (2) The woman (is sleeping / sleeping) in the room will wake up in an hour.

   (3) Do you know the girl (is walking / walking) along the street?

   (4) The man sitting by the window (is waiting / waiting) for his wife.

   (5) Those books lying on the desk (are / being) very interesting.

   (6) Tom was taking out some chairs (were broken / broken) during the earthquake.

   (7) The idea (was discussed / discussed) yesterday will be important for your plan.

2. 다음 빈칸에 주어진 단어를 적절한 형태로 쓰시오.

   (1) The people in the town love the church _____ in 1890. (build)

   (2) The book _____ in 1940 has many interesting stories. (write)

   (3) Harry has been _____ to watch TV for an hour. (allow)

   (4) Look at the girl _____ the tall building. (climb)

   (5) This picture _____ at the top of the mountain shows wonderful scenery. (take)

2 접속사 since와 though

> • **Since** it rained heavily, the station was closed. 심하게 비가 와서 역이 문을 닫았다.

■ 형태: **Since/Though** + 주어+동사 ~, 주어+동사
　　　　주어+동사 ~ **since/though** + 주어+동사

　의미: **since** = ~이기 때문에, ~한 이래로
　　　　though = 비록 ~이지만

■ since는 종속접속사로 주절의 이유나 근거를 나타내어 '~이기 때문에, ~해서'의 의미를 나타낸다. since는 부사절을 유도하며 since가 유도하는 부사절은 주절의 앞이나 뒤에 쓰인다.

- **Since** I ate a whole pizza, I am full.
  = I am full since I ate a whole pizza. 피자 한 판을 다 먹었기 때문에 나는 배가 부르다.

- **Since** it is hot, I want to drink something cold.
  = I want to drink something cold since it is hot. 날씨가 더워서 나는 차가운 것을 마시고 싶다.

cf. She has lived here **since** she moved to this city. 그녀는 이 도시로 이사한 이후로 여기에서 살고 있다.
　　(since = ~한 이래로)

■ 접속사 though는 although와 함께 '비록 ~이기는 하지만, ~할지라도'의 의미로, 주절과 대조되거나 상반되는 내용을 나타내는 양보의 접속사이다. though와 although는 부사절을 유도한다.

- **Though** I ate a whole pizza, I am still hungry.
  = I am still hungry **though** I ate a whole pizza. 비록 내가 피자 한 판을 다 먹었지만, 나는 여전히 배가 고프다.

- I am tired **though** I slept enough last night.
  = **Though** I slept enough last night, I am tired. 비록 어젯밤에 충분히 잤지만, 나는 피곤하다.

핵심 Check

3. 다음 주어진 문장에 어울리는 것을 고르시오.

(1) (Since / Though) you finished your homework, you may go out and play.

(2) (Since / Though) he had prepared a lot, he failed at the tryout.

(3) I don't want to go to the party (though / since) I have no one to talk with.

(4) (Though / Since) he was smiling, he didn't look that happy.

(5) It is sunny (though / since) it is cold.

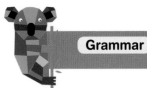

01 다음 빈칸에 들어갈 말로 알맞은 것은?

> Who is the man _____ by the door?

① stand   ② stood   ③ to stand
④ standing   ⑤ is standing

02 다음 중 밑줄 친 부분의 쓰임이 어색한 것을 고르시오.

① The boy <u>wearing</u> a baseball cap is my brother.
② Do you know the child <u>crying</u> in the room?
③ Look at the man <u>climbing</u> the high mountain.
④ I like every food <u>cooking</u> by my grandmother.
⑤ He is carrying a basket <u>filled</u> with cherries.

03 다음 〈보기〉의 밑줄 친 부분과 쓰임이 같은 것은?

> ┤ 보기 ├
>
> This is a photo <u>taken</u> last weekend.

① He has a lovely daughter <u>named</u> Elizabeth.
② I <u>helped</u> her clean the cage made of wood.
③ The cat <u>watched</u> us from a chair painted green.
④ Ants <u>produced</u> a special chemical for communication.
⑤ Mary <u>used</u> the smartphone for three years.

04 다음 우리말을 영어로 바르게 옮긴 것은?

> 비록 날씨가 춥지만 나는 차가운 것을 마시고 싶다.

① It is cold though I want to drink something cold.
② Though it is hot, I want to drink something hot.
③ Since it is cold, I want to drink something cold.
④ Though it is cold, I want to drink something cold.
⑤ Though I want to drink something cold, it is cold.

05 다음 괄호 안에서 알맞은 말을 고르시오.

(1) The man [wears / wearing] a white shirt is my uncle.
(2) I ate the whole cake [though / since] I really liked cake.

서답형

01 〈보기〉를 참고하여 주어진 두 문장을 한 문장으로 연결하여 쓰시오.

┌─ 보기 ─┐
- The book was written by her.
- The book is easy to read.
➡ The book written by her is easy to read.

(1) • The man was running along the road.
   • The man was asking for help.
   ➡ _____
   _____

(2) • The boy was eating lunch.
   • He was sitting on the floor.
   ➡ _____
   _____

(3) • The man was reading a book.
   • He told us to be quiet.
   ➡ _____
   _____

(4) • The boys were allowed to watch TV.
   • They were eating snacks.
   ➡ _____
   _____

02 다음 중 밑줄 친 부분의 쓰임이 어색한 것을 고르시오.

① I am tired though I slept enough last night.
② Though I ate a whole pizza, I am still hungry.
③ I stayed home though I felt tired.
④ Since I am tired, I will stop working.
⑤ Though he was full, he ate more cake.

서답형

03 다음 괄호 안에서 알맞은 말을 고르시오.

(1) The photos [taken / taking] by him show some sailing boats.
(2) The kid [walk / walking] across the garden is my brother.
(3) Do you know the man [inviting / invited] to the party?
(4) [Though / Since] I met him before, I was pleased to see him again.
(5) [Though / Since] I had lunch, I am still hungry.

04 다음 중 밑줄 친 부분의 쓰임이 어색한 것을 고르시오.

① The story is about endangered animals in the Arctic areas.
② I like the picture showing a skinny polar bear.
③ A watermelon is a ball-shaped fruit that has sweet and juicy flesh in it.
④ Look at the sun rising over the sea.
⑤ Though it rained heavily, he didn't go out.

05 다음 우리말을 영어로 바르게 옮긴 것은?

저기에서 노래하는 사람을 보아라.

① Look at the man sings over there.
② Look at the man singing over there.
③ Singing over there the man looking.
④ Looking at the man singing over there.
⑤ Look at the man to sing over there.

06 다음 중 밑줄 친 부분의 쓰임이 <u>다른</u> 하나를 고르시오.

① Those books <u>written</u> by James are very interesting.
② We saw the picture <u>taken</u> at the top.
③ He <u>found</u> a picture showing the image of a person.
④ Animals <u>found</u> in the mountain were eating grass.
⑤ The <u>frightened</u> child ran into the room.

07 다음 중 밑줄 친 부분의 쓰임이 <u>어색한</u> 것을 고르시오.

① An airplane is a <u>flying</u> machine that can take you to a faraway place.
② The girl <u>singing</u> over there is Nancy.
③ I helped her clean the cage <u>made</u> of glass.
④ The woman <u>moving</u> the table is my sister.
⑤ There is a picture <u>paint</u> by a parrot.

08 다음 빈칸에 들어갈 말로 알맞은 것은?

> _____ it rained heavily, the station was closed.

① Although
② While
③ Whether
④ Since
⑤ If

09 다음 우리말을 영어로 바르게 옮긴 것은?

> 나는 그녀가 요리한 음식을 모두 좋아한다.

① I like every food cooked by her.
② She likes all the food I cooked.
③ She likes every food cooked by her.
④ I like every food cook by her.
⑤ I like every food cooking by her.

서답형

10 다음 우리말에 맞게 괄호 안에 주어진 어휘를 바르게 배열 하시오. (필요하면 어형을 바꿀 것)

(1) 아이 한 명이 해변에서 놀고 있었다. (was, playing, the beach, there, a boy, on)
   ➡ _____

(2) 나는 나무로 만들어진 벤치에 앉았다. (the bench, wood, make, of, sat, on, I)
   ➡ _____

(3) 나는 너무 어리기 때문에 그 영화를 볼 수 없다. (I, watch, too young, am, the film, can't, I, since) (since로 시작할 것)
   ➡ _____

서답형

11 다음 괄호 안에서 알맞은 말을 고르시오.

(1) This is a cake (make / made) by him this morning.
(2) I visited a castle (built / building) a hundred years ago.
(3) I cleaned the wall (painting / painted) yellow.
(4) The taxi driver (moving / moved) the bag is very kind.
(5) The woman watched us from a car (wash / washed) this morning.

12 다음 중 밑줄 친 부분의 쓰임이 <u>어색한</u> 것을 고르시오.

① The children <u>wearing</u> a baseball cap are my friends.
② Do you know the girl <u>playing</u> in the room?
③ Look at the man <u>running</u> over the hill.
④ An essay <u>wrote</u> carefully will receive a high grade.
⑤ <u>Since</u> it was raining, we didn't go out.

13 다음 중 밑줄 친 부분의 쓰임이 <u>다른</u> 하나를 고르시오.

① The boy <u>singing</u> a song is my nephew.
② I know the child <u>crying</u> loudly.
③ The parrot <u>sitting</u> on the tree said, "Hurry up."
④ She enjoyed <u>talking</u> to her friends after the class.
⑤ The man <u>walking</u> into the room said hello to me.

14 다음 중 밑줄 친 부분의 쓰임이 <u>어색한</u> 것을 고르시오.

① In the room, I saw a picture <u>drawn</u> by him.
② That is the tower <u>built</u> by her last year.
③ The girl <u>sitting</u> under the tree called my name.
④ I like every book <u>written</u> by him.
⑤ I don't like the gift <u>gave</u> to me.

[15~16] 다음 빈칸에 들어갈 말로 알맞은 것은?

15

Like humans, they live almost everywhere in the world, except a few extremely cold places _____ Antarctica.

① include
② included
③ includes
④ including
⑤ have included

16

_____ he knows how to drive a car, he doesn't like to drive a car.

① Though
② Since
③ While
④ Whether
⑤ Unless

17 다음 밑줄 친 것 중에서 쓰임이 <u>다른</u> 하나는?

① Tom was tired <u>since</u> he walked for a long distance.
② <u>Since</u> it was very cold, I had to put on the jacket.
③ My mother made a cake <u>since</u> it was my birthday.
④ She has lived here <u>since</u> 2005.
⑤ I won't travel by train <u>since</u> I don't like the noise.

18 다음 빈칸에 들어가기에 적절한 것은?

Jane is _____ though she slept enough last night.

① free
② glad
③ busy
④ tired
⑤ happy

01 다음 우리말에 맞게 괄호 안에 주어진 어휘를 바르게 배열하시오. (필요한 어휘 변형 및 어휘 추가 가능)

(1) 그는 그에게 보내진 메시지를 읽지 않았다.
(read, send, the message, to him, he, didn't)

➡ _____

_____

(2) 농구하고 있는 아이들은 내 친구들이다.
(be, the children, my friends, play basketball)

➡ _____

_____

(3) 그는 내 동생에 의해 그려진 그림을 보고 있었다. (was looking at, by, paint, he, the picture, my brother)

➡ _____

_____

(4) 그 책이 너무 재미있어서 나는 그 책을 어젯밤에 읽기를 끝냈다. (the book, so, finished, was, reading the book, interesting, since, I, last night) (since로 시작할 것)

➡ _____

_____

(5) 나는 배가 고팠지만 음식을 먹지 않았다. (I, hungry, eat, was, didn't, though, I, the food) (though로 시작할 것)

➡ _____

_____

02 다음 밑줄 친 단어 대신 쓸 수 있는 단어를 쓰시오. (한 단어)

Though he was busy, he helped me.

➡ _____

03 다음 문장에 주어진 단어를 적절한 형태로 빈칸에 쓰시오.

(1) The man _____ by the tree was Ann's husband. (sit)

(2) Those books _____ on the desk are very difficult to read. (lie)

(3) He has to fix the door _____ a few days ago. (break)

(4) A picture _____ the top of the mountain was wonderful. (show)

(5) He was eating cookies _____ by his mother. (make)

04 다음 주어진 문장의 빈칸에 접속사 since와 though 중에서 적절한 것을 쓰시오.

(1) _____ it is cold, I want to drink something hot.

(2) _____ it rains, I'll go out with my friends.

(3) _____ I am tired, I want to go home early.

(4) _____ I am tired, I will stay up late and enjoy Friday night.

05 다음 우리말과 의미가 같도록 영작할 때 빈칸에 알맞은 말을 〈조건〉에 맞게 쓰시오.

┌─ 조건 ─┐
'bark'를 사용하여 문장을 완성할 것.

거리에서 짖고 있는 개 한 마리가 있다.
= There is _____ _____ _____ on the street.

06 다음 문장에서 어법상 어색한 부분을 바르게 고쳐 문장을 다시 쓰시오.

> The man walked his dogs is a famous singer.

➡ _____

07 다음 우리말에 맞게 빈칸에 알맞은 말을 쓰시오.

> 나는 방금 먹었기 때문에 배고프지 않다.
> ➡ I'm not hungry _____ I have just eaten.

➡ _____

08 다음 주어진 문장을 〈보기〉와 같이 분사가 있는 한 문장으로 다시 쓰시오.

> ┌─ 보기 ─┐
> • The children are watching TV.
> • They will help you.
> ➡ <u>The children watching TV will help you.</u>

(1) • The church was built 100 years ago.
    • It has beautiful stained glass.
    ➡ _____
    _____

(2) • The car was rolling down the road.
    • It made a loud noise.
    ➡ _____
    _____

(3) • The woman is cooking apple pies.
    • She will give them to you.
    ➡ _____
    _____

(4) • The photos were taken by Ann.
    • They show some wild birds.
    ➡ _____
    _____

(5) • The message was sent to him.
    • He was reading the message.
    ➡ _____
    _____

09 다음 대화의 우리말에 해당하는 문장을 영어로 옮길 때 빈칸에 들어가기에 적절한 단어를 쓰시오.

> B: Which picture do you think is better?
> G: <u>나는 여윈 북극곰을 보여 주는 사진이 마음에 들어.</u>(= I like the one _____ a skinny polar bear).

➡ _____

10 다음 문장에서 어색한 것을 바로 잡으시오.

(1) Mike was reading the newspaper send to him this morning.
    _____ ➡ _____

(2) Did the children like the actor sung on the stage?
    _____ ➡ _____

(3) The animals eaten plants are called beavers.
    _____ ➡ _____

Reading

The Amazing Ants

For the science project, our group has chosen very special insects.
<u>현재완료</u>

- They are very social.

- They are as old as the T-Rex.
  as+형용사/부사+as: '~만큼 …한', 원급 비교 표현

- They appear in Aesop's stories.

- They use a special chemical to communicate.
  '의사소통하기 위해', to부정사의 부사적 용법(목적)

Can you guess what they are? Yes, the answer is ants. We want to
guess의 목적어 역할을 하는 간접의문문. '의문사+주어+동사'의 어순

share with you what we have learned about these insects.
관계대명사 what(선행사 포함): '~하는 것'   현재완료   = ants

How Many Ants Are on Earth?

We often see ants come out of nowhere. Like humans, they live
지각동사+목적어+목적보어(동사원형)

almost everywhere in the world, except a few extremely cold places
a little(×)

including Antarctica. As of 2018, there were over 7 billion people on
billions(×)

Earth. Then, how about ants? According to scientists, there are about
= what about   ~에 의하면   약

one million ants for every human in the world. Though each ant hardly
'비록 ~이지만'(양보를 나타내는 접속사)   거의 ~ 않다

weighs anything, one million ants are as heavy as a human being
비교하는 두 대상의 특성이 동등함을 나타내는 원급 비교 구문

weighing about 62 kilograms.
명사를 뒤에서 수식하는 분사구 = who weighs about 62 kilograms

insect 곤충
social 사회적인, 사교적인
appear 나타나다, (글 속에) 나오다
chemical 화학물질
share 공유하다
out of nowhere 어디선지 모르게, 느닷없이
except ~을 제외하고
extremely 극심하게
including ~을 포함하여
as of ~ 현재, ~일자로
billion 십억
million 백만 (1,000,000)
hardly 거의 ~ 않다
human being 사람, 인간
weigh 무게가 나가다

 확인문제

● 다음 문장이 본문의 내용과 일치하면 T, 일치하지 않으면 F를 쓰시오.

1 Ants are very social. ☐

2 The T-Rex is older than ants. ☐

3 Ants often come out of nowhere. ☐

4 Ants live almost everywhere in the world including Antarctica. ☐

5 There are about one million ants for every human in the world. ☐

6 One million ants are heavier than a human being weighing about 62 kilograms. ☐

What Is the Ant Society Like?

Ants live in colonies which have lots of residents living together.
Within a colony, there are usually three different types of ants. There is the queen, and what she does her entire life is lay eggs. The second type of ant is the male that helps the queen produce these eggs. The third type of ant is the worker. Worker ants are all female and do very important jobs, like caring for eggs, defending the colony, and collecting food.

How Do Ants Communicate?

Though ants do not speak like humans, they actually have a "language." Ants produce a chemical called a pheromone to communicate with one another. By using the chemical, they can exchange information about food or danger. Ants also use touch for communication. For example, if an ant finds food, it passes on the good news by rubbing its body on its neighbor. Since an ant has legs covered with very sensitive hairs, it can sense even the smallest touch.

colony (동식물의) 군락, 군집
resident 거주자
entire 전체의
lay eggs 알을 낳다
male 남성의, 수컷의
produce 생산하다, 만들어 내다
female 여성의, 암컷의
defend 방어하다
one another 서로
exchange 교환하다
pass on 전달하다
rub 문지르다, 비비다
sensitive 예민한, 민감한

확인문제

● 다음 문장이 본문의 내용과 일치하면 T, 일치하지 <u>않으면</u> F를 쓰시오.

1 Within a colony, there are usually three different types of ants. ☐

2 What the queen does her entire life is care for eggs. ☐

3 The male helps the queen produce the eggs. ☐

4 Worker ants are all male. ☐

5 Ants produce a chemical called a pheromone to communicate with one another. ☐

6 Since an ant has wings covered with very sensitive hairs, it can sense even the smallest touch. ☐

FUN FACTS ABOUT ANTS

01 Some Queen ants live up to 30 years.

02 Some ants can carry things that are 50 times their own body
= which   50배
weight.

03 Ants do not have lungs but breathe through small holes in their
~을 통해서
bodies.

04 An ant has two stomachs. One stomach holds food for itself, and
둘 중 하나   재귀대명사
the other holds food to share with others.
둘 중 다른 하나   = other ants

05 Most ants can swim and live 24 hours underwater.
물속에서(부사)

up to ~까지

weight 몸무게, 체중

lung 폐

breathe 호흡하다

hole 구멍

stomach 위

underwater 수중에서

확인문제

● 다음 문장이 본문의 내용과 일치하면 T, 일치하지 않으면 F를 쓰시오.

1 Most Queen ants live up to more than 30 years. ☐

2 Ants have small holes in their bodies. ☐

3 An ant has another stomach to share food with other ants. ☐

● 우리말을 참고하여 빈칸에 알맞은 말을 쓰시오.

1 The _____ Ants

2 _____ _____ _____ _____, our group _____ _____ very special insects.

3 They are very _____.

4 They are _____ _____ _____ the T-Rex.

5 They _____ in Aesop's stories.

6 They use _____ _____ _____ to communicate.

7 Can you guess _____ _____ _____?

8 Yes, _____ _____ is ants.

9 We want to _____ _____ you _____ we have learned about these insects.

10 _____ _____ _____ Are on Earth?

11 We often see ants come _____ _____ _____.

12 _____ _____, they live almost everywhere in the world, _____ a few extremely cold places _____ _____.

13 _____ _____ _____, there were over 7 billion people on Earth.

14 Then, _____ _____ ants?

15 _____ _____ _____, there are about one million ants _____ _____ _____ in the world.

16 Though each ant _____ _____ _____, one million ants are _____ _____ _____ a human being weighing about 62 kilograms.

17 What _____ the Ant Society _____?

18 Ants live in colonies _____ _____ lots of residents _____ together.

19 _____ a colony, there are usually _____ _____ _____ of ants.

1	놀라운 개미
2	과학 프로젝트를 위해, 우리 모둠은 매우 특별한 곤충을 선택했습니다.
3	그들은 매우 사회적입니다.
4	그들은 티라노사우루스만큼 오래되었습니다.
5	그들은 이솝 이야기에 등장합니다.
6	그들은 의사소통하기 위해 특별한 화학물질을 사용합니다.
7	그들이 어떤 곤충인지 추측할 수 있나요?
8	네. 정답은 개미입니다.
9	저희들은 이 곤충에 관해 알게 된 것을 여러분과 함께 나누고 싶습니다.
10	지구상에는 얼마나 많은 개미가 있을까?
11	우리는 종종 난데없이 나타나는 개미들을 본다.
12	인간처럼, 개미도 남극을 포함한 일부 극도로 추운 곳을 제외한 전 세계 거의 모든 곳에 살고 있다.
13	2018년 현재, 지구상에 70억이 넘는 인구가 있었다.
14	그렇다면. 개미는 어떨까?
15	과학자들에 의하면, 세상에는 사람 한 명당 약 백만 마리의 개미가 있다.
16	개미 한 마리는 거의 무게가 나가지 않지만 백만 마리의 개미는 체중이 약 62kg인 사람 한 명과 무게가 같다.
17	개미 사회는 어떠할까?
18	개미는 많은 거주자가 함께 사는 군집을 이루어 산다.
19	군집 안에는 보통 세 가지 다른 종류의 개미가 있다.

20 There is the queen, and _____ _____ _____ her entire life is lay eggs.

21 The second type of ant is the male that helps the queen _____ _____ _____.

22 _____ _____ _____ of ant is the worker.

23 Worker ants are all female and do very important jobs, _____ _____ for eggs, _____ the colony, and _____ food.

24 _____ Do Ants Communicate?

25 Though ants do not speak _____ _____, they _____ _____ a "language."

26 Ants produce a chemical _____ a pheromone _____ _____ _____ one another.

27 _____ _____ the chemical, they can _____ _____ about food or danger.

28 Ants also use touch _____ _____.

29 _____ _____, if an ant finds food, it passes on the good news _____ _____ its body _____ its neighbor.

30 Since an ant has legs _____ _____ very sensitive hairs, it can sense _____ _____ _____ _____.

31 _____ _____ ABOUT ANTS

32 01 Some Queen ants live _____ _____ 30 years.

33 02 Some ants can carry things that are _____ _____ _____ _____ _____.

34 03 Ants do not have lungs but _____ _____ _____ _____ in their bodies.

35 04 An ant has _____ _____.

36 _____ stomach holds food _____ _____, and _____ _____ holds food to share with others.

37 05 _____ _____ can swim and live 24 hours _____.

● 우리말을 참고하여 본문을 영작하시오.

1   놀라운 개미
➡ _____

2   과학 프로젝트를 위해, 우리 모둠은 매우 특별한 곤충을 선택했습니다.
➡ _____

3   그들은 매우 사회적입니다.
➡ _____

4   그들은 티라노사우루스만큼 오래되었습니다.
➡ _____

5   그들은 이솝 이야기에 등장합니다.
➡ _____

6   그들은 의사소통하기 위해 특별한 화학물질을 사용합니다.
➡ _____

7   그들이 어떤 곤충인지 추측할 수 있나요?
➡ _____

8   네. 정답은 개미입니다.
➡ _____

9   저희들은 이 곤충에 관해 알게 된 것을 여러분과 함께 나누고 싶습니다.
➡ _____

10   지구상에는 얼마나 많은 개미가 있을까?
➡ _____

11   우리는 종종 난데없이 나타나는 개미들을 본다.
➡ _____

12   인간처럼, 개미도 남극을 포함한 일부 극도로 추운 곳을 제외한 전 세계 거의 모든 곳에 살고 있다.
➡ _____

13   2018년 현재, 지구상에 70억이 넘는 인구가 있었다.
➡ _____

14   그렇다면. 개미는 어떨까?
➡ _____

15   과학자들에 의하면, 세상에는 사람 한 명당 약 백만 마리의 개미가 있다.
➡ _____

16   개미 한 마리는 거의 무게가 나가지 않지만 백만 마리의 개미는 체중이 약 62kg인 사람 한 명과
무게가 같다.
➡ _____
_____

17   개미 사회는 어떠할까?
➡ _____

18   개미는 많은 거주자가 함께 사는 군집을 이루어 산다.
➡ _____

19 군집 안에는 보통 세 가지 다른 종류의 개미가 있다.

➡ _____

20 여왕개미가 있고. 그녀가 평생 하는 일은 알을 낳는 것이다.

➡ _____

21 두 번째 종류는 여왕이 알을 낳는 것을 돕는 수개미이다.

➡ _____

22 세 번째 종류는 일개미이다.

➡ _____

23 일개미는 모두 암컷인데, 알을 돌보고, 군집을 방어하며, 먹이를 모으는 것과 같은 매우 중요한 일을 한다.

➡ _____

_____

24 개미는 어떻게 의사소통할까?

➡ _____

25 개미들이 인간처럼 말을 하는 것은 아니지만, 그들은 실제로 '언어'를 가지고 있다.

➡ _____

26 개미는 서로 소통하기 위해 '페로몬'이라고 불리는 화학물질을 분비한다.

➡ _____

27 그 화학물질을 사용하여 그들은 먹이나 위험에 관한 정보를 교환할 수 있다.

➡ _____

28 개미는 또한 의사소통을 위해 접촉을 이용한다.

➡ _____

29 예를 들어, 먹이를 발견할 경우 개미는 자기 몸을 이웃의 개미에게 문질러서 좋은 소식을 전달한다.

➡ _____

30 개미는 (자극에) 매우 민감한 털로 덮인 다리가 있기 때문에, 아주 미세한 접촉도 감지할 수 있다.

➡ _____

31 개미에 관한 재미있는 사실

➡ _____

32 01 어떤 여왕개미는 30년까지 살 수 있다.

➡ _____

33 02 어떤 개미들은 자기 몸무게의 50배에 달하는 것을 들 수 있다.

➡ _____

34 03 개미는 폐가 없지만, 몸에 있는 작은 구멍을 통해 호흡한다.

➡ _____

35 04 개미는 위가 두 개 있다.

➡ _____

36 하나에는 자신의 먹이를 저장하고 다른 하나에는 다른 개미들과 함께 나눌 먹이를 저장한다.

➡ _____

37 05 대부분의 개미는 수영할 수 있고 물속에서 24시간 동안 살 수 있다.

➡ _____

[01~03] 다음 글을 읽고 물음에 답하시오.

For the science project, our group has chosen very special insects.

• They are very social.
• They are as old as the T-Rex.
• They appear in ⓐAesop's stories.
• They use a special chemical ⓑto communicate.

Can you guess what they are? Yes, the answer is ants. We want to share with you what we have learned about these insects.

01 위 글의 밑줄 친 ⓐAesop's stories가 속하는 문학 장르로 알맞은 것을 고르시오.

① poem   ② essay
③ fable   ④ play
⑤ scenario

02 아래 〈보기〉에서 위 글의 밑줄 친 ⓑto communicate와 to부정사의 용법이 다른 것의 개수를 고르시오.

┌─── 보기 ───┐

① You have to study hard to pass the exam.
② He tried to help the poor man.
③ She was surprised to hear the news.
④ She awoke to find herself famous.
⑤ Her dream is to be a dancer.

└──────────┘

① 1개 ② 2개 ③ 3개 ④ 4개 ⑤ 5개

03 위 글의 뒤에 올 내용으로 가장 알맞은 것을 고르시오.

① 과학 프로젝트 과제 선택 과정 설명
② 과학 프로젝트 과제 조사 방법 설명
③ 개미와 티라노사우루스의 비교
④ 의사소통에 필요한 매체 발표
⑤ 모둠이 개미에 관해 알게 된 것 발표

[04~06] 다음 글을 읽고 물음에 답하시오.

What Is the Ant Society Like?

(A)Ants live in colonies which has lots of residents living together. Within a colony, there are usually three different types of ants. There is the queen, and what she does her entire life is ___ⓐ___ eggs. The second type of ant is the male that helps the queen produce these eggs. The third type of ant is the worker. Worker ants are all female and do very important jobs, like caring for eggs, defending the colony, and collecting food.

04 위 글의 빈칸 ⓐ에 들어갈 알맞은 말을 모두 고르시오.

① to lay   ② laid
③ lie   ④ lay
⑤ lying

서답형

05 위 글의 밑줄 친 (A)에서 어법상 틀린 부분을 찾아 고치시오.

_____ ➡ _____

서답형

06 주어진 영영풀이에 해당하는 단어를 본문에서 찾아 쓰시오.

┌──────────────────────┐
a group of organisms of the same type living or growing together
└──────────────────────┘

➡ _____

[07~09] 다음 글을 읽고 물음에 답하시오.

How Many Ants Are on Earth?

We often see ants come out of nowhere. Like humans, they live almost everywhere in the world, ⓐ a few extremely cold places including Antarctica. As of 2018, there were over 7 billion people on Earth. Then, how about ants? According to scientists, there are about one million ants ⓑ every human in the world. Though each ant hardly weighs anything, one million ants are as heavy as a human being ©weighing about 62 kilograms.

07 위 글의 빈칸 ⓐ와 ⓑ에 들어갈 전치사가 바르게 짝지어진 것은?

	ⓐ	ⓑ			ⓐ	ⓑ
①	for	– from		②	except	– for
③	in	– for		④	for	– to
⑤	except	– from				

08 위 글의 밑줄 친 ©weighing과 문법적 쓰임이 같은 것을 모두 고르시오.

① My hobby is collecting stamps.
② The boy reading a book in the room is Ben.
③ Do you know the girl speaking English over there?
④ She left without saying a word.
⑤ Who is the boy playing baseball?

According to the passage, which is NOT true?

① Ants can live even in very cold places.
② As of 2018, over 7 billion people were living on Earth.
③ The number of ants is about one million times more than that of humans.
④ Each ant hardly weighs anything.
⑤ The weight of one million ants is about 62 kilograms.

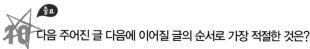

다음 주어진 글 다음에 이어질 글의 순서로 가장 적절한 것은?

Though ants do not speak like humans, they actually have a "language."

(A) Ants also use touch for communication. For example, if an ant finds food, it passes on the good news by rubbing its body on its neighbor.

(B) Ants produce a chemical called a pheromone to communicate with one another. By using the chemical, they can exchange information about food or danger.

(C) Since an ant has legs covered with very sensitive hairs, it can sense even the smallest touch.

① (A) – (C) – (B) ② (B) – (A) – (C)
③ (B) – (C) – (A) ④ (C) – (A) – (B)
⑤ (C) – (B) – (A)

[11~12] 다음 글을 읽고 물음에 답하시오.

How Do Ants Communicate?

 Though ants do not speak like humans, they actually have a "language." Ants produce a chemical called a pheromone to communicate with one another. By using the chemical, they can exchange information about food or danger. Ants also use touch for communication. For example, if an ant finds food, it passes on ⓐthe good news by rubbing its body on its neighbor. Since an ant has legs covered with very sensitive hairs, it can sense even the smallest touch.

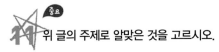 위 글의 주제로 알맞은 것을 고르시오.

① the way in which ants communicate
② how to produce a pheromone
③ various kinds of chemicals
④ the reason ants exchange information
⑤ the right way to use touch

서답형
12 위 글의 밑줄 친 ⓐthe good news의 내용을 우리말로 쓰시오.

➡ _____

[13~15] 다음 글을 읽고 물음에 답하시오.

 We often see ants come out of nowhere. Like humans, they live almost everywhere in the world, except a few extremely cold places including Antarctica. As of 2018, there were over 7 billion people on Earth. Then, how about ants? According to scientists, there are about one million ants for every human in the world. (A)Though each ant hardly weighs anything, one million ants are as heavy as a human being ⓐ _____ about 62 kilograms.

13 위 글의 빈칸 ⓐ에 weigh를 알맞은 형태로 쓰시오.

➡ _____

14 위 글의 밑줄 친 (A)Though와 바꿔 쓸 수 있는 말을 모두 고르시오.

① In spite of   ② Although
③ Even though   ④ Despite
⑤ As though

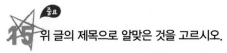 위 글의 제목으로 알맞은 것을 고르시오.

① How Do Ants Communicate?
② Have You Ever Seen Ants?
③ What Is the Ant Society Like?
④ How Many Ants Are There on Earth?
⑤ Can Ants Live in Antarctica?

[16~18] 다음 글을 읽고 물음에 답하시오.

What Is the Ant Society Like?

 Ants live in colonies (A)[where / which] have lots of residents living together. Within a colony, there are usually three different types of ants. There is the queen, and ⓐ what she does her entire life is lay eggs. The second type of ant is the male that helps the queen (B)[produce / producing] these eggs. The (C)[third / three] type of ant is the worker. Worker ants are all female and do very important jobs, like ⓑcaring for eggs, defending the colony, and collecting food.

16 위 글의 괄호 (A)~(C)에서 문맥이나 어법상 알맞은 낱말을 골라 쓰시오.

➡ (A) _____ (B) _____ (C) _____

17 위 글의 밑줄 친 ⓐwhat과 문법적 쓰임이 같은 것을 모두 고르시오.

① What do you think of that film?

② What I said is true.

③ I always do what I believe is right.

④ What a beautiful house!

⑤ Do you know what this is?

18 위 글의 밑줄 친 ⓑcaring for와 바꿔 쓸 수 있는 말을 모두 고르시오.

① looking after   ② taking after

③ making sure   ④ taking care of

⑤ looking for

[19~21] 다음 글을 읽고 물음에 답하시오.

FUN FACTS ABOUT ANTS

01 Some Queen ants live ⓐup to 30 years.

02 Some ants can carry things that are 50 (A)[hours / times] their own body weight.

03 Ants do not have lungs but breathe through small holes in their bodies.

04 An ant has two stomachs. One stomach holds food for itself, and (B)[others / the other] holds food to share with (C)[others / the other].

05 Most ants can swim and live 24 hours underwater.

19 위 글의 밑줄 친 ⓐup to와 가장 가까운 의미로 쓰인 것을 고르시오.

① He's not up to the job.

② What's she up to?

③ The temperature went up to 35°C.

④ It's up to her to finish the work.

⑤ Her latest book isn't up to her usual standard.

20 위 글의 괄호 (A)~(C)에서 문맥이나 어법상 알맞은 낱말을 골라 쓰시오.

➡ (A) _____ (B) _____ (C) _____

21 위 글을 읽고 알 수 없는 것을 고르시오.

① 여왕개미의 수명

② 개미의 몸무게

③ 개미의 호흡 방법

④ 개미의 위의 개수

⑤ 개미가 물속에서 살 수 있는 시간

[22~23] 다음 글을 읽고 물음에 답하시오.

How Do Ants Communicate?

Though ants do not speak like humans, they actually have a "language." Ants produce a chemical called a pheromone to communicate with one another. By (A)using the chemical, they can exchange information about food or danger. Ants also use touch for communication. ____ⓐ____, if an ant finds food, it passes on the good news by rubbing its body on its neighbor. Since an ant has legs covered with very sensitive hairs, it can sense even the smallest touch.

22 위 글의 빈칸 ⓐ에 들어갈 알맞은 말을 고르시오.

① Therefore   ② For example

③ In fact   ④ However

⑤ In other words

23 아래 〈보기〉에서 위 글의 밑줄 친 (A)using과 문법적 쓰임이 다른 것의 개수를 고르시오.

┌─── 보기 ───
│ ① Why are you <u>using</u> the chemical?
│ ② When did you finish <u>using</u> the chemical?
│ ③ How about <u>using</u> the chemical?
│ ④ I saw him <u>using</u> the chemical.
│ ⑤ She stopped <u>using</u> the chemical.
└───

① 1개 ② 2개 ③ 3개 ④ 4개 ⑤ 5개

[24~25] 다음 글을 읽고 물음에 답하시오.

Mosquito	
Home	Mosquitoes like warm weather and they are easily found in places with still water.
Life Span	Males usually live for about five ____ⓐ____ seven days, while females can live for two weeks ____ⓐ____ a month.
Food	Mosquitoes mainly feed ____ⓑ____ fruit and plant nectar, but the female mosquitoes also drink the blood of other animals.
Fun Facts	• A mosquito can drink blood up to three times its weight. • Female mosquitoes can lay up to 300 eggs at a time.

24 위 글의 빈칸 ⓐ와 ⓑ에 들어갈 전치사가 바르게 짝지어진 것은?

　　　ⓐ　ⓑ　　　　　　ⓐ　ⓑ
① for – on　　　② to – by
③ to – on　　　④ for – to
⑤ on – by

25 Which question CANNOT be answered after reading the passage?

① Where can we find mosquitoes easily?
② How long do male mosquitoes usually live?
③ Why can female mosquitoes live longer than males?
④ Do male mosquitoes drink the blood of other animals?
⑤ How many eggs can female mosquitoes lay at a time?

[26~28] 다음 글을 읽고 물음에 답하시오.

FUN FACTS ABOUT ANTS
01 Some Queen ants live up to 30 years.
02 Some ants can carry things ⓐ<u>자기 몸무게의 50배에 달하는</u>.
03 Ants do not have lungs but breathe through small holes in their bodies.
04 An ant has two stomachs. One stomach holds food for itself, and the other holds food to share with others.
05 Most ants can swim and live 24 hours underwater.

26 위 글의 밑줄 친 ⓐ의 우리말에 맞게 주어진 어휘를 이용하여 8단어로 영작하시오.

┌─────────────────────────
│ that, body weight
└─────────────────────────

➡ _____

27 개미가 호흡하는 법을 우리말로 쓰시오.

➡ _____

28 개미의 위의 역할을 우리말로 쓰시오.

➡ _____
_____

[01~03] 다음 글을 읽고 물음에 답하시오.

> For the science project, our group has chosen very special insects.
>
> • They are very social.
> • They are as old as the T-Rex.
> • They appear in Aesop's stories.
> • They use a special chemical (A)to communicate.
>
> (B)그것들이 무엇인지 추측할 수 있나요? Yes, the answer is ants. We want to share with you _____ⓐ_____ we have learned about these insects.

01 Fill in the blank ⓐ with a suitable word.

➡ _____

02 위 글의 밑줄 친 (A)to communicate를 다음과 같이 바꿔 쓸 때 빈칸에 들어갈 알맞은 말을 쓰시오.

➡ _____ _____ to communicate
= _____ _____ to communicate
= _____ _____ _____ they _____ communicate
= _____ _____ they _____ communicate

03 위 글의 밑줄 친 (B)의 우리말에 맞게 주어진 어휘를 알맞게 배열하시오.

| what / you / guess / they / can / are / ? |

➡ _____

[04~06] 다음 글을 읽고 물음에 답하시오.

> **How Many Ants Are on Earth?**
>
> We often see ants come ⓐ난데없이. Like humans, they live almost everywhere in the world, except a few extremely cold places including Antarctica. ⓑ2018년 현재, there were over 7 billion people on Earth. Then, ⓒhow about ants? According to scientists, there are about one million ants for every human in the world. ⓓSince each ant hardly weighs anything, one million ants are as heavy as a human being weighing about 62 kilograms.

04 위 글의 밑줄 친 ⓐ와 ⓑ의 우리말에 맞게 각각 3단어로 영작하시오.

➡ ⓐ _____ ⓑ _____

05 위 글의 밑줄 친 ⓒhow about ants?를 다음과 같이 바꿔 쓸 때 빈칸에 들어갈 알맞은 말을 쓰시오. (3단어)

➡ _____ _____ _____ are there on Earth?

06 위 글의 밑줄 친 ⓓ에서 흐름상 어색한 단어를 찾아 고치시오.

_____ ➡ _____

[07~09] 다음 글을 읽고 물음에 답하시오.

What Is the Ant Society Like?

Ants live in colonies which have lots of residents ⓐ living together. Within a colony, there are usually ⓑ three different types of ants. There is the queen, and what she does her entire life is lay eggs. The second type of ant is the male that helps the queen produce these eggs. The third type of ant is the worker. Worker ants are all female and do very important jobs, ⓒ like caring for eggs, defending the colony, and collecting food.

07 위 글의 밑줄 친 ⓐ living을 관계대명사를 사용하여 두 단어로 고치시오.

➡ _____

08 위 글의 밑줄 친 ⓑ three different types of ants가 가리키는 것을 본문에서 찾아 쓰시오.

➡ _____, _____, _____

09 위 글의 밑줄 친 ⓒ like를 두 단어로 바꿔 쓰시오.

➡ _____

[10~12] 다음 글을 읽고 물음에 답하시오.

How Do Ants Communicate?

ⓐ Though ants do not speak like humans, they actually have a "language." Ants produce a chemical (A)[calling / called] a pheromone to communicate with one another. By using the chemical, they can (B)[change / exchange] information about food or danger. Ants also use touch for communication. For example, if an ant finds food, it passes on the good news by rubbing its body on its neighbor. Since an ant has legs (C)[covering / covered] with very sensitive hairs, it can sense even the smallest touch.

10 위 글의 괄호 (A)~(C)에서 문맥이나 어법상 알맞은 낱말을 골라 쓰시오.

➡ (A) _____ (B) _____ (C) _____

11 위 글의 밑줄 친 ⓐ를 다음과 같이 바꿔 쓸 때 빈칸에 들어갈 알맞은 접속사를 쓰시오.

➡ Ants do not speak like humans, _____ they actually have a "language."

12 위 글의 내용을 다음과 같이 정리하고자 한다. 빈칸 (A)와 (B)에 들어갈 알맞은 단어를 본문에서 찾아 쓰시오.

Ants can communicate with one another by using the (A)_____ called a pheromone and (B)_____.

구석구석

Communicate: Speak

A: Which do you prefer, pizza or fried chicken?
선호를 묻는 말로 'Which do you like. A or B?' 형태이다.

B: I like pizza better. I can choose the toppings I like. How about you?
'the toppings I like'는 '내가 좋아하는 토핑'이라는 뜻으로 목적격 관계대명사가 생략되었다.

A: I like fried chicken better.

C: Me, too. I'm a meat lover.
'Me. too.'는 동의하는 말로 'So do I.'라고 할 수 있다.

구문해설 • How about you? 너는 어떠니? (권유, 제안, 상대의 의견 요청)

A: 피자와 치킨 중 어느 것을 좋아하니?

B: 피자를 더 좋아해. 나는 내가 좋아하는 토핑을 고를 수 있어. 너는 어떠니?

A: 나는 프라이드 치킨을 더 좋아해.

C: 나도 그래. 나는 고기를 좋아해.

My Speaking Portfolio

M: Honeybees are easily found in warm places which have many plants
be+과거분사: 수동태 　　　　　　　　주격관계대명사
and flowers. A queen lives up to five years, but worker bees only live for
　　　　　　　　　　　　　～까지
about seven weeks. Honeybees go from flower to flower to collect food. A
약　　　　　　　　　　　　from A to B: A에서 B로　to부정사의 부사적 용법-목적(～하기 위하여)
worker bee makes hundreds of trips to produce a small amount of honey.
　　　　　　　　　　　　　　　　to부정사의 부사적 용법-목적(～하기 위하여)
By moving around, honeybees help plants grow.
move around: 옮겨 다니다　　　　　help+목적어+동사원형

구문해설 • collect: 모으다 • hundred: 백, 100 • hundreds of: 수백의 • amount: 양
• grow: 성장하다

남: 꿀벌은 식물과 꽃이 많은 따뜻한 곳에서 쉽게 발견된다. 여왕벌은 5년까지 살지만, 일벌은 겨우 7주 정도만 산다. 꿀벌은 먹이를 모으기 위해 꽃에서 꽃으로 옮겨 다닌다. 일벌은 적은 양의 꿀을 만들기 위해 수백 번의 이동을 한다. 여기저기 옮겨 다니면서 꿀벌은 식물이 성장하는 것을 돕는다.

Wrap Up – Reading

Ants seem to be busy all the time and never rest. But this is not true. Worker
～인 것처럼 보인다　　　　　　　　　개미는 항상 바쁘고 전혀 휴식을 취하지 않는 것처럼 보이는 것
ants rest by taking very short naps about 250 times a day. Each of these naps
　　　　　　　　　　　　　　　　　　= per(～당, ～마다)
lasts only about a minute. This means that the worker ants sleep for about four
　　　　　　　　　　　앞의 내용, 즉 일개미는 하루에 약 250번의 짧은 잠을 자며 이 잠은 불과 1분 정도 이어진다는 사실을 가리킨다.
hours each day. On the other hand, queen ants fall asleep 90 times a day, and
　　　　　　　　　　반면에　　　　　　　　　잠들다
they sleep for about six minutes at a time. This means that they sleep for about
　　　　　　　　　　　　　　　　　　동사 means의 목적어를 이끄는 접속사로, 생략할 수 있다.
nine hours each day. In short, ants sleep and rest just like us though they do so
　　　　　　　　= In brief: 즉, 간단히 말해서　　　　　　양보를 나타내는 접속사(비록 ～이지만)　　　= sleep
in a different way.　　　　　　　　　　　　　　　　　　　　　　　　　　　　and rest

구문해설 • seem to: ～인 것처럼 보이다 • nap: 낮잠 • last: 지속되다 • all the time: 항상

개미는 항상 바쁘고 전혀 휴식을 취하지 않는 것처럼 보인다. 하지만 이것은 사실이 아니다. 일개미는 하루에 약 250번의 짧은 잠을 자며 휴식을 취한다. 이 잠은 불과 1분 정도 이어진다. 이것은 일개미가 하루에 4시간 정도 잠을 잔다는 의미이다. 반면에, 여왕개미는 하루에 90번 잠을 자고, 한 번에 약 6분 동안 잠을 잔다. 이것은 여왕개미가 하루에 약 9시간 동안 잠을 잔다는 것을 의미한다. 즉, 방식이 다르기는 하지만 개미도 우리처럼 잠을 자고 휴식을 취한다.

영역별 핵심문제

Words & Expressions

01 다음 영영풀이에 해당하는 단어를 고르시오.

> to try to answer a question or form an opinion when you are not sure whether you will be correct

① guess　　② chase　　③ decide
④ defend　　⑤ produce

02 다음 대화의 빈칸에 들어갈 말을 고르시오.

> B: Amber, how do you like the camp?
> G: It's great. I'm having a lot of fun.
> B: Me, too. The talent show last night was really _____.

① boring　　② sad　　③ worried
④ great　　⑤ disappointed

03 다음 빈칸에 들어갈 말로 적절한 것을 고르시오.

> Sometimes I get lost not because it's too _____ but because it's too bright.

① shiny　　② heavy　　③ dark
④ colorful　　⑤ extreme

04 다음 중 밑줄 친 부분의 뜻풀이가 바르지 <u>않은</u> 것은?

① By the way, did you <u>decide</u> on the afternoon program? (결정하다)
② They had a <u>talent show</u>. (장기 자랑)
③ Frank saw <u>wild</u> birds and insects in the woods. (야생의)
④ Can you guess how many <u>bees</u> live there? (꿀벌)
⑤ I don't <u>like</u> noisy music. (~ 같은)

Conversation

[05~06] 다음 대화의 빈칸에 들어갈 말을 고르시오.

05
> B: Sora, can you take a look at these pictures?
> G: What are these for?
> B: I'm trying to _____ a picture for my story in the school newspaper.

① choose　　② take　　③ draw
④ give　　⑤ like

06
> A: Which do like better, dogs or cats?
> B: I like dogs better. They are more friendly. How about you?
> C: _____
> D: Me, too. Cats are much cleaner than dogs.

① I like dogs better.
② I like cats better.
③ I play more often with my dogs.
④ Why do you like cats better?
⑤ I kept dogs in my house.

07 다음 대화에 이어지는 순서가 바르게 배열된 것을 고르시오.

> B: The talent show last night was really great.
> G: Yeah. By the way, did you decide on the afternoon program?

(A) Great. I heard we'll have a hiking guide.

(B) No, I haven't yet. Which do you think is better, hiking or swimming?

(C) I'll go hiking because we can see wild birds and insects in the woods.

(D) I'll join you. I like birds and insects.

① (A) – (C) – (D) – (B)
② (D) – (B) – (A) – (C)
③ (B) – (C) – (D) – (A)
④ (C) – (A) – (B) – (D)
⑤ (C) – (B) – (D) – (A)

[08~11] 다음 대화를 읽고 물음에 답하시오.

A: I heard birds are having a ___(A)___ these days. Can you tell us more?

B: Sure. The cities are too bright at night. Many birds lose their way.

A: _____(B)_____ Is there anything we can do to help them?

B: Yes. First, we should turn off unnecessary lights at night. Also we should hold the Earth Hour campaign regularly.

A: Those are good points. I think (C)새를 보호하는 것에 관하여 진지해져야 할 시간이라고. (time, it's, get, protect, serious)

08 빈칸 (A)에 들어갈 알맞은 말을 고르시오.

① flying chance   ② hard time
③ great friend   ④ new mate
⑤ wonderful time

09 빈칸 (B)에 알맞은 말을 고르시오.

① Me, too.
② You can say that again.
③ I'm pleased with it.
④ How nice of you!
⑤ That's too bad.

10 밑줄 친 (C)의 우리말을 영어로 옮기시오. (주어진 단어를 이용할 것.)

➡ _____

11 위 대화의 내용과 일치하지 <u>않는</u> 것은?

① Many birds are having trouble finding their way.
② Many birds lose their way due to the bright cities during the day.
③ For the birds, we should turn off unnecessary lights at night.
④ Holding the Earth Hour campaign regularly will be helpful for the birds.
⑤ They are talking about protecting birds.

Grammar

12 다음 빈칸에 들어갈 말로 알맞은 것은?

| Do you know the child _____ on the bed? |

① to sleep   ② sleep
③ slept   ④ sleeping
⑤ be sleeping

13 다음 우리말을 영어로 바르게 옮긴 것은?

> 나는 나이가 어리기 때문에 차를 운전할 수 없다.

① Since I cannot drive a car, I am young.
② Since I am young, I cannot drive a car.
③ I am young since I cannot drive a car.
④ Though I am young, I cannot drive a car.
⑤ Though I cannot drive a car, I am young.

14 다음 〈보기〉의 밑줄 친 부분과 쓰임이 다른 것은?

> ┌─ 보기 ├─
> Who is the lady underline{playing} tennis with Mark?

① I like the picture underline{showing} wonderful mountain tops.
② The man underline{talking} on the phone is my teacher.
③ I don't mind your brother underline{talking} in this room.
④ She met a man underline{speaking} Italian.
⑤ There was a car underline{running} on the road.

[15~16] 다음 빈칸에 들어가기에 적절한 것은?

15

> _____ ants do not speak like humans, they actually have a "language."

① Though   ② Since   ③ Because
④ Unless   ⑤ After

16

> Ants produce a chemical _____ a pheromone to communicate with one another.

① calls   ② calling   ③ called
④ to call   ⑤ is called

17 다음 우리말에 맞게 괄호 안에 주어진 어휘를 바르게 배열하시오. (필요하면 어형을 바꿀 것)

(1) 나는 그 가수에 의해서 불리는 모든 노래를 좋아한다. (like, song, sing, every, I, the singer, by)

➡ _____

(2) 그는 침대에서 자는 아이를 깨우지 않으려고 애썼다. (he, to wake up, not, tried, the baby, on the bed, sleep)

➡ _____

_____

18 다음 〈보기〉의 밑줄 친 부분과 쓰임이 같은 것은?

> ┌─ 보기 ├─
> The kid underline{wearing} a baseball cap is my nephew.

① He enjoyed underline{meeting} them.
② Do you know the child underline{crying} at the door?
③ His hobby is underline{listening} to music.
④ I don't mind your underline{making} noises.
⑤ He finished underline{reading} the book.

19 다음 대화를 읽고 어법상 틀린 부분을 찾아 알맞게 고쳐 쓰시오.

> B: Sora, can you take a look at these pictures?
> G: What are these for?
> B: I'm trying to choose a picture for my story in the school newspaper.
> G: What's your story about?
> B: Nature's future.
> G: Can you tell me more about it?
> B: It's about endangering animals in the Arctic areas.
> G: That sounds interesting.

_____ ➡ _____

20 다음 우리말을 영어로 올바르게 옮긴 것은?

> 나는 조심스럽게 일하는 그 여자를 좋아한다.

① I like the woman works very carefully.
② I like carefully the woman working.
③ The woman likes my working very carefully.
④ The woman I like works very carefully
⑤ I like the woman working very carefully.

21 다음 중 밑줄 친 부분의 쓰임이 어색한 것을 고르시오.

① An essay written carefully will receive a high grade.
② Though it rained heavily, we had to stop playing soccer.
③ Though it was very warm, she didn't take off her coat.
④ Since I am a middle school student, I cannot drive a car.
⑤ Since you don't have any evidence, you cannot punish him.

22 잘못된 부분을 바르게 고쳐 문장을 다시 쓰시오.

(1) He is carrying a basket filling with cherries.

➡ _____

(2) Though it is cold, I want to drink something hot.

➡ _____

(3) I am tired since I slept enough last night.

➡ _____

[23~25] 다음 글을 읽고 물음에 답하시오.

How Many Ants Are on Earth?
  We often see ants come out of nowhere. (①) ⓐLike humans, they live almost everywhere in the world, except a few extremely cold places including Antarctica. (②) As of 2018, there were over 7 billion people on Earth. (③) According to scientists, there are about one million ants for every human in the world. (④) Though each ant hardly weighs anything, ⓑone million ants are as heavy as a human being weighing about 62 kilograms. (⑤)

23 위 글의 ①~⑤ 중 다음 주어진 문장이 들어갈 알맞은 위치는?

> Then, how about ants?

①   ②   ③   ④   ⑤

24 위 글의 밑줄 친 ⓐLike와 의미가 같은 것을 고르시오.

① He is very like his father.
② Do you like swimming?
③ There are fruits like apples and pears.
④ She responded in like manner.
⑤ I, like everyone else, want to live long.

25 다음 중 밑줄 친 ⓑ의 의미를 바르게 이해한 사람을 고르시오.

① 진수: A human being weighing about 62 kilograms is heavier than one million ants.
② 희라: The weight of one million ants is about 62 kilograms.

③ 민규: One million ants are less heavy than a human being weighing about 62 kilograms.

④ 영진: A human being weighing about 62 kilograms isn't so heavy as one million ants.

⑤ 송미: One million ants are heavier than a human being weighing about 62 kilograms.

[26~28] 다음 글을 읽고 물음에 답하시오.

How Do Ants Communicate?

Though ants do not speak like humans, they actually have a "___ⓐ___." Ants produce a chemical called a pheromone to communicate with one another. By using the chemical, they can exchange information about food or danger. Ants also use touch for communication. For example, if an ant finds food, it passes on the good news by rubbing its body on its neighbor. ⓑSince an ant has legs covered with very sensitive hairs, it can sense even the smallest touch.

26 위 글의 빈칸 ⓐ에 들어갈 알맞은 말을 고르시오.

① letter ② rule
③ symbol ④ language
⑤ culture

27 위 글의 밑줄 친 ⓑSince와 같은 의미로 쓰인 것을 모두 고르시오.

① Since she is attractive, she is loved by many people.
② She's been off work since Tuesday.
③ We've lived here since 1994.
④ Since I'm busy, I can't go there.
⑤ I haven't eaten since breakfast.

28 According to the passage, which is NOT true?

① Ants do not speak like humans.
② Ants can communicate with one another by using a pheromone.
③ Ants also use touch for communication.
④ The legs of an ant are covered with very sensitive hairs.
⑤ Ants can't sense the smallest touch.

[29~30] 다음 글을 읽고 물음에 답하시오.

ⓐHoneybees are easily found in warm places where have many plants and flowers. A queen lives up to five years, but worker bees only live for about seven weeks. Honeybees go from flower to flower to collect food. A worker bee makes hundreds of trips to produce a small amount of honey. By moving around, honeybees help plants grow.

29 위 글의 밑줄 친 ⓐ에서 어법상 틀린 부분을 찾아 고치시오.

_____ ➡ _____

30 본문의 내용과 일치하도록 다음 빈칸 (A)와 (B)에 알맞은 단어를 쓰시오.

To produce a small amount of (A)_____, a worker bee makes (B)_____ _____ _____, and by doing so helps plants pollinate.

*pollinate: 수분(受粉)하다, 가루받이를 하다

출제율 90%

01 다음 짝지어진 단어의 관계가 같도록 빈칸에 알맞은 말을 쓰시오. (주어진 철자로 시작할 것)

> choose : select – offer : p_____

출제율 95%

02 다음 주어진 단어를 이용해 빈칸을 완성하시오.

> G: What's your story about?
> B: It's about _____ animals in the Arctic areas.

➡ _____ (danger)

출제율 90%

03 다음 밑줄 친 단어와 의미가 가장 가까운 단어를 고르시오.

> The photograph of the insects was <u>unbelievable</u>.

① incredible   ② colorful
③ wonderful   ④ worried
⑤ puzzled

[04~05] 다음 대화의 빈칸에 들어갈 말을 고르시오.

출제율 95%

04
> G: What do you do in your free time?
> B: I listen to music like EDM or hip-hop.
> G: Which do you like better?
> B: I _____ hip-hop.
> G: Why?
> B: Well, it sounds more exciting.

① decide   ② write
③ make   ④ prefer
⑤ support

출제율 95%

05 내용상 다음 빈칸에 들어가기에 적절한 것은?

> Ants also use touch for communication. For example, if an ant finds food, it _____ the good news by rubbing its body on its neighbor.

① gives up   ② gets over
③ passes on   ④ looks after
⑤ waits for

출제율 85%

06 다음 영영풀이에 해당하는 단어를 고르시오.

> to decide which one of a number of things or people you want

① take   ② bring
③ choose   ④ call
⑤ reside

[07~08] 다음 빈칸에 들어갈 말로 적절한 것을 고르시오.

출제율 95%

07
> Bees live together in a _____. It usually has a large number of residents in it.

① support   ② colony
③ forest   ④ village
⑤ society

출제율 90%

08
> Elephants are social animals. _____ elephants help each other look after their babies.

① Kind   ② Careful
③ Female   ④ Male
⑤ Adult

B: ⓐAmber, how do you like the camp?

G: It's great. I'm having a lot of fun.

B: Me, too. ⓑThe talent show last night was really terrible.

G: Yeah. By the way, did you decide on the afternoon program?

B: ⓒNo, I haven't yet. Which do you think is better, hiking or swimming?

G: ⓓI'll go hiking because we can see wild birds and insects in the woods.

B: I'll join you. I like birds and insects.

G: Great. ⓔI heard we'll have a hiking guide.

09 밑줄 친 ⓐ~ⓔ 중에서 흐름상 어색한 문장을 고르시오.

① ⓐ　　② ⓑ　　③ ⓒ　　④ ⓓ　　⑤ ⓔ

10 위 대화를 읽고, 대답할 수 없는 것은?

① Where are they at the moment?

② What was last night's program?

③ What will they do this afternoon?

④ Where can they swim?

⑤ Who will help them hike this afternoon?

[11~12] 다음 대화의 빈칸에 들어갈 말을 고르시오.

11

A: Which do you like better, sci-fi movies or horror movies?

B: I like sci-fi movies better. How about you?

A: I like horror movies better.

C: _____ Horror movies are more exciting.

① So am I.　　② Nor am I.

③ I don't agree.　　④ Me, too.

⑤ I like sci-fi movies.

12

G: Guess what I'm talking about.

B: Okay. Go ahead.

G: It's a common machine that you can see at home.

B: Well, can you tell me more?

G: _____

B: Now I know what it is.

① It helps you wash clothes.

② I don't know much about it.

③ Would you ask me more?

④ How about asking someone else?

⑤ You can guess what I am saying.

13 다음 〈보기〉의 밑줄 친 부분과 쓰임이 같은 것은?

┤ 보기 ├

We saw a big eagle flying above us.

① Learning English is very important.

② His wish is traveling around the world.

③ I hate speaking in front of other people.

④ A police officer is guarding the entrance.

⑤ What is your secret for winning the contest?

14 주어진 단어를 이용하여 빈칸에 적절한 형태로 쓰시오.

Since an ant has legs _____ with very sensitive hairs, it can sense even the smallest touch. (cover)

15 다음 중 밑줄 친 부분이 어법상 어색한 것은?

① Be careful with the boiling water.
② What is the language speaking in Mexico?
③ The boy playing basketball is my brother.
④ Look at the sleeping baby. He's so cute!
⑤ These are the pictures painted by Picasso.

16 다음 빈칸에 알맞은 것은?

> This is the novel _____ by Albert Camus.

① write ② wrote ③ written
④ writing ⑤ to write

17 다음 빈칸에 들어갈 말로 알맞은 것은?

> _____ he was ill, he had to cancel the appointment.

① Whether ② Since ③ Unless
④ Until ⑤ Although

18 다음 빈칸에 들어갈 말로 알맞은 것은?

> (A) I ate a whole pizza _____ I was on a diet.
> (B) _____ it is hot, I want to drink something cold.

	(A)	(B)
①	since	Though
②	since	Although
③	unless	Since
④	though	Since
⑤	though	Unless

[19~21] 다음 글을 읽고 물음에 답하시오.

What Is the Ant Society Like?

Ants live in colonies which have lots of residents living together. Within a colony, there are usually three different types of ants. There is the queen, and what she does her entire life is lay eggs. The second type of ant is the male (A)that helps the queen produce these eggs. The third type of ant is the worker. Worker ants are all female and do very important jobs, like ⓐ _____ for eggs, ⓑ _____ the colony, and ⓒ _____ food.

19 위 글의 빈칸 ⓐ~ⓒ에 care, defend, collect를 각각 알맞은 형태로 쓰시오.

➡ ⓐ _____ ⓑ _____ ⓒ _____

20 아래 〈보기〉에서 위 글의 밑줄 친 (A)that과 문법적 쓰임이 같은 것의 개수를 고르시오.

> ┌ 보기 ┐
> ① The climate of Seoul is like that of Paris.
> ② He is the first man that came here.
> ③ This is the watch that I bought yesterday.
> ④ This is my sister and that is my cousin.
> ⑤ Is this the farm that they spoke of?

① 1개 ② 2개 ③ 3개 ④ 4개 ⑤ 5개

21 According to the passage, which is NOT true?

① In ants' colonies, there are lots of residents living together.
② Usually three different types of ants are within a colony.
③ The queen lays eggs during her entire life.

④ The male helps the queen to produce the eggs.

⑤ Worker ants are all male.

[22~24] 다음 글을 읽고 물음에 답하시오.

How Do Ants Communicate?

Though ants do not speak like humans, they actually have a "language." Ants produce a chemical called a pheromone ⓐ to communicate with one another. By using the chemical, they can exchange information about food or danger. Ants also use touch for communication. For example, if an ant finds food, it passes on the good news by rubbing its body on its neighbor. Since an ant has legs covered with very sensitive hairs, ⓑit can sense even the smallest touch.

출제율 95%

22 위 글의 밑줄 친 ⓐto communicate와 to부정사의 용법이 같은 것을 모두 고르시오.

① The girl grew up to be an artist.

② It isn't easy to remember all the rules.

③ Kate must be stupid to believe Jake.

④ We need a house to live in.

⑤ His job is to take pictures.

출제율 95%

23 위 글의 밑줄 친 ⓑit이 가리키는 것을 본문에서 찾아 쓰시오.

➡ _____

출제율 90%

24 본문의 내용과 일치하도록 다음 빈칸에 알맞은 단어를 쓰시오.

An ant can sense even the smallest touch thanks to its _____ covered with very sensitive hairs.

[25~26] 다음 글을 읽고 물음에 답하시오.

Ants seem to be busy all the time and never rest. But (A)this is not true. Worker ants rest by taking very short naps about 250 times a day. Each of these naps lasts only about a minute. (B)This means that the worker ants sleep for about four hours each day. ___ⓐ___, queen ants fall asleep 90 times a day, and they sleep for about six minutes at a time. (C)This means that they sleep for about nine hours each day. ___ⓑ___, ants sleep and rest just like us though they do so in a different way.

출제율 90%

25 위 글의 빈칸 ⓐ와 ⓑ에 들어갈 알맞은 말을 고르시오.

① Thus – To sum up

② On the other hand – In short

③ As a result – In brief

④ Therefore – In short

⑤ On the other hand – However

출제율 100%

26 위 글의 밑줄 친 (A)this, (B)This, (C)This가 가리키는 내용을 각각 우리말로 쓰시오.

➡ (A) _____

_____

(B) _____

_____

(C) _____

_____

서술형 실전문제

01 다음 영영풀이에 해당하는 단어를 쓰시오.

> a small creature such as a fly or ant, that has six legs, and sometimes wings

➡ _____

02 다음 밑줄 친 단어와 의미가 같은 단어를 쓰시오. (주어진 철자로 시작할 것)

> I'm trying to <u>choose</u> a picture for my story in the school newspaper.

➡ s_____

03 다음 우리말에 맞게 빈칸에 알맞은 말을 쓰시오.

(1) 그런데 너는 오후 프로그램을 결정했니?

➡ By the way, did you _____ on the afternoon program?

(2) 좋은 추측입니다. 하지만 저것은 5만 마리가 넘는 벌을 수용할 만큼 커요.

➡ Good guess, but it's big enough to _____ over 50,000 bees.

04 다음 중 〈보기〉에 있는 단어를 사용하여 자연스러운 문장을 만드시오.

> ┌─ 보기 ─┐
> chemical ants information language

(1) _____ live in colonies.

(2) Though ants do not speak like humans, they actually have a "_____."

(3) Ants produce a _____ called a pheromone to communicate with one another.

(4) By using the chemical, they can exchange _____ about food or danger.

05 다음 대화의 빈칸에 들어갈 말로 알맞은 것은?

> A: Which do you like better, soccer or baseball?
> B: I like soccer better. Soccer is more exciting. How about you?
> A: I like baseball _____. I'm a big fan of the Lions.
> C: Are you? I'm a big fan of the Lions, too.

➡ _____

06 다음 우리말과 의미가 같도록 빈칸에 알맞은 말을 쓰시오. (단, 괄호 안에 주어진 단어가 있을 경우 활용할 것)

(1) 벽을 파란색으로 칠하는 남자를 보아라.

➡ Look at the man _____ the wall blue. (paint)

(2) John은 Tom이 만든 피자를 먹고 있다.

➡ John is eating the pizza _____ by Tom. (make)

(3) 파티에 초대된 사람들이 파티를 즐기고 있다.

➡ The people _____ to the party are enjoying themselves.

07 다음 우리말을 영어로 옮길 때 빈칸에 적절한 단어를 쓰시오. (주어진 철자로 시작할 것)

> 나이가 아주 많지만 그녀는 음식을 직접 요리한다.
> = T_____ she is very old, she cooks food herself.

How Many Ants Are on Earth?

We often see ants come (A)[into / out of] nowhere. Like humans, they live (B)[most / almost] everywhere in the world, except a few extremely cold places including Antarctica. As of 2018, there were over 7 billion (C)[people / peoples] on Earth. Then, how about ants? According to scientists, there are about one million ants for every human in the world. ⓐ각각의 개미는 거의 무게가 나가지 않지만, one million ants are as heavy as a human being weighing about 62 kilograms.

08 위 글의 괄호 (A)~(C)에서 문맥상 알맞은 낱말을 골라 쓰시오.

➡ (A) _____ (B) _____ (C) _____

09 위 글의 밑줄 친 ⓐ의 우리말에 맞게 주어진 어휘를 이용하여 6단어로 영작하시오.

each, hardly, anything

➡ _____

10 How many ants are there for each person in the world? Answer in English in a full sentence. (6 words)

➡ _____

How Do Ants Communicate?

Though ants do not speak like humans, they actually have a "language." Ants produce a chemical (A)called a pheromone to communicate with one another. By ___ⓐ___ the chemical, they can exchange information about food or danger. (B)Ants also use touch for communication. For example, if an ant finds food, it passes on the good news by ___ⓑ___ its body on its neighbor. Since an ant has legs (C)covered with very sensitive hairs, it can sense even the smallest touch.

11 위 글의 빈칸 ⓐ와 ⓑ에 use와 rub를 각각 알맞은 형태로 쓰시오.

➡ ⓐ _____ ⓑ _____

12 위 글의 밑줄 친 (A)와 (C) 앞에 생략된 말을 각각 쓰시오.

➡ (A) _____ (C) _____

13 위 글의 밑줄 친 (B)의 예를 우리말로 설명하시오.

➡ _____

01 신체를 나타내는 말이 포함된 표현을 찾아 문장을 만들어 봅시다.

eye	nose	ear	face	heart	arm

(1) I'll _____ your dog while you're away. ~을 지켜보다, ~을 감시하다

(2) Mike _____ today. 표정이 우울하다

(3) When the teacher talked about the camp schedule, everyone _____. 경청했다

(4) I'll _____ this offer. ~을 거절하다

(5) Try to _____ these English idioms. 암기하다

(6) It will _____ to buy a new car. 비싼 값을 치르다

02 다음 문장의 빈칸에 since나 though를 쓰시오.

(1) _____ it rained heavily, the soccer match was canceled.

(2) I don't want to go to the party _____ I have no one to talk with.

(3) _____ he was smiling, he didn't look that happy.

(4) It is sunny _____ it is cold.

03 다음 내용을 바탕으로 꿀벌에 관한 보고서를 쓰시오.

Home: Honeybees are found in warm places around the world.

Life Span: A queen lives up to five years, but worker bees only live for about seven weeks.

Food Collection: Honeybees visit flowers to collect food.

Fun Facts:

• A worker bee makes hundreds of trips to produce a small amount of honey.

• By moving around, honeybees help plants grow.

Honeybees are easily found in (A)_____ which have many plants and flowers. A queen lives up to (B)_____, but worker bees only live for (C)_____. Honeybees go from flower to flower (D)_____. A worker bee makes (E)_____ to produce a small amount of honey. By moving around, honeybees help plants (F)_____.

단원별 모의고사

01 다음 짝지어진 단어의 관계가 같도록 빈칸에 알맞은 말을 쓰시오. (주어진 철자로 시작할 것)

> defend : attack = male : f_____

02 다음 짝지어진 단어의 관계가 같도록 빈칸에 알맞은 말을 쓰시오. (주어진 철자로 시작할 것)

> unbelievable : incredible =
> choose : s_____

03 다음 영영풀이에 해당하는 단어를 고르시오.

> to provide something that people need or want

① offer
② receive
③ make
④ buy
⑤ produce

04 다음 대화의 빈칸에 들어갈 말을 고르시오.

> A: Which do you prefer to take, the bus or the subway?
> B: I _____ to take the subway better.

① select
② offer
③ prefer
④ like
⑤ choose

05 다음 빈칸에 들어갈 말로 적절한 것을 고르시오.

> Within a _____, there are usually three different types of ants.

① village
② value
③ colony
④ forest
⑤ tree

06 다음 〈보기〉에서 적절한 단어를 골라 주어진 문장을 완성하시오.

> ┤ 보기 ├
> exchange   sensitive   colonies   weighs

(1) Each ant hardly _____ anything.
(2) Ants live in _____ which have lots of residents living together.
(3) By using the chemical, ants can _____ information about food.
(4) An ant has legs covered with very _____ hairs.

07 다음 중 밑줄 친 부분의 뜻풀이가 바르지 <u>않은</u> 것은?

① Some ants can carry things that are <u>50 times</u> their own body weight. (50배)
② Most ants can swim and live 24 hours <u>underwater</u>. (수중에서)
③ Ants <u>breathe</u> through small holes in their bodies. (숨 쉬다)
④ The machine can take you to a <u>faraway</u> place. (멀리 떨어진)
⑤ What <u>chemical</u> do ants use to communicate? (화학적인)

08 다음 밑줄 친 단어와 의미가 가장 가까운 단어를 고르시오.

> This beehive is big enough to <u>hold</u> over 50,000 bees.

① contain
② produce
③ chase
④ provide
⑤ prefer

[09~11] 다음 대화를 읽고 물음에 답하시오.

A: I heard birds are having a hard time these days. Can you tell us more?

B: Sure. The cities are too bright at night. Many birds lose their way.

A: That's too bad. (A)우리가 그들을 돕기 위해 무언가 할 수 있는 것이 있니?(can, is, there, do, anything, we, help, them, to)

B: Yes. First, we should _____ (B) _____ unnecessary lights at night. Also we should hold the Earth Hour campaign regularly.

A: Those are good points. I think it's time to get serious about protecting birds.

09 주어진 단어를 배열하여 (A)의 우리말에 해당하는 영어 문장을 완성하시오.

➡ _____

10 대화의 흐름으로 보아 (B)에 들어가기에 가장 적절한 것은?

① catch on
② turn around
③ get over
④ care for
⑤ turn off

11 According to the dialogue, which one is NOT true?

① Birds are having trouble finding food.
② Birds lose their way because the cities are too bright at night.
③ We should turn off unnecessary lights at night.
④ We should get serious about protecting birds.
⑤ We should hold the Earth Hour campaign regularly.

12 다음 대화의 순서가 바르게 배열된 것을 고르시오.

W: Everyone, look at this chestnut tree. This is the oldest tree in these woods.

B: Can you tell me how old it is?

W: It's about 150 years old.

B: Wow! It's ten times my age.

G: Ms. Oh, is that a beehive up in the tree?

(A) Good guess, but it's big enough to hold over 50,000 bees.

(B) Yes. Can you guess how many bees live there?

(C) 500 bees?

B: G: Unbelievable!

① (A) – (C) – (B)
② (B) – (A) – (C)
③ (B) – (C) – (A)
④ (C) – (A) – (B)
⑤ (C) – (B) – (A)

13 짝지어진 대화가 어색한 것을 고르시오.

① A: Which picture do you like better?
　 B: I like the one showing a mountain.
② A: I like dogs better. They are more friendly. How about you?
　 B: Why do you like dogs better?
③ A: What are you drawing?
　 B: An elephant.
④ A: What are sunglasses?
　 B: They are things that you wear on your face.
⑤ A: Can you tell me more about it?
　 B: It's a flying machine that can take you to a faraway place.

[14~16] 다음 대화를 읽고 물음에 답하시오.

B: Amber, how do you like the camp?

G: It's great. I'm having a lot of fun.

B: Me, too. The talent show last night was really great.

G: Yeah. _____(A)_____, did you decide on the afternoon program?

B: No, I haven't yet. Which do you think is better, hiking or swimming?

G: I'll go hiking because we can see wild birds and insects in the woods.

B: _____(B)_____ I like birds and insects.

G: Great. I heard we'll have a hiking guide.

B: Sounds good.

14 빈칸 (A)에 들어갈 알맞은 말을 고르시오.

① However
② By the way
③ For example
④ In the end
⑤ First of all

15 위 대화의 빈칸 (B)에 들어가기에 알맞은 것은?

① Neither am I.
② So am I.
③ I don't agree.
④ I'll join you.
⑤ You can say that again.

16 위 대화의 내용과 일치하지 않는 것은?

① 소녀의 이름은 Amber이다.
② 소년은 어젯밤 장기 자랑이 재미있었다.
③ 소녀는 오후 프로그램을 결정하지 못했다.
④ 소년은 새와 곤충을 좋아한다.
⑤ 산행 가이드가 있을 것이다.

17 다음 〈보기〉의 밑줄 친 부분과 쓰임이 다른 것은?

┌─── 보기 ───┐
I know a woman underline{working} at the bank.
└────────────┘

① All the windows facing the street were shut.
② Do you know the boy walking around the garden?
③ The baby sleeping in the room will wake up in an hour.
④ They enjoyed jogging in the park.
⑤ We will take the train arriving at platform.

18 다음 우리말을 영어로 바르게 옮긴 것은?

┌────────────────────────────┐
│ 시간이 별로 없지만 너를 도와줄게. │
└────────────────────────────┘

① Though I have time, I can't help you.
② Though I help you, I don't have much time.
③ Since I don't have much time, I won't help you.
④ Since I don't have much time, I will help you.
⑤ Though I don't have much time, I will help you.

19 다음 중 밑줄 친 부분의 쓰임이 어색한 것을 고르시오.

① Since it rained heavily, the soccer match was canceled.
② Since she was ill, she didn't go to the party.
③ I don't want to go to the party though I have no one to talk with.
④ Though you don't like him, you must be polite.
⑤ Though he was young, he was not afraid at all.

[20~21] 다음 글을 읽고 물음에 답하시오.

How Many Ants Are on Earth?

We often see ants ____ⓐ____ out of nowhere. Like humans, they live almost everywhere in the world, except a few extremely cold places including Antarctica. As of 2018, there were over 7 (A)[billion / billions] people on Earth. Then, (B)[how about / why don't you] ants? According to scientists, there are about one million ants for every human in the world. Though each ant (C)[hard / hardly] weighs anything, one million ants are as heavy as a human being weighing about 62 kilograms.

20 위 글의 빈칸 ⓐ에 들어갈 알맞은 말을 <u>모두</u> 고르시오.

① to come   ② come
③ came   ④ will come
⑤ coming

21 위 글의 괄호 (A)~(C)에서 문맥이나 어법상 알맞은 낱말을 골라 쓰시오.

➡ (A) _____ (B) _____ (C) _____

[22~23] 다음 글을 읽고 물음에 답하시오.

Ants live in colonies which have lots of residents living together. Within a colony, there are usually ⓐ<u>three different types of ants</u>. There is the queen, and what she does her entire life is lay eggs. The second type of ant is the male that helps the queen produce these eggs. The third type of ant is the worker. Worker ants are all female and do very important jobs, like caring for eggs, defending the colony, and collecting food.

22 위 글의 제목으로 알맞은 것을 고르시오.

① Funny Facts About Ants
② What Is the Ant Society Like?
③ How Do Ants Communicate?
④ Why Do Ants Live in Colonies?
⑤ How Many Ants Are on Earth?

23 위 글의 밑줄 친 ⓐ가 하는 일을 각각 우리말로 쓰시오.

➡ 여왕개미: _____
　수개미: _____
　일개미: _____
　_____

[24~25] 다음 글을 읽고 물음에 답하시오.

How Do Ants Communicate?

Though ants do not speak like humans, they actually have a "language." Ants produce a chemical called a pheromone to communicate with one another. By using ⓐ<u>the chemical</u>, they can exchange information about food or danger. Ants also use touch for communication. For example, if an ant finds food, it passes on the good news by rubbing its body on its neighbor. ⓑ<u>Since an ant has legs covered with very sensible hairs, it can sense even the smallest touch.</u>

24 위 글의 밑줄 친 ⓐthe chemical이 가리키는 것을 본문에서 찾아 쓰시오.

➡ _____

25 위 글의 밑줄 친 ⓑ에서 문맥상 낱말의 쓰임이 적절하지 <u>않</u>은 것을 찾아 알맞게 고치시오.

_____ ➡ _____

Reading for Fun 1

The Full Jar

Key Words

- □ **fill** [fil] ⑧ 채우다, 메우다
- □ **full** [ful] ⑲ 가득 찬
- □ **health** [helθ] ⑲ 건강
- □ **jar** [dʒɑːr] ⑲ 병, 항아리
- □ **lose** [luːz] (**lost–lost**) ⑧ 잃어버리다
- □ **matter** [mǽtər] ⑧ 중요하다
- □ **open** [óupən] ⑲ 열려 있는, 막혀 있지 않은
- □ **pour** [pɔːr] ⑧ 붓다, 따르다
- □ **raise** [reiz] ⑧ ∼을 들어 올리다
- □ **reply** [riplái] ⑧ 대답하다
- □ **roll** [roul] ⑧ 굴러가다

- □ **room** [ruːm] ⑲ 공간, 여지
- □ **same** [seim] ⑲ 같은
- □ **seem** [seim] ⑧ …으로 보이다, …(인 것) 같다, …(인 것)으로 생각 되다
- □ **shake** [ʃeik] (**shook–shaken**) ⑧ 흔들다
- □ **space** [speis] ⑲ (비어 있는) 공간
- □ **spend** [spend] ⑧ 소비하다, 쓰다
- □ **stand** [stænd] (**stood–stood**) ⑧ 서 있다
- □ **suddenly** [sʌ́dnli] ⑨ 갑자기
- □ **though** [ðou] ⑳ 비록 ∼일지라도, ∼이지만
- □ **value** [vǽljuː] ⑧ ∼을 높이 평가하다, 중시하다

Key Expressions

- □ **a bottle of** ∼ ∼ 한 병
- □ **fill A with B** B로 A를 채우다
- □ **out of** ∼ 밖으로, ∼로부터
- □ **pick up** ∼을 집어올리다
- □ **pour A into B** A를 B에 붓다

- □ **spend A on B** A를 B하는 데 소비하다[쓰다]
- □ **take care of** ∼ ∼을 돌보다, ∼에 신경을 쓰다
- □ **take out** ∼을 꺼내다
- □ **watch+목적어+동사원형(ing)** 목적어가 ∼하는 것을 보다

Word Power

※ 다의어

□ **matter**

(명사)

1. 문제, 일, 사건

It's an extremely important **matter**. (그건 매우 중요한 문제이다.)

2. 어려움, 곤란, 걱정

You look sad. What's the **matter**? (너 슬퍼 보인다. 무슨 어려운 일이 있니?)

(동사) 중요하다

Money is the only thing that **matters** to them. (돈은 그들에게 중요한 유일한 것이다.)

□ **value**

(명사) 가치, 값어치

The **value** of the painting is not known. (그 그림의 값어치는 알려지지 않았다.)

(동사) ~을 높이 평가하다, 중시하다

You must **value** your health. (넌 건강을 중요시해야 한다.)

English Dictionary

□ **fill** 채우다, 메우다
→ to make something full
무언가를 가득 차게 만들다

□ **full** 가득 찬
→ having or containing a lot of something
어떤 것을 많이 가지고 있거나 보유하고 있는

□ **jar** 병, 항아리
→ a glass container with a lid and a wide top, especially one in which food is sold or kept
특히 그 안에 음식을 담아 팔거나 보관하는, 뚜껑과 넓은 윗부분을 가진 유리 용기

□ **lose** 잃어버리다
→ to fail to keep or to maintain; cease to have, either physically or in an abstract sense
유지하거나 간직하지 못하다; 물리적으로나 추상적인 의미에서 가지는 것을 중단하다

□ **reply** 대답하다
→ to say or write something as an answer to someone or something
누군가 또는 어떤 것에 대한 대답으로 무언가를 말하거나 쓰다

□ **shake** 흔들다
→ to hold it and move it quickly backwards and forwards or up and down.
어떤 것을 잡고 앞뒤로 또는 위아래로 빠르게 움직이다

□ **space** (비어 있는) 공간
→ an empty area
비어 있는 공간

□ **spend** 소비하다
→ to pay money for things that you want
원하는 것들을 위해 돈을 지불하다

□ **suddenly** 갑자기
→ quickly and without any warning
빠르고 경고 없이

□ **take care of** ~ ~을 돌보다, ~에 신경을 쓰다
→ to make sure that you are/somebody is safe, well, healthy, etc.; look after yourself/somebody
당신이나 누군가가 확실히 안전하고, 건강하도록 하게 하다; 당신 자신이나 다른 사람을 돌보다

Reading

교과서

The Full Jar

Mr. Jenkins stood before his class. He had a large jar and a big bag
~ 앞에
on the teacher's desk. When the class began, he picked up the jar and
= picked the jar up
started to fill it with **golf balls** from the bag. He asked the students, "Is
= the jar
the jar full?" They all said, "Yes."

The teacher took a box of **small stones** out of the bag and poured
~ 밖으로
them into the jar. He shook the jar a little, and the stones rolled into the
= small stones   shake의 과거   a few(×)
open areas between the golf balls. He asked the same question and got
= "Is the jar full?"
the same answer from his students.
= "Yes."

Next, the teacher took out a bottle of **sand** and poured it into the jar.
the sand
After he watched the sand fill the spaces between the stones, he asked
지각동사(watched)+목적어+원형부정사
once more, "Is the jar full?" All the students replied, "Yes."

Suddenly Mr. Jenkins took a can of **apple juice** out of the bag. He
poured the apple juice into the jar, and his students watched it fill the
└ pour A into B: B 안으로 A를 붓다 ┘   지각동사(watched)+목적어+원형부정사
spaces in the sand.

full 가득한

teacher's desk 교탁

pick up 집어 들다

pour 붓다

shake 흔들다

roll into 굴러 들어가다

take out ~을 꺼내다

fill 채우다, 메우다

space 공간

suddenly 갑자기

📎 확인문제

● 다음 문장이 본문의 내용과 일치하면 T, 일치하지 않으면 F를 쓰시오.

1   Mr. Jenkins had a large jar and a big bag on the teacher's desk. ☐

2   Mr. Jenkins picked up the jar and started to put small stones into it first. ☐

3   Mr. Jenkins shook the jar a little to let the stones roll into the open areas between
the golf balls. ☐

4   Mr. Jenkins put the sand into the jar before putting small stones. ☐

5   Lastly, Mr. Jenkins poured the apple juice into the jar. ☐

6   Mr. Jenkins and his students watched the apple juice spill over the jar. ☐

"Now," the teacher said, "I want you to understand that your life
_{want+목적어+to부정사}

is just like the jar. The golf balls are what is most important in life:
_{be like: ~와 같다} _{= the thing that[which]}

your family, your friends, your health, and your dreams. Even when

everything else is lost, your life can still be full. The stones are the
_{be lost: 사라지다, 없어지다} _{be동사, 조동사 뒤, 일반동사 앞에 위치}

other things valued by people, like your job, your house, and your car.
_{= that[which] are valued} _{= such as: ~와 같은}

The sand is all the small things."

"If you put the sand into the jar first," he said, "there's no room
_{공간, 여지}

for the stones or the golf balls. The same goes for life. If you
_{~도 마찬가지이다}

spend all your time and energy on the small things, you will never have
_{spend+시간, 돈+on+명사}

room for what is really important to you. Take care of the balls first —
_{공간, 여지} _{= the thing which[that] really matters}

the things that really matter."
_{= the things that are really important}

One student sitting in the back raised her hand and asked, "What
_{= who is sitting} _{rose(×)}

does the apple juice mean?" Mr. Jenkins smiled, "I'm glad you asked.

It just shows that though your life may seem full, there's always room
_{= The apple juice} _{비록 ~이지만} _{~할지도 모른다} _{공간, 여지}

for a cool drink with a friend."

---

health 건강

value 소중하게[가치 있게] 생각하다[여기다]

small 사소한, 대수롭지 않은

room 여지

take care of ~을 신경 쓰다

raise 들다, 올리다

though 비록 ~이지만

 확인문제

- 다음 문장이 본문의 내용과 일치하면 T, 일치하지 <u>않으면</u> F를 쓰시오.

1 Mr. Jenkins said, "The golf balls are what is most important in life." ☐

2 Mr. Jenkins said, "When everything else is lost, your life can't be full." ☐

3 Mr. Jenkins said, "The stones are the other things valued by people." ☐

4 Though you spend all your time and energy on the small things, you will have room

    for what is really important to you. ☐

5 Mr. Jenkins told the students to take care of the balls first, not the sand. ☐

6 A friend with whom you can have some apple juice is most important in life. ☐

● 우리말을 참고하여 빈칸에 알맞은 말을 쓰시오.

1 The _____ Jar

2 Mr. Jenkins stood _____ _____ _____.

3 He had _____ _____ _____ and a big bag on the teacher's desk.

4 When the class began, he picked up the jar and started to _____ it _____ **golf balls** _____ _____ _____.

5 He asked the students, "_____ _____ _____ _____?"

6 _____ _____ said, "Yes."

7 The teacher took a box of **small stones** _____ _____ _____ _____ and _____ _____ into the jar.

8 He shook the jar _____ _____, and the stones _____ _____ the open areas between the golf balls.

9 He asked _____ _____ _____ and got _____ _____ _____ from his students.

10 Next, the teacher _____ _____ a bottle of **sand** and it _____ the jar.

11 After he watched the sand _____ the spaces between the stones, he asked _____ _____, "Is the jar full?"

12 All the students _____, "Yes."

13 Suddenly Mr. Jenkins took a can of **apple juice** _____ _____ _____ _____.

1	가득 찬 병
2	Jenkins 선생님이 교실 앞에 섰다.
3	교탁 위에는 큰 병과 커다란 가방이 놓여 있었다.
4	수업이 시작하자, 선생님은 병을 집어 들고 가방에서 꺼낸 골프공으로 채우기 시작했다.
5	그는 학생들에게 "병이 가득 찼나요?"라고 질문했다.
6	학생들은 모두 "예."라고 대답했다.
7	선생님은 가방에서 작은 돌 한 상자를 끄집어내어 병 안에 부었다.
8	그가 병을 살짝 흔들자, 돌들이 골프공 사이의 틈새로 굴러 들어갔다.
9	그는 같은 질문을 했고 학생들에게서 같은 대답을 들었다.
10	그런 다음, 선생님은 모래 병을 꺼내 병 안에 부었다.
11	모래가 돌 사이의 공간을 채우는 것을 지켜보고 나서 그는 "이 병이 가득 찼나요?"라고 한 번 더 물었다.
12	모든 학생들이 "예."라고 답했다.
13	갑자기 Jenkins 선생님은 가방에서 사과 주스 한 캔을 꺼냈다.

14 He poured the apple juice into the jar, and his students watched it
_____ _____ _____ in the sand.

15 "Now," the teacher said, "I want you to understand that your life
_____ _____ _____ the jar.

16 The golf balls are _____ _____ _____ _____ in life:
your family, your friends, your health, and your dreams.

17 Even when everything else _____ _____, your life can still
be full.

18 The stones are the other things _____ by people, like your job,
your house, and your car.

19 The sand is _____ _____ _____ _____."

20 "If you put the sand into the jar first," he said, "_____ _____
_____ _____ the stones or the golf balls.

21 _____ _____ _____ _____ life.

22 If you _____ all your time and energy _____ the small
things, you will never have room for _____ _____ _____
_____ to you.

23 _____ _____ _____ the balls first — the things that really
_____."

24 One student _____ in the back _____ her hand and asked,
"What does the apple juice mean?"

25 Mr. Jenkins smiled, "I'm glad _____ _____.

26 It just shows that though your life may _____ _____, there's
always _____ _____ a cool drink with a friend."

14 그는 사과 주스를 병 안에 부었고, 학생들은 주스가 모래 사이의 빈틈을 채우는 것을 지켜보았다.

15 "자, 이제," 선생님이 말했다. "여러분의 인생이 병과 같다는 것을 이해하기 바랍니다.

16 골프공은 여러분의 가족, 친구, 건강, 꿈과 같이 인생에서 가장 중요한 것이랍니다.

17 다른 모든 것을 잃게 될 때라도 여러분의 인생은 여전히 가득 차 있을 수 있습니다.

18 돌은 여러분의 직업, 집, 자동차처럼 사람들이 소중하게 여기는 다른 것들에 해당합니다.

19 모래는 온갖 사소한 것들이랍니다."

20 "만약 병에 모래를 먼저 채우면, 돌이나 골프공을 채울 공간이 없게 됩니다.

21 인생도 똑같습니다.

22 여러분의 시간과 에너지를 사소한 것에 모두 허비한다면 여러분에게 진정으로 중요한 것을 채울 공간은 절대로 없을 겁니다.

23 골프공, 즉 정말로 중요한 것들을 먼저 챙기기 바랍니다."라고 선생님이 말했다.

24 뒤에 앉아 있던 학생 하나가 손을 들고 질문했다. "사과 주스는 무슨 뜻입니까?"

25 Jenkins 선생님은 미소 지었다. "질문을 해줘서 기뻐요.

26 그것은, 여러분의 인생이 가득 차 보일지라도 친구와 시원한 음료수를 나눌 여유는 늘 있다는 점을 보여 줍니다."

● 우리말을 참고하여 본문을 영작하시오.

1 가득 찬 병

➡ _____

2 Jenkins 선생님이 교실 앞에 섰다.

➡ _____

3 교탁 위에는 큰 병과 커다란 가방이 놓여 있었다.

➡ _____

4 수업이 시작하자, 선생님은 병을 집어 들고 가방에서 꺼낸 골프공으로 채우기 시작했다.

➡ _____

5 그는 학생들에게 "병이 가득 찼나요?"라고 질문했다.

➡ _____

6 학생들은 모두 "예."라고 대답했다.

➡ _____

7 선생님은 가방에서 작은 돌 한 상자를 끄집어내어 병 안에 부었다.

➡ _____

8 그가 병을 살짝 흔들자, 돌들이 골프공 사이의 틈새로 굴러 들어갔다.

➡ _____

9 그는 같은 질문을 했고 학생들에게서 같은 대답을 들었다.

➡ _____

10 그런 다음, 선생님은 모래 병을 꺼내 병 안에 부었다.

➡ _____

11 모래가 돌 사이의 공간을 채우는 것을 지켜보고 나서 그는 "이 병이 가득 찼나요?"라고 한 번 더 물었다.

➡ _____

12 모든 학생들이 "예."라고 답했다.

➡ _____

13 갑자기 Jenkins 선생님은 가방에서 사과 주스 한 캔을 꺼냈다.

➡ _____

14 그는 사과 주스를 병 안에 부었고, 학생들은 주스가 모래 사이의 빈틈을 채우는 것을 지켜보았다.

➡ _____

15 "자, 이제," 선생님이 말했다. "여러분의 인생이 병과 같다는 것을 이해하기 바랍니다.

➡ _____

16 골프공은 여러분의 가족, 친구, 건강, 꿈과 같이 인생에서 가장 중요한 것이랍니다.

➡ _____

17 다른 모든 것을 잃게 될 때라도 여러분의 인생은 여전히 가득 차 있을 수 있습니다.

➡ _____

18 돌은 여러분의 직업, 집, 자동차처럼 사람들이 소중하게 여기는 다른 것들에 해당합니다.

➡ _____

19 모래는 온갖 사소한 것들이랍니다."

➡ _____

20 "만약 병에 모래를 먼저 채우면, 돌이나 골프공을 채울 공간이 없게 됩니다.

➡ _____

21 인생도 똑같습니다.

➡ _____

22 여러분의 시간과 에너지를 사소한 것에 모두 허비한다면 여러분에게 진정으로 중요한 것을 채울 공간은 절대로 없을 겁니다.

➡ _____

_____

23 골프공, 즉 정말로 중요한 것들을 먼저 챙기기 바랍니다."라고 선생님이 말했다.

➡ _____

24 뒤에 앉아 있던 학생 하나가 손을 들고 질문했다. "사과 주스는 무슨 뜻입니까?"

➡ _____

25 Jenkins 선생님은 미소 지었다. "질문을 해줘서 기뻐요.

➡ _____

26 그것은, 여러분의 인생이 가득 차 보일지라도 친구와 시원한 음료수를 나눌 여유는 늘 있다는 점을 보여 줍니다."

➡ _____

01 다음 빈칸에 공통으로 들어갈 말을 쓰시오.

> • Who's _____ care of the dog while you're away?
> • The officer started _____ her notebook out.

02 다음 밑줄 친 부분과 바꿔 쓸 수 있는 말을 쓰시오. (v로 시작할 것)

> The more we study the document, the more we <u>appreciate</u> the wisdom of the men who wrote it.

➡ _____

03 다음 빈칸에 알맞은 단어를 〈보기〉에서 골라 쓰시오.

> ┌─ 보기 ─┐
> full   same   suddenly

(1) He sits in the _____ chair every night.
(2) I _____ realized that there was someone following me.
(3) Don't talk with your mouth _____.

04 다음 영영풀이에 해당하는 말을 주어진 철자로 시작하여 쓰시오.

> an empty area

➡ s_____

05 다음 밑줄 친 부분의 쓰임이 자연스럽지 <u>않은</u> 것을 찾아 고치시오.

> ⓐ We're spending a lot more <u>on food</u> than we used to.
> ⓑ She filled the bowl <u>with warm water</u>.
> ⓒ Jill watched the children <u>to build</u> sandcastles.

_____ ➡ _____

06 다음 우리말에 맞도록 빈칸에 알맞은 말을 쓰시오. (철자가 주어진 경우 주어진 철자로 시작할 것.)

(1) 교수가 이름을 불렀을 때 그 학생은 얼굴을 들었다.
➡ The student _____ her head when the professor called her name.
(2) 나는 뭐라고 대답해야 할지 몰랐다.
➡ I did not know what to r_____.

07 우리말 해석에 맞게 주어진 단어를 알맞게 배열하시오.

(1) 그들은 이미 많은 시간과 돈을 이 프로젝트에 쏟아부었다. (poured, and, project, already, a, money, this, they've, of, into, time, lot)
➡ _____
_____

(2) 공기가 장미의 향기로 채워졌다. (scent, filled, air, the, the, was, roses, of, with)
➡ _____
_____

(3) 네가 그걸 어떻게 하든 중요하지 않다. (it, it, you, how, matter, not, does, do)
➡ _____
_____

08 다음 문장을 어법에 맞게 고쳐 쓰시오.

(1) I can play the piano a few.

➔ _____

_____

(2) I often watch him to play tennis.

➔ _____

(3) The symbols stand for that we all want:
beauty, fame, and wealth.

➔ _____

_____

(4) Can you make yourself understand in
French?

➔ _____

_____

(5) She is not the one wears sunglasses
indoors to avoid eye contact.

➔ _____

_____

09 다음 두 문장을 같은 뜻을 갖는 한 문장으로 바꿔 쓰시오.

(1) • Herold is the boy.

• He is dancing to the music.

➔ _____

(2) • There were many soldiers.

• They were injured in the war.

➔ _____

(3) • We had a special dish.

• It was made with milk and ice.

➔ _____

10 다음 우리말을 괄호 안에 주어진 어휘를 이용하여 영작하시오.

(1) 그녀는 안경을 쓴 소녀와 이야기를 나누고 있
다. (talk, wear, glasses, 8단어)

➔ _____

(2) 그녀는 그가 창문을 여는 소리를 들었다.
(open, hear, 6단어)

➔ _____

11 다음 두 문장을 〈보기〉와 같이 지각동사를 이용하여 한 문
장으로 완성하시오.

┌─ 보기 ├
• He saw his dog.
• She was sleeping under the table.
→ He saw his dog sleeping under the
table.
└──────────────────────────────

(1) • Robert watched a thief.

• He stole a lady's bag.

➔ _____

(2) • Theresa heard her dog.

• He was barking loudly.

➔ _____

[12~14] 다음 글을 읽고 물음에 답하시오.

Mr. Jenkins stood before his class. He had a
large jar and a big bag on the teacher's desk.
When the class began, he picked up the jar
and started to fill it with **golf balls** from the
bag. He asked the students, "Is the jar full?"
They all said, "Yes."

The teacher took a box of **small stones** out
of the bag and poured them into the jar. He
shook the jar a little, and the stones rolled
into the open areas between the golf balls.
He asked ⓐthe same question and got ⓑthe
same answer from his students.

12 다음 문장에서 위 글의 내용과 다른 부분을 찾아서 고치시오. (두 군데)

> Mr. Jenkins picked up a jar and put small stones into it first, and then put golf balls into it, too.

_____ ➡ _____

_____ ➡ _____

13 위 글의 밑줄 친 ⓐthe same question과 ⓑthe same answer가 가리키는 것을 각각 본문에서 찾아 쓰시오.

➡ ⓐ _____ ⓑ _____

14 Why did Mr. Jenkins shake the jar a little after he poured small stones into the jar? Fill in the blanks with suitable words.

➡ He shook the jar a little to let the stones _____ _____ the open areas between _____ _____ _____.

[15~17] 다음 글을 읽고 물음에 답하시오.

"Now," the teacher said, "I want you to understand that your life is just like the jar. The golf balls are ___ⓐ___ is most important in life: your family, your friends, your health, and your dreams. Even when everything else is lost, your life can still be full. The stones are the other things valued by people, ⓑlike your job, your house, and your car. The sand is all the small things."

15 Fill in the blank ⓐ with a suitable word.

➡ _____

16 위 글의 밑줄 친 ⓑlike와 바꿔 쓸 수 있는 두 단어를 쓰시오.

➡ _____

17 위 글의 골프공, 돌들, 모래가 상징하는 것을 각각 우리말로 쓰시오.

➡ (1) _____
(2) _____
(3) _____

[18~20] 다음 글을 읽고 물음에 답하시오.

"If you put ⓐthe sand into the jar first," he said, "there's no room for ⓑthe stones or the golf balls. ⓒThe same goes for life. ⓓIf you spend all your time and energy on the small things, you will never have a room for what is really important to you. Take care of the balls first — the things that really matter."

18 위 글의 밑줄 친 ⓐ와 ⓑ가 상징하는 것을 본문에서 찾아 각각 쓰시오.

➡ ⓐ _____
ⓑ _____
_____

19 밑줄 친 ⓒ의 의미를 우리말로 자세히 설명하시오.

➡ _____
_____
_____

20 위 글의 밑줄 친 ⓓ에서 어법상 틀린 부분을 찾아 고치시오.

➡ _____ ➡ _____

01 빈칸에 들어갈 말이 나머지 넷과 다른 하나를 고르시오.

① There is an important _____ we need to discuss.
② Stacey _____ all her free time painting.
③ Does it _____ what I think?
④ It was clear that she wanted to discuss the _____.
⑤ It doesn't _____ what you wear, as long as you look neat and tidy.

02 빈칸 (A)와 (B)에 들어갈 말로 알맞은 것끼리 짝지어진 것을 고르시오.

- We stood at the counter, filling our bowls ___(A)___ salad.
- They spend quite a lot of money ___(B)___ eating out each week.

　　(A)　　(B)`　　　　(A)　　(B)
① to　 – on　　　② to　 – in
③ with – on　　　④ with– with
⑤ out　– in

03 다음 영영풀이가 나타내는 말을 고르시오.

to make sure that you are/somebody is safe, well, healthy, etc.; look after yourself/somebody

① put down　　② take out
③ take care of　　④ come across
⑤ turn down

04 밑줄 친 부분과 바꿔 쓸 수 있는 말을 쓰시오.

My suitcase was so full that I didn't have room for anything else.

➡ _____

05 다음 우리말에 맞도록 빈칸에 알맞은 말을 쓰시오. (철자가 주어진 경우 주어진 철자로 시작할 것)

(1) 냉장고에서 맥주 한 병 갖다 주시겠어요?
➡ Would you get _____ beer from the refrigerator for me?
(2) 만약에 신용카드를 잃어버린다면, 이 번호로 즉시 전화하세요.
➡ If you _____ your credit card, phone this number immediately.
(3) 내일은 오후 내내 그의 스케줄이 비어 있다.
➡ His schedule is o_____ all afternoon tomorrow.
(4) 그들은 아주 가난할지라도 함께 행복해 보인다.
➡ T_____ they are so poor, they seem happy together.

06 다음 중 어법상 어색한 것은?

① I just felt the building shaking.
② How you play the game is that really counts.
③ She noticed her husband injured during the game.
④ Though he often talks big, I love him so much.
⑤ It is a full year since I left home.

07 다음 문장을 어법에 맞게 고쳐 쓰시오.

(1) He quickly gets bored with his toys and wants them replacing with new ones.

➡ _____
_____

(2) The ball went over the fence and they looked at it flew through the air.

➡ _____
_____

(3) I cannot find the book what I just put on the table.

➡ _____
_____

(4) He addressed himself to her despite he was shy.

➡ _____
_____

08 다음 빈칸에 들어갈 괄호 안에 주어진 동사의 형태가 <u>다른</u> 하나는?

① They watched him _____ the bank. (enter)

② We saw her _____ the heavy box. (carry)

③ He didn't hear them _____ that night. (fight)

④ She wanted me _____ her with her homework. (help)

⑤ Do you want to know what made me _____ mad? (get)

09 다음 중 어법상 적절한 것은?

① The golf balls are that is most important in life.

② There's no rooms for the stones or the golf balls.

③ She watched him carry out his duties, always with a smile.

④ They were seating on each side of the upper platform.

⑤ Because summer is a fun season, I can't stand the heat!

10 다음을 같은 뜻을 갖는 문장으로 바꿔 쓰시오.

(1) The pen is something that I wanted to buy.

➡ _____

(2) The student sitting in the back raised her hand.

➡ _____
_____

[11~13] 다음 글을 읽고 물음에 답하시오.

Mr. Jenkins stood before his class. He had a large jar and a big bag on the teacher's desk. When the class began, he picked up the jar and started to fill (A)it with **golf balls** from the bag. He asked the students, "Is the jar full?" They all said, "Yes."

The teacher took a box of **small stones** ⓐ _____ the bag and poured (B)them into the jar. He shook the jar a little, and the stones rolled ⓑ _____ the open areas between the golf balls. He asked the same question and got the same answer from his students.

📝 출제율 90%

11 위 글의 밑줄 친 (A)it과 (B)them이 가리키는 것을 각각 본문에서 찾아 쓰시오.

➡ (A) _____ (B) _____

📝 출제율 95%

12 위 글의 빈칸 ⓐ와 ⓑ에 들어갈 전치사가 바르게 짝지어진 것은?

	ⓐ	ⓑ		ⓐ	ⓑ
①	from	– on	②	on	– into
③	out of	– on	④	from	– by
⑤	out of	– into			

📝 출제율 100%

13 According to the passage, which is NOT true?

① Mr. Jenkins had a large jar and a big bag on the teacher's desk.

② Mr. Jenkins asked the students if the jar was full after he filled the jar with golf balls.

③ The students answered that the jar was full.

④ Mr. Jenkins couldn't pour the small stones into the jar as it was full.

⑤ Mr. Jenkins shook the jar a little to let the small stones enter the open areas between the golf balls.

[14~15] 다음 글을 읽고 물음에 답하시오.

Next, the teacher took out a bottle of **sand** and poured ⓐit into the jar. After he watched the sand fill the spaces between the stones, he asked once more, "Is the jar full?" All the students replied, "Yes."

Suddenly Mr. Jenkins took a can of **apple juice** out of the bag. He poured the apple juice into the jar, and his students watched ⓑit fill the spaces in the sand.

📝 출제율 90%

14 위 글의 내용과 일치하도록 다음 빈칸 (A)와 (B)에 알맞은 단어를 쓰시오. 단, (B)에는 주어진 영영풀이를 참고하여 철자 r로 시작하는 단어를 쓰시오.

> Though the jar seemingly looked (A)_____, there was (B)_____ for the sand and the apple juice to enter.
>
> *seemingly: 외견상으로, 겉보기에는
>
> • (B)에 들어갈 단어의 영영풀이: enough empty space for people or things to be fitted in

📝 출제율 95%

15 위 글의 밑줄 친 ⓐit과 ⓑit이 가리키는 것을 각각 본문에서 찾아 쓰시오.

➡ ⓐ _____

　　ⓑ _____

[16~18] 다음 글을 읽고 물음에 답하시오.

"Now," the teacher said, "I want you to understand that your life is just (A)like the jar. The golf balls are what is most important in life: your family, your friends, your health, and your dreams. Even when everything else is lost, your life can still be full. The stones are the other things ⓐ _____ by people, like your job, your house, and your car. The sand is all the small things."

golf balls, small stones, sand

📝 출제율 95%

16 위 글의 빈칸 ⓐ에 value를 알맞은 형태로 쓰시오.

➡ _____

17 위 글의 밑줄 친 (A)like와 같은 의미로 쓰인 것을 고르시오.

① Would you like a drink?

② She responded in like manner.

③ He doesn't like asking his parents for help.

④ He's very like his father.

⑤ You should do it like this.

18 다음 중 위 글의 내용을 올바르게 이해하지 <u>못한</u> 사람을 고르시오.

┤ 보기 ├

① 정호: 셋 중에서 크기가 가장 큰 골프공은 인생에서 가장 중요한 것을 상징하는 거야.

② 상준: 그렇지 않아. 골프공은 가장 크기 때문에, 집과 같은 큰 물체를 상징하는 거야.

③ 지윤: 아니야. 사람들이 소중하게 여기는 집과 같은 것들을 상징하는 것은, 크기가 두 번째인 돌이야.

④ 민규: 그래. 그리고 돌은 직업이나 차를 상징하는 것이기도 해.

⑤ 은희: 그리고 온갖 사소한 것들을 상징하는 것은 모래야.

① 정호   ② 상준   ③ 지윤

④ 민규   ⑤ 은희

[19~21] 다음 글을 읽고 물음에 답하시오.

"If you put the sand into the jar first," he said, "there's no room for the stones or the golf balls. ⓐ인생도 똑같습니다. If you spend all your time and energy on the small things, you will never have ⓑroom for what is really important to you. Take care of the balls first — ⓒthe things that really matter."

19 위 글의 밑줄 친 ⓐ의 우리말에 맞게 5단어로 영작하시오.

➡ _____

20 위 글의 밑줄 친 ⓑroom과 같은 의미로 쓰인 것을 <u>모두</u> 고르시오.

① I think Simon is in his room.

② This table takes up too much room.

③ He walked out of the room and slammed the door.

④ They had to sit in the waiting room for an hour.

⑤ There could be no room for doubt.

21 위 글의 밑줄 친 ⓒ를 다음과 같이 바꿔 쓸 때 빈칸에 들어갈 알맞은 단어를 쓰시오.

➡ the things that _____ really _____

[22~24] 다음 글을 읽고 물음에 답하시오.

One student (A)[sitting / to sit] in the back ⓐraised her hand and asked, "What does ⓑthe apple juice mean?" Mr. Jenkins smiled, "I'm glad you asked. It just (B)[sees / shows] that though your life may seem (C)[empty / full], there's always room for a cool drink with a friend."

22 위 글의 괄호 (A)~(C)에서 문맥이나 어법상 알맞은 낱말을 골라 쓰시오.

➡ (A) _____ (B) _____ (C) _____

23 위 글의 밑줄 친 ⓐraised와 같은 의미로 쓰인 것을 고르시오.

① The book raised many important questions.

② I was raised as a city boy.

③ She raised her eyes from her work.

④ We raised money for charity.

⑤ They raised an income tax.

24 위 글의 밑줄 친 ⓑthe apple juice가 상징하는 것을 우리말로 쓰시오.

➡ _____

Lesson 3

Be Positive, Be Happy

 의사소통 기능

- 주제 소개하기
  A: I'd like to talk about Frida Kahlo.

- 이유 묻고 답하기
  A: I want to spend more time on social media.
  B: What makes you say that?
  A: I can make more friends from around the world.

 언어 형식

- 현재완료진행형
  Jake **has been sleeping** all afternoon.

- so ~ that ... 구문
  It was **so** cold **that** I put on my coat.

Key Words

- **appearance**[əpíərəns] 명 외모, 출현
- **argue**[ɑ́ːrgjuː] 동 주장하다
- **artificial**[ɑ̀ːrtəfíʃəl] 형 인공적인
- **as**[əz] 접 ~처럼
- **besides**[bisáidz] 부 그 외에도
- **boring**[bɔ́ːriŋ] 형 지루한
- **bother**[báðər] 동 성가시게 하다
- **cause**[kɔːz] 명 원인
- **chemical**[kémikəl] 명 화학물질
- **common**[kámən] 형 흔한
- **effect**[ifékt] 명 효과
- **focus**[fóukəs] 동 집중하다
- **friendship**[fréndʃip] 명 우정
- **gloomy**[glúːmi] 형 우울한
- **grade**[greid] 명 성적
- **helpful**[hélpfəl] 형 도움이 되는
- **improve**[imprúːv] 동 개선하다
- **leave**[liːv] 동 남겨두다
- **left-handed hitter** 좌타자

- **matter**[mǽtər] 동 문제가 되다, 중요하다
- **media**[míːdiə] 명 매체
- **method**[méθəd] 명 방법
- **nervous**[nə́ːrvəs] 형 불안한
- **patient**[péiʃənt] 형 인내하는
- **positive**[pázətiv] 형 긍정적인
- **produce**[prədjúːs] 동 생산하다
- **relieve**[rilíːv] 동 덜다
- **relieved**[rilíːvd] 형 안심이 되는
- **salty**[sɔ́ːlti] 형 짠
- **scary**[skɛ́əri] 형 무서운
- **schoolwork**[skúlwərk] 명 학교 공부
- **scream**[skriːm] 동 소리를 지르다
- **sleepy**[slíːpi] 형 졸리는
- **spend**[spend] 동 쓰다, 소비하다
- **stressed**[strest] 형 스트레스 받은
- **tidy**[táidi] 형 깔끔한
- **well-known** 형 유명한
- **work**[wəːrk] 동 효과가 있다

Key Expressions

- **according to** ~에 따르면
- **as long as** ~하는 한
- **at bat** 타석에
- **at the same time** 동시에
- **at the top of my lungs** 있는 힘껏
- **break a promise** 약속을 어기다
- **deal with** ~을 다루다, 처리하다
- **decide on** ~에 대하여 결정하다
- **feel like** ~ ~하고 싶은 기분이 들다
- **feel low** 우울하게 느끼다
- **forget to** ~할 것을 잊어버리다
- **get stressed** 스트레스 받다
- **get upset** 속이 상하다
- **have difficulty -ing** ~에 어려움이 있다

- **in other ways** 다른 방식으로
- **instead of** ~ ~ 대신에
- **make sense** 의미가 통하다
- **put down** 내려놓다
- **put on** 입다
- **something else** 다른 어떤 것
- **stress ~ out** 스트레스를 받아 지치게 하다
- **take a deep breath** 심호흡을 하다
- **take time out** 시간을 내다, 쉬다
- **thanks to** ~ 덕택에
- **that way** 그런 식으로
- **the next time** 다음 번 ~할 때
- **used to** ~하곤 했다
- **work on a team** 한 팀으로 일하다

Word Power

※ 서로 비슷한 뜻을 가진 어휘

- ☐ **artificial** 인공적인 : **manufactured** 제조된
- ☐ **bother** 성가시게 하다 : **disturb** 방해하다
- ☐ **common** 흔한 : **normal** 보통의
- ☐ **gloomy** 우울한 : **cheerless** 활기 없는
- ☐ **nervous** 불안한 : **unstable** 불안한
- ☐ **relieve** 덜다 : **ease** 편하게 하다
- ☐ **scream** 소리를 지르다 : **shout** 소리치다
- ☐ **tidy** 깔끔한 : **neat** 깨끗한

- ☐ **boring** 지루한 : **dull** 지루한
- ☐ **cause** 원인 : **reason** 이유
- ☐ **effect** 결과 : **outcome** 결과
- ☐ **improve** 개선하다 : **develop** 개발하다
- ☐ **patient** 인내하는 : **tolerant** 참을성 있는
- ☐ **matter** 중요하다 : **count** 중요하다
- ☐ **sleepy** 졸리는 : **drowsy** 졸리는
- ☐ **produce** 생산하다 : **manufacture** 제작하다

※ 서로 반대의 뜻을 가진 어휘

- ☐ **agree** 동의하다 ↔ **disagree** 동의하지 않다
- ☐ **cause** 원인 ↔ **effect** 결과
- ☐ **gloomy** 우울한 ↔ **cheerful** 활발한
- ☐ **positive** 긍정적인 ↔ **negative** 부정적인
- ☐ **relieved** 안심이 되는 ↔ **worried** 걱정되는
- ☐ **tidy** 깔끔한 ↔ **messy** 어질러진

- ☐ **artificial** 인공적인 ↔ **natural** 자연적인
- ☐ **common** 흔한 ↔ **rare** 흔하지 않은
- ☐ **nervous** 불안한 ↔ **calm** 차분한
- ☐ **produce** 생산하다 ↔ **consume** 소모하다
- ☐ **patient** 인내하는 ↔ **impatient** 조바심을 내는

English Dictionary

☐ **appearance** 외모
→ the way someone or something looks to other people
어떤 사람 또는 어떤 것이 다른 사람에게 보여지는 방식

☐ **argue** 주장하다
→ to disagree with someone in words, often in an angry way
말로 또는 종종 화가 나서 다른 사람의 의견에 반박하다

☐ **artificial** 인공적인
→ not made of natural things
자연적인 것들로 만들어지지 않은

☐ **bother** 성가시게 하다
→ to make someone feel slightly worried, upset, or concerned
다른 사람이 좀 걱정되거나 불편하게 느끼도록 만들다

☐ **cause** 원인
→ a person, event, or thing that makes something happen
무엇인가가 일어나도록 만드는 사람, 사건 또는 사물

☐ **effect** 효과
→ a change that is caused by an event, action, etc.
사건이나 행위 등에 의해서 생겨난 변화

☐ **gloomy** 우울한
→ sad because you think the situation will not improve
상황이 나아지지 않을 것이라고 생각해서 슬픈

☐ **improve** 개선하다
→ to make something better, or to become better
어떤 것을 더 좋게 만들거나 더 좋아지다

☐ **positive** 긍정적인
→ expressing support, agreement, or approval
지지, 동의, 찬성을 표현하는

☐ **tidy** 깔끔한
→ neatly arranged with everything in the right place
모든 것이 제자리에 단정하게 정돈된

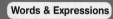

서답형

[01~02] 다음 짝지어진 단어의 관계가 같도록 빈칸에 알맞은 말을 쓰시오. (주어진 철자로 시작할 것)

01

| cause : effect = a_____ : natural |

02 중요

| patient : impatient = n_____ : calm |

03 다음 영영풀이에 해당하는 단어를 고르시오.

| to disagree with someone in words, often in an angry way |

① argue   ② grow

③ destroy   ④ support

⑤ produce

04 중요 다음 중 밑줄 친 부분의 뜻풀이가 바르지 <u>않은</u> 것은?

① I'd like to talk about true <u>friendship</u>. (우정)

② I think it's going to be a <u>boring</u> talk show. (지루한)

③ What makes you feel the most <u>stressed</u>? (스트레스를 받은)

④ Problems with friends <u>took</u> second place with 15.3%. (차지했다)

⑤ I understand. I <u>used to</u> feel that way, too. (사용했다)

05 다음 대화의 빈칸에 들어갈 말로 적절한 것을 고르시오.

> **A:** I'd like to talk about the effects of artificial light.
> **B:** Oh, I have _____ problems at night.

① eating   ② reading

③ running   ④ driving

⑤ sleeping

06 중요 문장의 빈칸에 알맞은 것으로 짝지어진 것은?

> • Jane put _____ a new skirt.
> • This book deals _____ educational problems.

① on – with   ② on – to

③ in – with   ④ to – for

⑤ for – from

07 중요 다음 중 〈보기〉에 있는 단어를 사용하여 자연스러운 문장을 만들 수 <u>없는</u> 것은?

> ┤ 보기 ├
> scary   spend   bothering   gloomy

① What's _____ you the most these days?

② We have _____ to eat.

③ Good horror movies are so _____ that I scream a lot.

④ Some people _____ time with friends when they feel low.

⑤ This is a very _____ situation.

01 다음 빈칸에 공통으로 들어갈 단어를 쓰시오.

- I'm studying for the math test, Mom. Grades stress me _____.
- "Me Time" on her calendar. This means she takes some time _____ for herself.

➡ _____

02 다음 밑줄 친 단어와 의미상 반대가 되는 단어를 주어진 철자로 시작하여 쓰시오.

His brother has a <u>rare</u> disease.

➡ c_____

03 다음 주어진 단어를 이용해 빈칸을 완성하시오.

What makes you feel the most _____?

➡ _____ (stress)

04 다음 우리말에 맞게 빈칸에 알맞은 말을 쓰시오.

(1) 오늘 학급 티셔츠에 대하여 이야기합시다. 우리는 디자인을 정해야 합니다.
➡ Today, let's talk about the class T-shirt. We have to _____ on the design.

(2) 나는 인공조명의 효과에 대하여 이야기하고 싶습니다.
➡ I'd like to talk about the effects of _____ light.

(3) 시험 공부가 나를 졸리게 만들어.
➡ Studying for tests makes me _____.

05 다음 영영풀이에 해당하는 단어를 쓰시오. (주어진 철자로 시작할 것)

not real or not made of natural things but made to be like something that is real or natural

➡ a_____

06 다음 빈칸에 공통으로 들어가기에 적절한 한 단어를 쓰시오.

- I try to forget about problems. It is a good way to deal _____ my feelings.
- Some people spend time _____ friends when they feel low.

➡ _____

07 다음 중 〈보기〉의 적절한 단어를 넣어 의미상 자연스러운 문장을 완성하시오.

보기
drinking relax happy deep counting

(1) I'd like to talk about some good ways to _____ when you get upset.
(2) First, it's good to take _____ breaths.
(3) Second, _____ to ten is a great idea.
(4) Also, _____ cold water helps.
(5) Lastly, thinking _____ thoughts can help.

Conversation

① 주제 소개하기

A I'd like to talk about Frida Kahlo. Frida Kahlo에 대하여 이야기하겠습니다.

■ 무엇인가를 하려고 할 때 'I'd like to ~'라고 한다. 지금부터 상대에게 새로운 주제를 소개하려고 할 때 '~에 대하여 말씀드리겠습니다.'라는 의미로 'I'd like to talk about ~'라고 한다.

• I'd like to talk about true friendship. 진정한 우정에 관하여 말씀드리겠습니다.

• Today, I'd like to talk to you about teen stress. 오늘 청소년의 스트레스에 관하여 말씀드리겠습니다.

■ 주제를 소개할 때 'I'd like to talk about ~'라고 할 수도 있지만 'Let's talk about ~'라고 하거나 'would like to' 대신 will, want to를 사용하여 'Today, I will talk about ~' 또는 'I want to talk about ~'라고 할 수도 있다.

■ 격식을 차려서 소개할 때는 'I'd like to give a presentation about ~'나 'I'd like to give you an introduction about ~'라고 할 수도 있다.

주제 소개하는 여러 가지 표현

• I'd like to talk about ~. ~에 대하여 말씀드리겠습니다.

• I want to talk about ~. ~에 대하여 말씀드리고 싶습니다.

• I will talk about ~. ~에 대하여 말씀드리겠습니다.

• Let's talk about ~. ~에 대하여 이야기해 봅시다.

핵심 Check

1. 다음 우리말과 일치하도록 빈칸에 알맞은 말을 쓰시오.

(1) **A:** I'd like to _____ about Spanish art. (스페인 예술에 대하여 말씀드리겠습니다.)

B: Okay, I'm ready. You may start. (좋아요. 준비됐습니다. 시작하세요.)

(2) **B1:** Today, _____ talk about the class T-shirt. We have to decide on the design.
(오늘 학급 티셔츠에 대하여 이야기해 보자. 우리는 디자인을 정해야 해.)

G: Let me show you some designs on the screen. (화면으로 디자인을 몇 개 보여줄게.)

B2: We have to choose a T-shirt with short sleeves. (우리는 반팔 티셔츠를 골라야 해.)

B1: What makes you say that? (무슨 이유로 그렇게 말하는 거야?)

B2: _____ we'll wear the T-shirt on Sports Day. It's in June.
(우리가 체육대회 때 티셔츠를 입기 때문이야. 그건 6월에 열려.)

G: That makes _____. What about this green one?
(그 말이 맞아. 이 초록색 티셔츠는 어때?)

② 이유 묻고 답하기

> **A** I want to spend more time on social media. 나는 소셜 미디어에 시간을 더 쓰고 싶어.
>
> **B** What makes you say that? 왜 그런 말을 하니?
>
> **A** I can make more friends from around the world.
> 나는 전 세계로부터 더 많은 친구를 사귈 수 있어.

- 상대방의 말을 듣고 그 이유를 묻는 표현은 'What makes you say that?'이나 'What makes you say so?' 이다. '무엇 때문에 그런 말을 하니?'의 의미로 상대방이 한 말의 이유를 확인하기 위하여 묻는 표현이다.

  - M: I'd like to talk about true friendship. 진정한 우정에 대하여 말씀드리겠습니다.
  - B: I think it's going to be a boring talk show. 지루한 토크쇼가 되겠군.
  - G: What makes you say so? 왜 그런 말을 하니?

- 이유를 물어볼 때는 'What makes you say that?'/ 'What makes you say so?'/ 'What makes you think so?' 등으로 물어볼 수 있다. 대답할 때는 단순히 자기 생각이나 이유를 말하면 되고, Because를 붙여서 말해도 된다.

이유 묻고 답하기

이유 묻기
- What makes you say that? 무엇 때문에 그런 말을 하니?
- What makes you say so?
- What makes you think so? 무엇 때문에 그렇게 생각하니?
- I wonder what makes you say that. 무엇 때문에 그런 말을 하는지 궁금해.

대답
- Because ~

핵심 Check

2. 다음 우리말과 일치하도록 빈칸에 알맞은 말을 쓰시오.

W: What are you doing, Oliver?

B: I'm studying for the math test, Mom. Grades stress me (A)_____.
(성적 때문에 스트레스를 받아 지쳐요.)

W: I understand. I (B)_____ to feel that way, too. (나도 또한 그렇게 느꼈지.)

B: Really? I didn't know that.

W: Yeah, but a little stress was helpful for me.

B: (C)_____ makes you say that? (무엇 때문에 그렇게 말씀하세요?)

W: I got stressed when I had an exam, but at the same time it made me (D)_____
and try harder. (동시에 그것이 집중하고 더 열심히 공부하도록 만들었지.)

 Listen & Answer Dialog 1

W: Today, ❶I'd like to talk to you about teen stress. ❷What makes you feel the most stressed? ❸About 9,000 teens answered this question. ❹As you can see, schoolwork was the most common cause of stress. Over half of the students said schoolwork stresses them the most. Problems with friends ❺took second place with 15.3%. ❻Next came family and worries about the future. 8.2% of the students said they ❼get stressed because of their appearance.

W: 오늘, 저는 여러분에게 십 대들의 스트레스에 관해 말씀드리려고 합니다. 여러분에게 가장 많이 스트레스를 주는 것은 무엇인가요? 약 9,000명의 십 대들이 이 질문에 답했습니다. 보시다시피, 학업이 스트레스의 가장 흔한 원인이었습니다. 절반이 넘는 학생들은 학업이 스트레스를 가장 많이 준다고 말했습니다. 친구들과의 문제는 15.3%로 2위를 차지했습니다. 다음은 가족, 그리고 장래에 대한 걱정 순이었습니다. 8.2%의 학생들은 외모 때문에 스트레스를 받는다고 말했습니다.

❶ would like to ~ = ~하고 싶다, ~하겠다
❷ 'What makes you ~?'는 '무엇이 ~하도록 만들었느냐?'의 의미로 이유를 물어보는 표현이다. Why를 사용할 수도 있지만 직설적인 느낌을 주어서 대화가 어색한 느낌을 줄 수도 있을 때는 'What ~?'으로 물어보는 것이 자연스럽다.
❸ about ~ = 약 ~
❹ As ~ (접속사) = ~다시피
❺ take ~ place = ~째 자리를 차지하다
❻ 부사 Next로 시작하는 문장에서 '부사+동사+주어'의 순서로 도치되어 있다. 주어는 'family and worries about the future'이다.
❼ 'get stressed'는 be동사 대신 get을 사용하여 수동의 의미로 사용하고 있다.

Check(√) True or False

(1) Schoolwork was the most common cause of stress.   T ☐ F ☐

(2) Problems with friends were the second common cause of stress.   T ☐ F ☐

 Listen & Answer Dialog 2

W: What are you doing, Oliver?

B: I'm studying for the math test, Mom. Grades stress me out.

W: I understand. I used to feel that way, too.

B: Really? I didn't know that.

W: Yeah, but a little stress was helpful for me.

B: What makes you say that?

W: I got stressed when I had an exam, but at the same time it made me ❶focus and try harder.

B: I see. Did stress help you in other ways?

W: Yes, ❷it helped improve my memory.

W: 뭐 하고 있니, Oliver?
B: 수학 시험이 있어서 공부하고 있어요, 엄마. 성적이 제게 스트레스를 줘요.
W: 이해한단다. 나도 그렇게 느끼곤 했거든.
B: 정말요? 그러신 줄 몰랐어요.
W: 그래, 하지만 약간의 스트레스는 내게 도움이 되기도 했단다.
B: 왜 그렇게 말씀하세요?
W: 나는 시험이 있을 때 스트레스를 받았지만, 동시에 그 스트레스가 나를 집중하고 더 열심히 노력하게 했거든.
B: 그렇군요. 스트레스가 다른 방식으로 엄마에게 도움이 된 적이 있나요?
W: 그럼, 내 기억력을 높이는 데 도움을 주었단다.

❶ 사역동사 made의 목적격보어로 focus와 try는 원형부정사로 사용되었다.
❷ = it helped (me) (to) improve my memory.

Check(√) True or False

(3) The boy is studying for the math test.   T ☐ F ☐

(4) Mom didn't get stressed when she had an exam.   T ☐ F ☐

Listen More

B1: Today, let's talk about the class T-shirt. We have to ❶decide on the design.

G: ❷Let me show you some designs on the screen.

B2: We have to choose a T-shirt with short sleeves.

B1: ❸What makes you say that?

B2: Because we'll wear the T-shirt on Sports Day. It's in June.

G: That ❹makes sense. ❺What about this green one?

B2: I like it. The bee on the T-shirt is so cute.

G: And it's not expensive.

B1: Yes. I think it's the best one.

❶ decide on ~ = ~에 대하여 결정하다
❷ Let me ~. = ~하겠습니다.
❸ 'What makes you ~?'는 이유를 묻는 질문이기 때문에 대답에 Because를 사용해서 대답할 수 있다.
❹ make sense = 의미가 통하다, 말이 되다
❺ 'What about ~?'는 '~은 어때?'의 의미로 상대의 의견을 묻거나 권유할 때 쓰는 표현이다.

 Speak – Talk in groups.

Hi. Today, I'd like to talk about Frida Kahlo. She was a Mexican painter. ❶One of her most ❷ well-known paintings is *Viva la Vida*.

❶ 'one of the[소유격]+최상급 복수명사'의 형태로 '가장 ~한 것 중 하나'의 의미이다.
❷ well-known은 '잘 알려진'의 의미로 famous와 동의어이다.

 Speak – Talk in pairs.

A: I want to ❶spend more time on social media.

B: What makes you say that?

A: I can ❷make more friends from around the world.

B: That makes sense.

❶ 보통 'spend 시간 -ing'의 구문으로 쓰지만 명사와 함께 사용할 때는 'spend 시간 on 명사'의 형태로 쓰기도 한다.
❷ make friends = 친구를 사귀다

 My Speaking Portfolio Step 3

I'd like to talk about some good ways ❶to relax when you ❷get upset. First, ❸it's good to take deep breaths. Second, ❹counting to ten is a great idea. Also, drinking cold water helps. Lastly, thinking happy thoughts can help.

❶ to relax는 명사 ways를 수식하는 부정사의 형용사적 용법이다.
❷ get upset = 화가 나다, 속상하다
❸ 'it is ~ to부정사'의 형태로 가주어, 진주어의 구문이다.
❹ 'counting to ten', 'drinking cold water', 'thinking happy thoughts'는 모두 동명사가 주어로 사용되었다.

 Wrap Up – Listening & Speaking 1

W: Hello, teens. I'm Dr. Broccoli. Last time, I talked about different foods ❶that are good for your health. Today, I'd like to talk about healthy eating habits. First, ❷try to eat slowly. Second, ❸it's important to ❹stop eating when you're full.

❶ that은 주격 관계대명사로 선행사는 different foods로 복수이다.
❷ try to ~ = ~하려고 노력하다, 애쓰다
❸ it is ~ to부정사의 가주어, 진주어 구문이다.
❹ stop -ing = ~하기를 중단하다

 Wrap Up – Listen & Speaking 2

G: ❶Why don't we make a sport club?

B: ❷Sounds good. Let's make a baseball club.

G: Well, I think a basketball club is a better idea.

B: ❸What makes you say that?

G: ❹All we need is a ball to play basketball.

❶ Why don't we ~? = 우리 ~하는 게 어때? (권유나 제안의 표현이다.)
❷ '(It) sounds good.'에서 It을 생략한 말이다.
❸ 상대방의 말에 대하여 이유를 물어보고 있다.
❹ 'All we need'는 'all that we need'에서 목적격 관계대명사 that을 생략하고 쓴 단수 주어이다. '우리가 필요한 것이라고는 ~뿐이다.'의 의미로 쓴다.

다음 우리말과 일치하도록 빈칸에 알맞은 말을 쓰시오.

Listen and Answer – Dialog 1

W: Today, I'd like to _____ to you _____ teen stress. _____ makes you _____ the most _____? _____ 9,000 teens _____ this question. _____ you can _____, schoolwork was the most _____ _____ of stress. _____ half of the students said schoolwork _____ them the most. _____ with friends _____ second place _____ 15.3%. _____ came family and _____ about the future. 8.2% of the students said they _____ _____ because of their _____.

Listen and Answer – Dialog 2

W: _____ are you doing, Oliver?

B: I'm _____ _____ the math test, Mom. _____ stress me out.

W: I understand. I _____ _____ feel that _____, too.

B: Really? I didn't _____ that.

W: Yeah, but a little _____ was _____ for me.

B: _____ makes you say that?

W: I _____ _____ when I had an exam, but _____ the same time it made me _____ and try harder.

B: I see. Did stress _____ you in other ways?

W: Yes, it helped _____ my memory.

Listen More – Listen and choose.

B1: Today, let's _____ about the class T-shirt. We have to _____ on the design.

G: _____ me show you some _____ on the screen.

B2: We have to _____ a T-shirt with _____ sleeves.

B1: What makes you _____ that?

B2: _____ we'll _____ the T-shirt on Sports Day. It's in June.

G: That _____ _____. What _____ this green one?

B2: I like it. The bee on the T-shirt is so _____.

G: And it's not _____.

B1: Yes. I think it's the best one.

W: 오늘, 저는 여러분에게 십 대들의 스트레스에 관해 말씀드리려고 합니다. 여러분에게 가장 많이 스트레스를 주는 것은 무엇인가요? 약 9,000명의 십 대들이 이 질문에 답했습니다. 보시다시피, 학업이 스트레스의 가장 흔한 원인이었습니다. 절반이 넘는 학생들은 학업이 스트레스를 가장 많이 준다고 말했습니다. 친구들과의 문제는 15.3%로 2위를 차지했습니다. 다음은 가족, 그리고 장래에 대한 걱정 순이었습니다. 8.2%의 학생들은 외모 때문에 스트레스를 받는다고 말했습니다.

W: 뭐 하고 있니, Oliver?
B: 수학 시험이 있어서 공부하고 있어요, 엄마. 성적이 제게 스트레스를 줘요.
W: 이해한단다. 나도 그렇게 느끼곤 했거든.
B: 정말요? 그러신 줄 몰랐어요.
W: 그래, 하지만 약간의 스트레스는 내게 도움이 되기도 했단다.
B: 왜 그렇게 말씀하세요?
W: 나는 시험이 있을 때 스트레스를 받았지만, 동시에 그 스트레스가 나를 집중하고 더 열심히 노력하게 했거든.
B: 그렇군요. 스트레스가 다른 방식으로 엄마에게 도움이 된 적이 있나요?
W: 그럼, 내 기억력을 높이는 데 도움을 주었단다.

B1: 오늘은 학급 티셔츠에 관해 이야기해 보자. 우리는 디자인을 정해야 해.
G: 화면으로 몇 가지 디자인을 보여 줄게.
B2: 우리는 반팔 티셔츠를 골라야 해.
B1: 무슨 이유로 그렇게 말하는 거야?
B2: 우리가 체육대회 때 티셔츠를 입기 때문이야. 그건 6월에 열려.
G: 그 말이 맞아. 이 초록색 티셔츠는 어때?
B2: 나는 마음에 들어. 티셔츠 위의 벌 그림이 정말 귀여워.
G: 그리고 비싸지 않아.
B1: 맞아. 그게 제일 좋겠어.

Speak – Talk in groups.

Hi. Today, I'd like to _____ about Frida Kahlo. She was a Mexican painter. _____ of her most _____ paintings is *Viva la Vida*.

Speak – Talk in pairs.

A: I want to _____ more time on social media.

B: What _____ you say that?

A: I can _____ more friends from around the world.

B: That _____ sense.

My Speaking Portfolio Step 3

I'd _____ to talk about some good ways to _____ when you get _____. First, it's good to _____ _____ breaths. Second, _____ to ten is a great idea. Also, _____ cold water helps. _____, thinking happy thoughts can help.

Wrap Up – Listening & Peaking 1

W: Hello, teens. I'm Dr. Broccoli. Last time, I _____ about different _____ that _____ _____ for your health. Today, I'd _____ _____ talk about _____ _____ habits. First, try to eat _____. Second, it's important to stop _____ when you're full.

Wrap Up – Listening & Speaking 2

G: Why _____ we _____ a sport club?

B: Sounds good. Let's _____ a baseball club.

G: Well, I think a _____ club is a better idea.

B: What makes you _____ that?

G: All _____ _____ is a ball to play basketball.

안녕하세요. 오늘은 Frida Kahlo에 대하여 이야기하겠습니다. 그녀는 멕시코인 화가입니다. 그녀의 가장 유명한 그림 중 하나는 Viva la Vida입니다.

A: 나는 소셜 미디어에 더 많은 시간을 쓰고 싶어.
B: 왜 그렇게 생각하니?
A: 나는 전 세계로부터 더 많은 친구를 사귈 수 있어.
B: 옳은 말이야.

여러분이 화가 났을 때 긴장을 풀 수 있는 방법에 관하여 이야기하겠습니다. 첫째, 심호흡을 하는 것이 좋습니다. 둘째, 열까지 세는 것은 좋은 생각입니다. 또한 차가운 물을 마시는 것도 도움이 됩니다. 마지막으로 행복한 생각을 하는 것이 도움이 됩니다.

여: 안녕하세요, 십 대 여러분. 저는 Broccoli 박사입니다. 지난 시간에, 건강에 좋은 다양한 음식에 관해 이야기했죠. 오늘은 건강한 식습관에 관해 이야기하고자 합니다. 먼저, 천천히 먹으려고 노력하세요. 둘째, 배가 부르면 그만 먹는 것이 중요합니다.

G: 우리 운동 동아리를 만드는 게 어때?
B: 좋아. 야구 동아리를 만들자.
G: 글쎄, 농구 동아리가 더 좋은 생각인 것 같아.
B: 왜 그렇게 말하는 거야?
G: 농구를 하기 위해 우리에게 필요한 건 농구공뿐이잖아.

[01~02] 다음 대화의 빈칸에 들어갈 말을 고르시오.

01

M: I'd like to talk _____ true friendship.

A: I think it's going to be a boring talk show.

B: What makes you say so?

① to   ② with   ③ for

④ about   ⑤ by

02

A: I want to spend more time on social media.

B: _____ makes you say that?

A: I can make more friends from around the world.

B: That makes sense.

① Why   ② What   ③ When

④ Who   ⑤ Which

[03~04] 다음 글을 읽고 물음에 답하시오.

Hello, teens. I'm Dr. Broccoli. Last time, I _____(A)_____ about different foods that are good for your health. Today, I'd like to talk about healthy eating habits. First, try to eat slowly. Second, it's important to stop eating when you're full.

03 빈칸 (A)에 들어갈 알맞은 말을 고르시오.

① studied   ② talked   ③ chose

④ took   ⑤ thought

04 위 글의 내용과 일치하지 <u>않는</u> 것은?

① The speaker's name is Broccoli.

② The speaker is a doctor.

③ He will talk about different foods.

④ We should eat slowly for our health.

⑤ When we feel full, we had better stop eating.

[01~03] 다음 대화를 읽고 물음에 답하시오.

W: What are you doing, Oliver?

B: I'm studying for the math test, Mom. Grades stress me out.

W: I understand. I used to feel (A)that way, too.

B: Really? I didn't know that.

W: Yeah, but a little stress was helpful for me.

B: (B)왜 그렇게 말씀을 하세요? (what, say, that)

W: I got stressed when I had an exam, but at the same time it made me focus and try harder.

B: I see. Did stress help you in other ways?

W: Yes, it helped improve my memory.

01 밑줄 친 (A)가 가리키는 것을 우리말로 쓰시오.

➡ _____

02 (B)의 주어진 우리말을 영어 문장으로 쓰시오. (주어진 단어 반드시 포함)

➡ _____

03 According to the dialogue, which one is NOT true?

① Oliver is studying for the math test.

② Oliver's mom also felt stressed about grades.

③ Oliver knew a little stress was helpful.

④ Stress helped Oliver's mom try harder.

⑤ Oliver's mom got stressed when she had an exam.

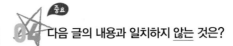

04 다음 글의 내용과 일치하지 않는 것은?

W: Today, I'd like to talk to you about teen stress. What makes you feel the most stressed? About 9,000 teens answered this question. As you can see, schoolwork was the most common cause of stress. Over half of the students said schoolwork stresses them the most. Problems with friends took second place with 15.3%. Next came family and worries about the future. 8.2% of the students said they get stressed because of their appearance.

① The topic of this talk is 'teen stress.'

② The largest number of students feel stressed about schoolwork.

③ Problems with friends are the most common cause of stress.

④ Over half of the students get stressed because of schoolwork.

⑤ 8.2% of the students get stressed because of their appearance.

05 다음 대화의 순서가 바르게 배열된 것을 고르시오.

(A) I can make more friends from around the world.

(B) I want to spend more time on social media.

(C) What makes you say that?

① (A) – (C) – (B)   ② (B) – (A) – (C)

③ (B) – (C) – (A)   ④ (C) – (A) – (B)

⑤ (C) – (B) – (A)

[06~07] 다음 대화를 읽고 물음에 답하시오.

> G: Why don't we make a sport club?
> B: _____(A)_____ Let's make a baseball club.
> G: Well, I think a basketball club is a better idea.
> B: What makes you say that?
> G: All we need is a ball to play basketball.

06 빈칸 (A)에 들어가기에 적절하지 <u>않은</u> 것은?

① That's a good idea.
② Sounds good.
③ Yes, I agree.
④ I can't agree with you more.
⑤ I'm not with you.

07 Which one is true about the dialogue?

① The girl suggests making a sport club.
② The girl wants to make a baseball club.
③ The boy suggests making a basketball club.
④ The girl agrees with the boy's idea.
⑤ Just a ball is needed to play baseball.

[08~09] 다음 대화의 빈칸에 들어갈 말을 고르시오.

08
> W: What are you doing, Oliver?
> B: I'm studying for the math test, Mom. Grades _____ me out.
> W: I understand. I used to feel that way, too.

① stress   ② take
③ get   ④ work
⑤ bring

09
> W: A little stress was _____ for me.
> B: What makes you say that?
> W: I got stressed when I had an exam, but at the same time it made me focus and try harder.
> B: I see. Did stress help you in other ways?
> W: Yes, it helped improve my memory.

① hopeful   ② helpful   ③ careful
④ stressful   ⑤ tiring

서답형

10 다음 대화의 빈칸에 들어갈 말을 〈보기〉에서 골라 순서대로 배열하시오.

> B1: Today, let's talk about the class T-shirt. We have to decide on the design.
> G: Let me show you some designs on the screen.
> B2: _____
> B1: _____
> B2: Because we'll wear the T-shirt on Sports Day. It's in June.
> G: That makes sense.
> _____
> B2: I like it. The bee on the T-shirt is so cute.
> G: _____
> B1: Yes. I think it's the best one.

┤ 보기 ├
(A) What makes you say that?
(B) We have to choose a T-shirt with short sleeves.
(C) And it's not expensive.
(D) What about this green one?

➡ _____

[01~03] 다음 글을 읽고 물음에 답하시오.

W: Today, I'd like to talk to you about teen stress. (A)여러분에게 가장 많이 스트레스를 주는 것은 무엇인가요? About 9,000 teens answered this question. As you can see, schoolwork was the most common cause of stress. Over half of the students said schoolwork stresses them the most. Problems with friends took second place with 15.3%. (B)다음은 가족, 그리고 장래에 관한 걱정 순이었습니다. 8.2% of the students said they get stressed because of their appearance.

01 (A)에 주어진 우리말에 해당하는 영어 문장을 완성하시오. 〈보기〉의 단어를 포함할 것) (7 words)

┌─ 보기 ├─
stressed   make   feel
└────────────┘

➡ _____

02 다음 단어를 배열하여 (B)의 의미에 해당하는 영어 문장을 완성하시오.

(1) Next로 시작할 것.
(2) family, the future, about, worries, came, and를 배열할 것.

➡ _____

03 위 글을 읽고 다음 질문에 대한 답을 완성하시오.

What is the most common cause of stress for teens?

➡ The most common cause of stress for teens is _____.

[04~05] 다음 대화를 읽고 물음에 답하시오.

W: What are you doing, Oliver?
B: I'm studying for the math test, Mom. Grades stress me out.
W: I understand. I used to feel that way, too.
B: Really? I didn't know ⓐthat.
W: Yeah, but a little stress was helpful for me.
B: What makes you say that?
W: I got stressed when I had an exam, but ___ⓑ___ the same time it made me focus and try harder.
B: I see. Did stress help you in other ways?
W: Yes, it helped improve my memory.

04 위 대화의 밑줄 친 ⓐ가 가리키는 것을 우리말로 쓰시오.

➡ _____

05 위 대화의 빈칸 ⓑ에 알맞은 전치사를 쓰시오.

➡ _____

06 다음 밑줄 친 우리말을 영어로 쓰시오. (it으로 시작하고 breaths를 포함할 것)

I'd like to talk about some good ways to relax when you get upset. First, 심호흡을 하는 것이 좋습니다. Second, counting to ten is a great idea. Also, drinking cold water helps. Lastly, thinking happy thoughts can help.

➡ _____

교과서
Grammar

① 현재완료진행형

> • Jake **has been sleeping** all afternoon. Jake는 오후 내내 자고 있다.

- 형태: have/has been -ing
  의미: ~하고 있다

- 현재완료진행형은 과거에서 지금까지 계속된 현재완료의 상황과 지금도 지속되고 있는 진행형을 결합한 것으로 '과거에 시작해서 지금까지 계속되었고, 지금도 진행하고 있는 동작'을 나타낸다. 현재완료진행형에서 '~ 이래로'는 since로 나타내고, '~ 동안'은 for로 나타낸다.
  - I **'ve been using** this method for the past several months. 나는 지난 몇 달 동안 이 방법을 사용하고 있다.
  - She **has been waiting** for his call for two hours. 그녀는 두 시간 동안 그의 전화를 기다리고 있다.

- 현재완료진행형은 현재까지 계속되고 있는 동작을 나타낼 때 사용한다. 상태 동사는 진행 시제를 쓸 수 없기 때문에 현재완료진행형으로 나타내지 않는다. 현재완료진행형은 현재완료와 마찬가지로 명백한 과거 표현과는 같이 쓸 수 없다.
  - I **have been learning** English since I was 10. 나는 10살 이후로 영어를 배우고 있다.
  - Ann **has been living** in this city since she was born. Ann은 태어난 이래로 이 도시에 살고 있다.

핵심 Check

1. 다음 주어진 단어를 적절한 형태로 쓰시오.

(1) He's been _____ for a job since last month. (look)

(2) I've been _____ 'Me Time' on my calendar for two months. (write)

(3) Plum has been _____ with us since last winter. (live)

2. 다음 주어진 문장을 한 문장으로 적절하게 완성하시오.

(1) They have waited for him to arrive and they are still waiting.

  ➡ They _____ for him to arrive.
  (그들은 그가 도착하기를 기다리고 있다.)

(2) He started to read the book two hours ago. He is still reading the book.

  ➡ He _____ the book for two hours.
  (그는 두 시간 동안 그 책을 읽고 있다.)

❷ so ~ that ... 구문

> • It was **so** cold **that** I put on my coat. 날씨가 너무 추워서 나는 코트를 입었다.

- 형태: so 형용사/부사 that 주어+동사

  의미: 너무 ~해서 …하다

- 'so ~ that …' 구문은 '너무 ~해서 …하다'의 의미로 원인과 결과를 나타내는 표현이다. so와 that 사이에는 형용사나 부사를 써야 한다.

  - Good horror movies are **so** scary **that** I scream a lot.
    좋은 공포 영화는 너무 무서워서 나는 소리를 많이 지른다.

  - While I fish, I'm **so** focused **that** I can leave all my worries behind.
    낚시를 하는 동안 나는 너무 집중하여 걱정을 뒤로 미뤄놓을 수 있다.

  - When she's **so** stressed **that** her life looks gloomy, she cleans her room.
    그녀가 너무 스트레스를 받아 삶이 우울해 보일 때, 그녀는 방청소를 한다.

- so와 that 사이에는 형용사나 부사를 써야 하지만, 명사구를 써야 할 때는 so가 아니라 such를 써서 'such (a)+형용사+명사 that ~'의 형태가 된다.

  - It was **such** an interesting novel **that** I finished reading it last night.
    그것은 너무 재미있는 소설이어서 나는 어젯밤에 그것을 다 읽었다.

  - It was **such** a delicious cake **that** he wanted to have some more.
    그것은 너무 맛있는 케이크여서 그는 좀 더 먹기를 원했다.

- 'so that'은 '그래서 ~'의 의미로 결과를 나타내는 부사절을 유도한다. 'so that 주어 can/will ~'은 '~하기 위하여'의 의미로 목적을 나타내는 부사절을 유도한다.

핵심 Check

3. 다음 주어진 문장에서 적절한 것을 고르시오.

(1) The book was (so / such) interesting that he read it again.

(2) It was (so / such) a heavy bag that I couldn't move it.

4. 다음 주어진 문장을 'so ~ that'을 이용하여 한 문장으로 다시 쓰시오.

(1) Because it was too cold, we didn't go out.

= It was ＿＿＿＿ ＿＿＿＿ ＿＿＿＿ ＿＿＿＿ ＿＿＿＿ go out.

(2) Since the jacket was very expensive, he didn't buy it.

= The jacket was ＿＿＿＿ ＿＿＿＿ ＿＿＿＿ ＿＿＿＿ ＿＿＿＿ buy it.

(3) Because the wind was very strong, they stopped fishing.

= The wind was ＿＿＿＿ ＿＿＿＿ ＿＿＿＿ ＿＿＿＿ ＿＿＿＿ fishing.

01 다음 빈칸에 어법상 적절한 것은?

> I have been _____ in this city since I was born.

① lived   ② lives   ③ live
④ to live   ⑤ living

02 다음 중 어법상 <u>어색한</u> 것은?

① Today, I'd like to talk to you about teen stress.
② What makes you feel the most stressed?
③ Let me show you some designs on the screen.
④ It's so noisy that she wants to shut the window.
⑤ French fries are so salty that I won't eat.

03 다음 〈보기〉의 두 문장을 현재완료진행형을 사용하여 한 문장으로 연결하시오. (단, 숫자는 한 단어로 취급하며, 총 12단어로 주어진 문장을 완성하시오.)

> ┤ 보기 ├
> • James started teaching English 20 years ago.
> • He is still teaching at this middle school.

➡ James _____ .

04 다음 문장의 빈칸에 들어갈 알맞은 말을 차례대로 쓰시오.

> I was _____ tired _____ I fell asleep on the bus.

05 다음 빈칸에 어법상 적절한 것은?

> It was so _____ that they stopped sailing.

① windy   ② fog   ③ wind
④ rain   ⑤ rained

01 〈보기〉를 참고하여 주어진 단어를 이용하여 두 문장을 한 문장으로 쓰시오.

> ┌ 보기 ┐
> • They started to play basketball two hours ago.
> • They are still playing basketball. (for)
> ➡ <u>They have been playing basketball for two hours.</u>

(1) • She sat on the bench an hour ago.
　• She is still sitting on the bench. (for)
➡ _____
_____

(2) • She began to work at the store in 2010.
　• She is still working at the store. (since)
➡ _____

(3) • Tom started cleaning the room this morning.
　• He is still cleaning the room. (since)
➡ _____
_____

02 다음 중 빈칸에 들어갈 be동사의 형태가 <u>다른</u> 하나는?

① I have _____ living in this city since I was born.
② The house _____ painted red yesterday.
③ She has _____ reading a book for two hours.
④ They have _____ playing soccer for forty minutes.
⑤ We have _____ running along the river for an hour.

03 다음 빈칸에 어법상 적절한 것은?

> Sam has _____ sleeping all afternoon.

① be　　　　　② being
③ been　　　　④ was
⑤ are

04 다음 괄호 안에 주어진 어구들을 바르게 배열하여 문장을 완성하시오.

> (I've / 'Me Time' / my calendar / been / for / writing / on / two months)

➡ _____
_____

05 다음 〈보기〉에서 어법상 <u>어색한</u> 문장의 개수는?

> ┌ 보기 ┐
> ⓐ My sister is old enough to ride a bike.
> ⓑ My fathet was too sleepy to drive.
> ⓒ It was such fine that we went outside.
> ⓓ Thinking happy thoughts can help.
> ⓔ She has been lived here for 5 years.

① 1개　② 2개　③ 3개　④ 4개　⑤ 5개

06 다음 밑줄 친 부분의 쓰임이 나머지와 <u>다른</u> 하나는?

① It's so noisy <u>that</u> he closed the door.
② The food is so salty <u>that</u> I don't want it.
③ I am so hungry <u>that</u> I will eat a whole pizza.
④ I know the boy <u>that</u> is walking to me.
⑤ The line is so long <u>that</u> I won't wait in line.

07 다음 중 밑줄 친 부분이 어법상 어색한 것은?

① It's good to take deep breaths.
② She has been running for an hour.
③ Counting to ten is a great idea.
④ Drink cold water helps.
⑤ Some people spend time with friends when they feel low.

서답형

08 〈보기〉를 참고하여 주어진 두 문장을 한 문장으로 연결하여 쓰시오.

┌─ 보기 ├─
• She bought the flowers.
• The flowers were very beautiful.
➡ The flowers were so beautiful that she bought them.
└──────

(1) • She went to bed early.
    • She was very tired.
    ➡ _____
    _____

(2) • The cake looked very delicious.
    • He decided to buy it.
    ➡ _____
    _____

(3) • The story was very interesting.
    • He read it in a day.
    ➡ _____
    _____

서답형

09 다음 우리말을 영어로 옮길 때 빈칸에 알맞은 말을 쓰시오.

┌──────
방이 너무 더워서 그는 창문을 열었다.
└──────

➡ It was so hot in the room _____ he opened the window.

10 다음 우리말을 영어로 옮긴 것 중 어색한 것은?

① 청소년들의 스트레스에 관하여 말씀드리겠습니다.
➡ I'd like to talk to you about teen stress.

② 무엇이 가장 스트레스를 받게 했습니까?
➡ What makes you feel the most stressed?

③ 그는 한 시간 동안 방에서 음악을 듣고 있다.
➡ He was been listening to music in the room for an hour.

④ 약 9천 명의 청소년이 이 질문에 대답을 했다.
➡ About 9,000 teens answered this question.

⑤ 날씨가 너무 추워서 나는 두꺼운 코트를 입었다.
➡ It was so cold that I wore a thick coat.

11 다음 중 밑줄 친 부분의 쓰임이 어색한 것을 고르시오.

① It was so a nice day that he went out for a walk.
② He felt so tired that he went home early.
③ The cake was so delicious that I wanted to have some more.
④ It was so hot that I drank some cold water.
⑤ The mountain was so high that we couldn't climb it.

서답형

12 다음 괄호 안에서 알맞은 말을 고르시오.

(1) They have [being / been] eating lunch.
(2) He has been [cleaned / cleaning] the room.
(3) The bag was [so / such] heavy that he couldn't move it.
(4) He was [so / such] busy that he couldn't help her.

13 다음 중 어법상 어색한 것을 고르시오.

① She has been watching TV for an hour.

② He has been living here since 2010.

③ They have known each other since 20 years.

④ The weather was so hot that we went to the lake.

⑤ She spoke so fast that we couldn't understand her.

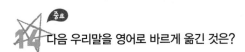

14 다음 우리말을 영어로 바르게 옮긴 것은?

그는 너무 고통스러워 잠을 잘 수가 없었다.

① He was very painful that could sleep.

② He was so painful that he couldn't sleep.

③ It was so painful that he can't sleep.

④ He was such painful that he couldn't sleep.

⑤ He couldn't sleep so that he was painful.

15 다음 중 밑줄 친 부분의 쓰임이 어색한 것을 고르시오.

① They have been married for 2005.

② We have been waiting for him since last January.

③ They have been eating lunch for 30 minutes.

④ She has been living here since 2011.

⑤ She has been doing the dishes since she finished dinner.

16 다음 우리말을 영어로 바르게 옮긴 것은?

그 차는 너무 오래 되어서 빨리 달릴 수 없었다.

① It was such an old car that it couldn't run fast.

② It was so old car that it could run fast.

③ It was such old a car that it couldn't run fast.

④ It ran so fast that it was very old car.

⑤ It was so an old car that it couldn't run fast.

17 다음 중 어법상 어색한 것은?

① I've been using this method for a long time.

② I know that he hasn't finished the work yet.

③ My uncle graduated from college two years ago.

④ He has been looking for a job since last year.

⑤ She has finished reading a book yesterday.

18 다음 두 문장을 한 문장으로 쓸 때 빈칸에 알맞은 말을 쓰시오.

- He began watching TV five hours ago.
- He is still watching TV now.

➡ He _____ _____ _____ TV for five hours.

01 다음 우리말에 맞게 괄호 안에 주어진 어휘를 바르게 배열하시오.

(1) 그녀는 이 학교에서 10년 동안 영어를 가르치고 있다.

(teaching, she, been, 10 years, has, English, for, at this school)

➡ _____

_____

(2) 어젯밤부터 비가 내리고 있다.

(it, raining, since, has, last, been, night)

➡ _____

_____

(3) 그가 차를 너무 빠르게 몰아서 그의 아버지가 그에게 차를 천천히 운전하라고 말했다.

(he, his father, drove the car, so, told, that, him, fast, slowly, to drive)

➡ _____

_____

02 다음 주어진 문장을 아래와 같이 바꾸어 쓸 때 적절한 말을 쓰시오.

> The mountain was so high that they couldn't climb it.
> = It was such _____ _____
> that they couldn't climb it.

03 다음 문장의 빈칸에 우리말의 의미에 맞게 채우시오.

(1) Mike has been doing his homework all day.

➡ _____ his homework all day?

(Mike는 하루 종일 그의 숙제를 하고 있는 중이니?)

(2) Jack has been playing the computer game since last night.

➡ _____ the computer game since last night.

(Jack은 지난밤부터 지금까지 계속해서 컴퓨터 게임을 해오고 있지는 않다.)

04 다음 빈칸에 주어진 단어를 적절한 형태로 쓰시오.

(1) She has been _____ on the phone for an hour. (talk)

(2) He has _____ lying on the bed since this morning. (be)

05 다음 두 문장을 한 문장으로 만들 때 빈칸을 완성하시오. (단, 반드시 been을 사용할 것)

> • Chris started playing tennis two hours ago.
> • He is still playing tennis.
> ➡ Chris _____
> _____.

06 다음 주어진 두 문장을 한 문장으로 연결할 때 빈칸에 알맞은 말을 쓰시오.

> He is very rich. He can buy anything
> = He is _____ _____ that he can buy anything.

07 다음 우리말을 〈조건〉에 맞게 영작하시오.

> 그녀는 매우 친절해서 모두가 그녀를 좋아한다.

> ┤ 조건 ├
> 1. 'so ... that' 구문을 활용할 것.
> 2. 8단어의 완전한 문장으로 쓸 것.

➡ _____

08 다음 괄호 안에서 알맞은 단어를 골라 〈보기〉와 같이 두 문장을 한 문장으로 바꿔 쓰시오.

> ┤ 보기 ├
> • My father started repairing his car two hours ago.
> • He is still repairing it now. (for/since)
> ➡ <u>My father has been repairing his car for two hours.</u>

> • Ann and I started studying Chinese last week.
> • We are still studying it now. (for/since)

➡ _____

_____

09 다음 빈칸에 알맞은 말을 넣어 문장을 완성하시오.

(1) He felt too tired. He stopped working.
   ➡ He felt _____ _____ that he stopped working.

(2) Because the box was too heavy, the child couldn't move it.
   ➡ The box was so _____ _____ the child couldn't move it.

(3) Since the pizza was very delicious, they wanted more.
   ➡ The pizza was so delicious _____ _____ _____ _____.

10 다음 두 문장을 한 문장으로 만들 때 빈칸에 들어갈 알맞은 말을 쓰시오.

> • My brother started using a computer two hours ago.
> • He is still using it.
> ➡ My brother _____ a computer for two hours.

11 다음 괄호 안에 주어진 단어들을 바르게 배열하여 문장을 다시 쓰시오.

> Some people (with / spend / when / time / feel / they / friends / low).

➡ _____

_____

12 다음 주어진 문장이 같은 의미가 되도록 so, that을 사용하여 다시 쓰시오.

(1) She is too hungry. She can't swim any more.
   ➡ _____

   _____

(2) Because the car was very old, it couldn't run fast.
   ➡ _____

   _____

(3) Since it was very cold, he put on his coat.
   ➡ _____

   _____

Say Goodbye to Stress

Some people spend time with friends when they feel low. Others eat special foods to feel better. Still others simply sleep for a while. How do you deal with stress? Here are some stories about people who suggest different ways.

Mina (15, Daejeon)

Sometimes my friends give me stress by saying bad things about me, breaking promises, or arguing over small things. When this happens, I watch horror movies! Good horror movies are so scary that I scream a lot. I guess that screaming at the top of my lungs helps me feel better. Also, thanks to scary scenes and sound effects, I can forget about what bothers me. I've been using this method for the past several months, and it really works.

Junho (14, Yeosu)

My uncle graduated from college two years ago. He lives with my family, and he's been looking for a job for some time. I know that he's stressed out, but he always tries to be positive by going fishing. He never gets upset when he doesn't catch any fish. He says, "While I fish, I'm so focused that I can leave all my worries behind. Besides, it teaches me to be patient." I'm sure that focusing on one thing helps us forget about something else.

feel low 기운이 없다, 무기력하다
for a while 잠깐, 잠시 동안
suggest 제안하다, 제시하다
break (약속 등을) 어기다
argue over ~을 두고 논쟁하다
scream 비명을 지르다
thanks to ~덕분에
scene 장면
effect 효과
bother 괴롭히다
method 방법
work 효과가 나다[있다]
graduate 졸업하다
stress out 스트레스를 받다
focused 집중한, 집중적인
worry 걱정거리, 걱정(되는 일)
patient 참을성[인내심] 있는

확인문제

● 다음 문장이 본문의 내용과 일치하면 T, 일치하지 않으면 F를 쓰시오.

1　When Mina's friends give her stress, she watches horror movies. ☐

2　Screaming at the top of her lungs prevents Mina from feeling better. ☐

3　Junho's uncle has been looking for a job for some time. ☐

4　Junho's uncle gets upset when he doesn't catch any fish. ☐

Dobin (16, Seoul)

My sister, a second-year student in high school, has a wonderful way
to stay free from stress. She feels a lot of stress from schoolwork, but
my mother seems to like the situation for a good reason. It is because
cleaning is my sister's number-one way to make life better! When
she's so stressed that her life looks gloomy, she cleans her room. She
says, "As I clean my room, I feel like I'm also relieving stress. When
my room looks tidy, my life looks brighter."

Yulia (14, Ansan)

Let me tell you what my mother does about her stress. She feels
stressed by all the things she has to do at work and at home. When
she's under stress, she writes "Me Time" on her calendar. This means
she takes some time out for herself. She reads a book, watches a
movie, or talks with her friends. She says, "It doesn't really matter
what I do, as long as it's something I like. I've been writing 'Me Time'
on my calendar for two months, and I feel much better."

Which methods will work for you? Try some of these ideas yourself,
and find your best way to say goodbye to stress.

way 방법
stay free from ~으로부터 벗어나다
schoolwork 학교 공부
situation 상황
reason 이유
gloomy 우울한
relieve 없애[덜어]주다
tidy 깔끔한
bright 밝은
feel stressed 스트레스를 받다
take some time out 잠깐 시간을 갖다
matter 중요하다
method 방법

 확인문제

● 다음 문장이 본문의 내용과 일치하면 T, 일치하지 않으면 F를 쓰시오.

1 Dobin's sister is a second-year student in high school. ☐

2 Dobin's sister doesn't have any ways to stay free from stress. ☐

3 When Dobin's mother is so stressed, she cleans her room. ☐

4 Yulia's mother feels stressed by all the things she must do at work and at home. ☐

5 When Yulia's mother is under stress, she writes "Me Time" on her calendar. ☐

6 It really matters what Yulia's mother should do as it's something she doesn't like. ☐

● 우리말을 참고하여 빈칸에 알맞은 말을 쓰시오.

1 Say _____ to Stress

2 Some people spend time with friends when they _____ _____.

3 _____ eat special foods _____ _____ _____.

4 _____ _____ simply sleep for a while.

5 How do you _____ _____ stress?

6 Here are some stories about people who _____ _____ _____.

Mina (15, Daejeon)

7 Sometimes my friends give me stress by _____ bad things about me, _____ promises, or _____ over small things.

8 _____ _____ _____, I watch horror movies!

9 Good horror movies are _____ scary _____ I scream a lot.

10 I guess that screaming _____ _____ _____ _____ _____ _____ helps me feel better.

11 Also, _____ _____ scary scenes and sound effects, I can forget about _____ _____ _____.

12 _____ _____ _____ this method for the past several months, and it really _____.

Junho (14, Yeosu)

13 My uncle _____ _____ college two years ago.

14 He lives with my family, and _____ _____ _____ _____ a job for some time.

15 I know that _____ _____ _____, but he always tries to be positive _____ _____ _____.

16 He never _____ _____ when he doesn't catch any fish.

17 He says, "While I fish, I'm _____ focused _____ I _____ _____ all my worries _____.

18 _____, it teaches me _____ _____ patient."

---

1 스트레스와 이별하라

2 어떤 사람들은 울적할 때 친구들과 시간을 보낸다.

3 다른 사람들은 기분이 좋아지도록 특별한 음식을 먹는다.

4 또 다른 사람들은 그저 잠시 잠을 자기도 한다.

5 여러분은 스트레스를 어떻게 다루는가?

6 여기 다양한 방법을 제안하는 사람들의 이야기가 있다.

미나 (15살, 대전)

7 때때로 내 친구들은 나에 관해 나쁜 말을 하거나, 약속을 어기거나, 혹은 사소한 일을 두고 언쟁을 하며 내게 스트레스를 준다.

8 이럴 때, 나는 공포 영화를 본다!

9 훌륭한 공포 영화는 너무 무서워서 나는 소리를 많이 지르게 된다.

10 있는 힘껏 소리 지르는 것은 내 기분이 나아지는 데 도움이 된다고 생각한다.

11 또한, 무서운 장면과 음향 효과 덕분에 나를 괴롭히는 것들을 잊을 수 있다.

12 나는 지난 몇 달간 이 방법을 써오고 있는데, 효과가 아주 좋다.

준호 (14살, 여수)

13 우리 삼촌은 2년 전에 대학을 졸업했다.

14 삼촌은 우리 가족과 함께 살고 있고, 얼마 전부터 직장을 구하고 있다.

15 나는 삼촌이 스트레스를 받고 있지만 낚시를 다니며 긍정적으로 지내려고 항상 노력한다는 것을 안다.

16 물고기를 한 마리도 잡지 못했을 때에도 삼촌은 절대 속상해하지 않는다.

17 삼촌은 "낚시하는 동안, 나는 아주 몰입해서 모든 걱정을 잊을 수 있어.

18 게다가 낚시는 나에게 인내를 가르쳐 준단다."라고 말한다

19 I'm sure that _____ _____ one thing helps us _____ about something else.

Dobin (16, Seoul)

20 My sister, a _____ student in high school, has a wonderful way to stay _____ _____ stress.

21 She feels a lot of stress from schoolwork, but my mother _____ _____ _____ the situation _____ _____ _____ _____.

22 It is because cleaning is my sister's _____ _____ to make life better!

23 When she's _____ stressed _____ her life looks gloomy, she cleans her room.

24 She says, "As I clean my room, I _____ _____ I'm also _____ stress.

25 When my room _____ _____, my life _____ _____."

Yulia (14, Ansan)

26 Let me tell you _____ my mother does about her stress.

27 She feels stressed by _____ _____ _____ _____ _____ _____ _____ at work and at home.

28 When _____ _____ _____, she writes "Me Time" on her calendar.

29 This means she _____ _____ _____ _____ for herself.

30 She _____ a book, _____ a movie, or _____ with her friends.

31 She says, "It doesn't really _____ what I do, _____ _____ _____ it's something I like.

32 _____ _____ _____ 'Me Time' on my calendar for two months, and I feel much better."

33 Which methods will _____ _____ _____?

34 Try some of these ideas yourself, and find your best way _____ _____ _____ _____ _____.

도빈 (16살, 서울)

20 고등학교 2학년인 우리 누나에게는 스트레스에서 벗어나는 훌륭한 방법이 있다.

21 누나가 학업 때문에 많은 스트레스를 받지만, 그럴 만한 이유로 우리 어머니는 그 상황을 좋아하시는 것 같다.

22 그것은 바로, 청소가 누나의 삶을 향상하는 최고의 방법이기 때문이다.

23 스트레스를 너무 많이 받아서 인생이 우울해 보일 때, 누나는 방을 청소한다.

24 누나는 "방을 청소하면서 스트레스도 해소되는 것 같아.

25 내 방이 깔끔해 보이면 내 삶도 더 밝아 보여."라고 말한다.

Yulia (14살, 안산)

26 우리 어머니께서 스트레스를 어떻게 다루시는지 소개하려고 한다.

27 어머니는 직장과 집에서 해야 하는 온갖 일로 인해 스트레스를 받으신다.

28 스트레스를 받을 때면 어머니는 달력에 '나만의 시간'이라고 적으신다.

29 이것은 어머니 자신을 위해 잠깐 시간을 낸다는 의미이다.

30 어머니는 책을 읽거나, 영화를 보거나, 친구들과 이야기를 나누신다.

31 어머니는 "내가 좋아하는 것이라면, 무엇을 하는지는 별로 중요하지 않아.

32 나는 두 달째 달력에 '나만의 시간'을 적어 왔고, 기분이 훨씬 좋아졌어."라고 말씀하신다.

33 어떤 방법이 여러분에게 효과가 있을까?

34 이 아이디어 중 몇 개를 직접 해 보고, 스트레스와 이별하는 자신만의 최고의 방법을 찾아라.

● 우리말을 참고하여 본문을 영작하시오.

1 스트레스와 이별하라
➡ _____

2 어떤 사람들은 울적할 때 친구들과 시간을 보낸다.
➡ _____

3 다른 사람들은 기분이 좋아지도록 특별한 음식을 먹는다.
➡ _____

4 또 다른 사람들은 그저 잠시 잠을 자기도 한다.
➡ _____

5 여러분은 스트레스를 어떻게 다루는가?
➡ _____

6 여기 다양한 방법을 제안하는 사람들의 이야기가 있다.
➡ _____

미나 (15살, 대전) Mina (15, Daejeon)

7 때때로 내 친구들은 나에 관해 나쁜 말을 하거나, 약속을 어기거나, 혹은 사소한 일을 두고 언쟁을 하며 내게 스트레스를 준다.
➡ _____
_____

8 이럴 때, 나는 공포 영화를 본다!
➡ _____

9 훌륭한 공포 영화는 너무 무서워서 나는 소리를 많이 지르게 된다.
➡ _____

10 있는 힘껏 소리 지르는 것은 내 기분이 나아지는 데 도움이 된다고 생각한다.
➡ _____

11 또한, 무서운 장면과 음향 효과 덕분에 나를 괴롭히는 것들을 잊을 수 있다.
➡ _____

12 나는 지난 몇 달간 이 방법을 써 오고 있는데, 효과가 아주 좋다.
➡ _____

준호 (14살, 여수) Junho (14, Yeosu)

13 우리 삼촌은 2년 전에 대학을 졸업했다.
➡ _____

14 삼촌은 우리 가족과 함께 살고 있고, 얼마 전부터 직장을 구하고 있다.
➡ _____

15 나는 삼촌이 스트레스를 받고 있지만 낚시를 다니며 긍정적으로 지내려고 항상 노력한다는 것을 안다.
➡ _____

16 물고기를 한 마리도 잡지 못했을 때에도 삼촌은 절대 속상해 하지 않는다.
➡ _____

17 삼촌은 "낚시하는 동안, 나는 아주 몰입해서 모든 걱정을 잊을 수 있어.

➡ _____

18 게다가 낚시는 나에게 인내를 가르쳐 준단다."라고 말한다.

➡ _____

19 한 가지 일에 집중하는 것이 다른 무언가를 잊는 데 도움이 된다고 나는 확신한다.

➡ _____

도빈 (16살, 서울) Dobin (16, Seoul)

20 고등학교 2학년인 우리 누나에게는 스트레스에서 벗어나는 훌륭한 방법이 있다.

➡ _____

21 누나가 학업 때문에 많은 스트레스를 받지만, 그럴 만한 이유로 우리 어머니는 그 상황을 좋아하시는 것 같다.

➡ _____

22 그것은 바로, 청소가 누나의 삶을 향상하는 최고의 방법이기 때문이다.

➡ _____

23 스트레스를 너무 많이 받아서 인생이 우울해 보일 때, 누나는 방을 청소한다.

➡ _____

24 누나는 "방을 청소하면서 스트레스도 해소되는 것 같아.

➡ _____

25 내 방이 깔끔해 보이면 내 삶도 더 밝아 보여."라고 말한다.

➡ _____

Yulia (14살, 안산) Yulia (14, Ansan)

26 우리 어머니께서 스트레스를 어떻게 다루시는지 소개하려고 한다.

➡ _____

27 어머니는 직장과 집에서 해야 하는 온갖 일로 인해 스트레스를 받으신다.

➡ _____

28 스트레스를 받을 때면 어머니는 달력에 '나만의 시간'이라고 적으신다.

➡ _____

29 이것은 어머니 자신을 위해 잠깐 시간을 낸다는 의미이다.

➡ _____

30 어머니는 책을 읽거나, 영화를 보거나, 친구들과 이야기를 나누신다.

➡ _____

31 어머니는 "내가 좋아하는 것이라면, 무엇을 하는지는 별로 중요하지 않아.

➡ _____

32 나는 두 달째 달력에 '나만의 시간'을 적어 왔고, 기분이 훨씬 좋아졌어."라고 말씀하신다.

➡ _____

33 어떤 방법이 여러분에게 효과가 있을까?

➡ _____

34 이 아이디어 중 몇 개를 직접 해 보고, 스트레스와 이별하는 자신만의 최고의 방법을 찾아라.

➡ _____

[01~03] 다음 글을 읽고 물음에 답하시오.

Mina (15, Daejeon)

Sometimes my friends give me stress by ①saying bad things about me, ②breaking promises, or ③arguing over small things. When this happens, I watch horror movies! Good horror movies are so scary that I scream a lot. I guess that ④screaming at the top of my lungs helps me feel better. Also, thanks to scary scenes and sound effects, I can forget about what bothers me. I've been ⑤using this method for the past several months, and it really ⓐworks.

01 위 글의 밑줄 친 ①~⑤ 중에서 문법적 쓰임이 나머지 넷과 다른 것은?

①   ②   ③   ④   ⑤

02 위 글의 밑줄 친 ⓐworks와 같은 의미로 쓰인 것을 고르시오.

① He works for an engineering company.

② This medicine works pretty well.

③ I like the works of Tolstoy.

④ They didn't finish the public works.

⑤ This machine works by electricity.

03 According to the passage, which is NOT true?

① Sometimes Mina feels stressed when her friends say bad things about her.

② When Mina feels stressed, she watches horror movies.

③ Good horror movies are too scary to make Mina scream a lot.

④ Screaming at the top of her lungs helps Mina feel better.

⑤ Scary scenes and sound effects in horror movies help Mina forget about what bothers her.

[04~06] 다음 글을 읽고 물음에 답하시오.

Junho (14, Yeosu)

My uncle graduated ___ⓐ___ college two years ago. He lives with my family, and (A)he's been looking for a job for some time. I know that he's stressed out, but he always tries to be positive by going fishing. He never gets upset when he doesn't catch any fish. He says, "While I fish, I'm so focused that I can leave all my worries behind. Besides, it teaches me to be patient." I'm sure that focusing ___ⓑ___ one thing helps us forget about something else.

04 위 글의 빈칸 ⓐ와 ⓑ에 들어갈 전치사가 바르게 짝지어진 것은?

  ⓐ   ⓑ   ⓐ   ⓑ

① at – for   ② from – on

③ in – on   ④ at – to

⑤ from – for

05 위 글에서 알 수 있는 준호의 삼촌 성격으로 가장 알맞은 것을 고르시오.

① passive   ② impatient

③ optimistic   ④ generous

⑤ negative

06 위 글의 밑줄 친 (A)에 쓰인 것과 같은 용법의 현재완료가 쓰인 문장을 모두 고르시오.

① How many times have you considered moving to New York?

② She has been studying English for five years.

③ It has just stopped snowing.

④ Have you ever practiced playing the piano?

⑤ I have been cleaning the house since this morning.

[07~10] 다음 글을 읽고 물음에 답하시오.

Dobin (16, Seoul)

My sister, a second-year student in high school, has (a)a wonderful way to stay free from stress. She feels a lot of stress from schoolwork, but my mother seems to like the situation for a good reason. It is (A)[because / why] cleaning is my sister's number-one way to make life better! When she's so stressed that her life (B)[looks / looks like] gloomy, she cleans her room. She says, "(b)As I clean my room, I feel like I'm also (C)[increasing / relieving] stress. When my room looks ____ⓐ____, my life looks brighter."

서답형

07 주어진 영영풀이를 참고하여 빈칸 ⓐ에 철자 t로 시작하는 단어를 쓰시오.

| neat and arranged in an organized way |

➡ _____

서답형

08 위 글의 밑줄 친 (a)a wonderful way가 가리키는 것을 본문에서 찾아 쓰시오.

➡ _____

서답형

09 위 글의 괄호 (A)~(C)에서 문맥이나 어법상 알맞은 낱말을 골라 쓰시오.

➡ (A) _____ (B) _____ (C) _____

10 위 글의 밑줄 친 (b)As와 같은 의미로 쓰인 것을 고르시오.

① Do in Rome as the Romans do.

② He runs as fast as you.

③ As he entered the room, he cried.

④ As I was tired, I soon fell asleep.

⑤ It can be used as a knife.

[11~13] 다음 글을 읽고 물음에 답하시오.

Yulia (14, Ansan)

Let me tell you what my mother does about her stress. She feels stressed by all the things she has to do at work and at home. When she's under stress, she writes "Me Time" on her calendar. This means she takes some time out for herself. She reads a book, watches a movie, or talks with her friends. She says, "ⓐIt doesn't really matter what I do, as long as ⓑit's something I like. I've been writing 'Me Time' on my calendar for two months, and I feel much better."

서답형

11 위 글의 밑줄 친 ⓐIt과 ⓑit이 공통으로 가리키는 것을 본문에서 찾아 쓰시오.

➡ _____

중요

12 위 글의 제목으로 알맞은 것을 고르시오.

① Causes of Yulia's Mom's Stress

② Yulia's Mom's Ways to Deal with Stress

③ How to Write "Me Time" on the Calendar

④ What Really Matters When You Feel Stressed?

⑤ How to Spend "Me Time" Effectively

13 Which question CANNOT be answered after reading the passage?

① By what does Yulia's mother feel stressed?

② When Yulia's mother is under stress, what does she do?

③ What's the meaning of writing "Me Time" on the calendar?

④ How often does Yulia's mother have "Me Time"?

⑤ How long has Yulia been writing 'Me Time' on her calendar?

[14~17] 다음 글을 읽고 물음에 답하시오.

Mina (15, Daejeon)

Sometimes my friends give me stress by saying bad things about me, breaking promises, or arguing over small things. (①) Good horror movies are so scary that I scream a lot. (②) I guess that ⓐ있는 힘껏 소리 지르는 것은 helps me feel better. (③) Also, thanks to scary scenes and sound effects, I can forget about ⓑwhat bothers me. (④) I've been using this method for the past several months, and it really works. (⑤)

14 위 글의 흐름으로 보아, 주어진 문장이 들어가기에 가장 적절한 곳은?

> When this happens, I watch horror movies!

①　　　②　　　③　　　④　　　⑤

15 위 글의 밑줄 친 ⓐ의 우리말에 맞게 주어진 어휘를 이용하여 7단어로 영작하시오.

> top, lungs

➡ _____

16 위 글의 밑줄 친 ⓑwhat과 문법적 쓰임이 같은 것을 모두 고르시오.

① What kind of music do you like?

② He knows what it is to be in debt.

③ What you need is a good meal.

④ He is not what he was.

⑤ What are you looking at?

위 글의 주제로 알맞은 것을 고르시오.

① many causes of stress

② friends saying bad things

③ how to deal with stress

④ the benefit of horror movies

⑤ scary sound effects in horror movies

[18~20] 다음 글을 읽고 물음에 답하시오.

Junho (14, Yeosu)

My uncle graduated from college two years ago. He lives with my family, and he's been looking for a job for some time. I know that he's stressed out, but he always tries to be positive by going ___ⓐ___ . He never gets upset when he doesn't catch any fish. He says, "While I fish, I'm so focused that I can leave all my worries behind. ___ⓑ___ , it teaches me to be patient." I'm sure that focusing on one thing helps us forget about something else.

서답형

18 위 글의 빈칸 ⓐ에 fish를 알맞은 형태로 쓰시오.

➡ _____

19 위 글의 빈칸 ⓑ에 들어갈 알맞은 말을 고르시오.

① Instead　　　② Besides

③ However　　　④ For example

⑤ By contrast

20 다음 빈칸 (A)~(C)에 알맞은 단어를 넣어 준호의 삼촌에 대한 소개를 완성하시오.

> Junho's uncle has been looking for (A)_____ _____ for some time. Though he is stressed out, he always tries to be optimistic by (B)_____ _____, and he never (C)_____ _____ when he catches no fish.

[21~23] 다음 글을 읽고 물음에 답하시오.

Dobin (16, Seoul)

My sister, a second-year student in high school, has a wonderful way ⓐto stay free from stress. She feels ⓑa lot of stress from schoolwork, but ⓒmy mother seems to like the situation for a good reason. It is because cleaning is my sister's number-one way to make life better! When she's so stressed that her life looks gloomy, she cleans her room. She says, "As I clean my room, I feel like I'm also relieving stress. When my room looks tidy, my life looks brighter."

21 아래 〈보기〉에서 위 글의 밑줄 친 ⓐto stay와 to부정사의 용법이 다른 것의 개수를 고르시오.

> ┌── 보기 ──┐
> ① His mother lived to be ninety years old.
> ② I don't have any friends to talk with.
> ③ My dream is to travel around the world.
> ④ It is important to use your time well.
> ⑤ She came here to meet Jake.

① 1개 ② 2개 ③ 3개 ④ 4개 ⑤ 5개

22 위 글의 밑줄 친 ⓑa lot of와 바꿔 쓸 수 없는 말을 모두 고르시오.

① many   ② much
③ a number of   ④ lots of
⑤ a great deal of

23 다음 빈칸 (A)와 (B)에 알맞은 단어를 넣어 밑줄 친 ⓒ의 이유를 완성하시오.

> It's because when Dobin's sister is so stressed that her life looks gloomy, she (A)_____ _____ _____.
> Cleaning is her number-one way to (B)_____ _____ _____.

[24~25] 다음 글을 읽고 물음에 답하시오.

> Which methods will ⓐwork for you? ⓑTry some of these ideas yourself, and find your best way to say hello to stress.

24 위 글의 밑줄 친 ⓐwork와 의미가 같은 것을 모두 고르시오.

① Taking care of a baby is hard work.
② Do you know how to work the coffee machine?
③ The pills the doctor gave me don't work on me.
④ She had been out of work for a year.
⑤ My plan didn't work well in practice.

25 위 글의 밑줄 친 ⓑ에서 흐름상 어색한 부분을 찾아 고치시오.

_____ ➡ _____

[01~03] 다음 글을 읽고 물음에 답하시오.

Mina (15, Daejeon)

Sometimes my friends give me stress by
___ⓐ___ bad things about me, ___ⓑ___ promises,
or ___ⓒ___ over small things. When this
happens, I watch horror movies! ⓓ훌륭한 공포
영화는 너무 무서워서 나는 소리를 많이 지르게 된다.
I guess that screaming at the top of my lungs
helps me feel better. Also, thanks to scary
scenes and sound effects, I can forget about
what bothers me. I've been using this method
for the past several months, and it really works.

01 위 글의 빈칸 ⓐ~ⓒ에 say, break, argue를 각각 알맞은
형태로 쓰시오.

➡ ⓐ _____ ⓑ _____ ⓒ _____

02 위 글의 밑줄 친 ⓓ의 우리말에 맞게 주어진 어휘를 알맞게
배열하시오.

> I / so / are / a lot / scary / scream / good
> horror movies / that

➡ _____

03 다음 빈칸 (A)와 (B)에 알맞은 단어를 넣어 미나의 스트레스
해소 방법에 대한 소개를 완성하시오.

> When Mina feels stressed, she watches
> (A)_____ _____ and screams at the
> top of (B)_____ _____.

[04~06] 다음 글을 읽고 물음에 답하시오.

Junho (14, Yeosu)

My uncle graduated from college two years
ago. He lives with my family, and he's been
looking for a job (A)[for / since] some time.

I know that he's stressed out, but he always
tries to be (B)[positive / negative] by going
fishing. He never gets upset when he doesn't
catch any fish. He says, "While I fish, I'm
(C)[so / such] focused that I can leave all
my worries behind. ⓐBesides, it teaches me
being patient." I'm sure that focusing on one
thing helps us forget about something else.

04 위 글의 괄호 (A)~(C)에서 문맥이나 어법상 알맞은 낱말을
골라 쓰시오.

➡ (A) _____ (B) _____ (C) _____

05 위 글의 밑줄 친 ⓐ에서 어법상 틀린 부분을 찾아 고치시오.

_____ ➡ _____

06 다음 문장에서 위 글의 내용과 다른 부분을 찾아서 고치시오.

> Junho's uncle has no difficulty finding a
> job.

_____ ➡ _____

[07~09] 다음 글을 읽고 물음에 답하시오.

Yulia (14, Ansan)

Let me tell you ___ⓐ___ my mother does
about her stress. She feels stressed by all the
things she has to do at work and at home.
When she's under stress, she writes "Me
Time" on her calendar. This means she takes
some time out for herself. She reads a book,
watches a movie, or talks with her friends.
She says, "It doesn't really matter ___ⓑ___ I
do, ⓒas long as it's something I like. ⓓI've
been writing 'Me Time' on my calendar for
two months, and I feel much better."

07 위 글의 빈칸 ⓐ와 ⓑ에 공통으로 들어갈 알맞은 단어를 쓰시오.

➡ _____

08 위 글의 밑줄 친 ⓒas long as와 바꿔 쓸 수 있는 말을 쓰시오.

➡ _____

09 위 글의 밑줄 친 ⓓ를 다음과 같이 바꿔 쓸 때 빈칸에 들어갈 알맞은 단어를 쓰시오.

➡ I started to write 'Me Time' on my calendar _____ _____ ago, and I am still _____ it on my calendar.

[10~12] 다음 글을 읽고 물음에 답하시오.

Dobin (16, Seoul)

My sister, a second-year student in high school, has a wonderful way to stay ⓐ<u>free from</u> stress. She feels a lot of stress from schoolwork, but my mother seems to like ⓑ <u>the situation</u> for a good reason. It is because cleaning is my sister's number-one way to make life better! When she's so stressed that her life looks gloomy, she cleans her room. She says, "As I clean my room, I feel like I'm also relieving stress. When my room looks tidy, my life looks brighter."

10 위 글의 밑줄 친 ⓐ<u>free from</u>과 바꿔 쓸 수 있는 한 단어를 쓰시오.

➡ _____

11 위 글의 밑줄 친 ⓑ가 가리키는 상황을 우리말로 쓰시오.

➡ _____

12 본문의 내용과 일치하도록 다음 빈칸 (A)와 (B)에 알맞은 단어를 쓰시오.

- Cause of Dobin's Sister's Stress:
  (A) _____
- Dobin's Sister's Method to Relieve Stress:
  (B) _____ _____ _____

[13~15] 다음 글을 읽고 물음에 답하시오.

Yulia (14, Ansan)

Let me (A)[tell / telling] you what my mother does about her stress. She feels stressed by all the things she has to do at work and at home. When she's (B)[over / under] stress, she writes "ⓐMe Time" on her calendar. This means she takes some time out for (C)[her / herself]. She reads a book, watches a movie, or talks with her friends. She says, "It doesn't really matter what I do, as long as it's something I like. I've been writing 'Me Time' on my calendar for two months, and I feel ⓑ<u>much</u> better."

13 위 글의 괄호 (A)~(C)에서 문맥이나 어법상 알맞은 낱말을 골라 쓰시오.

➡ (A) _____ (B) _____ (C) _____

14 위 글의 밑줄 친 ⓐMe Time의 의미를 우리말로 쓰시오.

➡ _____

15 위 글의 밑줄 친 ⓑmuch와 바꿔 쓸 수 있는 말을 쓰시오. (두 개)

➡ _____

해석

Words in Action

1. Tests stress me out. Grades give me more stress.
   stress ~ out (스트레스로) ~을 지치게 하다
2. Worry less, smile more. Worry never helps.
   worry (동사) 걱정하다   (명사) 걱정
3. I work hard. I have a lot of work to do.
   work (동사) 일하다   (명사) 일
4. I need a change. I will change my hairstyle.
   change (명사) 변화   기분전환 (동사) 바꾸다
5. I caught just a few fish. I want to fish some more.
   fish (명사) 물고기   (동사) 낚시하다

구문해설 • **need a change** 기분 전환이 필요하다

1. 시험은 나를 지치게 해. 성적은 나에게 더 많은 스트레스를 준다.
2. 걱정은 줄이고 더 많이 웃어라. 걱정은 전혀 도움이 되지 않아.
3. 나는 열심히 일한다. 나는 할 일이 많다.
4. 나는 기분 전환이 필요하다. 나는 헤어스타일을 바꿀 것이다.
5. 나는 겨우 물고기 몇 마리를 잡았다. 나는 몇 마리 더 낚고 싶다.

Speak – Get ready.

1. I want to spend more/less time on social media.
   spend time on ~ = ~에 시간을 쓰다
2. Working on a team can be difficult/helpful.
   difficult/helpful 어려운/유익한
3. I like watching/playing sports better.
4. Having a part-time job as a teen can be good/bad.
   십대일 때   좋은/나쁜

구문해설 • **working on a team** 팀을 이루어 일하는 것

1. 나는 소셜미디어에 더 많은/적은 시간을 보내기를 원한다.
2. 팀을 이루어 일하는 것은 어려울 수 있다/도움이 될 수 있다.
3. 나는 스포츠 보는 것을/하는 것을 더 좋아한다.
4. 십대일 때 아르바이트를 하는 것은 좋다/나쁘다.

Wrap Up – Reading

Are you stressed or feeling low? Then here is some good news for you. A few simple steps can help you! First, go outdoors and get plenty of sunlight.
= measures   = much
According to scientists, this helps produce a special chemical in your brain,
= to produce
and the chemical makes you feel happy! Another thing you can do is exercise.
사역동사 make+목적어+동사원형   = to exercise
This helps produce even more of the "happiness chemical." Try these simple
= to produce   비교급 강조(훨씬)
tips the next time you feel low. Instead of sitting in front of a screen, go
다음에 ~할 때에는   Instead of+동명사
outdoors and run around in the sun!

구문해설 • **low**: 기분이 저조한 • **step**: 조치 • **outdoors**: 옥외[야외]에서
• **according to**: ~에 따르면 • **chemical**: 화학 물질 • **instead of**: ~ 대신에

스트레스를 받았거나 기분이 우울한가? 그렇다면 여기 당신에게 좋은 소식이 있다. 간단한 몇 가지 절차가 도움이 될 것이다! 첫째, 밖에 나가서 충분한 양의 햇볕을 쬐라. 과학자들에 따르면 이것이 뇌 속에 특별한 화학물질을 만드는 데 도움을 주고, 이 화학물질은 당신을 행복하게 만든다고 한다! 당신이 할 수 있는 또 다른 일은 운동이다. 이것은 훨씬 더 많은 '행복 화학물질'을 만드는 데 도움을 준다. 다음에 당신이 우울하다면 이 간단한 조언을 시도해 보라. 화면 앞에 앉아 있는 대신, 밖에 나가 태양 아래에서 뛰어다녀라!

영역별 핵심문제

01 다음 영영풀이에 해당하는 단어를 고르시오.

> the way someone or something looks to other people

① appearance ② program
③ patient ④ view
⑤ scene

02 다음 짝지어진 단어의 관계가 같도록 빈칸에 알맞은 말을 쓰시오. (주어진 철자로 시작할 것)

> agree : disagree = a_____ : natural

03 다음 대화의 빈칸에 들어갈 말로 적절한 것을 고르시오.

> A: I want to spend more time on social media.
> B: What makes you say that?
> A: I can _____ more friends from around the world.

① invite ② make
③ help ④ visit
⑤ call

04 다음 밑줄 친 단어와 의미가 가장 가까운 것을 고르시오.

> He looked quite cheerless.

> A: This is a very ①gloomy situation.
> B: What's ②bothering you?
> A: We ③have nothing to eat.
> B: Don't ④worry. We can have ⑤free pizza.

05 다음 대화의 순서가 바르게 배열된 것을 고르시오.

> G: Why don't we make a sport club?
> B: Sounds good. Let's make a baseball club.
> (A) What makes you say that?
> (B) Well, I think a basketball club is a better idea.
> (C) All we need is a ball to play basketball.

① (A) – (C) – (B) ② (B) – (A) – (C)
③ (B) – (C) – (A) ④ (C) – (A) – (B)
⑤ (C) – (B) – (A)

06 다음 글의 내용과 일치하는 것은?

> I'd like to talk about some good ways to relax when you get upset. First, it's good to take deep breaths. Second, counting to ten is a great idea. Also, drinking cold water helps. Lastly, thinking happy thoughts can help.

① 글의 주제는 화를 푸는 방법이다.
② 심호흡을 하는 것은 건강에 좋다.
③ 열까지 세는 것은 소화를 도와준다.
④ 화가 났을 때는 말을 하지 마라.
⑤ 행복한 생각은 명상에 도움이 된다.

07

다음 대화의 빈칸에 들어가기에 적절한 단어를 주어진 철자로 시작하여 쓰시오.

> A: I want to spend more time on social media.
> B: What makes you say that?
> A: I can make more friends from around the world.
> B: That m_____ sense.

08

다음 빈칸 ⓐ~ⓔ에 들어갈 말로 가장 어색한 것은?

> B1: Today, let's talk about the class T-shirt. We have to decide on the design.
> G: _____ⓐ_____
> B2: We have to choose a T-shirt with short sleeves.
> B1: _____ⓑ_____
> B2: Because we'll wear the T-shirt on Sports Day. _____ⓒ_____
> G: _____ⓓ_____ What about this green one?
> B2: I like it. The bee on the T-shirt is so cute.
> G: And _____ⓔ_____
> B1: Yes. I think it's the best one.

① ⓐ Let me show you some designs on the screen.
② ⓑ What makes you say that?
③ ⓒ It's in November.
④ ⓓ That makes sense.
⑤ ⓔ it's not expensive.

[09~11] 다음 대화를 읽고 물음에 답하시오.

> W: What are you doing, Oliver?
> B: I'm studying for the math test, Mom. ___(A)___ stress me out.
> W: I understand. I used to feel that way, too.
> B: Really? I didn't know that.
> W: Yeah, but a little stress was helpful for me.
> B: (B)What makes you say that?
> W: I got stressed when I had an exam, but at the same time it made me focus and try harder.
> B: I see. Did stress ___(C)___ you in other ways?
> W: Yes, it helped improve my memory.

09

빈칸 (A)에 들어갈 가장 알맞은 말을 고르시오.

① Homework
② Grades
③ Clothes
④ Friends
⑤ Foods

10

밑줄 친 (B)와 바꿔 쓸 수 있는 것을 고르시오.

① What makes you think so?
② Why do you study so hard?
③ What is the cause of your stress?
④ How can you avoid this stress?
⑤ When will the stress be away?

11

빈칸 (C)에 알맞은 말을 쓰시오.

➡ _____

Grammar

12

다음 빈칸에 어법상 적절한 것은?

> I am _____ hungry that I want to eat *ramyeon*.

① such
② very
③ too
④ so
⑤ quite

[13~14] 다음 괄호 안에 주어진 단어들을 바르게 배열하여 문장을 완성하시오.

13

[I guess / screaming / that / of my lungs / at the top / me / helps / feel better].

➡ _____

_____

14

Let me [what / you / my mother / tell / about / does / her stress].

➡ Let me _____

_____.

15 다음 〈보기〉에서 어법상 <u>어색한</u> 문장의 개수는?

┌─ 보기 ─┐

ⓐ My sister has a wonderful way to stay free from stress.

ⓑ She feels a lot of stress from schoolwork.

ⓒ My mother seems to like the situation for a good reason.

ⓓ She has been using this method when she was a child.

ⓔ She was so happy that she sang out.

① 1개 ② 2개 ③ 3개 ④ 4개 ⑤ 5개

[16~17] 다음 빈칸에 들어가기에 적절한 것은?

16

Tom has been living with us _____ last winter.

① after   ② before   ③ while
④ since   ⑤ for

17

It was so cloudy _____ he took his umbrella.

① that   ② what   ③ which
④ while   ⑤ when

18 다음 우리말을 영어로 바르게 옮긴 것은?

┌──────────────────────────┐
│ 그는 너무 기뻐서 마음껏 소리를 질렀다. │
└──────────────────────────┘

① She was so happy what she screamed loudly.

② She felt so pleased that she screamed at the top of her lungs.

③ She was such happy that she screamed at the top of her lungs.

④ She screamed at the top of her lungs that she was so happy.

⑤ She was happy so that she screamed at the top of her lungs.

19 다음 대화에서 어법상 <u>어색한</u> 것을 2개 찾아 고치시오.

┌──────────────────────────────┐
│ W: Little stress was helpful for me.   │
│ B: What makes you say that?   │
│ W: I got stressed when I had an exam, but │
│   at the same time it made me focus and │
│   try harder.   │
│ B: I see. Did stress help you in other   │
│   ways?   │
│ W: Yes, it helped improving my memory.   │
└──────────────────────────────┘

(1) _____ ➡ _____
(2) _____ ➡ _____

20 다음 중 어법상 어색한 것은?

① Problems with friends took second place with 15.3%.
② Next family and worries about the future came.
③ My mother takes some time out for herself.
④ They eat special foods to feel better.
⑤ I'd like to talk about some good ways to relax when you get upset.

21 다음 우리말을 영어로 옮긴 것 중 어색한 것은?

① 또 다른 사람들은 단지 잠시 잠을 잔다.
   → Still others simply sleep for a while.
② 집이 너무 조용해서 그는 TV를 켰다.
   → The house was so quiet that he turned on the TV.
③ 왜 그런 생각을 하십니까?
   → Why makes you think so?
④ 당신은 스트레스를 어떻게 처리합니까?
   → How do you deal with stress?
⑤ 이 녹색은 어떻습니까?
   → What about this green one?

22 다음 중 문장의 의미가 나머지와 다른 하나는?

① She was so honest that she couldn't tell a lie.
② She was too honest to tell a lie.
③ She couldn't tell a lie because she was very honest.
④ She was very honest, so she couldn't tell a lie.
⑤ She was very honest though she told a lie.

[23~26] 다음 글을 읽고 물음에 답하시오.

_____ⓐ_____ people spend time with friends when they feel low. Others eat special foods (A)to feel better. _____ⓑ_____ others simply sleep for a while. (B)What do you deal with stress? Here are some stories about people _____ⓒ_____ suggest different ways.

23 위 글의 빈칸 ⓐ~ⓒ에 들어갈 알맞은 단어를 각각 쓰시오.

➡ ⓐ _____ ⓑ _____ ⓒ _____

24 위 글의 밑줄 친 (A)to feel과 to부정사의 용법이 같은 것을 모두 고르시오.

① I worked hard to pass the test.
② There are many books to read.
③ It is hard for me to study English.
④ She must be mad to say so.
⑤ I don't know where to go.

25 위 글의 밑줄 친 (B)에서 어법상 틀린 부분을 찾아 고치시오.

_____ ➡ _____

26 위 글의 뒤에 올 내용으로 가장 알맞은 것을 고르시오.

① 스트레스의 주된 원인들
② 스트레스를 다루는 방법들 소개
③ 친구들과 즐거운 시간을 보내는 방법들
④ 스트레스를 없애는 음식들 소개
⑤ 효과적인 수면 방법들

[27~28] 다음 글을 읽고 물음에 답하시오.

Junho (14, Yeosu)
My uncle graduated from college two years ago. He lives with my family, and he's been looking for a job for some time. I know that

he's stressed out, but he always tries to be positive by going fishing. He never gets upset when he doesn't catch any fish. He says, "While I fish, I'm so focused that I can leave all my worries behind. Besides, it teaches me to be patient." I'm sure that ⓐ한 가지 일에 집중하는 것이 다른 무엇인가를 잊는 데 도움이 된다.

27 위 글의 밑줄 친 ⓐ의 우리말에 맞게 한 단어를 보충하여, 주어진 어휘를 알맞게 배열하시오.

> helps / thing / about / focusing / us / else / something / one / forget

➡ _____

_____

28 According to the passage, which is NOT true?

① Junho's uncle lives with Junho's family.

② Junho's uncle has not found a job yet.

③ Junho's uncle is stressed out and has a negative attitude.

④ While Junho's uncle fishes, he's so focused that he can leave all his worries behind.

⑤ Fishing teaches Junho's uncle to be patient.

[29~30] 다음 글을 읽고 물음에 답하시오.

Dobin (16, Seoul)

My sister, a second-year student in high school, has a wonderful way to stay free ____ⓐ____ stress. She feels a lot of stress from schoolwork, but my mother seems to like the situation for a good reason. It is because cleaning is my sister's number-one way to make life better! When she's so stressed that her life looks gloomy, she cleans her room.

She says, "As I clean my room, I feel like I'm also relieving stress. ⓑ내 방이 깔끔해 보이면 내 삶도 더 밝아 보여."

29 위 글의 빈칸 ⓐ에 알맞은 것은?

① from   ② to   ③ over

④ with   ⑤ along

30 위 글의 밑줄 친 ⓑ의 우리말에 맞게 주어진 어휘를 이용하여 9단어로 영작하시오.

> When, tidy, brighter

➡ _____

[31~32] 다음 글을 읽고 물음에 답하시오.

Use Your Five Senses
and Stay Free from Stress

Eye	Look at the sky when you are outdoors.
___ⓐ___	Drink some tea.
Hand	Give your friend a high-five.
___ⓑ___	Smell fresh flowers.
Ear	Listen to your favorite song.

31 Fill in the blanks ⓐ and ⓑ with suitable words.

➡ ⓐ _____ ⓑ _____

32 위 글의 '오감을 사용한 스트레스 해소법'에 해당하지 않는 것은?

① 야외에 있을 때는 식물들을 보아라.

② 약간의 차를 마셔라.

③ 친구에게 하이 파이브를 해주어라.

④ 신선한 꽃 냄새를 맡아라.

⑤ 좋아하는 노래를 들어라.

✏ 출제율 90%

01 다음 짝지어진 단어의 관계가 같도록 빈칸에 알맞은 말을 쓰시오. (주어진 철자로 시작할 것)

> bright : clever = b_____ : dull

✏ 출제율 90%

02 다음 영영풀이에 해당하는 단어를 고르시오.

> to make someone feel slightly worried, upset, or concerned

① bother
② produce
③ please
④ depress
⑤ frighten

✏ 출제율 95%

03 다음 문장의 빈칸에 알맞은 것으로 짝지어진 것은?

> • Did you decide _____ the menu?
> • I met a lot of nice people, thanks _____ you.

① to – on
② for – at
③ to – from
④ on – to
⑤ on – with

✏ 출제율 100%

04 다음 중 〈보기〉에 있는 단어를 사용하여 자연스러운 문장을 만들 수 없는 것은?

> ┌─ 보기 ─┐
> positive   graduated   forget   focused

① My uncle _____ from college two years ago.
② I know that he's _____ out by the work.
③ He always tries to be _____ by going fishing.
④ While I fish, I'm so _____ that I can leave all my worries behind.
⑤ I'm sure that focusing on one thing helps us _____ about something else.

[05~06] 다음 빈칸에 들어갈 말로 적절한 것을 고르시오.

✏ 출제율 95%

05
> Good horror movies are so _____ that I scream a lot.

① boring
② scary
③ gloomy
④ patient
⑤ difficult

✏ 출제율 95%

06
> I guess that screaming at the top of my _____ helps me feel better. Also, thanks to scary scenes and sound effects, I can forget about what bothers me.

① nose
② height
③ sizes
④ fingers
⑤ lungs

✏ 출제율 95%

07 다음 짝지어진 단어의 관계가 같도록 빈칸에 알맞은 말을 쓰시오. (주어진 철자로 시작할 것)

> cause : effect = tidy : m_____

✏ 출제율 95%

08 다음 중 밑줄 친 부분의 뜻풀이가 바르지 않은 것은?

① <u>Grades</u> stress me out. (학년)
② Yeah, but a little stress was <u>helpful</u> for me. (유익한)
③ At the same time it made me <u>focus</u> and try harder. (집중하다)
④ I <u>see</u>. Did stress help you in other ways? (이해하다)
⑤ Yes, it helped <u>improve</u> my memory. (향상하다)

09 다음 영영풀이에 해당하는 단어를 고르시오.

> able to wait calmly for a long time or to accept difficulties without becoming angry

① patient ② stressed
③ sleepy ④ gloomy
⑤ positive

10 다음 우리말에 맞게 빈칸에 알맞은 말을 쓰시오.

(1) 고등학교 2학년인 누나는 스트레스를 없애는 좋은 방법을 가지고 있다.
➡ My sister, a second-year student in high school, has a wonderful way to stay _____ from stress.

(2) 엄마는 그 상황을 정당한 이유로 좋아하는 것 같다.
➡ My mother seems to like the situation for a good _____.

(3) 그녀는 너무 스트레스를 받아서 삶이 우울해 보일 때 방을 청소한다.
➡ When she's so stressed that her life looks _____, she cleans her room.

11 다음 대화의 내용과 일치하는 것은?

> G: Why don't we make a sport club?
> B: Sounds good. Let's make a baseball club.
> G: Well, I think a basketball club is a better idea.
> B: What makes you say that?
> G: All we need is a ball to play basketball.

① The girl wants to make a sport club.
② The boy doesn't like to make a sport club.
③ The girl wants to make a baseball club.
④ The girl agrees with the boy about a baseball club.
⑤ The girl and the boy like baseball a lot.

[12~14] 다음 대화를 읽고 물음에 답하시오.

> B1: Today, let's talk about the class T-shirt. We have to decide on the design.
> G: Let me show you some designs on the screen.
> B2: We have to choose a T-shirt __(A)__ short sleeves.
> B1: What makes you say that?
> B2: Because we'll wear the T-shirt on Sports Day. It's in June.
> G: That makes sense. What about this green one?
> B2: I like it. The bee on the T-shirt is so cute.
> G: _____(B)_____
> B1: Yes. I think it's the best one.

12 위 대화의 빈칸 (A)에 알맞은 것은?

① on ② with ③ for
④ from ⑤ over

13 위 대화의 흐름으로 보아 (B)에 들어가기에 적절한 것은?

① And it's so large.
② But it's too colorful.
③ But how about this one?
④ And it's very dark.
⑤ And it's not expensive

출제율 95%

14 위 대화의 내용과 일치하지 <u>않는</u> 것은?

① They are talking about the T-shirt.

② They are choosing the design.

③ They chose a T-shirt which has short sleeves.

④ They will wear the T-shirt in spring.

⑤ They may choose a green T-shirt.

출제율 90%

15 다음 빈칸에 어법상 적절한 것은?

> He lives with my family, and he's been _____ for a job for some time.

① looked   ② looks

③ to look   ④ being looked

⑤ looking

출제율 90%

16 다음 중 어법상 <u>어색한</u> 것은?

① How do you deal with stress?

② Here are some stories about people who suggest different ways.

③ The girl has been playing the piano since an hour.

④ As you can see, schoolwork was the most common cause of stress.

⑤ About 9,000 teens answered this question.

출제율 90%

17 다음 〈보기〉에서 어법상 <u>어색한</u> 문장의 개수는?

> ┌─── 보기 ───┐
>
> ⓐ I was so busy that I didn't eat lunch.
>
> ⓑ She has been running around the playground for an hour.
>
> ⓒ The bag was so expensive that she couldn't buy.
>
> ⓓ He was such tired that he stopped working.
>
> ⓔ He was reading a book since this morning.

① 1개   ② 2개   ③ 3개   ④ 4개   ⑤ 5개

[18~20] 다음 글을 읽고 물음에 답하시오.

Mina (15, Daejeon)

Sometimes my friends give me stress by saying bad things about me, breaking promises, or arguing over small things. When (A)this happens, I watch horror movies! Good horror movies are so scary that I scream a lot. I guess that screaming at the top of my lungs helps me feel better. Also, thanks to scary scenes and sound effects, I can forget about what bothers me. I've been ___ (B) ___ this method for the past several months, and it really works.

출제율 95%

18 위 글의 밑줄 친 (A)this가 가리키는 내용을 우리말로 쓰시오.

➡ _____

_____

출제율 95%

19 위 글의 빈칸 (B)에 use를 알맞은 형태로 쓰시오.

➡ _____

출제율 95%

20 What TWO things in horror movies help Mina forget about the thing which bothers her? Answer in English.

➡ ① _____ ② _____

[21~22] 다음 글을 읽고 물음에 답하시오.

Junho (14, Yeosu)

My uncle (A)[graduated / graduated from] college two years ago. He lives with my family, and he's been looking for a job for some time. I know that he's stressed out, but he always tries to be positive by going fishing. He never gets (B)[relaxed / upset] when he doesn't catch any fish. He says, "While I fish, I'm so focused that I can leave all my worries behind. ⓐBesides, it teaches me to be (C) [patient / impatient]." I'm sure that focusing on one thing helps us forget about something else.

---

21 위 글의 괄호 (A)~(C)에서 문맥이나 어법상 알맞은 낱말을 골라 쓰시오.

➡ (A) _____ (B) _____ (C) _____

---

22 위 글의 밑줄 친 ⓐBesides와 바꿔 쓸 수 <u>없는</u> 말을 모두 고르시오.

① Therefore   ② In addition to
③ Moreover   ④ What's more
⑤ Furthermore

[23~25] 다음 글을 읽고 물음에 답하시오.

Yulia (14, Ansan)

Let me tell you what my mother does about her stress. She feels stressed by all the things she has to do at work and at home. When she's under stress, she writes "Me Time" on her calendar. (A)<u>This means she takes some time out for her.</u> She reads a book, watches a movie, or talks with her friends. She says, "(B)<u>It doesn't really matter</u> what I do, as long as it's something I like. I've been writing 'Me Time' on my calendar for two months, and I feel much better."

---

23 위 글의 밑줄 친 (A)에서 어색한 것을 고치시오.

_____ ➡ _____

---

24 위 글의 밑줄 친 (B)를 다음과 같이 바꿔 쓸 때 빈칸에 들어갈 알맞은 단어를 쓰시오.

➡ It isn't really _____

---

25 위 글의 내용과 일치하도록 다음 빈칸 (A)와 (B)에 알맞은 단어를 쓰시오.

> • Cause of Yulia's Mother's Stress:
> (A) _____ _____ _____ _____
> _____ _____ _____ at work
> and at home
> • Yulia's Mother's Method to Relieve Stress:
> (B) having "_____ _____"

[26~27] 다음 글을 읽고 물음에 답하시오.

Are you stressed or feeling low? Then here is some good news for you. A few simple steps can help you! First, go outdoors and get plenty of sunlight. According to scientists, (A)<u>this</u> helps produce a special chemical in your brain, and the chemical makes you feel happy! Another thing you can do is exercise. (B)<u>This</u> helps produce even more of the "happiness chemical." Try these simple tips the next time you feel low.   ⓐ   sitting in front of a screen, go outdoors and run around in the sun!

---

26 위 글의 빈칸 ⓐ에 들어갈 알맞은 말을 고르시오.

① Besides   ② Instead of
③ Along with   ④ In spite of
⑤ In addition

---

27 위 글의 밑줄 친 (A)this와 (B)This가 가리키는 것을 각각 본문에서 찾아 쓰시오. ((A)는 동명사를 사용하여 답하시오.)

➡ (A) _____
(B) _____

[01~02] 다음 짝지어진 단어의 관계가 같도록 빈칸에 알맞은 말을 쓰시오. (주어진 철자로 시작할 것)

01

bother : disturb = cause : r_____

02

cheap : expensive = relieved : w_____

03 다음 영영풀이에 해당하는 단어를 주어진 철자로 시작하여 쓰시오.

a change that is caused by an event, action, etc.

➡ e_____

[04~06] 다음 대화를 읽고 물음에 답하시오.

W: What are you doing, Oliver?
B: I'm studying for the math test, Mom. Grades stress me out.
W: I understand. I used to feel ⓐthat way, too.
B: Really? I didn't know that.
W: Yeah, but a little stress was ⓑhelp for me.
B: What ⓒ____ you say that?
W: I got stressed when I had an exam, but at the same time it made me focus and try harder.
B: I see. Did stress help you in other ways?
W: Yes, it helped improve my memory.

04 위 대화의 밑줄 친 ⓐ를 본문에 나오는 한 단어로 바꿔 쓰시오.

➡ _____

05 위 대화의 밑줄 친 ⓑ를 알맞은 형으로 고치시오.

➡ _____

06 위 대화의 빈칸 ⓒ에 알맞은 말을 쓰시오.

➡ _____

[07~08] 다음 글을 읽고 물음에 답하시오.

W: Today, I'd like to talk to you about teen stress. What makes you feel the most stressed? About 9,000 teens answered ⓐthis question. As you can see, schoolwork was the most common cause of stress. Over half of the students said schoolwork stresses them the most. Problems with friends took second place with 15.3%. Next came family and worries about the future. 8.2% of the students said they get stressed because of their ⓑappear.

07 위 글의 밑줄 친 ⓐthis question의 내용을 우리말로 구체적으로 쓰시오.

➡ _____

08 밑줄 친 ⓑappear를 알맞은 형으로 고치시오.

➡ _____

09 다음 〈보기〉의 두 문장을 현재완료진행시제를 사용하여 한 문장으로 연결하시오.

┤ 보기 ├
• My mother started cooking dinner at 6:00.
• My mother is still cooking dinner.

➡ _____

10 다음 〈보기〉의 두 문장을 적절한 단어를 사용하여 한 문장으로 쓰시오.

> ┌── 보기 ──
> • He was very excited.
> • He shouted for the team.

➡ He was _____ excited _____ he shouted for the team.

[11~13] 다음 글을 읽고 물음에 답하시오.

> **Mina (15, Daejeon)**
>
> Sometimes my friends give me stress by saying bad things about me, breaking promises, or arguing over small things. When this (A)[happens / is happened], I watch horror movies! Good horror movies are __ⓐ__ scary __ⓑ__ I scream a lot. I guess that screaming at the top of my lungs (B)[help / helps] me feel better. Also, thanks to scary scenes and sound effects, I can forget about (C)[that / what] bothers me. I've been using this method for the past several months, and ⓒit really works.

11 Fill in the blanks ⓐ and ⓑ with the suitable words.

➡ ⓐ _____ ⓑ _____

12 위 글의 괄호 (A)~(C)에서 어법상 알맞은 낱말을 골라 쓰시오.

➡ (A) _____ (B) _____ (C) _____

13 위 글의 밑줄 친 ⓒit이 가리키는 것을 본문에서 찾아 쓰시오.

➡ _____

[14~16] 다음 글을 읽고 물음에 답하시오.

> **Junho (14, Yeosu)**
>
> My uncle graduated from college two years ago. He lives with my family, and ⓐhe's been looking for a job for some time. I know that he's stressed out, but he always tries to be positive by going fishing. He never gets upset when he doesn't catch any fish. He says, "While I fish, ⓑI'm so focused that I can leave all my worries behind. Besides, it teaches me to be patient." I'm sure that focusing on one thing helps us forget about something else.

14 위 글의 밑줄 친 ⓐ를 다음과 같이 바꿔 쓸 때 빈칸에 들어갈 알맞은 단어를 쓰시오.

➡ he started to look for a job some time _____, and he _____ still _____ for a job

15 위 글의 밑줄 친 ⓑ를 단문으로 고칠 때, 빈칸에 들어갈 알맞은 단어를 쓰시오.

➡ I'm focused _____ _____ leave all my worries behind.

16 다음 빈칸 (A)와 (B)에 알맞은 단어를 넣어 준호 삼촌의 구직 활동으로 인한 스트레스 해소 방법을 완성하시오.

> Junho's uncle goes (A)_____, which enables him to have a (B)_____ attitude though he has a hard time finding a job.
>
> *attitude: 태도

01 다음 대화의 빈칸에 알맞은 말을 넣어 대화를 완성해 봅시다.

A: What's the matter?

B: I've been _____ all day.

A: You need a _____. Why don't you go to the river and fish?

B: That's a good idea.

......

A: What's the matter this time?

B: I haven't caught a _____. It _____ me out.

A: Don't _____. You'll catch one soon.

02 다음 항목들을 'have been -ing'를 사용하여 말해 봅시다.

since I was ten -
- live in this city
- hang out with my best friend
- learn English
- play the guitar
- use this computer

➡ I _____ since I was ten.

03 다음 그림을 바탕으로 오감을 사용한 스트레스 해소법을 소개하는 포스터를 완성하시오.

Use Your Five Senses and Stay Free from Stress

(A)_____: Look at the sky when you are outdoors.

(B)_____: Drink some tea.

(C)_____: Give your friend a high-five.

(D)_____: Smell fresh flowers.

(E)_____: Listen to your favorite song.

단원별 모의고사

01 다음 짝지어진 단어의 관계가 같도록 빈칸에 알맞은 것은?

> tidy : neat = _____ : shout

① affect ② scream ③ laugh
④ sense ⑤ weep

02 다음 영영풀이에 해당하는 단어를 고르시오.

> to make something better, or to become better

① produce ② present ③ stress
④ improve ⑤ decide

03 다음 중 밑줄 친 부분의 뜻풀이가 바르지 <u>않은</u> 것은?

① This is a very <u>gloomy</u> situation. (우울한)
② What's <u>bothering</u> you? (괴롭히는)
③ We can have <u>free</u> pizza here. (공짜의)
④ I'm so <u>relieved</u>. (안심이 되는)
⑤ Let's be <u>patient</u> and wait for our food. (조바심이 나는)

04 다음 대화의 순서가 바르게 배열된 것을 고르시오.

> A: I want to spend more time on social media.
> (A) I can make more friends from around the world.
> (B) What makes you say that?
> (C) That makes sense.

① (A) – (C) – (B) ② (B) – (A) – (C)
③ (B) – (C) – (A) ④ (C) – (A) – (B)
⑤ (C) – (B) – (A)

05 다음 대화의 문맥상 또는 어법상 어색한 것을 찾아 고치시오.

> W: What are you doing, Oliver?
> B: I'm ①studying for the math test, Mom. Grades stress me out.
> W: I understand. I ②used to feel that way, too.
> B: Really? I didn't know that.
> W: Yeah, but a little stress was ③helpful for me.
> B: What makes you ④say that?
> W: I got ⑤stress when I had an exam, but at the same time it made me focus and try harder.
> B: I see. Did stress help you in other ways?
> W: Yes, it helped improve my memory.

_____ ➡ _____

06 다음 대화의 내용과 일치하지 <u>않는</u> 것은?

> B1: Today, let's talk about the class T-shirt. We have to decide on the design.
> G: Let me show you some designs on the screen.
> B2: We have to choose a T-shirt with short sleeves.
> B1: What makes you say that?
> B2: Because we'll wear the T-shirt on Sports Day. It's in June.
> G: That makes sense. What about this green one?
> B2: I like it. The bee on the T-shirt is so cute.
> G: And it's not expensive.
> B1: Yes. I think it's the best one.

① 오늘의 주제는 티셔츠 디자인 결정이다.

② 그들은 안내책자를 보고 디자인을 결정할 것이다.

③ 소매가 짧은 셔츠 디자인을 결정할 것이다.

④ 고르려고 하는 셔츠는 비싸지 않다.

⑤ 티셔츠에는 꿀벌 그림이 있다.

07 다음 중 어법상 <u>어색한</u> 문장은?

① He has been working for two hours.

② It was so cold that we stayed home.

③ He is a such kind boy that I like him.

④ He has been singing for two hours.

⑤ She has lived here for ten years.

08 다음 〈보기〉와 같이 주어진 두 문장을 한 문장으로 바꾸어 쓰시오.

┤ 보기 ├

• I started working at the Chinese restaurant six months ago.

• I am still working there.

➡ I have been working at the Chinese restaurant for six months.

• My father started repairing his car this morning.

• He is still repairing it now.

➡ _____

_____

09 다음 빈칸에 어법상 적절한 것은?

I've been using this method _____ the past several months, and it really works.

① for   ② since

③ before   ④ after

⑤ during

10 다음 문장에 들어가기에 적절한 것은?

Because the soup was too hot, he decided to eat it later.

= The soup was _____ _____ _____ he decided to eat it later.

11 다음 괄호 안에 주어진 어구를 바르게 배열하여 문장을 완성하시오.

(1) I'd (to / some / talk / ways / like / about / you / good / when / relax / upset / to / get).

➡ I'd _____

_____.

(2) While I (focused / fish, / I / I'm / so / that / all my worries / can leave / behind).

➡ While I _____

_____.

12 다음 중 어법상 <u>어색한</u> 문장은?

① She has been doing the dishes since half an hour.

② He has been playing the piano for two hours.

③ We have been waiting for him since this morning.

④ He has been living in the house for three years.

⑤ They have been studying for the test for three hours.

13 다음 〈보기〉에서 어법상 어색한 문장의 개수는?

보기

ⓐ Last time, I talked about different foods that are good for your health.

ⓑ Ann was such hungry that she wanted to eat *ramyeon*.

ⓒ Today, I'd like to talk about healthy eating habits.

ⓓ First, it's important to stop eating when you're full.

ⓔ The weather is so fine which I can go to the park today.

ⓕ I have been read this novel for three hours.

① 1개　② 2개　③ 3개　④ 4개　⑤ 5개

[14~15] 다음 글을 읽고 물음에 답하시오.

Mina (15, Daejeon)

ⓐSometimes my friends give me stress by saying bad things about me, keeping promises, or arguing over small things. When this happens, I watch horror movies! Good horror movies are so scary that I scream a lot. I guess that screaming at the top of my lungs helps me feel better. Also, thanks to scary scenes and sound effects, I can forget about ⓑwhat bothers me. I've been using this method for the past several months, and it really works.

14 위 글의 밑줄 친 ⓐ에서 흐름상 어색한 부분을 찾아 고치시오.

_____ ➡ _____

15 위 글의 밑줄 친 ⓑwhat을 3 단어로 바꿔 쓰시오.

➡ _____

[16~17] 다음 글을 읽고 물음에 답하시오.

Junho (14, Yeosu)

My uncle graduated from college two years ago. He lives with my family, and he's been looking for a job for some time. I know that he's stressed out, but he always tries to be positive by going fishing. He never gets upset when he doesn't catch any fish. He says, "ⓐWhile I fish, I'm so focused that I can leave all my worries behind. Besides, ⓑit teaches me to be patient." I'm sure that focusing on one thing helps us forget about something else.

16 위 글의 밑줄 친 ⓐWhile과 같은 의미로 쓰인 것을 모두 고르시오.

① I fell asleep while I was reading.

② Where have you been all this while?

③ The walls are green, while the ceiling is white.

④ Did anyone call while I was away?

⑤ Some are rich, while others are poor.

17 위 글의 밑줄 친 ⓑ가 가리키는 것을 한 단어로 쓰시오.

➡ _____

[18~19] 다음 글을 읽고 물음에 답하시오.

Dobin (16, Seoul)

My sister, a second-year student in high school, has a wonderful way to stay free ⓐ_____ stress. She feels a lot of stress ⓑ_____ schoolwork, but my mother seems to like the situation for a good reason.

It is because cleaning is my sister's number-one way to make life better! When she's so stressed that her life looks gloomy, she cleans her room. She says, "As I clean my room, I feel like I'm also relieving stress. When my room looks tidy, my life looks brighter."

18 위 글의 빈칸 @와 ⓑ에 공통으로 들어갈 알맞은 전치사를 쓰시오.

➡ _____

19 According to the passage, which is NOT true?

① Dobin's sister is a second-year student in high school.
② When Dobin's sister feels much stress, Dobin's mother doesn't like it.
③ Cleaning is Dobin's sister's number-one way to make life better.
④ When Dobin's sister is so stressed that her life looks gloomy, she cleans her room.
⑤ As Dobin's sister cleans her room, she feels like she's also relieving stress.

[20~22] 다음 글을 읽고 물음에 답하시오.

Yulia (14, Ansan)

Let me tell you what my mother does about her stress. She feels stressed by all the things she has to do at work and at home. When she's under stress, she writes "Me Time" on her calendar. This means she takes some time out for herself. She reads a book, watches a movie, or talks with her friends. She says,

@This doesn't really matter what I do, as long as it's something I like. ⓑI've been writing 'Me Time' on my calendar for two months, and I feel much better."

20 위 글의 밑줄 친 @에서 어법상 <u>틀린</u> 부분을 찾아 고치시오.

_____ ➡ _____

21 위 글의 밑줄 친 ⓑ에 쓰인 것과 같은 용법의 현재완료가 쓰인 문장의 개수를 고르시오.

┌─── 보기 ───┐
① Have you ever seen it before?
② She has gone to Paris.
③ I have just solved the problem.
④ How long have you known each other?
⑤ He hasn't finished it yet.
└────────┘

① 1개　② 2개　③ 3개　④ 4개　⑤ 5개

22 위 글의 내용으로 보아 대답할 수 <u>없는</u> 질문은?

① What does Yulia tell you about?
② What kind of job does Yulia's mother have?
③ What does Yulia's mother do when she is stressed?
④ What does Yulia's mother write on her calendar?
⑤ How long has Yulia been writing 'Me Time' on her calendar?

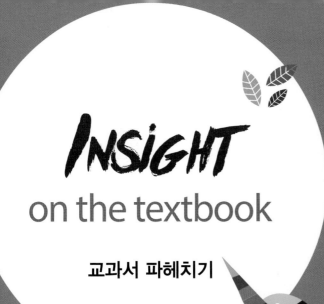

INSIGHT
on the textbook

교과서 파헤치기

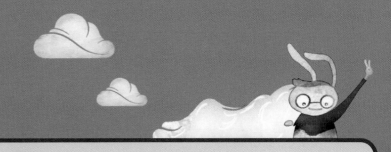

※ 다음 영어를 우리말로 쓰시오.

01 pack _____

02 appear _____

03 priceless _____

04 chase _____

05 realize _____

06 prepare _____

07 chew _____

08 serve _____

09 jealous _____

10 relax _____

11 repay _____

12 hurry _____

13 chest _____

14 allowance _____

15 include _____

16 speechless _____

17 palace _____

18 invention _____

19 faraway _____

20 worthless _____

21 servant _____

22 present _____

23 merchant _____

24 subject _____

25 tool _____

26 delighted _____

27 spice _____

28 puzzled _____

29 trade _____

30 valuable _____

31 whisper _____

32 pleased _____

33 kitten _____

34 wonder _____

35 after a while _____

36 thanks to ~ _____

37 chase A away _____

38 take care of ~ _____

39 get over _____

40 all day long _____

41 have two left feet _____

42 take ~ hard _____

43 be sure that ~ _____

※ 다음 우리말을 영어로 쓰시오.

01 추적하다		22 주다, 선사하다	
02 기쁜		23 속삭이다	
03 비옷		24 포함하다	
04 상품		25 소중한	
05 서두르다		26 당황스러운	
06 나타나다		27 씹다	
07 말문이 막힌		28 깨닫다	
08 하인		29 준비하다	
09 용돈		30 발명, 발명품	
10 멀리 떨어진		31 질투하는	
11 새끼 고양이		32 음식을 날라 주다	
12 도구, 연장		33 가치 없는	
13 보물, 보석		34 소중한	
14 무역하다, 교역하다		35 극복하다	
15 갚다		36 하루 종일	
16 상인		37 ~을 돌보다	
17 짐을 꾸리다, 가득 채우다		38 동작이 어색하다, 몸치이다	
18 상자, 가슴		39 행운을 빌어!	
19 향료		40 ~ 덕택에	
20 쉬다		41 A를 쫓아내다	
21 궁전		42 ~을 확신하다	
		43 시간을 알아보다	

※ 다음 영영풀이에 알맞은 단어를 <보기>에서 골라 쓴 후, 우리말 뜻을 쓰시오.

1 _____ : a young cat: _____

2 _____ : extremely valuable or important: _____

3 _____ : the official home of a king, queen, president, etc.: _____

4 _____ : to make someone or something part of a larger group: _____

5 _____ : someone who buys and sells goods in large quantities: _____

6 _____ : to pay back the money that you have borrowed from somebody:

   _____

7 _____ : a precious stone such as a diamond, ruby, etc.: _____

8 _____ : to put things into cases, bags etc ready for a trip somewhere: _____

9 _____ : to quickly follow someone or something in order to catch them:

   _____

10 _____ : an amount of money that you are given regularly or for a special

   purpose: _____

11 _____ : to speak very quietly to somebody so that other people cannot hear what

   you are saying: _____

12 _____ : a film, television programme, computer game etc that has pictures, clay

   models etc that seem to be really moving: _____

13 _____ : a large strong box that you use to store things in or to move your

   personal possessions from one place to another: _____

14 _____ : someone, especially in the past, who was paid to clean someone's house,

   cook for them, answer the door etc.: _____

15 _____ : something such as a hammer, saw, shovel, etc. that you hold in your

   hand and use for a particular task: _____

16 _____ : to bite food into small pieces in your mouth with your teeth to make it

   easier to swallow: _____

보기			
chase	servant	jewel	chew
include	kitten	tool	priceless
repay	merchant	palace	pack
whisper	animation	allowance	chest

※ 다음 우리말과 일치하도록 빈칸에 알맞은 말을 쓰시오.

Listen – Listen and Answer – Dialog 1

G: Hey, Minjun. _____ a _____!

B: Hi, Sora. I'm _____ we're in the _____ _____.

G: I _____, _____. We're now in our _____ _____ in middle school. _____ do you _____?

B: I'm _____ _____ _____ that there'll be more schoolwork.

G: Me, too. We also _____ _____ think about our _____ school.

B: _____ _____ of school do you _____ in _____?

G: I'm _____ of an animation high school. I love _____.

Listen – Listen and Answer – Dialog 2

G: Oliver, _____ _____ are you _____ to _____?

B: I'm not _____. _____ _____ you, Sora?

G: I want _____ _____ the school dance club.

B: Really? But I _____ you're _____ _____ an animation high school.

G: Right, but I _____ some time _____ _____. We all _____ to do something _____ _____ _____ stress.

B: _____ _____ _____ that again.

G: _____ _____ you join me? It'll be fun.

B: No, _____. Dancing is not _____ _____. I have _____ _____ _____.

Listen More – Listen and say

B: Jimin, look! That red phone _____ _____ _____!

G: You can _____ _____ again! Mom would love it _____ a _____ _____.

B: I _____ _____ _____ it _____.

G: _____ me _____. It _____ 40,000 won.

B: Really? That's so _____.

G: I don't _____. Look! It _____ _____ a wallet, _____.

B: Oh, I didn't see that. Then _____ _____ it for Mom.

G: Okay. I'm _____ _____ something _____ for Mom.

B: _____ _____ I.

Speak - Talk in pairs.

A: Did you _____ the _____ _____?

B: Yes. It's _____ _____ _____ all day _____.

A: Really? I'm _____ I can _____ my new _____.

B: _____ _____ you.

A: 일기예보 들었니?
B: 들었어. 하루 종일 비가 올 거야.
A: 정말! 새 비옷을 입을 수 있어 기뻐.
B: 좋겠다.

Speak - Talk in groups.

A: I think _____ _____ _____ day of the _____ is Monday.

B: You _____ _____ that _____.

C: I _____ _____ so. Thursday is the _____ _____.

D: I _____. We have all the _____ _____ on Thursday.

A: 나는 가장 지루한 날이 월요일이라고 생각해.
B: 네 말이 맞아.
C: 나는 그렇게 생각하지 않아. 목요일이 가장 지루해.
D: 나도 동의해. 우리는 목요일에 어려운 과목이 모두 있어.

My Speaking Portfolio

1. B1: _____ do you do in your _____ time? I _____ to music.
   I think it's the _____ _____. I can't _____ _____ it.

2. G: I think chocolate is the _____ _____. It makes me _____ _____. It also helps me _____ _____ when I study.

3. B2: Many people will _____ that paper is the greatest invention. _____ _____ paper, we all can _____ books and _____ things _____.

1. B1: 여러분은 여가 시간에 무엇을 하나요? 나는 음악을 듣습니다. 나는 음악이 가장 위대한 발명품이라고 생각합니다. 나는 음악 없이는 살 수 없습니다.

2. G: 나는 초콜릿이 가장 위대한 발명품이라고 생각합니다. 초콜릿은 내가 기분이 좋아지도록 해 줍니다. 그것은 또한 내가 공부할 때 더 잘 집중하도록 도와줍니다.

3. B2: 종이가 가장 위대한 발명품이라는 데 많은 사람이 동의할 것입니다. 종이 덕분에 우리는 모두 책을 읽고 무언가를 적을 수 있습니다.

Wrap up - Listening & Speaking ⑤

B: You _____ so _____. What's _____ _____?

G: Oh, I'm just _____ for the school play tomorrow.

B: _____ do you _____ _____ it?

G: I'm _____ I may _____ a _____.

B: I'm _____ you'll do well. _____ a _____!

G: Thanks.

B: 너 진지해 보인다. 무슨 일이니?
G: 아, 그냥 내일 있을 학교 연극을 연습하는 중이야.
B: 기분이 어때?
G: 실수할까 봐 걱정돼.
B: 너는 틀림없이 잘할 거야. 행운을 빌어!
G: 고마워.

Wrap up - Listening & Speaking ⑥

G: _____ you _____ about Mr. Oh?

B: No. _____ _____ him?

G: He _____ first _____ in the TV quiz show.

B: It's not _____. He _____ _____ know about everything.

G: You can say that again! He's a _____ _____.

G: 오 선생님에 관해 들었니?
B: 아니. 선생님에 관해 뭘?
G: 선생님이 TV 퀴즈 쇼에서 우승하셨대.
B: 놀랄 일도 아니지. 선생님은 모든 것에 관해 알고 계신 것 같아.
G: 맞아! 걸어 다니는 사전이시지.

※ 다음 우리말에 맞도록 대화를 영어로 쓰시오.

Listen – Listen and Answer – Dialog 1

G: _____

B: _____

G: _____

B: _____

G: _____

B: _____

G: _____

G: 야, 민준아. 정말 놀랍다!
B: 안녕, 소라야. 우리가 같은 반에 있어서 기뻐.
G: 나도 그래. 우리 이제 중학교의 마지막 학년이야. 기분이 어떠니?
B: 공부할 게 더 많을 것 같아서 조금 걱정이야.
G: 나도 그래. 고등학교에 대해서도 생각해야 하지.
B: 너는 어떤 학교를 마음에 두고 있니?
G: 나는 애니메이션 고등학교를 생각하고 있어. 내가 그림 그리는 걸 좋아하거든.

Listen – Listen and Answer – Dialog 2

G: _____

B: _____

G: _____

B: _____

G: _____

B: _____

G: _____

B: _____

G: Oliver, 넌 어느 동아리에 들어갈 거니?
B: 잘 모르겠어. 소라, 너는?
G: 난 학교 춤 동아리에 가입하고 싶어.
B: 정말? 하지만 네가 애니메이션 고등학교를 준비하고 있다고 들었는데.
G: 그렇긴 한데, 좀 쉴 시간이 필요해. 우리 모두 스트레스를 극복하려면 뭔가를 할 필요가 있잖아.
B: 전적으로 동의해.
G: 너 나랑 함께하는 게 어때? 재미있을 거야.
B: 고맙지만 사양할게. 춤은 내게 맞지 않아. 난 몸치야.

Listen More – Listen and say

B: _____

G: _____

B: _____

G: _____

B: _____

G: _____

B: _____

G: _____

B: _____

B: 지민아, 봐! 저 빨간 전화기 케이스 멋지다!
G: 정말 그렇다! 생신 선물로 어머니께서 좋아하실 거야.
B: 난 가격이 얼마인지 궁금해.
G: 어디 보자. 가격은 40,000원이야.
B: 정말? 그거 너무 비싸다!
G: 난 동의하지 않아. 봐! 이건 지갑 역할도 해.
B: 아, 그건 못 봤어. 그럼 어머니를 위해 그걸 사자.
G: 알았어. 어머니께 뭔가 특별한 것을 사 드리게 되어 기뻐.
B: 나도 그래.

Speak - Talk in pairs.

A: _____

B: _____

A: _____

B: _____

A: 일기예보 들었니?
B: 들었어. 하루 종일 비가 올 거야.
A: 정말! 새 비옷을 입을 수 있어 기뻐.
B: 좋겠다.

Speak - Talk in groups.

A: _____

B: _____

C: _____

D: _____

A: 나는 가장 지루한 날이 월요일이라고 생각해.
B: 네 말이 맞아.
C: 나는 그렇게 생각하지 않아. 목요일이 가장 지루해.
D: 나도 동의해. 우리는 목요일에 어려운 과목이 모두 있어.

My Speaking Portfolio

1. B1: _____
   _____

2. G: _____
   _____

3. B2: _____
   _____

1. B1: 여러분은 여가 시간에 무엇을 하나요? 나는 음악을 듣습니다. 나는 음악이 가장 위대한 발명품이라고 생각합니다. 나는 음악 없이는 살 수 없습니다.
2. G: 나는 초콜릿이 가장 위대한 발명품이라고 생각합니다. 초콜릿은 내가 기분이 좋아지도록 해 줍니다. 그것은 또한 내가 공부할 때 더 잘 집중하도록 도와줍니다.
3. B2: 종이가 가장 위대한 발명품이라는 데 많은 사람이 동의할 것입니다. 종이 덕분에 우리는 모두 책을 읽고 무언가를 적을 수 있습니다.

Wrap up - Listening & Speaking ⑤

B: _____

G: _____

B: _____

G: _____

B: _____

G: _____

B: 너 진지해 보인다. 무슨 일이니?
G: 아, 그냥 내일 있을 학교 연극을 연습하는 중이야.
B: 기분이 어때?
G: 실수할까 봐 걱정돼.
B: 너는 틀림없이 잘할 거야. 행운을 빌어!
G: 고마워.

Wrap up - Listening & Speaking ⑥

G: _____

B: _____

G: _____

B: _____

G: _____

G: 오 선생님에 관해 들었니?
B: 아니. 선생님에 관해 뭘?
G: 선생님이 TV 퀴즈 쇼에서 우승하셨대.
B: 놀랄 일도 아니지. 선생님은 모든 것에 관해 알고 계신 것 같아.
G: 맞아! 걸어 다니는 사전이시지.

※ 다음 우리말과 일치하도록 빈칸에 알맞은 것을 골라 쓰시오.

1 A _____ _____
A. Gift   B. Priceless

2 Long _____, an _____ _____ lived _____ Genoa, Italy.
A. in   B. merchant   C. ago   D. honest

3 His name was Antonio, and he went to different _____ to _____ his family _____ _____.
A. support   B. trading   C. by   D. places

4 One day, he _____ his ship _____ _____ and visited a _____ island.
A. faraway   B. filled   C. goods   D. with

5 There he _____ tools for _____ and books _____ _____.
A. nuts   B. traded   C. spices   D. for

6 _____ _____ Antonio, the islanders could get _____ they _____.
A. to   B. needed   C. thanks   D. what

7 One night, Antonio had _____ _____ the island's _____ at her _____.
A. palace   B. dinner   C. queen   D. with

8 When dinner was _____, rats _____, and some servants _____ them _____ with sticks.
A. chased   B. served   C. away   D. appeared

9 Antonio was _____ _____ that _____ were rats in the _____.
A. surprised   B. palace   C. greatly   D. there

10 He asked, "_____ _____ _____ _____ on this island?"
A. cats   B. are   C. no   D. there

11 The queen _____ _____.
A. puzzled   B. looked

12 "What is a _____?" _____ _____.
A. she   B. cat   C. asked

13 The merchant _____ to _____, "What the islanders here need is _____ tools or books, _____ cats."
A. not   B. himself   C. said   D. but

14 He _____ two cats _____ his ship and _____ them _____ free.
A. let   B. brought   C. run   D. from

1 소중한 선물

2 먼 옛날 이탈리아 제노바에 정직한 상인 한 명이 살았다.

3 그의 이름은 Antonio로, 그는 교역으로 가족을 부양하기 위해 여러 곳을 다녔다.

4 어느 날 그는 배에 상품을 가득 싣고 머나먼 섬으로 갔다.

5 거기서 그는 공구를 향신료와 바꾸었고, 책을 견과류와 바꾸었다.

6 Antonio 덕에 섬사람들은 필요한 것을 얻을 수 있었다.

7 어느 날 밤, Antonio는 궁전에서 그 섬의 여왕과 저녁 식사를 했다.

8 식사가 나왔을 때 쥐들이 나타났고, 하인 몇 명이 막대기로 쥐를 쫓아내었다.

9 Antonio는 궁전에 쥐가 있다는 사실에 무척 놀랐다.

10 그는 "이 섬에는 고양이가 없습니까?"라고 물었다.

11 여왕은 어리둥절한 것처럼 보였다.

12 "고양이가 뭔가요?"라고 그녀가 물었다.

13 상인은 "여기 섬사람들이 필요로 하는 것은 공구나 책이 아니라 고양이야."라고 혼자 중얼거렸다.

14 그는 배에서 고양이 두 마리를 데리고 와서, 자유롭게 돌아다니도록 풀어놓았다.

15 "_____ amazing animals!" cried the queen _____ she saw all the rats _____ _____.

    A. run   B. what   C. when   D. away

16 She gave Antonio a _____ that was _____ _____ _____.

    A. filled   B. chest   C. jewels   D. with

17 _____ in Italy, Antonio _____ his friends about his _____ _____.

    A. good   B. back   C. told   D. fortune

18 Luigi, the _____ _____ in Genoa, _____ the story and was _____.

    A. heard   B. merchant   C. jealous   D. richest

19 "Cats _____ _____," Luigi _____.

    A. thought   B. worthless   C. are

20 "I'll _____ the queen _____ is really _____.

    A. what   B. bring   C. valuable

21 I'm _____ that the _____ will give _____ more _____."

    A. me   B. sure   C. jewels   D. queen

22 Luigi _____ his ship _____ wonderful paintings and _____ _____ of art.

    A. with   B. works   C. packed   D. other

23 He _____ the _____ to the _____.

    A. gifts   B. took   C. island

24 To get a _____ to meet the queen, he told the _____ a _____ that he was a _____ friend of Antonio's.

    A. lie   B. chance   C. islanders   D. good

25 When the queen _____ about Luigi, she _____ him to her _____ for _____.

    A. invited   B. heard   C. dinner   D. palace

26 Before _____ down at the table, Luigi _____ the queen _____ all his gifts, and the queen thanked him _____ and again.

    A. with   B. sitting   C. again   D. presented

27 "I'll _____ you _____ a _____ gift," said the queen.

    A. with   B. repay   C. priceless

28 Luigi _____ the queen _____ in a servant's _____.

    A. whisper   B. watched   C. ear

15 "정말 놀라운 동물이네요!" 쥐가 모두 도망가는 것을 보자 여왕이 감탄하였다.

16 그녀는 Antonio에게 보석이 가득한 상자를 주었다.

17 이탈리아로 돌아와서, Antonio는 자신에게 일어난 행운을 친구들에게 이야기했다.

18 제노바에서 가장 부유한 상인인 Luigi는 그 이야기를 듣고 시샘이 일었다.

19 "고양이는 쓸모없어." Luigi가 생각했다.

20 "난 여왕에게 정말로 귀중한 것을 가지고 갈 거야.

21 틀림없이 여왕이 내게 더 많은 보석을 줄 거야."

22 Luigi는 멋진 그림들과 다른 예술 작품을 배에 실었다.

23 그는 선물을 섬으로 가지고 갔다.

24 여왕을 만날 기회를 얻기 위해서, 그는 자신이 Antonio의 친한 친구라고 섬사람들에게 거짓말을 했다.

25 Luigi에 관해 듣고, 여왕은 그를 궁전으로 저녁 식사에 초대했다.

26 식탁에 앉기 전에 Luigi는 여왕에게 자신이 가져온 온갖 선물을 전했고, 여왕은 그에게 여러 차례 감사하다고 했다.

27 "당신께 값진 선물로 보답하겠습니다."라고 여왕이 말했다.

28 Luigi는 여왕이 하인의 귀에 대고 속삭이는 것을 지켜보았다.

29 He _____ _____ and _____.

A. excited　　　B. became　　　C. hopeful

30 He was sure that he would _____ _____ _____ _____ Antonio.

A. more　　　B. receive　　　C. than　　　D. jewels

31 After a _____, the servant _____ with a box, and the queen _____ it _____ Luigi.

A. returned　　　B. while　　　C. presented　　　D. to

32 _____ Luigi _____ the box, he was _____.

A. opened　　　B. when　　　C. speechless

33 _____ was a _____ in the _____.

A. box　　　B. there　　　C. kitten

34 "Antonio _____ us the _____ cats, and we now have some _____," said the _____.

A. kittens　　　B. priceless　　　C. queen　　　D. gave

35 "In _____ for the wonderful gifts you gave us, we want to give you _____ is _____ _____ to us."

A. what　　　B. return　　　C. valuable　　　D. most

36 Luigi _____ that, in the queen's _____, the kitten was _____ _____ more than all the jewels in the world.

A. mind　　　B. far　　　C. realized　　　D. worth

37 He _____ to _____ _____ with the gift.

A. look　　　B. tried　　　C. pleased

38 He knew that was the _____ _____ _____ _____.

A. to　　　B. right　　　C. do　　　D. thing

39 Luigi did not _____ _____ a _____ _____.

A. home　　　B. man　　　C. richer　　　D. return

40 But he was _____ a _____ _____.

A. wiser　　　B. surely　　　C. one

29 그는 흥분되고 기대에 부풀었다.

30 그는 Antonio보다 많은 보석을 받게 될 거라고 확신했다.

31 잠시 후에 하인이 상자 하나를 가지고 돌아왔고, 여왕은 그것을 Luigi에게 주었다.

32 상자를 열어본 Luigi는 말문이 막혔다.

33 상자 안에는 새끼 고양이 한 마리가 들어 있었다.

34 "Antonio가 우리에게 매우 귀한 고양이들을 줬는데, 이제 새끼 고양이 몇 마리가 생겼어요."라고 여왕이 말했다.

35 "당신이 우리에게 준 멋진 선물에 보답하는 뜻에서, 우리에게 가장 값진 것을 당신에게 드리고 싶어요."

36 여왕의 생각에는 세상의 온갖 보석보다 새끼 고양이가 훨씬 더 가치 있다는 것을 Luigi는 깨달았다.

37 그는 선물에 대해 기뻐하는 표정을 지으려고 애썼다.

38 그게 올바른 행동이라는 것을 그는 알았다.

39 Luigi는 더 부유한 사람이 되어 집으로 돌아오지는 않았다.

40 하지만 그는 분명히 더 현명한 사람이 되었다.

※ 다음 우리말과 일치하도록 빈칸에 알맞은 것을 골라 쓰시오.

1 A _____ _____

2 Long ago, _____ _____ _____ _____ in Genoa, Italy.

3 His name was Antonio, and he went to different places _____ _____ _____ _____ _____ _____.

4 One day, he _____ his ship _____ goods and visited a _____ _____.

5 There he _____ tools _____ spices and books _____ nuts.

6 _____ _____ Antonio, the islanders could get _____ they _____.

7 One night, Antonio _____ _____ _____ the island's queen at her palace.

8 When dinner _____ _____, rats _____, and some servants _____ _____ _____ _____ _____.

9 Antonio was _____ _____ that _____ _____ rats in the palace.

10 He asked, "_____ _____ _____ _____ on this island?"

11 The queen _____ _____.

12 "What is a cat?" _____ _____.

13 The merchant _____ _____ _____, "_____ the islanders here need is _____ tools or books, _____ cats."

14 He _____ two cats _____ his ship and _____ _____ _____ _____.

---

1 소중한 선물

2 먼 옛날 이탈리아 제노바에 정직한 상인 한 명이 살았다.

3 그의 이름은 Antonio로, 그는 교역으로 가족을 부양하기 위해 여러 곳을 다녔다.

4 어느 날 그는 배에 상품을 가득 싣고 머나먼 섬으로 갔다.

5 거기서 그는 공구를 향신료와 바꾸었고, 책을 견과류와 바꾸었다.

6 Antonio 덕에 섬사람들은 필요한 것을 얻을 수 있었다.

7 어느 날 밤, Antonio는 궁전에서 그 섬의 여왕과 저녁 식사를 했다.

8 식사가 나왔을 때 쥐들이 나타났고, 하인 몇 명이 막대기로 쥐를 쫓아내었다.

9 Antonio는 궁전에 쥐가 있다는 사실에 무척 놀랐다.

10 그는 "이 섬에는 고양이가 없습니까?"라고 물었다.

11 여왕은 어리둥절한 것처럼 보였다.

12 "고양이가 뭔가요?"라고 그녀가 물었다.

13 상인은 "여기 섬사람들이 필요로 하는 것은 공구나 책이 아니라 고양이야."라고 혼자 중얼거렸다.

14 그는 배에서 고양이 두 마리를 데리고 와서, 자유롭게 돌아다니도록 풀어놓았다.

15 "_____ _____ animals!" cried the queen when she saw all the rats _____ _____.

16 She gave Antonio a chest that _____ _____ _____ jewels.

17 _____ _____ Italy, Antonio told his friends about his _____ _____.

18 Luigi, _____ _____ _____ in Genoa, _____ the story and was _____.

19 "Cats are _____," Luigi _____.

20 "I'll bring the queen _____ is really _____.

21 _____ _____ that the queen will give me _____ _____."

22 Luigi _____ his ship _____ wonderful paintings and other _____ _____ _____.

23 He _____ the gifts _____ the island.

24 _____ _____ a chance to meet the queen, he told the islanders a lie that he was _____ _____ _____ _____ _____.

25 When the queen _____ _____ Luigi, she _____ him _____ her palace for dinner.

26 Before _____ down at the table, Luigi _____ the queen _____ all his gifts, and the queen _____ him _____ _____ _____.

27 "I'll _____ you _____ a _____ gift," said the queen.

28 Luigi _____ the queen _____ in a servant's ear.

15 "정말 놀라운 동물이네요!" 쥐가 모두 도망가는 것을 보자 여왕이 감탄하였다.

16 그녀는 Antonio에게 보석이 가득한 상자를 주었다.

17 이탈리아로 돌아와서, Antonio는 자신에게 일어난 행운을 친구들에게 이야기했다.

18 제노바에서 가장 부유한 상인인 Luigi는 그 이야기를 듣고 시샘이 일었다.

19 "고양이는 쓸모없어." Luigi가 생각했다.

20 "난 여왕에게 정말로 귀중한 것을 가지고 갈 거야.

21 틀림없이 여왕이 내게 더 많은 보석을 줄 거야."

22 Luigi는 멋진 그림들과 다른 예술 작품을 배에 실었다.

23 그는 선물을 섬으로 가지고 갔다.

24 여왕을 만날 기회를 얻기 위해서, 그는 자신이 Antonio의 친한 친구라고 섬사람들에게 거짓말을 했다.

25 Luigi에 관해 듣고, 여왕은 그를 궁전으로 저녁 식사에 초대했다.

26 식탁에 앉기 전에 Luigi는 여왕에게 자신이 가져온 온갖 선물을 전했고, 여왕은 그에게 여러 차례 감사하다고 했다.

27 "당신께 값진 선물로 보답하겠습니다."라고 여왕이 말했다.

28 Luigi는 여왕이 하인의 귀에 대고 속삭이는 것을 지켜보았다.

29 He became _____ and _____.

30 He _____ _____ that he would receive _____ _____ _____ Antonio.

31 _____ _____ _____, the servant returned with a box, and the queen _____ it _____ Luigi.

32 When Luigi _____ the box, he was _____.

33 There was a _____ in the box.

34 "Antonio gave us the _____ cats, and we now have some kittens," said the queen.

35 "_____ _____ _____ the wonderful gifts you gave us, we want to give you _____ _____ _____ _____ to us."

36 Luigi _____ that, in the queen's _____, the kitten was _____ _____ _____ _____ all the jewels in the world.

37 He tried to _____ _____ _____ the gift.

38 He knew that was the _____ _____ _____ _____.

39 Luigi did not _____ _____ a _____ man.

40 But he was _____ _____ _____ _____.

29 그는 흥분되고 기대에 부풀었다.

30 그는 Antonio보다 많은 보석을 받게 될 거라고 확신했다.

31 잠시 후에 하인이 상자 하나를 가지고 돌아왔고, 여왕은 그것을 Luigi에게 주었다.

32 상자를 열어본 Luigi는 말문이 막혔다.

33 상자 안에는 새끼 고양이 한 마리가 들어 있었다.

34 "Antonio가 우리에게 매우 귀한 고양이들을 줬는데, 이제 새끼 고양이 몇 마리가 생겼어요."라고 여왕이 말했다.

35 "당신이 우리에게 준 멋진 선물에 보답하는 뜻에서, 우리에게 가장 값진 것을 당신에게 드리고 싶어요."

36 여왕의 생각에는 세상의 온갖 보석보다 새끼 고양이가 훨씬 더 가치 있다는 것을 Luigi는 깨달았다.

37 그는 선물에 대해 기뻐하는 표정을 지으려고 애썼다.

38 그게 올바른 행동이라는 것을 그는 알았다.

39 Luigi는 더 부유한 사람이 되어 집으로 돌아오지는 않았다.

40 하지만 그는 분명히 더 현명한 사람이 되었다.

본문 Test

※ 다음 문장을 우리말로 쓰시오.

1 A Priceless Gift

➡ _____

2 Long ago, an honest merchant lived in Genoa, Italy.

➡ _____

3 His name was Antonio, and he went to different places to support his family by trading.

➡ _____

4 One day, he filled his ship with goods and visited a faraway island.

➡ _____

5 There he traded tools for spices and books for nuts.

➡ _____

6 Thanks to Antonio, the islanders could get what they needed.

➡ _____

7 One night, Antonio had dinner with the island's queen at her palace.

➡ _____

8 When dinner was served, rats appeared, and some servants chased them away with sticks.

➡ _____

9 Antonio was greatly surprised that there were rats in the palace.

➡ _____

10 He asked, "Are there no cats on this island?"

➡ _____

11 The queen looked puzzled.

➡ _____

12 "What is a cat?" she asked.

➡ _____

13 The merchant said to himself, "What the islanders here need is not tools or books, but cats."

➡ _____

14 He brought two cats from his ship and let them run free.

➡ _____

15 "What amazing animals!" cried the queen when she saw all the rats run away.

➡ _____

16 She gave Antonio a chest that was filled with jewels.

➡ _____

17 Back in Italy, Antonio told his friends about his good fortune.

➡ _____

18 Luigi, the richest merchant in Genoa, heard the story and was jealous.

➡ _____

19 "Cats are worthless," Luigi thought.

➡ _____

20 "I'll bring the queen what is really valuable.

➡ _____

21 I'm sure that the queen will give me more jewels."

➡ _____

22 Luigi packed his ship with wonderful paintings and other works of art.

➡ _____

23 He took the gifts to the island.

➡ _____

24 To get a chance to meet the queen, he told the islanders a lie that he was a good friend of Antonio's.

➡ _____

25 When the queen heard about Luigi, she invited him to her palace for dinner.

➡ _____

26 Before sitting down at the table, Luigi presented the queen with all his gifts, and the queen thanked him again and again.

➡ _____

27 "I'll repay you with a priceless gift," said the queen.

➡ _____

28 Luigi watched the queen whisper in a servant's ear.

➡ _____

29 He became excited and hopeful.

➡ _____

30 He was sure that he would receive more jewels than Antonio.

➡ _____

31 After a while, the servant returned with a box, and the queen presented it to Luigi.

➡ _____

32 When Luigi opened the box, he was speechless.

➡ _____

33 There was a kitten in the box.

➡ _____

34 "Antonio gave us the priceless cats, and we now have some kittens," said the queen.

➡ _____

35 "In return for the wonderful gifts you gave us, we want to give you what is most valuable to us."

➡ _____

36 Luigi realized that, in the queen's mind, the kitten was worth far more than all the jewels in the world.

➡ _____

37 He tried to look pleased with the gift.

➡ _____

38 He knew that was the right thing to do.

➡ _____

39 Luigi did not return home a richer man.

➡ _____

40 But he was surely a wiser one.

➡ _____

※ 다음 괄호 안의 단어들을 우리말에 맞도록 바르게 배열하시오.

1 (Priceless / Gift / A)
➡ _____

2 (ago, / long / honest / an / lived / merchant / Genoa, / in / Italy.)
➡ _____

3 (name / his / Antonio, / was / he / and / to / went / places / different / support / to / family / his / trading. / by)
➡ _____
_____

4 (day, / one / filled / he / ship / his / goods / with / and / a / visited / island. / faraway)
➡ _____

5 (he / there / tools / traded / spices / for / and / nuts. / for / books)
➡ _____

6 (to / thanks / Antonio, / islanders / the / get / could / what / needed. / they)
➡ _____

7 (night, / one / had / Antonio / with / dinner / the / queen / island's / at / palace. / her)
➡ _____

8 (dinner / when / served, / was / appeared, / rats / and / servants / some / them / chased / with / away / sticks.)
➡ _____
_____

9 (was / Antonio / surprised / greatly / there / that / rats / were / the / palace. / in)
➡ _____

10 (asked, / he / there / "are / cats / no / this / on / island?")
➡ _____

11 (queen / the / puzzled. / looked)
➡ _____

12 (is / "what / cat?" / a / asked. / she)
➡ _____

13 (merchant / the / to / said / himself, / the / "what / here / islanders / is / need / tools / not / books, / or / cats." / but)
➡ _____
_____

14 (brought / he / cats / two / his / from / ship / and / them / let / free. / run)
➡ _____

1 소중한 선물

2 먼 옛날 이탈리아 제노바에 정직한 상인 한 명이 살았다.

3 그의 이름은 Antonio로, 그는 교역으로 가족을 부양하기 위해 여러 곳을 다녔다.

4 어느 날 그는 배에 상품을 가득 싣고 머나먼 섬으로 갔다.

5 거기서 그는 공구를 향신료와 바꾸었고, 책을 견과류와 바꾸었다.

6 Antonio 덕에 섬사람들은 필요한 것을 얻을 수 있었다.

7 어느 날 밤, Antonio는 궁전에서 그 섬의 여왕과 저녁 식사를 했다.

8 식사가 나왔을 때 쥐들이 나타났고, 하인 몇 명이 막대기로 쥐를 쫓아내었다.

9 Antonio는 궁전에 쥐가 있다는 사실에 무척 놀랐다.

10 그는 "이 섬에는 고양이가 없습니까?"라고 물었다.

11 여왕은 어리둥절한 것처럼 보였다.

12 "고양이가 뭔가요?"라고 그녀가 물었다.

13 상인은 "여기 섬사람들이 필요로 하는 것은 공구나 책이 아니라 고양이야."라고 혼자 중얼거렸다.

14 그는 배에서 고양이 두 마리를 데리고 와서, 자유롭게 돌아다니도록 풀어놓았다.

15 (amazing / "what / animals!" / the / cried / queen / she / when / all / saw / rats / the / away. / run)

➡ _____

_____

16 (gave / she / a / Antonio / chest / was / that / with / filled / jewels.)

➡ _____

17 (in / back / Italy, / told / Antonio / friends / his / about / good / fortune. / his)

➡ _____

18 (the / Luigi / merchant / richest / Genoa, / in / the / heard / story / and / jealous. / was)

➡ _____

19 (are / "cats / worthless," / thought. / Luigi)

➡ _____

20 (bring / "I'll / queen / the / is / what / valuable. / really)

➡ _____

21 (sure / I'm / the / that / will / queen / me / give / jewels." / more)

➡ _____

22 (packed / Luigi / ship / his / wonderful / with / and / paintings / works / other / art. / of)

➡ _____

23 (took / he / gifts / the / to / island. / the)

➡ _____

24 (get / to / chance / a / meet / to / queen, / the / told / he / islanders / the / lie / a / that / was / he / a / friend / good / Antonio's. / of)

➡ _____

25 (the / when / heard / queen / Luigi, / about / invited / she / to / him / her / dinner. / for / palace)

➡ _____

26 (sitting / before / at / down / table, / the / presented / Luigi / queen / the / with / his / all / gifts, / and / queen / the / him / thanked / and / again / again.)

➡ _____

27 (repay / "I'll / with / you / priceless / a / gift," / the / said / queen.)

➡ _____

28 (watched / Luigi / the / whisper / queen / a / in / ear. / servant's)

➡ _____

15 "정말 놀라운 동물이네요!" 쥐가 모두 도망가는 것을 보자 여왕이 감탄하였다.

16 그녀는 Antonio에게 보석이 가득한 상자를 주었다.

17 이탈리아로 돌아와서, Antonio는 자신에게 일어난 행운을 친구들에게 이야기했다.

18 제노바에서 가장 부유한 상인인 Luigi는 그 이야기를 듣고 시샘이 일었다.

19 "고양이는 쓸모없어." Luigi가 생각했다.

20 "난 여왕에게 정말로 귀중한 것을 가지고 갈 거야.

21 틀림없이 여왕이 내게 더 많은 보석을 줄 거야."

22 Luigi는 멋진 그림들과 다른 예술 작품을 배에 실었다.

23 그는 선물을 섬으로 가지고 갔다.

24 여왕을 만날 기회를 얻기 위해서, 그는 자신이 Antonio의 친한 친구라고 섬사람들에게 거짓말을 했다.

25 Luigi에 관해 듣고, 여왕은 그를 궁전으로 저녁 식사에 초대했다.

26 식탁에 앉기 전에 Luigi는 여왕에게 자신이 가져온 온갖 선물을 전했고, 여왕은 그에게 여러 차례 감사하다고 했다.

27 "당신께 값진 선물로 보답하겠습니다."라고 여왕이 말했다.

28 Luigi는 여왕이 하인의 귀에 대고 속삭이는 것을 지켜보았다.

29 (became / he / hopeful. / and / excited)

➡ _____

30 (was / he / that / sure / would / he / more / receive / than / jewels / Antonio.)

➡ _____

31 (a / after / while, / servant / the / with / returned / box, / a / and / queen / the / it / presented / Luigi. / to)

➡ _____

_____

32 (Luigi / when / the / opened / box, / was / he / speechless.)

➡ _____

33 (was / there / kitten / a / the / box. / in)

➡ _____

34 (gave / us / "Antonio / the / cats, / priceless / and / now / we / some / have / kittens," / the / said / queen.)

➡ _____

_____

35 (return / "in / the / for / gifts / wonderful / gave / you / us, / want / we / give / to / what / you / valuable / most / us." / to)

➡ _____

_____

36 (realized / Luigi / that, / the / in / queen's / mind, / kitten / the / worth / was / more / far / than / the / all / jewels / the / world. / in)

➡ _____

_____

37 (tried / he / look / to / with / pleased / gift. / the)

➡ _____

38 (knew / he / was / that / the / thing / right / do. / to)

➡ _____

39 (did / Luigi / return / not / a / home / man. / richer)

➡ _____

40 (he / but / surely / was / one. / wiser / a)

➡ _____

---

29 그는 흥분되고 기대에 부풀었다.

30 그는 Antonio보다 많은 보석을 받게 될 거라고 확신했다.

31 잠시 후에 하인이 상자 하나를 가지고 돌아왔고, 여왕은 그것을 Luigi에게 주었다.

32 상자를 열어본 Luigi는 말문이 막혔다.

33 상자 안에는 새끼 고양이 한 마리가 들어 있었다.

34 "Antonio가 우리에게 매우 귀한 고양이들을 줬는데, 이제 새끼 고양이 몇 마리가 생겼어요."라고 여왕이 말했다.

35 "당신이 우리에게 준 멋진 선물에 보답하는 뜻에서, 우리에게 가장 값진 것을 당신에게 드리고 싶어요."

36 여왕의 생각에는 세상의 온갖 보석보다 새끼 고양이가 훨씬 더 가치 있다는 것을 Luigi는 깨달았다.

37 그는 선물에 대해 기뻐하는 표정을 지으려고 애썼다.

38 그게 올바른 행동이라는 것을 그는 알았다.

39 Luigi는 더 부유한 사람이 되어 집으로 돌아오지는 않았다.

40 하지만 그는 분명히 더 현명한 사람이 되었다.

※ 다음 우리말을 영어로 쓰시오.

1 소중한 선물

➡ _____

2 먼 옛날 이탈리아 제노바에 정직한 상인 한 명이 살았다.

➡ _____

3 그의 이름은 Antonio로, 그는 교역으로 가족을 부양하기 위해 여러 곳을 다녔다.

➡ _____

4 어느 날 그는 배에 상품을 가득 싣고 머나먼 섬으로 갔다.

➡ _____

5 거기서 그는 공구를 향신료와 바꾸었고, 책을 견과류와 바꾸었다.

➡ _____

6 Antonio 덕에 섬사람들은 필요한 것을 얻을 수 있었다.

➡ _____

7 어느 날 밤, Antonio는 궁전에서 그 섬의 여왕과 저녁 식사를 했다.

➡ _____

8 식사가 나왔을 때 쥐들이 나타났고, 하인 몇 명이 막대기로 쥐를 쫓아내었다.

➡ _____

9 Antonio는 궁전에 쥐가 있다는 사실에 무척 놀랐다.

➡ _____

10 그는 "이 섬에는 고양이가 없습니까?"라고 물었다.

➡ _____

11 여왕은 어리둥절한 것처럼 보였다.

➡ _____

12 "고양이가 뭔가요?"라고 그녀가 물었다.

➡ _____

13 상인은 "여기 섬사람들이 필요로 하는 것은 공구나 책이 아니라 고양이야."라고 혼자 중얼거렸다.

➡ _____

14 그는 배에서 고양이 두 마리를 데리고 와서, 자유롭게 돌아다니도록 풀어놓았다.

➡ _____

15 "정말 놀라운 동물이네요!" 쥐가 모두 도망가는 것을 보자 여왕이 감탄하였다.

➡ _____

16 그녀는 Antonio에게 보석이 가득한 상자를 주었다.

➡ _____

17 이탈리아로 돌아와서, Antonio는 자신에게 일어난 행운을 친구들에게 이야기했다.

➡ _____

18 제노바에서 가장 부유한 상인인 Luigi는 그 이야기를 듣고 시샘이 일었다.

➡ _____

19 "고양이는 쓸모없어." Luigi가 생각했다.

➡ _____

20 "난 여왕에게 정말로 귀중한 것을 가지고 갈 거야.

➡ _____

21 틀림없이 여왕이 내게 더 많은 보석을 줄 거야."

➡ _____

22 Luigi는 멋진 그림들과 다른 예술 작품을 배에 실었다.

➡ _____

23 그는 선물을 섬으로 가지고 갔다.

➡ _____

24 여왕을 만날 기회를 얻기 위해서, 그는 자신이 Antonio의 친한 친구라고 섬사람들에게 거짓말을 했다.

➡ _____

25 Luigi에 관해 듣고, 여왕은 그를 궁전으로 저녁 식사에 초대했다.

➡ _____

26 식탁에 앉기 전에 Luigi는 여왕에게 자신이 가져온 온갖 선물을 전했고, 여왕은 그에게 여러 차례 감사하다고 했다.

➡ _____

27 "당신께 값진 선물로 보답하겠습니다."라고 여왕이 말했다.

➡ _____

28 Luigi는 여왕이 하인의 귀에 대고 속삭이는 것을 지켜보았다.

➡ _____

29 그는 흥분되고 기대에 부풀었다.

➡ _____

30 그는 Antonio보다 많은 보석을 받게 될 거라고 확신했다.

➡ _____

31 잠시 후에 하인이 상자 하나를 가지고 돌아왔고, 여왕은 그것을 Luigi에게 주었다.

➡ _____

32 상자를 열어본 Luigi는 말문이 막혔다.

➡ _____

33 상자 안에는 새끼 고양이 한 마리가 들어 있었다.

➡ _____

34 "Antonio가 우리에게 매우 귀한 고양이들을 줬는데, 이제 새끼 고양이 몇 마리가 생겼어요."라고

여왕이 말했다.

➡ _____

35 "당신이 우리에게 준 멋진 선물에 보답하는 뜻에서, 우리에게 가장 값진 것을 당신에게 드리고 싶어요."

➡ _____

36 여왕의 생각에는 세상의 온갖 보석보다 새끼 고양이가 훨씬 더 가치 있다는 것을 Luigi는 깨달았다.

➡ _____

37 그는 선물에 대해 기뻐하는 표정을 지으려고 애썼다.

➡ _____

38 그게 올바른 행동이라는 것을 그는 알았다.

➡ _____

39 Luigi는 더 부유한 사람이 되어 집으로 돌아오지는 않았다.

➡ _____

40 하지만 그는 분명히 더 현명한 사람이 되었다.

➡ _____

※ 다음 우리말과 일치하도록 빈칸에 알맞은 말을 쓰시오.

My Speaking Portfolio

1. A: What is _____ _____ _____ in history?

2. B: _____ _____ the clock. We can't _____ _____ _____ without it.

3. C: I _____ really _____ _____ you. I think the cell phone is _____ _____ _____.

4. D: You can _____ _____ _____.

All Ears

1. M: 1. I _____ _____ _____ you _____ _____.

   2. I _____ _____ you _____ _____ the plan.

2. A: I'm _____ I can _____ _____ _____ _____.

3. B: You're _____ _____ the zoo? _____ _____ you.

4. A: I _____ I have _____ _____ _____ a snack.

5. B: I _____ _____. You must _____ _____ _____.

Wrap Up - Reading

1. Isabel _____ in a _____ _____ _____ Kakamega, Kenya.

2. In the past, she _____ _____ walk a _____ _____ every day _____ _____ clean water.

3. She sometimes _____ _____ _____ _____ the _____ _____ _____ _____.

4. Three months _____, she _____ a _____ _____ from a _____ _____.

5. It _____ _____ a thick straw.

6. Dirty water _____ _____ _____ _____, and clean water _____ _____ _____ _____ it.

7. Isabel _____ the straw _____.

8. Now, she does _____ _____ _____ _____.

9. She can go to school _____ _____.

10. So, the straw is _____ _____ _____ _____ to Isabel.

※ 다음 우리말을 영어로 쓰시오.

My Speaking Portfolio

1. A: 무엇이 역사상 가장 위대한 발명품이니?
➡ _____

2. B: 나는 시계라고 말하겠어. 그것이 없으면 시간을 알 수 없어.
➡ _____

3. C: 나는 동의하지 않아. 나는 휴대전화가 가장 위대한 발명품이라고 생각해.
➡ _____

4. D: 네 말이 맞아.
➡ _____

All Ears

1. M: 1. 나는 그 문제에 대하여 너에게 동의하지 않아.
➡ _____

　　2. 나는 네가 그 계획을 좋아하지 않는 다는 것을 알지 못했어.
➡ _____

2. 2. A: 나는 동물원에 갈 수 있어서 기뻐.
➡ _____

3. 3. B: 동물원에 가니? 좋겠구나.
➡ _____

4. 4. A: 나는 간식을 먹을 시간이 있다고 생각해.
➡ _____

5. 5. B: 나는 동의하지 않아. 너는 서둘러 되돌아가야 해.
➡ _____

Wrap Up - Reading

1. Isabel은 케냐의 Kakamega 인근 마을에 살고 있다.
➡ _____

2. 예전에 그녀는 깨끗한 물을 구하기 위해 매일 먼 거리를 걸어야 했다.
➡ _____

3. 그녀는 가끔 그녀가 마신 더러운 물로 인해 병에 걸리기도 했다.
➡ _____

4. 석달 전 그녀는 자원봉사자 한 명에게서 귀한 선물을 받았다.
➡ _____

5. 그것은 두꺼운 빨대처럼 생겼다.
➡ _____

6. 더러운 물이 빨대로 들어가면 깨끗한 물이 나온다.
➡ _____

7. Isabel은 그것을 어디나 가지고 다닌다.
➡ _____

8. 이제 그녀는 더 이상 병에 걸리지 않는다.
➡ _____

9. 매일 학교에 갈 수 있다.
➡ _____

10. 그래서 그 빨대는 Isabel에게 가장 귀중한 것이다.
➡ _____

※ 다음 영어를 우리말로 쓰시오.

01 rub

02 defend

03 chestnut

04 beehive

05 hold

06 unbelievable

07 endangered

08 Arctic

09 skinny

10 stripe

11 offer

12 entire

13 male

14 exchange

15 flesh

16 sensitive

17 faraway

18 lung

19 breathe

20 underwater

21 nap

22 protect

23 female

24 social

25 appear

26 chemical

27 except

28 extremely

29 including

30 billion

31 hardly

32 weigh

33 colony

34 resident

35 pass on

36 have a hard time

37 learn by heart

38 out of nowhere

39 cost an arm and a leg

40 one another

41 keep an eye on

42 have a long face

43 be all ears

※ 다음 우리말을 영어로 쓰시오.

01	줄무늬		22	무게가 나가다
02	북극의		23	군락, 군집
03	여윈, 두께가 얇은		24	전체의
04	~에 민감한, 예민한		25	남성의, 수컷의
05	벌집		26	방어하다
06	나타나다, (글 속에) 나오다		27	문지르다, 비비다
07	화학물질		28	여성의, 암컷의
08	수용하다, 지니다		29	폐
09	믿을 수 없는		30	호흡하다
10	살, 고기		31	수중의, 물속의
11	낮잠		32	생산하다, 만들어 내다
12	거주자		33	교환하다
13	멀리 떨어진		34	백만
14	밤		35	알을 낳다
15	~을 제외하고		36	어디선지 모르게, 느닷없이
16	보호하다		37	서로
17	극심하게		38	~을 지켜보다, ~을 감시하다
18	~을 포함하여		39	암기하다
19	위험에 처한, 멸종 위기의		40	어려움을 겪다
20	십억		41	~을 돌보다
21	거의 ~않다		42	경청하다
			43	표정이 우울하다

※ 다음 영영풀이에 알맞은 단어를 <보기>에서 골라 쓴 후, 우리말 뜻을 쓰시오.

1 _____ : to have a particular weight: _____

2 _____ : to protect somebody/something from attack: _____

3 _____ : relating to the most northern part of the world: _____

4 _____ : a structure where bees are kept for producing honey: _____

5 _____ : a short sleep, especially during the day: _____

6 _____ : very thin, especially in a way that you find unpleasant or ugly: _____

7 _____ : to take air into your lungs and send it out again through your nose or mouth: _____

8 _____ : a long narrow line of colour, that is a different colour from the areas next to it: _____

9 _____ : to decide which one of a number of things or people you want: _____

10 _____ : someone who lives or stays in a particular place: _____

11 _____ : to like someone or something more than someone or something else: _____

12 _____ : a large round fruit with hard green skin, red flesh, and black seeds: _____

13 _____ : a small creature such as a fly or ant, that has six legs, and sometimes wings: _____

14 _____ : a group of animals or plants of the same type that are living or growing together: _____

15 _____ : the act of giving someone something and receiving something else from them: _____

16 _____ : to put someone or something in a situation in which they could be harmed or damaged: _____

보기			
stripe	endangered	insect	colony
weigh	choose	watermelon	prefer
exchange	breathe	nap	skinny
resident	defend	beehive	Arctic

※ 다음 우리말과 일치하도록 빈칸에 알맞은 말을 쓰시오.

Listen – Listen and Answer – Dialog 1

B: Amber, _____ do you _____ the camp?

G: It's _____. I'm _____ _____ _____ _____ fun.

B: _____, too. The talent _____ last night was really _____.

G: Yeah. _____ _____ _____, did you _____ on the afternoon program?

B: No, I haven't _____. _____ do you _____ is _____, hiking or _____?

G: I'll go _____ because we can _____ _____ birds and _____ in the woods.

B: I'll _____ you. I like _____ and _____.

G: Great. I _____ we'll have a hiking _____.

B: Sounds good.

Listen – Listen and Answer – Dialog 2

W: Everyone, _____ at this _____ tree. This is _____ _____ tree in these _____.

B: Can you _____ me _____ _____ _____ _____ _____?

W: It's _____ 150 years old.

B: Wow! It's _____ _____ my _____.

G: Ms. Oh, is that a _____ _____ in the tree?

W: Yes. Can you _____ how many _____ _____ there?

G: 500 bees?

W: Good _____, but it's _____ _____ to _____ 50,000 bees.

B, G: _____!

Listen More - Listen and choose.

B: Sora, can you _____ a _____ _____ these pictures?

G: _____ are these _____?

B: I'm _____ to _____ a picture for my _____ in the school newspaper.

G: _____ your story _____?

B: Nature's _____.

G: Can you _____ me _____ _____ _____ it?

B: It's about _____ _____ in the _____ _____.

G: That _____ interesting.

B: _____ _____ do you _____ is _____?

G: I like the one _____ a _____ polar bear.

B: Amber, 캠프 어때?

G: 좋아. 아주 재미있어.

B: 나도 그래. 어젯밤 장기 자랑은 정말 멋졌어.

G: 맞아. 그런데 너는 오후 프로그램 결정했니?

B: 아니, 아직 못했어. 너는 산행과 수영 중에 뭐가 낫다고 생각해?

G: 숲에서 야생 조류와 곤충을 볼 수 있으니까 난 산행을 할 거야.

B: 나도 같이할게. 나는 새와 곤충을 좋아하거든.

G: 좋아. 산행 가이드가 있을 거라고 들었어.

B: 잘됐다.

W: 여러분, 이 밤나무를 보세요. 이것은 이 숲에서 가장 오래된 나무랍니다.

B: 그 나무가 몇 살인지 알려 주실 수 있나요?

W: 150살쯤 되었어요.

B: 와! 제 나이의 열 배군요.

G: 오 선생님, 나무 위에 있는 저것은 벌집인가요?

W: 맞아요. 벌이 저곳에서 몇 마리나 사는지 짐작할 수 있겠어요?

G: 500마리요?

W: 좋은 추측입니다. 하지만 저것은 5만 마리 이상을 수용할 만큼 커요.

B, G: 믿을 수 없어요!

B: 소라야, 이 사진들을 한번 봐 줄래?

G: 어디에 쓸 건데?

B: 학교 신문에 실을 내 이야기에 넣을 사진을 고르고 있어.

G: 네 이야기가 무엇에 관한 건데?

B: 자연의 미래.

G: 그것에 대해 더 말해 줄 수 있니?

B: 북극 지역에 사는 멸종 위기의 동물들에 관한 거야.

G: 흥미롭다.

B: 네 생각에는 어느 사진이 더 낫니?

G: 나는 여윈 북극곰을 보여 주는 사진이 마음에 들어.

Speak – Talk in groups.

A: _____ do _____ _____, dogs or cats?

B: I _____ dogs _____. They are more _____. _____ _____ you?

C: I _____ cats _____.

D: _____, too. Cats are _____ _____ than dogs.

Speak – Talk in pairs.

A: What _____ you _____?

B: An _____.

A: What's an elephant?

B: It's an _____.

A: Can you _____ _____ _____ _____ it?

B: It's a _____ animal _____ _____ a long nose and big ears.

My Speaking Portfolio Step 1

1. People _____ to the _____ and _____ the forest. Many of my friends have _____ their homes. I don't know _____ to go.

2. I get _____ _____ I have to _____ a big street. This morning I was _____ _____. I don't _____ _____ people are _____ _____ _____ _____.

3. I have a _____ _____. I _____ _____ _____ _____. I think it's _____ someone _____ _____ the sea.

4. Sometimes I _____ _____ not because it's _____ _____ but because it's _____ _____. When lights are too bright, I can't tell _____ _____ _____ _____.

Wrap Up – Listening & Speaking ⑤

G: What do you _____ in your _____ _____?

B: I _____ _____ music _____ EDM or hip-hop.

G: _____ do you _____ _____?

B: I _____ hip-hop.

G: Why?

B: Well, it _____ _____ _____.

※ 다음 우리말에 맞도록 대화를 영어로 쓰시오.

Listen – Listen and Answer – Dialog 1

B: _____

G: _____

B: _____

G: _____

B: _____

G: _____

B: _____

G: _____

B: _____

Listen – Listen and Answer – Dialog 2

W: _____

B: _____

W: _____

B: _____

G: _____

W: _____

G: _____

W: _____

B, G: _____

Listen More - Listen and choose.

B: _____

G: _____

B: _____

G: _____

B: _____

G: _____

B: _____

G: _____

B: _____

G: _____

Speak – Talk in groups.

A: _____

B: _____

C: _____

D: _____

A: 개와 고양이 중에 어느 것을 더 좋아하니?
B: 개를 더 좋아해. 그들이 더 친절해. 너는 어떠니?
C: 나는 고양이를 더 좋아해.
D: 나도 그래. 고양이가 개보다 훨씬 더 깨끗해.

Speak – Talk in pairs.

A: _____

B: _____

A: _____

B: _____

A: _____

B: _____

A: 너는 무엇을 그리고 있니?
B: 코끼리.
A: 코끼리가 뭐니?
B: 그것은 동물이야.
A: 그것에 대하여 더 말해 줄 수 있니?
B: 그것은 긴 코와 큰 귀를 가진 덩치 큰 동물이야.

My Speaking Portfolio Step 1

1. _____
   _____

2. _____
   _____

3. _____
   _____

4. _____
   _____

1. 사람들이 숲에 와서 삼림을 파괴해요. 내 친구들 중 많은 수가 집을 잃었어요. 나는 어디로 가야 할지 모르겠어요.
2. 나는 큰 길을 건너야 할 때마다 겁이 나요. 오늘 아침 나는 차에 치일 뻔했다고요. 사람들이 왜 그리 급한지 이해가 안 돼요.
3. 나는 배가 몹시 아파요. 나는 이상한 것을 먹었어요. 내 생각에 그것은 누군가 바다에 버린 것 같아요.
4. 때때로 나는 너무 어두워서가 아니라 너무 밝아서 길을 잃어요. 불빛이 너무 밝으면 나는 어디로 날아가야 할지 분간할 수 없어요.

Wrap Up - Listening & Speaking ⑤

G: _____

B: _____

G: _____

B: _____

G: _____

B: _____

여: 너는 한가한 시간에 뭘 하니?
남: 나는 EDM이나 힙합 같은 음악을 들어.
여: 어떤 것을 더 좋아하는데?
남: 나는 힙합을 더 좋아해.
여: 왜?
남: 글쎄. 그게 더 신나거든.

※ 다음 우리말과 일치하도록 빈칸에 알맞은 것을 골라 쓰시오.

1 The _____ _____
    A. Ants   B. Amazing

2 For the science _____, our group _____ _____ very special _____.
    A. chosen   B. project   C. has   D. insects

3 They are _____ _____.
    A. social   B. very

4 They are _____ _____ as the T-Rex.
    A. old   B. as

5 They _____ in Aesop's _____.
    A. stories   B. appear

6 They _____ a special _____ to _____.
    A. communicate   B. use   C. chemical

7 Can you _____ _____ they _____?
    A. are   B. what   C. guess

8 Yes, the _____ is _____.
    A. ants   B. answer

9 We want to _____ _____ you _____ we have _____ about these insects.
    A. what   B. share   C. learned   D. with

10 _____ _____ Ants Are _____ Earth?
    A. on   B. Many   C. How

11 We often see ants come _____ _____ _____.
    A. out   B. nowhere   C. of

12 _____ humans, they live almost everywhere in the world, _____ a few _____ cold places _____ Antarctica.
    A. except   B. like   C. including   D. extremely

13 _____ _____ 2018, there were _____ 7 _____ people on Earth.
    A. over   B. as   C. billion   D. of

14 Then, _____ _____ ants?
    A. about   B. how

15 _____ _____ scientists, there are _____ one million ants for _____ human in the world.
    A. every   B. according   C. about   D. to

16 Though each ant _____ weighs _____, one million ants are as _____ as a human being _____ about 62 kilograms.
    A. weighing   B. heavy   C. hardly   D. anything

17 What _____ the Ant Society _____?
    A. Like   B. Is

18 Ants live in _____ which have _____ of _____ _____ together.
    A. residents   B. colonies   C. living   D. lots

19 _____ a colony, there are usually _____ _____ _____ of ants.
    A. three   B. types   C. within   D. different

---

1 놀라운 개미

2 과학 프로젝트를 위해, 우리 모둠은 매우 특별한 곤충을 선택했습니다.

3 그들은 매우 사회적입니다.

4 그들은 티라노사우루스만큼 오래되었습니다.

5 그들은 이솝 이야기에 등장합니다.

6 그들은 의사소통하기 위해 특별한 화학물질을 사용합니다.

7 그들이 어떤 곤충인지 추측할 수 있나요?

8 네. 정답은 개미입니다.

9 저희들은 이 곤충에 관해 알게 된 것을 여러분과 함께 나누고 싶습니다.

10 지구상에는 얼마나 많은 개미가 있을까?

11 우리는 종종 난데없이 나타나는 개미들을 본다.

12 인간처럼, 개미도 남극을 포함한 일부 극도로 추운 곳을 제외한 전 세계 거의 모든 곳에 살고 있다.

13 2018년 현재, 지구상에 70억이 넘는 인구가 있었다.

14 그렇다면. 개미는 어떨까?

15 과학자들에 의하면, 세상에는 사람 한 명당 약 백만 마리의 개미가 있다.

16 개미 한 마리는 거의 무게가 나가지 않지만 백만 마리의 개미는 체중이 약 62kg인 사람 한 명과 무게가 같다.

17 개미 사회는 어떠할까?

18 개미는 많은 거주자가 함께 사는 군집을 이루어 산다.

19 군집 안에는 보통 세 가지 다른 종류의 개미가 있다.

20 There is the queen, and _____ she does her _____ life is _____ eggs.
A. entire   B. what   C. lay

21 The second _____ of ant is the _____ that helps the queen _____ these eggs.
A. male   B. produce   C. type

22 The _____ _____ of ant is the _____.
A. type   B. worker   C. third

23 Worker ants are all female and do very important jobs, _____ _____ for eggs, _____ the colony, and _____ food.
A. like   B. collecting   C. defending   D. caring

24 _____ Do Ants _____?
A. Communicate   B. How

25 _____ ants do not speak _____ _____, they have a "language."
A. like   B. though   C. actually   D. humans

26 Ants produce a chemical _____ a pheromone to _____ one _____.
A. another   B. called   C. with   D. communicate

27 _____ _____ the chemical, they can _____ _____ about food or danger.
A. using   B. information   C. by   D. exchange

28 Ants also use _____ _____ _____.
A. for   B. touch   C. communication

29 _____ example, if an ant finds food, it passes on the good news _____ its body _____ its neighbor.
A. on   B. rubbing   C. for   D. by

30 _____ an ant has legs _____ very sensitive hairs, it can sense even the _____ touch.
A. with   B. smallest   C. covered   D. since

31 _____ _____ ABOUT _____
A. ANTS   B. FACTS   C. FUN

32 01 Some Queen ants _____ _____ _____ 30 years.
A. up   B. live   C. to

33 02 Some ants can _____ things that are 50 _____ their own _____.
A. weight   B. carry   C. times   D. body

34 03 Ants do not have _____ but _____ _____ small holes in their bodies.
A. through   B. lungs   C. breathe

35 04 An _____ has two _____.
A. stomachs   B. ant

36 _____ stomach holds food for _____, and the _____ holds food to share _____ others.
A. other   B. itself   C. one   D. with

37 05 _____ _____ can swim and _____ 24 hours _____.
A. underwater   B. ants   C. live   D. most

20 여왕개미가 있고, 그녀가 평생 하는 일은 알을 낳는 것이다.

21 두 번째 종류는 여왕이 알을 낳는 것을 돕는 수개미이다.

22 세 번째 종류는 일개미이다.

23 일개미는 모두 암컷인데, 알을 돌보고, 군집을 방어하며, 먹이를 모으는 것과 같은 매우 중요한 일을 한다.

24 개미는 어떻게 의사소통할까?

25 개미들이 인간처럼 말을 하는 것은 아니지만, 그들은 실제로 '언어'를 가지고 있다.

26 개미는 서로 소통하기 위해 '페로몬'이라고 불리는 화학물질을 분비한다.

27 그 화학물질을 사용하여 그들은 먹이나 위험에 관한 정보를 교환할 수 있다.

28 개미는 또한 의사소통을 위해 접촉을 이용한다.

29 예를 들어, 먹이를 발견할 경우 개미는 자기 몸을 이웃의 개미에게 문질러서 좋은 소식을 전달한다.

30 개미는 (자극에) 매우 민감한 털로 덮인 다리가 있기 때문에, 아주 미세한 접촉도 감지할 수 있다.

31 개미에 관한 재미있는 사실

32 01 어떤 여왕개미는 30년까지 살 수 있다.

33 02 어떤 개미들은 자기 몸무게의 50배에 달하는 것을 들 수 있다.

34 03 개미는 폐가 없지만, 몸에 있는 작은 구멍을 통해 호흡한다.

35 04 개미는 위가 두 개 있다.

36 하나에는 자신의 먹이를 저장하고 다른 하나에는 다른 개미들과 함께 나눌 먹이를 저장한다.

37 05 대부분의 개미는 수영할 수 있고 물속에서 24시간 동안 살 수 있다.

※ 다음 우리말과 일치하도록 빈칸에 알맞은 말을 쓰시오.

1 The _____ _____

2 _____ _____ _____ _____, our group _____ _____ very _____ _____.

3 They are very _____.

4 They are _____ _____ _____ the T-Rex.

5 They _____ in _____ _____.

6 They use _____ _____ _____ to _____.

7 Can you _____ _____ _____ _____ _____?

8 Yes, _____ _____ is _____.

9 We want to _____ _____ you _____ we _____ _____ about these insects.

10 _____ _____ _____ Are _____ Earth?

11 We often see ants come _____ _____ _____.

12 _____ _____, they live almost everywhere in the world, _____ a few _____ cold places _____ _____.

13 _____ _____ _____, there were _____ 7 _____ _____ on Earth.

14 Then, _____ _____ ants?

15 _____ _____ _____, there are about one million ants _____ _____ _____ in the world.

16 Though each ant _____ _____ _____, one million ants are _____ _____ _____ a human _____ _____ about 62 kilograms.

17 What _____ the Ant Society _____?

18 Ants live in colonies _____ _____ lots of _____ _____ together.

19 _____ a _____, there are usually _____ _____ _____ of ants.

1 놀라운 개미

2 과학 프로젝트를 위해, 우리 모둠은 매우 특별한 곤충을 선택했습니다.

3 그들은 매우 사회적입니다.

4 그들은 티라노사우루스만큼 오래되었습니다.

5 그들은 이솝 이야기에 등장합니다.

6 그들은 의사소통하기 위해 특별한 화학물질을 사용합니다.

7 그들이 어떤 곤충인지 추측할 수 있나요?

8 네. 정답은 개미입니다.

9 저희들은 이 곤충에 관해 알게 된 것을 여러분과 함께 나누고 싶습니다.

10 지구상에는 얼마나 많은 개미가 있을까?

11 우리는 종종 난데없이 나타나는 개미들을 본다.

12 인간처럼, 개미도 남극을 포함한 일부 극도로 추운 곳을 제외한 전 세계 거의 모든 곳에 살고 있다.

13 2018년 현재, 지구상에 70억이 넘는 인구가 있었다.

14 그렇다면, 개미는 어떨까?

15 과학자들에 의하면, 세상에는 사람 한 명당 약 백만 마리의 개미가 있다.

16 개미 한 마리는 거의 무게가 나가지 않지만 백만 마리의 개미는 체중이 약 62kg인 사람 한 명과 무게가 같다.

17 개미 사회는 어떠할까?

18 개미는 많은 거주자가 함께 사는 군집을 이루어 산다.

19 군집 안에는 보통 세 가지 다른 종류의 개미가 있다.

20 There is the queen, and _____ _____ _____ her entire life is _____ _____.

21 The _____ _____ of ant is the _____ that helps the queen _____ _____ _____.

22 _____ _____ _____ of ant is the _____.

23 Worker ants are all female and do very important jobs, _____ _____ _____ eggs, _____ the colony, and _____ food.

24 _____ Do Ants _____?

25 _____ ants do not speak _____ _____, they _____ _____ a "language."

26 Ants produce a chemical _____ a pheromone _____ _____ _____ _____ _____.

27 _____ _____ the chemical, they can _____ _____ about food or _____.

28 Ants also use _____ _____ _____.

29 _____ _____, if an ant finds food, it passes on the good news _____ _____ its body _____ _____ _____.

30 Since an ant has legs _____ _____ very sensitive hairs, it can sense _____ _____ _____ _____.

31 _____ _____ ABOUT ANTS

32 01 Some Queen ants _____ _____ _____ 30 years.

33 02 Some ants can _____ _____ that are _____ _____ _____ _____ _____.

34 03 Ants do not have lungs but _____ _____ _____ _____ in their bodies.

35 04 An ant has _____ _____.

36 _____ stomach holds food _____ _____, and _____ holds food to _____ _____ others.

37 05 _____ _____ can swim and live 24 hours _____.

20 여왕개미가 있고. 그녀가 평생 하는 일은 알을 낳는 것이다.

21 두 번째 종류는 여왕이 알을 낳는 것을 돕는 수개미이다.

22 세 번째 종류는 일개미이다.

23 일개미는 모두 암컷인데, 알을 돌보고, 군집을 방어하며, 먹이를 모으는 것과 같은 매우 중요한 일을 한다.

24 개미는 어떻게 의사소통할까?

25 개미들이 인간처럼 말을 하는 것은 아니지만, 그들은 실제로 '언어'를 가지고 있다.

26 개미는 서로 소통하기 위해 '페로몬'이라고 불리는 화학물질을 분비한다.

27 그 화학물질을 사용하여 그들은 먹이나 위험에 관한 정보를 교환할 수 있다.

28 개미는 또한 의사소통을 위해 접촉을 이용한다.

29 예를 들어, 먹이를 발견할 경우 개미는 자기 몸을 이웃의 개미에게 문질러서 좋은 소식을 전달한다.

30 개미는 (자극에) 매우 민감한 털로 덮인 다리가 있기 때문에, 아주 미세한 접촉도 감지할 수 있다.

31 개미에 관한 재미있는 사실

32 01 어떤 여왕개미는 30년까지 살 수 있다.

33 02 어떤 개미들은 자기 몸무게의 50배에 달하는 것을 들 수 있다.

34 03 개미는 폐가 없지만, 몸에 있는 작은 구멍을 통해 호흡한다.

35 04 개미는 위가 두 개 있다.

36 하나에는 자신의 먹이를 저장하고 다른 하나에는 다른 개미들과 함께 나눌 먹이를 저장한다.

37 05 대부분의 개미는 수영할 수 있고 물속에서 24시간 동안 살 수 있다.

※ 다음 문장을 우리말로 쓰시오.

1 The Amazing Ants

➡ _____

2 For the science project, our group has chosen very special insects.

➡ _____

3 They are very social.

➡ _____

4 They are as old as the T-Rex.

➡ _____

5 They appear in Aesop's stories.

➡ _____

6 They use a special chemical to communicate.

➡ _____

7 Can you guess what they are?

➡ _____

8 Yes, the answer is ants.

➡ _____

9 We want to share with you what we have learned about these insects.

➡ _____

10 How Many Ants Are on Earth?

➡ _____

11 We often see ants come out of nowhere.

➡ _____

12 Like humans, they live almost everywhere in the world, except a few extremely cold places including Antarctica.

➡ _____

13 As of 2018, there were over 7 billion people on Earth.

➡ _____

14 Then, how about ants?

➡ _____

15 According to scientists, there are about one million ants for every human in the world..

➡ _____

16 Though each ant hardly weighs anything, one million ants are as heavy as a human being weighing about 62 kilograms.

➡ _____

17 What Is the Ant Society Like?

➡ _____

18 Ants live in colonies which have lots of residents living together.

➡ _____

19 Within a colony, there are usually three different types of ants.

➡ _____

20 There is the queen, and what she does her entire life is lay eggs.

➡ _____

21 The second type of ant is the male that helps the queen produce these eggs.

➡ _____

22 The third type of ant is the worker.

➡ _____

23 Worker ants are all female and do very important jobs, like caring for eggs, defending the colony, and collecting food.

➡ _____

24 How Do Ants Communicate?

➡ _____

25 Though ants do not speak like humans, they actually have a "language."

➡ _____

26 Ants produce a chemical called a pheromone to communicate with one another.

➡ _____

27 By using the chemical, they can exchange information about food or danger.

➡ _____

28 Ants also use touch for communication.

➡ _____

29 For example, if an ant finds food, it passes on the good news by rubbing its body on its neighbor.

➡ _____

30 Since an ant has legs covered with very sensitive hairs, it can sense even the smallest touch.

➡ _____

31 FUN FACTS ABOUT ANTS

➡ _____

32 01 Some Queen ants live up to 30 years.

➡ _____

33 02 Some ants can carry things that are 50 times their own body weight.

➡ _____

34 03 Ants do not have lungs but breathe through small holes in their bodies.

➡ _____

35 04 An ant has two stomachs.

➡ _____

36 One stomach holds food for itself, and the other holds food to share with others.

➡ _____

37 05 Most ants can swim and live 24 hours underwater.

➡ _____

Step4

※ 다음 괄호 안의 단어들을 우리말에 맞도록 바르게 배열하시오.

1 (Amazing / The / Ants)

➡ _____

2 (the / for / project, / science / group / our / chosen / has / special / very / insects.)

➡ _____

3 (are / they / social. / very)

➡ _____

4 (are / they / old / as / the / as / T-Rex.)

➡ _____

5 (appear / they / Aesop's / in / stories.)

➡ _____

6 (use / they / special / a / to / communicate. / chemical)

➡ _____

7 (you / can / what / guess / are? / they)

➡ _____

8 (yes, / answer / the / ants. / is)

➡ _____

9 (want / we / share / to / you / with / we / what / learned / have / these / insects. / about)

➡ _____

10 (Many / How / Are / Ants / Earth? / on)

➡ _____

11 (often / we / ants / see / out / come / nowhere. / of)

➡ _____

12 (humans, / like / live / they / everywhere / almost / the / in / world, / a / except / extremely / few / places / cold / Antarctica. / including)

➡ _____

➡ _____

13 (of / as / 2018, / were / there / 7 / over / people / billion / Earth. / on)

➡ _____

14 (how / then, / ants? / about)

➡ _____

1 놀라운 개미

2 과학 프로젝트를 위해, 우리 모둠은 매우 특별한 곤충을 선택했습니다.

3 그들은 매우 사회적입니다.

4 그들은 티라노사우루스만큼 오래되었습니다.

5 그들은 이솝 이야기에 등장합니다.

6 그들은 의사소통하기 위해 특별한 화학물질을 사용합니다.

7 그들이 어떤 곤충인지 추측할 수 있나요?

8 네. 정답은 개미입니다.

9 저희들은 이 곤충에 관해 알게 된 것을 여러분과 함께 나누고 싶습니다.

10 지구상에는 얼마나 많은 개미가 있을까?

11 우리는 종종 난데없이 나타나는 개미들을 본다.

12 인간처럼, 개미도 남극을 포함한 일부 극도로 추운 곳을 제외한 전 세계 거의 모든 곳에 살고 있다.

13 2018년 현재. 지구상에 70억이 넘는 인구가 있었다.

14 그렇다면. 개미는 어떨까?

15 (to / according / scientists, / are / there / one / about / million / for / ants / human / every / the / world. / in)

➡ _____

16 (each / though / hardly / ant / anything, / weighs / million / one / ants / as / are / heavy / a / as / being / human / about / weighing / kilograms. / 62)

➡ _____

17 (Is / What / Ant / the / Like? / Society)

➡ _____

18 (live / ants / colonies / in / have / which / of / lots / residents / together. / living)

➡ _____

19 (a / within / colony, / are / there / three / usually / types / different / ants. / of)

➡ _____

20 (is / there / queen, / the / what / and / does / she / entire / her / is / life / eggs. / lay)

➡ _____

21 (second / the / of / type / is / ant / male / the / that / the / helps / queen / these / produce / eggs.)

➡ _____

22 (third / the / of / type / ant / the / is / worker.)

➡ _____

23 (ants / worker / all / are / and / female / very / do / important / jobs, / caring / like / eggs, / for / the / defending / colony, / collecting / and / food.)

➡ _____

24 (Do / How / Communicate? / Ants)

➡ _____

25 (ants / though / not / do / speak / humans, / like / actually / they / a / "language." / have)

➡ _____

26 (produce / ants / chemical / a / called / pheromone / a / communicate / to / one / with / another.)

➡ _____

27 (using / by / chemical, / the / can / they / information / exchange / about / danger. / or / food)

➡ _____
_____

15 과학자들에 의하면, 세상에는 사람 한 명당 약 백만 마리의 개미가 있다.

16 개미 한 마리는 거의 무게가 나가지 않지만 백만 마리의 개미는 체중이 약 62kg인 사람 한 명과 무게가 같다.

17 개미 사회는 어떠할까?

18 개미는 많은 거주자가 함께 사는 군집을 이루어 산다.

19 군집 안에는 보통 세 가지 다른 종류의 개미가 있다.

20 여왕개미가 있고, 그녀가 평생 하는 일은 알을 낳는 것이다.

21 두 번째 종류는 여왕이 알을 낳는 것을 돕는 수개미이다.

22 세 번째 종류는 일개미이다.

23 일개미는 모두 암컷인데, 알을 돌보고, 군집을 방어하며, 먹이를 모으는 것과 같은 매우 중요한 일을 한다.

24 개미는 어떻게 의사소통할까?

25 개미들이 인간처럼 말을 하는 것은 아니지만, 그들은 실제로 '언어'를 가지고 있다.

26 개미는 서로 소통하기 위해 '페로몬'이라고 불리는 화학물질을 분비한다.

27 그 화학물질을 사용하여 그들은 먹이나 위험에 관한 정보를 교환할 수 있다.

28 (also / ants / touch / use / communication. / for)

➡ _____

29 (example, / for / an / if / finds / ant / food, / passes / it / the / on / good / by / news / rubbing / body / its / its / on / neighbor.)

➡ _____

_____

30 (an / since / has / ant / legs / with / covered / sensitive / very / hairs, / can / it / even / sense / smallest / the / touch.)

➡ _____

_____

31 (FACTS / FUN / ANTS / ABOUT)

➡ _____

32 (01 / Queen / Some / live / ants / up / 30 / to / years.)

➡ _____

33 (02 / ants / some / carry / can / that / things / are / times / 50 / own / their / weight. / body)

➡ _____

34 (03 / do / ants / have / not / but / lungs / through / breathe / holes / small / their / bodies. / in)

➡ _____

_____

35 (04 / ant / an / two / has / stomachs.)

➡ _____

36 (stomach / one / food / holds / itself, / for / and / other / the / food / holds / to / with / share / others.)

➡ _____

_____

37 (05 / ants / most / swim / can / and / 24 / live / underwater. / hours)

➡ _____

28 개미는 또한 의사소통을 위해 접촉을 이용한다.

29 예를 들어, 먹이를 발견할 경우 개미는 자기 몸을 이웃의 개미에게 문질러서 좋은 소식을 전달한다.

30 개미는 (자극에) 매우 민감한 털로 덮인 다리가 있기 때문에, 아주 미세한 접촉도 감지할 수 있다.

31 개미에 관한 재미있는 사실

32 01 어떤 여왕개미는 30년까지 살 수 있다.

33 02 어떤 개미들은 자기 몸무게의 50배에 달하는 것을 들 수 있다.

34 03 개미는 폐가 없지만, 몸에 있는 작은 구멍을 통해 호흡한다.

35 04 개미는 위가 두 개 있다.

36 하나에는 자신의 먹이를 저장하고 다른 하나에는 다른 개미들과 함께 나눌 먹이를 저장한다.

37 05 대부분의 개미는 수영할 수 있고 물속에서 24시간 동안 살 수 있다.

※ 다음 우리말을 영어로 쓰시오.

1 놀라운 개미
➡ _____

2 과학 프로젝트를 위해, 우리 모둠은 매우 특별한 곤충을 선택했습니다.
➡ _____

3 그들은 매우 사회적입니다.
➡ _____

4 그들은 티라노사우루스만큼 오래되었습니다.
➡ _____

5 그들은 이솝 이야기에 등장합니다.
➡ _____

6 그들은 의사소통하기 위해 특별한 화학물질을 사용합니다.
➡ _____

7 그들이 어떤 곤충인지 추측할 수 있나요?
➡ _____

8 네. 정답은 개미입니다.
➡ _____

9 저희들은 이 곤충에 관해 알게 된 것을 여러분과 함께 나누고 싶습니다.
➡ _____

10 지구상에는 얼마나 많은 개미가 있을까?
➡ _____

11 우리는 종종 난데없이 나타나는 개미들을 본다.
➡ _____

12 인간처럼, 개미도 남극을 포함한 일부 극도로 추운 곳을 제외한 전 세계 거의 모든 곳에 살고 있다.
➡ _____

13 2018년 현재, 지구상에 70억이 넘는 인구가 있었다.
➡ _____

14 그렇다면. 개미는 어떨까?
➡ _____

15 과학자들에 의하면, 세상에는 사람 한 명당 약 백만 마리의 개미가 있다.
➡ _____

16 개미 한 마리는 거의 무게가 나가지 않지만 백만 마리의 개미는 체중이 약 62kg인 사람 한 명과 무게가 같다.
➡ _____

17 개미 사회는 어떠할까?
➡ _____

18 개미는 많은 거주자가 함께 사는 군집을 이루어 산다.
➡ _____

19 군집 안에는 보통 세 가지 다른 종류의 개미가 있다.

➡ _____

20 여왕개미가 있고. 그녀가 평생 하는 일은 알을 낳는 것이다.

➡ _____

21 두 번째 종류는 여왕이 알을 낳는 것을 돕는 수개미이다.

➡ _____

22 세 번째 종류는 일개미이다.

➡ _____

23 일개미는 모두 암컷인데, 알을 돌보고, 군집을 방어하며, 먹이를 모으는 것과 같은 매우 중요한 일을 한다.

➡ _____

24 개미는 어떻게 의사소통할까?

➡ _____

25 개미들이 인간처럼 말을 하는 것은 아니지만, 그들은 실제로 '언어'를 가지고 있다.

➡ _____

26 개미는 서로 소통하기 위해 '페로몬'이라고 불리는 화학물질을 분비한다.

➡ _____

27 그 화학물질을 사용하여 그들은 먹이나 위험에 관한 정보를 교환할 수 있다.

➡ _____

28 개미는 또한 의사소통을 위해 접촉을 이용한다.

➡ _____

29 예를 들어, 먹이를 발견할 경우 개미는 자기 몸을 이웃의 개미에게 문질러서 좋은 소식을 전달한다.

➡ _____

30 개미는 (자극에) 매우 민감한 털로 덮인 다리가 있기 때문에, 아주 미세한 접촉도 감지할 수 있다.

➡ _____

31 개미에 관한 재미있는 사실

➡ _____

32 01 어떤 여왕개미는 30년까지 살 수 있다.

➡ _____

33 02 어떤 개미들은 자기 몸무게의 50배에 달하는 것을 들 수 있다.

➡ _____

34 03 개미는 폐가 없지만, 몸에 있는 작은 구멍을 통해 호흡한다.

➡ _____

35 04 개미는 위가 두 개 있다.

➡ _____

36 하나에는 자신의 먹이를 저장하고 다른 하나에는 다른 개미들과 함께 나눌 먹이를 저장한다.

➡ _____

37 05 대부분의 개미는 수영할 수 있고 물속에서 24시간 동안 살 수 있다.

➡ _____

※ 다음 우리말과 일치하도록 빈칸에 알맞은 말을 쓰시오.

Communicate: Speak

1. A: _____ do you _____, pizza or fried chicken?

2. B: I like pizza better. I can _____ _____ _____ _____
   _____. _____ _____ you?

3. A: I _____ fried chicken _____.

4. C: _____, _____. I'm a _____ _____.

1. A: 피자와 치킨 중 어느 것을 좋아하니?
2. B: 피자를 더 좋아해. 나는 내가 좋아하는 토핑을 고를 수 있어. 너는 어떠니?
3. A: 나는 프라이드 치킨을 더 좋아해.
4. C: 나도 그래. 나는 고기를 좋아해.

My Speaking Portfolio

1. M: Honeybees _____ _____ _____ in warm places which
   _____ _____ _____ and flowers.

2. A queen _____ _____ _____ five years, but worker bees
   _____ _____ _____ about seven weeks.

3. Honeybees go _____ flower _____ flower _____
   _____.

4. A worker bee makes _____ _____ trips to produce _____
   _____ _____ _____ honey.

5. _____ _____ _____, honeybees _____ plants _____.

1. 남: 꿀벌은 식물과 꽃이 많은 따뜻한 곳에서 쉽게 발견된다.
2. 여왕벌은 5년까지 살지만, 일벌은 겨우 7주 정도만 산다.
3. 꿀벌은 먹이를 모으기 위해 꽃에서 꽃으로 옮겨 다닌다.
4. 일벌은 적은 양의 꿀을 만들기 위해 수백 번의 이동을 한다.
5. 여기저기 옮겨 다니면서 꿀벌은 식물이 성장하는 것을 돕는다.

Wrap Up - Reading

1. Ants _____ _____ be busy _____ _____ _____ and
   never rest.

2. But this is _____ _____.

3. Worker ants _____ _____ _____ very short naps _____
   250 times _____ _____.

4. _____ _____ these naps _____ only _____ _____
   _____.

5. This means that the worker ants sleep _____ _____ _____
   _____ _____ _____.

6. _____ _____ _____ _____, queen ants _____ _____
   90 times a day, and they sleep for about six minutes _____
   _____ _____.

7. This means _____ they sleep _____ _____ _____ _____
   _____ _____.

8. _____ _____, ants sleep and rest just _____ us _____
   they do so _____ _____ _____ _____ _____.

1. 개미는 항상 바쁘고 전혀 휴식을 취하지 않는 것처럼 보인다.
2. 하지만 이것은 사실이 아니다.
3. 일개미는 하루에 약 250번의 짧은 잠을 자며 휴식을 취한다.
4. 이 잠은 불과 1분 정도 이어진다.
5. 이것은 일개미가 하루에 4시간 정도 잠을 잔다는 의미이다.
6. 반면에, 여왕개미는 하루에 90번 잠을 자고, 한 번에 약 6분 동안 잠을 잔다.
7. 이것은 여왕개미가 하루에 약 9시간 동안 잠을 잔다는 것을 의미한다.
8. 즉, 방식이 다르기는 하지만 개미도 우리처럼 잠을 자고 휴식을 취한다.

구석구석 지문 Test

※ 다음 우리말을 영어로 쓰시오.

Communicate: Speak

1. A: 피자와 치킨 중 어느 것을 좋아하니?
   ➡ _____

2. B: 피자를 더 좋아해. 나는 내가 좋아하는 토핑을 고를 수 있어. 너는 어떠니?
   ➡ _____

3. A: 나는 프라이드 치킨을 더 좋아해.
   ➡ _____

4. C: 나도 그래. 나는 고기를 좋아해.
   ➡ _____

My Speaking Portfolio

1. 남: 꿀벌은 식물과 꽃이 많은 따뜻한 곳에서 쉽게 발견된다.
   ➡ _____

2. 여왕벌은 5년까지 살지만, 일벌은 겨우 7주 정도만 산다.
   ➡ _____

3. 꿀벌은 먹이를 모으기 위해 꽃에서 꽃으로 옮겨 다닌다.
   ➡ _____

4. 일벌은 적은 양의 꿀을 만들기 위해 수백 번의 이동을 한다.
   ➡ _____

5. 여기저기 옮겨 다니면서 꿀벌은 식물이 성장하는 것을 돕는다.
   ➡ _____

Wrap Up - Reading

1. 개미는 항상 바쁘고 전혀 휴식을 취하지 않는 것처럼 보인다.
   ➡ _____

2. 하지만 이것은 사실이 아니다.
   ➡ _____

3. 일개미는 하루에 약 250번의 짧은 잠을 자며 휴식을 취한다.
   ➡ _____

4. 이 잠은 불과 1분 정도 이어진다.
   ➡ _____

5. 이것은 일개미가 하루에 4시간 정도 잠을 잔다는 의미이다.
   ➡ _____

6. 반면에, 여왕개미는 하루에 90번 잠을 자고, 한 번에 약 6분 동안 잠을 잔다.
   ➡ _____

7. 이것은 여왕개미가 하루에 약 9시간 동안 잠을 잔다는 것을 의미한다.
   ➡ _____

8. 즉, 방식이 다르기는 하지만 개미도 우리처럼 잠을 자고 휴식을 취한다.
   ➡ _____

※ 다음 영어를 우리말로 쓰시오.

01 raise	_____	16 seem	_____
02 golf ball	_____	17 room	_____
03 same	_____	18 shake	_____
04 health	_____	19 though	_____
05 reply	_____	20 value	_____
06 matter	_____	21 spend	_____
07 fill	_____	22 suddenly	_____
08 roll	_____	23 take out	_____
09 open	_____	24 pick up	_____
10 space	_____	25 a bottle of ~	_____
11 jar	_____	26 out of	_____
12 lose	_____	27 take care of ~	_____
13 stand	_____	28 pour A into B	_____
14 full	_____	29 spend A on B	_____
15 pour	_____	30 watch+목적어 +동사원형(ing)	_____
		31 fill A with B	_____

※ 다음 우리말을 영어로 쓰시오.

01 골프공

02 건강

03 중요하다

04 열려 있는, 막혀 있지 않은

05 ~을 들어 올리다

06 채우다, 메우다

07 흔들다

08 붓다, 따르다

09 가득 찬

10 (비어 있는) 공간

11 대답하다

12 ~을 높이 평가하다, 중시하다

13 같은

14 서 있다

15 병, 항아리

16 ~으로 보이다, ~(인 것) 같다

17 잃어버리다

18 비록 ~일지라도, ~이지만

19 갑자기

20 굴러가다

21 소비하다, 쓰다

22 공간, 여지

23 ~ 밖으로, ~ 로부터

24 ~을 집어올리다

25 ~ 한 병

26 ~을 꺼내다

27 A를 B에 붓다

28 목적어가 ~하는 것을 보다

29 A를 B하는 데 소비하다

30 ~에 신경을 쓰다, ~을 돌보다

31 B로 A를 채우다

※ 다음 영영풀이에 알맞은 단어를 <보기>에서 골라 쓴 후, 우리말 뜻을 쓰시오.

1 _____ : to be important: _____

2 _____ : an empty area: _____

3 _____ : to make something full: _____

4 _____ : quickly and without any warning: _____

5 _____ : having or containing a lot of something: _____

6 _____ : to pay money for things that you want: _____

7 _____ : to say or write something as an answer to someone or something:
_____

8 _____ : to hold it and move it quickly backwards and forwards or up and down:
_____

9 _____ : a glass container with a lid and a wide top, especially one in which food
is sold or kept: _____

10 _____ : to fail to keep or to maintain; cease to have, either physically or in an
abstract sense: _____

11 _____ : to evaluate or estimate the nature, quality, ability, extent, or significance
of: _____

12 _____ : to make sure that you are/somebody is safe, well, healthy, etc.; look after
yourself/somebody: _____

보기			
value	space	lose	take care of
fill	full	spend	reply
shake	suddenly	jar	matter

※ 다음 우리말과 일치하도록 빈칸에 알맞은 것을 골라 쓰시오.

1 The _____ _____

    A. Jar   B. Full

2 Mr. Jenkins _____ _____ his _____ .

    A. before   B. stood   C. class

3 He had a large _____ and a big bag _____ the teacher's _____ .

    A. jar   B. desk   C. on

4 When the class began, he _____ _____ the jar and started to _____ it _____ **golf balls** from the bag.

    A. up   B. fill   C. picked   D. with

5 He _____ the students, "Is the _____ _____ ?"

    A. full   B. asked   C. jar

6 _____ _____ _____ , "Yes."

    A. said   B. they   C. all

7 The teacher took a box of **small stones** _____ _____ the bag and _____ them _____ the jar.

    A. poured   B. out   C. into   D. of

8 He shook the jar a _____ , and the stones _____ _____ the open areas _____ the golf balls.

    A. little   B. into   C. between   D. rolled

9 He asked the _____ _____ and got the same _____ _____ his students.

    A. question   B. answer   C. same   D. from

10 Next, the teacher _____ _____ a bottle of **sand** and _____ it _____ the jar.

    A. out   B. poured   C. took   D. into

11 After he watched the sand _____ the spaces between the stones, he asked _____ _____ , "Is the jar _____ ?"

    A. once   B. full   C. fill   D. more

12 _____ _____ students _____ , "Yes."

    A. the   B. all   C. replied

13 _____ Mr. Jenkins _____ a can of **apple juice** _____ the bag.

    A. took   B. of   C. suddenly   D. out

---

1 가득 찬 병

2 Jenkins 선생님이 교실 앞에 섰다.

3 교탁 위에는 큰 병과 커다란 가방이 놓여 있었다.

4 수업이 시작하자, 선생님은 병을 집어 들고 가방에서 꺼낸 골프공으로 채우기 시작했다.

5 그는 학생들에게 "병이 가득 찼나요?"라고 질문했다.

6 학생들은 모두 "예."라고 대답했다.

7 선생님은 가방에서 작은 돌 한 상자를 끄집어내어 병 안에 부었다.

8 그가 병을 살짝 흔들자, 돌들이 골프공 사이의 틈새로 굴러 들어갔다.

9 그는 같은 질문을 했고 학생들에게서 같은 대답을 들었다.

10 그런 다음, 선생님은 모래 병을 꺼내 병 안에 부었다.

11 모래가 돌 사이의 공간을 채우는 것을 지켜보고 나서 그는 "이 병이 가득 찼나요?"라고 한 번 더 물었다.

12 모든 학생들이 "예."라고 답했다.

13 갑자기 Jenkins 선생님은 가방에서 사과 주스 한 캔을 꺼냈다.

14 He _____ the apple juice into the jar, and his students _____ it _____ the _____ in the sand.

    A. watched   B. spaces   C. poured   D. fill

15 "Now," the teacher said, "I want you to _____ _____ your life is _____ _____ the jar.

    A. like   B. that   C. just   D. understand

16 The golf balls are _____ _____ _____ _____ in life: your family, your friends, your health, and your dreams.

    A. most   B. what   C. important   D. is

17 _____ when everything else _____ _____, your life can still be _____.

    A. lost   B. full   C. even   D. is

18 The _____ are the _____ things _____ by people, _____ your job, your house, and your car.

    A. vauled   B. like   C. other   D. stones

19 The sand is _____ _____ _____ _____."

    A. the   B. all   C. things   D. small

20 "If you put the sand into the jar first," he said, "_____ _____ _____ _____ the stones or the golf balls.

    A. no   B. for   C. there's   D. room

21 The _____ _____ _____ life.

    A. goes   B. same   C. for

22 If you _____ all your time and energy _____ the small things, you will never have _____ for _____ is really important to you.

    A. what   B. on   C. room   D. spend

23 _____ _____ of the balls first — the _____ that really _____."

    A. care   B. things   C. take   D. matter

24 One student _____ in the back _____ her hand and asked, "What does the apple juice _____?"

    A. mean   B. raised   C. sitting

25 Mr. Jenkins _____, "I'm glad _____ _____.

    A. asked   B. smiled   C. you

26 It just shows that though your life may _____ _____, there's always _____ _____ a cool drink with a friend."

    A. full   B. for   C. room   D. seem

14 그는 사과 주스를 병 안에 부었고, 학생들은 주스가 모래 사이의 빈틈을 채우는 것을 지켜보았다.

15 "자, 이제." 선생님이 말했다. "여러분의 인생이 병과 같다는 것을 이해하기 바랍니다.

16 골프공은 여러분의 가족, 친구, 건강, 꿈과 같이 인생에서 가장 중요한 것이랍니다.

17 다른 모든 것을 잃게 될 때라도 여러분의 인생은 여전히 가득 차 있을 수 있습니다.

18 돌은 여러분의 직업, 집, 자동차처럼 사람들이 소중하게 여기는 다른 것들에 해당합니다.

19 모래는 온갖 사소한 것들이랍니다."

20 "만약 병에 모래를 먼저 채우면, 돌이나 골프공을 채울 공간이 없게 됩니다.

21 인생도 똑같습니다.

22 여러분의 시간과 에너지를 사소한 것에 모두 허비한다면 여러분에게 진정으로 중요한 것을 채울 공간은 절대로 없을 겁니다.

23 골프공, 즉 정말로 중요한 것들을 먼저 챙기기 바랍니다."라고 선생님이 말했다.

24 뒤에 앉아 있던 학생 하나가 손을 들고 질문했다. "사과 주스는 무슨 뜻입니까?"

25 Jenkins 선생님은 미소 지었다. "질문을 해줘서 기뻐요.

26 그것은, 여러분의 인생이 가득 차 보일지라도 친구와 시원한 음료수를 나눌 여유는 늘 있다는 점을 보여 줍니다."

※ 다음 우리말과 일치하도록 빈칸에 알맞은 것을 골라 쓰시오.

1 The _____ _____

2 Mr. Jenkins stood _____ _____ _____.

3 He had _____ _____ _____ and a big bag on the _____ _____.

4 When the class began, he _____ _____ the jar and started to _____ it _____ **golf balls** _____ _____ _____.

5 He asked the students, "_____ _____ _____ _____?"

6 _____ _____ said, "Yes."

7 The teacher took _____ _____ _____ **small stones** _____ _____ _____ and _____ _____ _____ the jar.

8 He shook the jar _____ _____, and the stones _____ _____ the _____ _____ between the golf balls.

9 He asked _____ _____ _____ and got _____ _____ _____ from his students.

10 Next, the teacher _____ _____ a bottle of **sand** and _____ it _____ the jar.

11 After he _____ the sand _____ the spaces between the stones, he asked _____ _____, "Is the jar _____?"

12 _____ _____ _____ _____, "Yes."

13 _____ Mr. Jenkins took a can of **apple juice** _____ _____ _____.

1 가득 찬 병

2 Jenkins 선생님이 교실 앞에 섰다.

3 교탁 위에는 큰 병과 커다란 가방이 놓여 있었다.

4 수업이 시작하자, 선생님은 병을 집어 들고 가방에서 꺼낸 골프공으로 채우기 시작했다.

5 그는 학생들에게 "병이 가득 찼나요?"라고 질문했다.

6 학생들은 모두 "예."라고 대답했다.

7 선생님은 가방에서 작은 돌 한 상자를 끄집어내어 병 안에 부었다.

8 그가 병을 살짝 흔들자, 돌들이 골프공 사이의 틈새로 굴러 들어갔다.

9 그는 같은 질문을 했고 학생들에게서 같은 대답을 들었다.

10 그런 다음, 선생님은 모래 병을 꺼내 병 안에 부었다.

11 모래가 돌 사이의 공간을 채우는 것을 지켜보고 나서 그는 "이 병이 가득 찼나요?"라고 한 번 더 물었다.

12 모든 학생들이 "예."라고 답했다.

13 갑자기 Jenkins 선생님은 가방에서 사과 주스 한 캔을 꺼냈다.

14 He _____ the apple juice _____ the jar, and his students watched it _____ _____ _____ in the sand.

15 "Now," the teacher said, "I _____ you to _____ that your life _____ _____ _____ the jar.

16 The golf balls are _____ _____ _____ _____ in life: your family, your friends, your _____, and your _____.

17 _____ _____ everything else _____ _____, your life can still be full.

18 The stones are the other things _____ by people, _____ your job, your house, and your car.

19 The sand is _____ _____ _____ _____."

20 "If you _____ the sand _____ the jar first," he said, "_____ _____ _____ _____ the stones or the golf balls.

21 _____ _____ _____ _____ life.

22 If you _____ all your time and energy _____ the small things, you will never have _____ for _____ _____ _____ _____ to you.

23 _____ _____ _____ the balls first — the things that really _____."

24 One student _____ in the back _____ her hand and asked, "_____ does the apple juice _____?"

25 Mr. Jenkins _____, "I'm glad _____ _____.

26 It just shows that though your life may _____ _____, there's always _____ _____ a cool drink with a friend."

14 그는 사과 주스를 병 안에 부었고, 학생들은 주스가 모래 사이의 빈틈을 채우는 것을 지켜보았다.

15 "자, 이제," 선생님이 말했다. "여러분의 인생이 병과 같다는 것을 이해하기 바랍니다.

16 골프공은 여러분의 가족, 친구, 건강, 꿈과 같이 인생에서 가장 중요한 것이랍니다.

17 다른 모든 것을 잃게 될 때라도 여러분의 인생은 여전히 가득 차 있을 수 있습니다.

18 돌은 여러분의 직업, 집, 자동차처럼 사람들이 소중하게 여기는 다른 것들에 해당합니다.

19 모래는 온갖 사소한 것들이랍니다."

20 "만약 병에 모래를 먼저 채우면, 돌이나 골프공을 채울 공간이 없게 됩니다.

21 인생도 똑같습니다.

22 여러분의 시간과 에너지를 사소한 것에 모두 허비한다면 여러분에게 진정으로 중요한 것을 채울 공간은 절대로 없을 겁니다.

23 골프공, 즉 정말로 중요한 것들을 먼저 챙기기 바랍니다."라고 선생님이 말했다.

24 뒤에 앉아 있던 학생 하나가 손을 들고 질문했다. "사과 주스는 무슨 뜻입니까?"

25 Jenkins 선생님은 미소 지었다. "질문을 해줘서 기뻐요.

26 그것은, 여러분의 인생이 가득 차 보일지라도 친구와 시원한 음료수를 나눌 여유는 늘 있다는 점을 보여 줍니다."

※ 다음 문장을 우리말로 쓰시오.

1 The Full Jar

➡ _____

2 Mr. Jenkins stood before his class.

➡ _____

3 He had a large jar and a big bag on the teacher's desk.

➡ _____

4 When the class began, he picked up the jar and started to fill it with golf balls from the bag.

➡ _____

5 He asked the students, "Is the jar full?"

➡ _____

6 They all said, "Yes."

➡ _____

7 The teacher took a box of small stones out of the bag and poured them into the jar.

➡ _____

8 He shook the jar a little, and the stones rolled into the open areas between the golf balls.

➡ _____

9 He asked the same question and got the same answer from his students.

➡ _____

10 Next, the teacher took out a bottle of and poured it into the jar.

➡ _____

11 After he watched the sand fill the spaces between the stones, he asked once more, "Is the jar full?"

➡ _____

12 All the students replied, "Yes."

➡ _____

13 Suddenly Mr. Jenkins took a can of apple juice out of the bag.

➡ _____

14 He poured the apple juice into the jar, and his students watched it fill the spaces in the sand.

➡ _____

15 "Now," the teacher said, "I want you to understand that your life is just like the jar.

➡ _____

16 The golf balls are what is most important in life: your family, your friends, your health, and your dreams.

➡ _____

17 Even when everything else is lost, your life can still be full.

➡ _____

18 The stones are the other things valued by people, like your job, your house, and your car.

➡ _____

19 The sand is all the small things."

➡ _____

20 "If you put the sand into the jar first," he said, "there's no room for the stones or the golf balls.

➡ _____

21 The same goes for life.

➡ _____

22 If you spend all your time and energy on the small things, you will never have room for what is really important to you.

➡ _____

➡ _____

23 Take care of the balls first — the things that really matter."

➡ _____

24 One student sitting in the back raised her hand and asked, "What does the apple juice mean?"

➡ _____

25 Mr. Jenkins smiled, "I'm glad you asked.

➡ _____

26 It just shows that though your life may seem full, there's always room for a cool drink with a friend."

➡ _____

※ 다음 괄호 안의 단어들을 우리말에 맞도록 바르게 배열하시오.

1 (Full / The / Jar)
➡ _____

2 (Jenkins / Mr. / before / stood / class. / his)
➡ _____

3 (had / he / large / a / jar / a / and / big / on / bag / the / desk. / teacher's)
➡ _____

4 (the / when / began, / class / he / up / picked / jar / the / and / to / started / fill / with / it / balls / golf / the / from / bag.)
➡ _____

5 (asked / he / students, / the / "is / full?" / jar / the)
➡ _____

6 (all / they / "yes." / said,)
➡ _____

7 (teacher / the / a / took / box / small / of / out / stones / of / bag / the / and / them / poured / into / jar. / the)
➡ _____

8 (shook / he / jar / the / little, / a / and / stones / the / into / rolled / open / the / areas / the / between / balls. / golf)
➡ _____
_____

9 (asked / he / same / the / question / and / the / got / answer / same / from / students. / his)
➡ _____

10 (the / next, / teacher / out / took / bottle / a / of / and / sand / it / poured / into / jar. / the)
➡ _____

11 (he / after / the / watched / sand / the / fill / spaces / the / between / stones, / asked / he / more, / once / "is / jar / the / full?")
➡ _____
_____

12 (the / all / replied, / students / "yes.")
➡ _____

13 (Mr. / suddenly / Jenkins / took / can / a / apple / of / juice / of / out / bag. / the)
➡ _____

14 (poured / he / apple / the / juice / the / into / jar, / his / and / watched / students / fill / it / spaces / the / the / sand. / in)
➡ _____
_____

1 가득 찬 병

2 Jenkins 선생님이 교실 앞에 섰다.

3 교탁 위에는 큰 병과 커다란 가방이 놓여 있었다.

4 수업이 시작하자, 선생님은 병을 집어 들고 가방에서 꺼낸 골프공으로 채우기 시작했다.

5 그는 학생들에게 "병이 가득 찼나요?"라고 질문했다.

6 학생들은 모두 "예."라고 대답했다.

7 선생님은 가방에서 작은 돌 한 상자를 끄집어내어 병 안에 부었다.

8 그가 병을 살짝 흔들자, 돌들이 골프공 사이의 틈새로 굴러 들어갔다.

9 그는 같은 질문을 했고 학생들에게서 같은 대답을 들었다.

10 그런 다음, 선생님은 모래 병을 꺼내 병 안에 부었다.

11 모래가 돌 사이의 공간을 채우는 것을 지켜보고 나서 그는 "이 병이 가득 찼나요?"라고 한 번 더 물었다.

12 모든 학생들이 "예."라고 답했다.

13 갑자기 Jenkins 선생님은 가방에서 사과 주스 한 캔을 꺼냈다.

14 그는 사과 주스를 병 안에 부었고, 학생들은 주스가 모래 사이의 빈틈을 채우는 것을 지켜보았다.

15 (the / "now," / said, / teacher / want / "I / to / want / you / understand / that / life / your / just / is / like / the / jar.)

➡ _____

_____

16 (golf / the / are / balls / what / most / is / important / life: / in / family, / your / friends, / your / and / health, / your / dreams. / your)

➡ _____

_____

17 (even / everything / when / is / else / lost, / life / your / can / be / still / full.)

➡ _____

18 (stones / the / the / are / things / other / valued / people, / by / your / like / job, / house, / your / and / car. / your)

➡ _____

19 (sand / the / all / is / small / the / things.")

➡ _____

20 ("if / put / you / the / into / sand / jar / the / first," / said, / he / no / "there's / room / the / for / stones / the / or / balls. / golf)

➡ _____

_____

21 (same / the / for / goes / life.)

➡ _____

22 (you / if / spend / time / your / all / energy / and / the / on / thiings, / small / will / you / have / never / room / what / for / is / important / really / you. / to)

➡ _____

_____

23 (care / of / take / first / the / balls / – / things / the / really / that / matter.")

➡ _____

24 (student / one / in / sitting / the / back / her / raised / hand / and / asked, / does / "what / apple / the / mean?" / juice)

➡ _____

_____

25 (Jenins / Mr. / smiled, / glad / "I'm / asked. / you)

➡ _____

26 (just / it / that / shows / your / though / life / seem / may / full, / always / there's / for / room / a / cool / with / drink / friend." / a)

➡ _____

_____

15 "자, 이제." 선생님이 말했다. "여러분의 인생이 병과 같다는 것을 이해하기 바랍니다.

16 골프공은 여러분의 가족, 친구, 건강, 꿈과 같이 인생에서 가장 중요한 것이랍니다.

17 다른 모든 것을 잃게 될 때라도 여러분의 인생은 여전히 가득 차 있을 수 있습니다.

18 돌은 여러분의 직업, 집, 자동차처럼 사람들이 소중하게 여기는 다른 것들에 해당합니다.

19 모래는 온갖 사소한 것들이랍니다."

20 "만약 병에 모래를 먼저 채우면, 돌이나 골프공을 채울 공간이 없게 됩니다.

21 인생도 똑같습니다.

22 여러분의 시간과 에너지를 사소한 것에 모두 허비한다면 여러분에게 진정으로 중요한 것을 채울 공간은 절대로 없을 겁니다.

23 골프공, 즉 정말로 중요한 것들을 먼저 챙기기 바랍니다."라고 선생님이 말했다.

24 뒤에 앉아 있던 학생 하나가 손을 들고 질문했다. "사과 주스는 무슨 뜻입니까?"

25 Jenkins 선생님은 미소 지었다. "질문을 해줘서 기뻐요.

26 그것은, 여러분의 인생이 가득 차 보일지라도 친구와 시원한 음료수를 나눌 여유는 늘 있다는 점을 보여 줍니다."

※ 다음 우리말을 영어로 쓰시오.

1 가득 찬 병

➡ _____

2 Jenkins 선생님이 교실 앞에 섰다.

➡ _____

3 교탁 위에는 큰 병과 커다란 가방이 놓여 있었다.

➡ _____

4 수업이 시작하자, 선생님은 병을 집어 들고 가방에서 꺼낸 골프공으로 채우기 시작했다.

➡ _____

5 그는 학생들에게 "병이 가득 찼나요?"라고 질문했다.

➡ _____

6 학생들은 모두 "예."라고 대답했다.

➡ _____

7 선생님은 가방에서 작은 돌 한 상자를 끄집어내어 병 안에 부었다.

➡ _____

8 그가 병을 살짝 흔들자, 돌들이 골프공 사이의 틈새로 굴러 들어갔다.

➡ _____

9 그는 같은 질문을 했고 학생들에게서 같은 대답을 들었다.

➡ _____

10 그런 다음, 선생님은 모래 병을 꺼내 병 안에 부었다.

➡ _____

11 모래가 돌 사이의 공간을 채우는 것을 지켜보고 나서 그는 "이 병이 가득 찼나요?"라고 한 번 더 물었다.

➡ _____

12 모든 학생들이 "예."라고 답했다.

➡ _____

13 갑자기 Jenkins 선생님은 가방에서 사과 주스 한 캔을 꺼냈다.

➡ _____

14 그는 사과 주스를 병 안에 부었고, 학생들은 주스가 모래 사이의 빈틈을 채우는 것을 지켜보았다.

➡ _____

15 "자, 이제," 선생님이 말했다. "여러분의 인생이 병과 같다는 것을 이해하기 바랍니다.

➡ _____

16 골프공은 여러분의 가족, 친구, 건강, 꿈과 같이 인생에서 가장 중요한 것이랍니다.

➡ _____

17 다른 모든 것을 잃게 될 때라도 여러분의 인생은 여전히 가득 차 있을 수 있습니다.

➡ _____

18 돌은 여러분의 직업, 집, 자동차처럼 사람들이 소중하게 여기는 다른 것들에 해당합니다.

➡ _____

19 모래는 온갖 사소한 것들이랍니다."

➡ _____

20 "만약 병에 모래를 먼저 채우면, 돌이나 골프공을 채울 공간이 없게 됩니다.

➡ _____

21 인생도 똑같습니다.

➡ _____

22 여러분의 시간과 에너지를 사소한 것에 모두 허비한다면 여러분에게 진정으로 중요한 것을 채울
공간은 절대로 없을 겁니다.

➡ _____

_____

23 골프공, 즉 정말로 중요한 것들을 먼저 챙기기 바랍니다."라고 선생님이 말했다.

➡ _____

24 뒤에 앉아 있던 학생 하나가 손을 들고 질문했다. "사과 주스는 무슨 뜻입니까?"

➡ _____

25 Jenkins 선생님은 미소 지었다. "질문을 해줘서 기뻐요.

➡ _____

26 그것은, 여러분의 인생이 가득 차 보일지라도 친구와 시원한 음료수를 나눌 여유는 늘 있다는 점을
보여 줍니다."

➡ _____

※ 다음 영어를 우리말로 쓰시오.

01	artificial	22	boring
02	bother	23	matter
03	cause	24	scary
04	relieved	25	produce
05	gloomy	26	effect
06	friendship	27	focus
07	helpful	28	salty
08	positive	29	sleepy
09	stressed	30	tidy
10	improve	31	work
11	appearance	32	schoolwork
12	scream	33	media
13	well-known	34	leave
14	relieve	35	used to
15	argue	36	thanks to
16	patient	37	at the same time
17	chemical	38	feel low
18	besides	39	according to
19	method	40	make sense
20	common	41	deal with
21	nervous	42	as long as
		43	have difficulty -ing

※ 다음 우리말을 영어로 쓰시오.

01 매체 _____

02 안심이 되는 _____

03 생산하다 _____

04 주장하다 _____

05 도움이 되는 _____

06 졸리는 _____

07 그 외에도 _____

08 집중하다 _____

09 개선하다 _____

10 소리를 지르다 _____

11 외모 _____

12 문제가 되다, 중요하다 _____

13 화학물질 _____

14 무서운 _____

15 흔한 _____

16 남겨두다 _____

17 불안한 _____

18 스트레스 받은 _____

19 인내하는 _____

20 방법 _____

21 유명한 _____

22 덜다 _____

23 지루한 _____

24 짠 _____

25 깔끔한 _____

26 효과가 있다 _____

27 우울한 _____

28 인공적인 _____

29 성가시게 하다 _____

30 원인 _____

31 긍정적인 _____

32 효과 _____

33 학교 공부 _____

34 우정 _____

35 ~에 따르면 _____

36 다른 방식으로 _____

37 ~하는 한 _____

38 ~할 것을 잊어버리다 _____

39 동시에 _____

40 ~ 대신에 _____

41 ~을 다루다, 처리하다 _____

42 약속을 어기다 _____

43 ~하곤 했다 _____

※ 다음 영영풀이에 알맞은 단어를 <보기>에서 골라 쓴 후, 우리말 뜻을 쓰시오.

1 _____ : a relationship between friends: _____

2 _____ : a particular way of doing something: _____

3 _____ : known about by a lot of people: _____

4 _____ : not real or not made of natural things: _____

5 _____ : a person, event, or thing that makes something happen: _____

6 _____ : a change that is caused by an event, action, etc.: _____

7 _____ : sad because you think the situation will not improve: _____

8 _____ : to make something better, or to become better: _____

9 _____ : expressing support, agreement, or approval: _____

10 _____ : to disagree with someone in words, often in an angry way: _____

11 _____ : neatly arranged with everything in the right place: _____

12 _____ : happening often; existing in large numbers or in many places:

_____

13 _____ : the way someone or something looks to other people: _____

14 _____ : to make someone feel slightly worried, upset, or concerned: _____

15 _____ : to shout something in a loud, high voice because of fear, anger, etc.:

_____

16 _____ : to give attention, effort, etc. to one particular subject, situation or person

rather than another: _____

보기			
cause	scream	artificial	bother
gloomy	appearance	method	focus
common	well-known	tidy	effect
argue	friendship	positive	improve

※ 다음 우리말과 일치하도록 빈칸에 알맞은 말을 쓰시오.

Listen and Answer – Dialog 1

W: Today, I'd like to _____ to you _____ teen stress. _____ _____ you _____ the most _____? _____ 9,000 teens _____ this question. _____ you can _____, schoolwork was the most _____ _____ of stress. _____ _____ _____ the students said schoolwork _____ them the most. _____ with friends _____ second place _____ 15.3%. _____ came family and _____ about the future. 8.2% of the students said they _____ _____ _____ _____ their _____.

W: 오늘, 저는 여러분에게 십 대들의 스트레스에 관해 말씀드리려고 합니다. 여러분에게 가장 많이 스트레스를 주는 것은 무엇인가요? 약 9,000명의 십 대들이 이 질문에 답했습니다. 보시다시피, 학업이 스트레스의 가장 흔한 원인이었습니다. 절반이 넘는 학생들은 학업이 스트레스를 가장 많이 준다고 말했습니다. 친구들과의 문제는 15.3%로 2위를 차지했습니다. 다음은 가족, 그리고 장래에 대한 걱정 순이었습니다. 8.2%의 학생들은 외모 때문에 스트레스를 받는다고 말했습니다.

Listen and Answer – Dialog 2

W: _____ are you _____, Oliver?

B: I'm _____ _____ the math test, Mom. _____ stress me out.

W: I understand. I _____ _____ feel that _____, _____.

B: Really? I didn't _____ that.

W: Yeah, but _____ _____ was _____ for me.

B: _____ _____ you _____ that?

W: I _____ _____ when I had an exam, but _____ _____ _____ _____ it made me _____ and _____ _____.

B: I see. Did stress _____ you _____ _____ _____?

W: Yes, it helped _____ my _____.

W: 뭐 하고 있니, Oliver?
B: 수학 시험이 있어서 공부하고 있어요, 엄마. 성적이 제게 스트레스를 줘요.
W: 이해한단다. 나도 그렇게 느끼곤 했거든.
B: 정말요? 그러신 줄 몰랐어요.
W: 그래, 하지만 약간의 스트레스는 내게 도움이 되기도 했단다.
B: 왜 그렇게 말씀하세요?
W: 나는 시험이 있을 때 스트레스를 받았지만, 동시에 그 스트레스가 나를 집중하고 더 열심히 노력하게 했거든.
B: 그렇군요. 스트레스가 다른 방식으로 엄마에게 도움이 된 적이 있나요?
W: 그럼, 내 기억력을 높이는 데 도움을 주었단다.

Listen More – Listen and choose.

B1: Today, let's _____ about the class T-shirt. We _____ _____ _____ on the design.

G: _____ me _____ you some _____ on the screen.

B2: We have to _____ a T-shirt with _____ _____.

B1: _____ _____ you _____ that?

B2: _____ we'll _____ the T-shirt on Sports Day. It's in June.

G: That _____ _____. What _____ this green one?

B2: I like it. The bee on the T-shirt is so _____.

G: And it's not _____.

B1: Yes. I think it's the _____ _____.

B1: 오늘은 학급 티셔츠에 관해 이야기해 보자. 우리는 디자인을 정해야 해.
G: 화면으로 몇 가지 디자인을 보여 줄게.
B2: 우리는 반팔 티셔츠를 골라야 해.
B1: 무슨 이유로 그렇게 말하는 거야?
B2: 우리가 체육대회 때 티셔츠를 입기 때문이야. 그건 6월에 열려.
G: 그 말이 맞아. 이 초록색 티셔츠는 어때?
B2: 나는 마음에 들어. 티셔츠 위의 벌 그림이 정말 귀엽다.
G: 그리고 비싸지 않아.
B1: 맞아. 그게 제일 좋겠어.

Speak – Talk in groups.

Hi. Today, I'd _____ _____ _____ about Frida Kahlo. She was a Mexican painter. _____ of her _____ _____ _____ is *Viva la Vida*.

안녕하세요. 오늘은 Frida Kahlo에 대하여 이야기하겠습니다. 그녀는 멕시코인 화가입니다. 그녀의 가장 유명한 그림 중 하나는 Viva la Vida입니다.

Speak – Talk in pairs.

A: I want to _____ more time on social media.

B: What _____ you _____ that?

A: I can _____ more friends from _____ _____ _____.

B: That _____ _____.

A: 나는 소셜 미디어에 더 많은 시간을 쓰고 싶어.
B: 왜 그렇게 생각하니?
A: 나는 전 세계로부터 더 많은 친구를 사귈 수 있어.
B: 옳은 말이야.

My Speaking Portfolio Step 3

I'd _____ to talk about some _____ _____ _____ _____ when you get _____. First, it's good to _____ _____ _____. Second, _____ to ten is a great idea. Also, _____ cold water helps. _____, _____ happy _____ can help.

여러분이 화가 났을 때 긴장을 풀 수 있는 방법에 관하여 이야기하겠습니다. 첫째, 심호흡을 하는 것이 좋습니다. 둘째, 열까지 세는 것은 좋은 생각입니다. 또한 차가운 물을 마시는 것도 도움이 됩니다. 마지막으로 행복한 생각을 하는 것이 도움이 됩니다.

Wrap Up – Listening & Speaking 1

W: Hello, teens. I'm Dr. Broccoli. Last time, I _____ about different _____ that _____ _____ for your health. Today, I'd _____ _____ talk about _____ _____ habits. First, try to eat _____. Second, it's important _____ _____ _____ when you're _____.

여: 안녕하세요, 십 대 여러분. 저는 Broccoli 박사입니다. 지난 시간에, 건강에 좋은 다양한 음식에 관해 이야기했죠. 오늘은 건강한 식습관에 관해 이야기하고자 합니다. 먼저, 천천히 먹으려고 노력하세요. 둘째, 배가 부르면 그만 먹는 것이 중요합니다.

Wrap Up – Listening & Speaking 2

G: Why _____ we _____ a sport club?

B: Sounds good. Let's _____ a baseball club.

G: Well, I think a _____ club is a _____ _____.

B: What _____ you _____ that?

G: All _____ _____ is a ball to play basketball.

G: 우리 운동 동아리를 만드는 게 어때?
B: 좋아. 야구 동아리를 만들자.
G: 글쎄, 농구 동아리가 더 좋은 생각인 것 같아.
B: 왜 그렇게 말하는 거야?
G: 농구를 하기 위해 우리에게 필요한 건 농구공뿐이잖아.

※ 다음 우리말에 맞도록 대화를 영어로 쓰시오.

Listen and Answer – Dialog 1

W: _____
_____
_____
_____
_____
_____

Listen and Answer – Dialog 2

W: _____

B: _____

W: _____

B: _____

W: _____

B: _____

W: _____

B: _____

W: _____

Listen More – Listen and choose.

B1: _____

G: _____

B2: _____

B1: _____

B2: _____

G: _____

B2: _____

G: _____

B1: _____

Speak – Talk in groups.

_____

_____

안녕하세요. 오늘은 Frida Kahlo에 대하여 이야기하겠습니다. 그녀는 멕시코인 화가입니다. 그녀의 가장 유명한 그림 중 하나는 Viva la Vida입니다.

Speak – Talk in pairs.

A: _____

B: _____

A: _____

B: _____

A: 나는 소셜 미디어에 더 많은 시간을 쓰고 싶어.
B: 왜 그렇게 생각하니?
A: 나는 전 세계로부터 더 많은 친구를 사귈 수 있어.
B: 옳은 말이야.

My Speaking Portfolio Step 3

_____

_____

_____

여러분이 화가 났을 때 긴장을 풀 수 있는 방법에 관하여 이야기하겠습니다. 첫째, 심호흡을 하는 것이 좋습니다. 둘째, 열까지 세는 것은 좋은 생각입니다. 또한 차가운 물을 마시는 것도 도움이 됩니다. 마지막으로 행복한 생각을 하는 것이 도움이 됩니다.

Wrap Up – Listening & Speaking 1

W: _____

_____

_____

여: 안녕하세요, 십 대 여러분. 저는 Broccoli 박사입니다. 지난 시간에, 건강에 좋은 다양한 음식에 관해 이야기했죠. 오늘은 건강한 식습관에 관해 이야기하고자 합니다. 먼저, 천천히 먹으려고 노력하세요. 둘째, 배가 부르면 그만 먹는 것이 중요합니다.

Wrap Up – Listening & Speaking 2

G: _____

B: _____

G: _____

B: _____

G: _____

G: 우리 운동 동아리를 만드는 게 어때?
B: 좋아. 야구 동아리를 만들자.
G: 글쎄, 농구 동아리가 더 좋은 생각인 것 같아.
B: 왜 그렇게 말하는 거야?
G: 농구를 하기 위해 우리에게 필요한 건 농구공뿐이잖아.

※ 다음 우리말과 일치하도록 빈칸에 알맞은 것을 골라 쓰시오.

1 Say _____ to _____
A. Stress   B. Goodbye

2 Some people _____ time _____ friends when they _____
_____.
A. feel   B. with   C. low   D. spend

3 _____ eat special foods to _____ _____.
A. feel   B. others   C. better

4 _____ simply sleep for a _____.
A. while   B. others   C. still

5 _____ do you _____ _____ stress?
A. deal   B. how   C. with

6 _____ are some stories about people who _____ _____.
_____.
A. different   B. suggest   C. ways   D. here

Mina (15, Daejeon)

7 Sometimes my friends give me stress _____ _____ bad things about me, _____ promises, or _____ over small things.
A. breaking   B. saying   C. arguing   D. by

8 _____ this _____, I watch _____ movies!
A. happens   B. horror   C. when

9 Good horror movies are _____ scary _____ I scream a _____.
A. that   B. so   C. lot

10 I guess that _____ at the _____ of my _____ helps me _____ better.
A. lungs   B. feel   C. top   D. screaming

11 Also, _____ to scary _____ and sound _____, I can forget about what _____ me.
A. bothers   B. scenes   C. effects   D. thanks

12 I've _____ _____ this _____ for the past several months, and it really _____.
A. method   B. usinig   C. works   D. been

Junho (14, Yeosu)

13 My uncle _____ _____ college two years _____.
A. from   B. ago   C. graduated

14 He lives _____ my family, and he's _____ _____ _____ a job for some time.
A. looking   B. with   C. for   D. been

15 I know that he's _____ _____, but he always tries to be positive by _____ _____.
A. out   B. fishing   C. stressed   D. going

16 He never _____ _____ when he doesn't _____ any _____.
A. catch   B. gets   C. fish   D. upset

17 He says, " _____ I fish, I'm _____ focused _____ I can leave all my worries _____.
A. behind   B. that   C. so   D. while

18 _____, it teaches me to _____ _____."
A. besides   B. patient   C. be

---

1 스트레스와 이별하라

2 어떤 사람들은 울적할 때 친구들과 시간을 보낸다.

3 다른 사람들은 기분이 좋아지도록 특별한 음식을 먹는다.

4 또 다른 사람들은 그저 잠시 잠을 자기도 한다.

5 여러분은 스트레스를 어떻게 다루는가?

6 여기 다양한 방법을 제안하는 사람들의 이야기가 있다.

미나 (15살, 대전)

7 때때로 내 친구들은 나에 관해 나쁜 말을 하거나, 약속을 어기거나, 혹은 사소한 일을 두고 언쟁을 하며 내게 스트레스를 준다.

8 이럴 때, 나는 공포 영화를 본다!

9 훌륭한 공포 영화는 너무 무서워서 나는 소리를 많이 지르게 된다.

10 있는 힘껏 소리 지르는 것은 내기분이 나아지는 데 도움이 된다고 생각한다.

11 또한, 무서운 장면과 음향 효과 덕분에 나를 괴롭히는 것들을 잊을 수 있다.

12 나는 지난 몇 달간 이 방법을 써 오고 있는데, 효과가 아주 좋다.

준호 (14살, 여수)

13 우리 삼촌은 2년 전에 대학을 졸업했다.

14 삼촌은 우리 가족과 함께 살고 있고, 얼마 전부터 직장을 구하고 있다.

15 나는 삼촌이 스트레스를 받고 있지만 낚시를 다니며 긍정적으로 지내려고 항상 노력한다는 것을 안다.

16 물고기를 한 마리도 잡지 못했을 때에도 삼촌은 절대 속상해하지 않는다.

17 삼촌은 "낚시하는 동안, 나는 아주 몰입해서 모든 걱정을 잊을 수 있어.

18 게다가 낚시는 나에게 인내를 가르쳐 준단다."라고 말한다

19 I'm _____ that _____ _____ one thing helps us _____ about something else.

    A. forget   B. on   C. sure   D. focusing

Dobin (16, Seoul)

20 My sister, a _____ student in high school, has a wonderful _____ to stay _____ _____ stress.

    A. free   B. second-year   C. from   D. way

21 She feels a lot of stress from schoolwork, but my mother _____ to _____ the situation _____ a good _____.

    A. seems   B. reason   C. for   D. like

22 It is _____ cleaning is my sister's _____ _____ to make life _____!

    A. because   B. way   C. number-one D. better

23 When she's _____ stressed _____ her life _____ _____, she cleans her room.

    A. gloomy   B. that   C. so   D. looks

24 She says, "_____ I clean my room, I _____ _____ I'm also _____ stress.

    A. relieving   B. as   C. like   D. feel

25 _____ my room looks _____, my life _____ _____."

    A. tidy   B. when   C. brighter   D. looks

Yulia (14, Ansan)

26 _____ me _____ you _____ my mother does about her stress.

    A. tell   B. what   C. let

27 She feels _____ by all the _____ she _____ to do at _____ and at home.

    A. has   B. stressed   C. work   D. things

28 When she's _____ _____, she _____ "Me Time" on her _____.

    A. writes   B. under   C. calendar   D. stress

29 This means she _____ some time _____ for _____.

    A. herself   B. takes   C. out

30 She _____ a book, _____ a movie, or _____ with her friends.

    A. watches   B. reads   C. talks

31 She says, "It doesn't really _____ what I do, _____ _____ _____ it's something I like.

    A. as   B. matter   C. as   D. long

32 I've _____ _____ 'Me Time' _____ my calendar for two months, and I feel _____ better."

    A. writing   B. much   C. on   D. been

33 _____ _____ will _____ _____ you?

    A. work   B. methods   C. which   D. for

34 _____ some of these ideas _____, and find your best _____ to say goodbye to _____.

    A. way   B. yourself   C. stress   D. try

---

19 한 가지 일에 집중하는 것이 다른 무언가를 잊는 데 도움이 된다고 나는 확신한다.

도빈 (16살, 서울)

20 고등학교 2학년인 우리 누나에게는 스트레스에서 벗어나는 훌륭한 방법이 있다.

21 누나가 학업 때문에 많은 스트레스를 받지만, 그럴 만한 이유로 우리 어머니는 그 상황을 좋아하시는 것 같다.

22 그것은 바로, 청소가 누나의 삶을 향상하는 최고의 방법이기 때문이다.

23 스트레스를 너무 많이 받아서 인생이 우울해 보일 때, 누나는 방을 청소한다.

24 누나는 "방을 청소하면서 스트레스도 해소되는 것 같아.

25 내 방이 깔끔해 보이면 내 삶도 더 밝아 보여."라고 말한다.

Yulia (14살, 안산)

26 우리 어머니께서 스트레스를 어떻게 다루시는지 소개하려고 한다.

27 어머니는 직장과 집에서 해야 하는 온갖 일로 인해 스트레스를 받으신다.

28 스트레스를 받을 때면 어머니는 달력에 '나만의 시간'이라고 적으신다.

29 이것은 어머니 자신을 위해 잠깐 시간을 낸다는 의미이다.

30 어머니는 책을 읽거나, 영화를 보거나, 친구들과 이야기를 나누신다.

31 어머니는 "내가 좋아하는 것이라면, 무엇을 하는지는 별로 중요하지 않아.

32 나는 두 달째 달력에 '나만의 시간'을 적어 왔고, 기분이 훨씬 좋아졌어."라고 말씀하신다.

33 어떤 방법이 여러분에게 효과가 있을까?

34 이 아이디어 중 몇 개를 직접 해 보고, 스트레스와 이별하는 자신만의 최고의 방법을 찾아라.

※ 다음 우리말과 일치하도록 빈칸에 알맞은 말을 쓰시오.

1 _____ _____ to Stress

2 Some people _____ _____ _____ friends when they _____ _____.

3 _____ eat special foods _____ _____ _____.

4 _____ _____ simply sleep _____ _____ _____.

5 How do you _____ _____ stress?

6 Here are some stories about people who _____ _____ _____.

Mina (15, Daejeon)

7 Sometimes my friends give me stress by _____ bad things about me, _____ promises, or _____ _____ small things.

8 _____ _____ _____, I watch horror movies!

9 Good horror movies are _____ scary _____ I scream a lot.

10 I guess that screaming _____ _____ _____ _____ _____ _____ me _____ better.

11 Also, _____ _____ scary _____ and sound _____, I can forget about _____ _____ _____.

12 _____ _____ _____ this method for the past _____ _____, and it really _____.

Junho (14, Yeosu)

13 My uncle _____ _____ college two years _____.

14 He lives with my family, and _____ _____ _____ _____ a job for some time.

15 I know that _____ _____ _____, but he _____ _____ to be positive _____ _____ _____.

16 He never _____ _____ when he doesn't catch any fish.

17 He says, "While I fish, I'm _____ focused _____ I _____ _____ all my _____ _____.

18 _____, it teaches me _____ _____ _____."

---

1 스트레스와 이별하라

2 어떤 사람들은 울적할 때 친구들과 시간을 보낸다.

3 다른 사람들은 기분이 좋아지도록 특별한 음식을 먹는다.

4 또 다른 사람들은 그저 잠시 잠을 자기도 한다.

5 여러분은 스트레스를 어떻게 다루는가?

6 여기 다양한 방법을 제안하는 사람들의 이야기가 있다.

미나 (15살, 대전)

7 때때로 내 친구들은 나에 관해 나쁜 말을 하거나, 약속을 어기거나, 혹은 사소한 일을 두고 언쟁을 하며 내게 스트레스를 준다.

8 이럴 때, 나는 공포 영화를 본다!

9 훌륭한 공포 영화는 너무 무서워서 나는 소리를 많이 지르게 된다.

10 있는 힘껏 소리 지르는 것은 내 기분이 나아지는 데 도움이 된다고 생각한다.

11 또한, 무서운 장면과 음향 효과 덕분에 나를 괴롭히는 것들을 잊을 수 있다.

12 나는 지난 몇 달간 이 방법을 써 오고 있는데, 효과가 아주 좋다.

준호 (14살, 여수)

13 우리 삼촌은 2년 전에 대학을 졸업했다.

14 삼촌은 우리 가족과 함께 살고 있고, 얼마 전부터 직장을 구하고 있다.

15 나는 삼촌이 스트레스를 받고 있지만 낚시를 다니며 긍정적으로 지내려고 항상 노력한다는 것을 안다.

16 물고기를 한 마리도 잡지 못했을 때에도 삼촌은 절대 속상해하지 않는다.

17 삼촌은 "낚시하는 동안, 나는 아주 몰입해서 모든 걱정을 잊을 수 있어.

18 게다가 낚시는 나에게 인내를 가르쳐 준단다."라고 말한다

19 I'm sure that _____ _____ one thing helps us _____ about _____ _____.

Dobin (16, Seoul)

20 My sister, a _____ student in high school, has a wonderful way _____ _____ _____ _____ stress.

21 She feels a lot of stress from schoolwork, but my mother _____ _____ _____ the situation _____ _____ _____ _____.

22 It is because cleaning is my sister's _____ _____ life better!

23 When she's _____ stressed _____ her life _____, she cleans her room.

24 She says, "_____ I clean my room, I _____ _____ I'm also _____ stress.

25 When my room _____ _____, my life _____ _____."

Yulia (14, Ansan)

26 _____ me tell you _____ my mother does about her stress.

27 She feels stressed by _____ _____ _____ _____ _____ _____ _____ _____ and at home.

28 When _____ _____ _____, she writes "Me Time" on her calendar.

29 This means she _____ _____ _____ _____ for herself.

30 She _____ a book, _____ a movie, or _____ with her friends.

31 She says, "It doesn't really _____ _____ I do, _____ _____ it's something I like.

32 _____ _____ _____ 'Me Time' on my calendar for two months, and I _____ _____ _____."

33 _____ methods will _____ _____ _____?

34 Try some of these ideas yourself, and find your best way _____ _____ _____ _____ _____.

19 한 가지 일에 집중하는 것이 다른 무언가를 잊는 데 도움이 된다고 나는 확신한다.

도빈 (16살, 서울)

20 고등학교 2학년인 우리 누나에게는 스트레스에서 벗어나는 훌륭한 방법이 있다.

21 누나가 학업 때문에 많은 스트레스를 받지만, 그럴 만한 이유로 우리 어머니는 그 상황을 좋아하시는 것 같다.

22 그것은 바로, 청소가 누나의 삶을 향상하는 최고의 방법이기 때문이다.

23 스트레스를 너무 많이 받아서 인생이 우울해 보일 때, 누나는 방을 청소한다.

24 누나는 "방을 청소하면서 스트레스도 해소되는 것 같아.

25 내 방이 깔끔해 보이면 내 삶도 더 밝아 보여."라고 말한다.

Yulia (14살, 안산)

26 우리 어머니께서 스트레스를 어떻게 다루시는지 소개하려고 한다.

27 어머니는 직장과 집에서 해야 하는 온갖 일로 인해 스트레스를 받으신다.

28 스트레스를 받을 때면 어머니는 달력에 '나만의 시간'이라고 적으신다.

29 이것은 어머니 자신을 위해 잠깐 시간을 낸다는 의미이다.

30 어머니는 책을 읽거나, 영화를 보거나, 친구들과 이야기를 나누신다.

31 어머니는 "내가 좋아하는 것이라면, 무엇을 하는지는 별로 중요하지 않아.

32 나는 두 달째 달력에 '나만의 시간'을 적어 왔고, 기분이 훨씬 좋아졌어."라고 말씀하신다.

33 어떤 방법이 여러분에게 효과가 있을까?

34 이 아이디어 중 몇 개를 직접 해 보고, 스트레스와 이별하는 자신만의 최고의 방법을 찾아라.

※ 다음 문장을 우리말로 쓰시오.

1 ▷ Say Goodbye to Stress

➡ _____

2 ▷ Some people spend time with friends when they feel low.

➡ _____

3 ▷ Others eat special foods to feel better.

➡ _____

4 ▷ Still others simply sleep for a while.

➡ _____

5 ▷ How do you deal with stress?

➡ _____

6 ▷ Here are some stories about people who suggest different ways.

➡ _____

미나 (15살, 대전) Mina (15, Daejeon)

7 ▷ Sometimes my friends give me stress by saying bad things about me, breaking promises, or arguing over small things.

➡ _____

8 ▷ When this happens, I watch horror movies!

➡ _____

9 ▷ Good horror movies are so scary that I scream a lot.

➡ _____

10 ▷ I guess that screaming at the top of my lungs helps me feel better.

➡ _____

11 ▷ Also, thanks to scary scenes and sound effects, I can forget about what bothers me.

➡ _____

12 ▷ I've been using this method for the past several months, and it really works.

➡ _____

준호 (14살, 여수) Junho (14, Yeosu)

13 ▷ My uncle graduated from college two years ago.

➡ _____

14 ▷ He lives with my family, and he's been looking for a job for some time.

➡ _____

15 ▷ I know that he's stressed out, but he always tries to be positive by going fishing.

➡ _____

16 ▷ He never gets upset when he doesn't catch any fish.

➡ _____

17 He says, "While I fish, I'm so focused that I can leave all my worries behind.

➡ _____

18 Besides, it teaches me to be patient."

➡ _____

19 I'm sure that focusing on one thing helps us forget about something else.

➡ _____

도빈 (16살, 서울) Dobin (16, Seoul)

20 My sister, a second-year student in high school, has a wonderful way to stay free from stress.

➡ _____

21 She feels a lot of stress from schoolwork, but my mother seems to like the situation for a good reason.

➡ _____

22 It is because cleaning is my sister's number-one way to make life better!

➡ _____

23 When she's so stressed that her life looks gloomy, she cleans her room.

➡ _____

24 She says, "As I clean my room, I feel like I'm also relieving stress.

➡ _____

25 When my room looks tidy, my life looks brighter."

➡ _____

Yulia (14살, 안산) Yulia (14, Ansan)

26 Let me tell you what my mother does about her stress.

➡ _____

27 She feels stressed by all the things she has to do at work and at home.

➡ _____

28 When she's under stress, she writes "Me Time" on her calendar.

➡ _____

29 This means she takes some time out for herself.

➡ _____

30 She reads a book, watches a movie, or talks with her friends.

➡ _____

31 She says, "It doesn't really matter what I do, as long as it's something I like.

➡ _____

32 I've been writing 'Me Time' on my calendar for two months, and I feel much better."

➡ _____

33 Which methods will work for you?

➡ _____

34 Try some of these ideas yourself, and find your best way to say goodbye to stress.

➡ _____

※ 다음 괄호 안의 단어들을 우리말에 맞도록 바르게 배열하시오.

1 (to / Say / Stress / Goodbye)
➡ _____

2 (people / some / time / spend / friends / with / they / when / low. / feel)
➡ _____

3 (eat / others / foods / special / feel / better. / to)
➡ _____

4 (others / still / sleep / simply / for / while. / a)
➡ _____

5 (do / how / you / with / stress? / deal)
➡ _____

6 (are / here / stories / some / people / about / suggest / who / ways. / different)
➡ _____

Mina (15, Daejeon)

7 (my / sometimes / friends / me / give / stress / saying / by / things / bad / me, / about / promises, / breaking / or / over / arguing / things. / small)
➡ _____

8 (this / when / happens, / watch / I / movies! / horror)
➡ _____

9 (horror / good / are / movies / scary / so / I / that / a / scream / lot.)
➡ _____

10 (guess / I / screaming / that / the / at / of / top / lungs / my / me / helps / better. / feel)
➡ _____

11 (thanks / also, / scary / to / scenes / and / effects, / sound / can / I / forget / what / about / me / bothers)
➡ _____

12 (been / I've / this / using / method / the / for / several / past / months, / and / really / it / works.)
➡ _____

Junho (14, Yeosu)

13 (uncle / my / from / graduated / college / ago. / years / two)
➡ _____

14 (lives / he / my / with / family, / he's / and / looking / been / for / job / a / for / time. / some)
➡ _____

15 (know / I / that / stressed / he's / out, / but / always / he / to / tries / be / positive / going / by / fishing.)
➡ _____

16 (never / he / upset / gets / he / when / catch / doesn't / fish. / any)
➡ _____

17 (says, / he / I / "while / fish, / so / I'm / that / focused / can / I / leave / all / worries / my / behind.)
➡ _____

18 (it / besides, / teaches / to / me / patient." / be)
➡ _____

1 스트레스와 이별하라

2 어떤 사람들은 울적할 때 친구들과 시간을 보낸다.

3 다른 사람들은 기분이 좋아지도록 특별한 음식을 먹는다.

4 또 다른 사람들은 그저 잠시 잠을 자기도 한다.

5 여러분은 스트레스를 어떻게 다루는가?

6 여기 다양한 방법을 제안하는 사람들의 이야기가 있다.

미나 (15살, 대전)

7 때때로 내 친구들은 나에 관해 나쁜 말을 하거나, 약속을 어기거나, 혹은 사소한 일을 두고 언쟁을 하며 내게 스트레스를 준다.

8 이럴 때, 나는 공포 영화를 본다!

9 훌륭한 공포 영화는 너무 무서워서 나는 소리를 많이 지르게 된다.

10 있는 힘껏 소리 지르는 것은 내 기분이 나아지는 데 도움이 된다고 생각한다.

11 또한, 무서운 장면과 음향 효과 덕분에 나를 괴롭히는 것들을 잊을 수 있다.

12 나는 지난 몇 달간 이 방법을 써 오고 있는데, 효과가 아주 좋다.

준호 (14살, 여수)

13 우리 삼촌은 2년 전에 대학을 졸업했다.

14 삼촌은 우리 가족과 함께 살고 있고, 얼마 전부터 직장을 구하고 있다.

15 나는 삼촌이 스트레스를 받고 있지만 낚시를 다니며 긍정적으로 지내려고 항상 노력한다는 것을 안다.

16 물고기를 한 마리도 잡지 못했을 때에도 삼촌은 절대 속상해하지 않는다.

17 삼촌은 "낚시하는 동안, 나는 아주 몰입해서 모든 걱정을 잊을 수 있어.

18 게다가 낚시는 나에게 인내를 가르쳐 준단다."라고 말한다

19 (sure / I'm / focusing / that / one / on / helps / thing / forget / us / something / about / else.)

➡ _____

Dobin (16, Seoul)

20 (sister, / my / second-year / a / in / student / school, / high / a / has / wonderful / to / way / free / stay / stress. / from)

➡ _____

21 (feels / she / lot / a / of / from / stress / schoolwork, / my / but / mother / to / seems / like / to / the / situation / for / good / a / reason.)

➡ _____

22 (is / it / cleaning / because / my / is / sister's / way / number-one / make / to / better! / life)

➡ _____

23 (she's / when / stressed / so / that / life / her / gloomy, / looks / cleans / she / room. / her)

➡ _____

24 (says, / she / "as / clean / I / room, / my / feel / I / like / I'm / releiving / stress. / also)

➡ _____

25 (my / when / room / tidy, / looks / life / my / brighter." / looks)

➡ _____

Yulia (14, Ansan)

26 (me / let / you / tell / what / mother / my / about / does / stress. / her)

➡ _____

27 (feels / she / by / stressed / all / things / the / has / she / to / at / do / work / and / home. / at)

➡ _____

28 (she's / when / stress, / under / writes / she / Time" / "Me / her / on / calender.)

➡ _____

29 (means / this / takes / she / time / some / for / out / herself.)

➡ _____

30 (reads / she / book, / a / watches / movie, / a / talks / or / her / with / friends.)

➡ _____

31 (says / she / "it / really / doesn't / what / matter / do, / I / long / as / it's / as / something / like. / I)

➡ _____

32 (been / I've / writing / Time' / 'Me / my / on / calender / two / for / months, / I / and / much / feel / better.")

➡ _____

33 (methods / which / work / will / you? / for)

➡ _____

34 (some / try / these / of / yourself, / ideas / and / your / find / way / best / say / to / goodbye / stress. / to)

➡ _____

_____

19 한 가지 일에 집중하는 것이 다른 무언가를 잊는 데 도움이 된다고 나는 확신한다.

도빈 (16살, 서울)

20 고등학교 2학년인 우리 누나에게는 스트레스에서 벗어나는 훌륭한 방법이 있다.

21 누나가 학업 때문에 많은 스트레스를 받지만, 그럴 만한 이유로 우리 어머니는 그 상황을 좋아하시는 것 같다.

22 그것은 바로, 청소가 누나의 삶을 향상하는 최고의 방법이기 때문이다.

23 스트레스를 너무 많이 받아서 인생이 우울해 보일 때, 누나는 방을 청소한다.

24 누나는 "방을 청소하면서 스트레스도 해소되는 것 같아.

25 내 방이 깔끔해 보이면 내 삶도 더 밝아 보여."라고 말한다.

Yulia (14살, 안산)

26 우리 어머니께서 스트레스를 어떻게 다루시는지 소개하려고 한다.

27 어머니는 직장과 집에서 해야 하는 온갖 일로 인해 스트레스를 받으신다.

28 스트레스를 받을 때면 어머니는 달력에 '나만의 시간'이라고 적으신다.

29 이것은 어머니 자신을 위해 잠깐 시간을 낸다는 의미이다.

30 어머니는 책을 읽거나, 영화를 보거나, 친구들과 이야기를 나누신다.

31 어머니는 "내가 좋아하는 것이라면, 무엇을 하는지는 별로 중요하지 않아.

32 나는 두 달째 달력에 '나만의 시간'을 적어 왔고, 기분이 훨씬 좋아졌어."라고 말씀하신다.

33 어떤 방법이 여러분에게 효과가 있을까?

34 이 아이디어 중 몇 개를 직접 해 보고, 스트레스와 이별하는 자신만의 최고의 방법을 찾아라.

※ 다음 우리말을 영어로 쓰시오.

1 스트레스와 이별하라

➡ _____

2 어떤 사람들은 울적할 때 친구들과 시간을 보낸다.

➡ _____

3 다른 사람들은 기분이 좋아지도록 특별한 음식을 먹는다.

➡ _____

4 또 다른 사람들은 그저 잠시 잠을 자기도 한다.

➡ _____

5 여러분은 스트레스를 어떻게 다루는가?

➡ _____

6 여기 다양한 방법을 제안하는 사람들의 이야기가 있다.

➡ _____

미나 (15살, 대전) Mina (15, Daejeon)

7 때때로 내 친구들은 나에 관해 나쁜 말을 하거나, 약속을 어기거나, 혹은 사소한 일을 두고 언쟁을 하며 내게 스트레스를 준다.

➡ _____

_____

8 이럴 때, 나는 공포 영화를 본다!

➡ _____

9 훌륭한 공포 영화는 너무 무서워서 나는 소리를 많이 지르게 된다.

➡ _____

10 있는 힘껏 소리 지르는 것은 내 기분이 나아지는 데 도움이 된다고 생각한다.

➡ _____

11 또한, 무서운 장면과 음향 효과 덕분에 나를 괴롭히는 것들을 잊을 수 있다.

➡ _____

12 나는 지난 몇 달간 이 방법을 써 오고 있는데, 효과가 아주 좋다.

➡ _____

준호 (14살, 여수) Junho (14, Yeosu)

13 우리 삼촌은 2년 전에 대학을 졸업했다.

➡ _____

14 삼촌은 우리 가족과 함께 살고 있고, 얼마 전부터 직장을 구하고 있다.

➡ _____

15 나는 삼촌이 스트레스를 받고 있지만 낚시를 다니며 긍정적으로 지내려고 항상 노력한다는 것을 안다.

➡ _____

16 물고기를 한 마리도 잡지 못했을 때에도 삼촌은 절대 속상해 하지 않는다.

➡ _____

17 삼촌은 "낚시하는 동안, 나는 아주 몰입해서 모든 걱정을 잊을 수 있어.

➡ _____

18 게다가 낚시는 나에게 인내를 가르쳐 준단다."라고 말한다.

➡ _____

19 한 가지 일에 집중하는 것이 다른 무언가를 잊는 데 도움이 된다고 나는 확신한다.

➡ _____

도빈 (16살, 서울) Dobin (16, Seoul)

20 고등학교 2학년인 우리 누나에게는 스트레스에서 벗어나는 훌륭한 방법이 있다.

➡ _____

21 누나가 학업 때문에 많은 스트레스를 받지만, 그럴 만한 이유로 우리 어머니는 그 상황을 좋아하시는 것 같다.

➡ _____

22 그것은 바로, 청소가 누나의 삶을 향상하는 최고의 방법이기 때문이다.

➡ _____

23 스트레스를 너무 많이 받아서 인생이 우울해 보일 때, 누나는 방을 청소한다.

➡ _____

24 누나는 "방을 청소하면서 스트레스도 해소되는 것 같아.

➡ _____

25 내 방이 깔끔해 보이면 내 삶도 더 밝아 보여."라고 말한다.

➡ _____

Yulia (14살, 안산) Yulia (14, Ansan)

26 우리 어머니께서 스트레스를 어떻게 다루시는지 소개하려고 한다.

➡ _____

27 어머니는 직장과 집에서 해야 하는 온갖 일로 인해 스트레스를 받으신다.

➡ _____

28 스트레스를 받을 때면 어머니는 달력에 '나만의 시간'이라고 적으신다.

➡ _____

29 이것은 어머니 자신을 위해 잠깐 시간을 낸다는 의미이다.

➡ _____

30 어머니는 책을 읽거나, 영화를 보거나, 친구들과 이야기를 나누신다.

➡ _____

31 어머니는 "내가 좋아하는 것이라면, 무엇을 하는지는 별로 중요하지 않아.

➡ _____

32 나는 두 달째 달력에 '나만의 시간'을 적어 왔고, 기분이 훨씬 좋아졌어."라고 말씀하신다.

➡ _____

33 어떤 방법이 여러분에게 효과가 있을까?

➡ _____

34 이 아이디어 중 몇 개를 직접 해 보고, 스트레스와 이별하는 자신만의 최고의 방법을 찾아라.

➡ _____

※ 다음 우리말과 일치하도록 빈칸에 알맞은 말을 쓰시오.

Words in Action

1. Tests _____ me _____. Grades give _____ _____ _____.

2. _____ _____, smile more. Worry _____ _____.

3. I work hard. I have _____ _____ _____ _____.

4. I need a _____. I will _____ _____ _____.

5. I _____ just _____ _____ fish. I want _____ _____ some more.

1. 시험은 나를 지치게 해. 성적은 나에게 더 많은 스트레스를 준다.
2. 걱정은 줄이고 더 많이 웃어라. 걱정은 전혀 도움이 되지 않아.
3. 나는 열심히 일한다. 나는 할 일이 많다.
4. 나는 기분 전환이 필요하다. 나는 헤어스타일을 바꿀 것이다.
5. 나는 겨우 물고기 몇 마리를 잡았다. 나는 몇 마리 더 낚고 싶다.

Speak – Get ready.

1. I want to _____ more/_____ _____ on social media.

2. _____ _____ a team _____ _____ difficult/_____.

3. I like _____/playing sports _____.

4. _____ a _____ _____ as a teen can be good/_____.

1. 나는 소셜미디어에 더 많은/적은 시간을 보내기를 원한다.
2. 팀을 이루어 일하는 것은 어려울 수 있다/도움이 될 수 있다.
3. 나는 스포츠 보는 것을/하는 것을 더 좋아한다.
4. 십대일 때 아르바이트를 하는 것은 좋다/나쁘다.

Wrap Up - Reading

1. Are you _____ or _____ _____?

2. Then here is _____ _____ _____ for you.

3. _____ _____ simple _____ can _____ you!

4. First, go _____ and get _____ _____ sunlight.

5. _____ _____ scientists, this helps _____ a special chemical _____ _____ _____, and the chemical _____ _____ _____ happy!

6. _____ _____ _____ _____ _____ _____ is exercise.

7. This helps _____ _____ _____ of the "_____ _____."

8. _____ these _____ _____ the next time you _____ _____.

9. _____ _____ _____ in _____ of a screen, go outdoors and _____ _____ in the sun!

1. 스트레스를 받았거나 기분이 우울한가?
2. 그렇다면 여기 당신에게 좋은 소식이 있다.
3. 간단한 몇 가지 절차가 도움이 될 것이다!
4. 첫째, 밖에 나가서 충분한 양의 햇볕을 쬐라.
5. 과학자들에 따르면 이것이 뇌 속에 특별한 화학물질을 만드는 데 도움을 주고, 이 화학물질은 당신을 행복하게 만든다고 한다!
6. 당신이 할 수 있는 또 다른 일은 운동이다.
7. 이것은 훨씬 더 많은 '행복 화학물질'을 만드는 데 도움을 준다.
8. 다음에 당신이 우울하다면 이 간단한 조언을 시도해 보라.
9. 화면 앞에 앉아 있는 대신, 밖에 나가 태양 아래에서 뛰어 다녀라!

※ 다음 우리말을 영어로 쓰시오.

Words in Action

1. 시험은 나를 지치게 해. 성적은 나에게 더 많은 스트레스를 준다.
➡ _____

2. 걱정은 줄이고 더 많이 웃어라. 걱정은 전혀 도움이 되지 않아.
➡ _____

3. 나는 열심히 일한다. 나는 할 일이 많다.
➡ _____

4. 나는 기분 전환이 필요하다. 나는 헤어스타일을 바꿀 것이다.
➡ _____

5. 나는 겨우 물고기 몇 마리를 잡았다. 나는 몇 마리 더 낚고 싶다.
➡ _____

Speak – Get ready.

1. 나는 소셜미디어에 더 많은/적은 시간을 보내기를 원한다.
➡ _____

2. 팀을 이루어 일하는 것은 어려울 수 있다/도움이 될 수 있다.
➡ _____

3. 나는 스포츠 보는 것을/하는 것을 더 좋아한다.
➡ _____

4. 십대일 때 아르바이트를 하는 것은 좋다/나쁘다.
➡ _____

Wrap Up - Reading

1. 스트레스를 받았거나 기분이 우울한가?
➡ _____

2. 그렇다면, 여기 당신에게 좋은 소식이 있다.
➡ _____

3. 간단한 몇 가지 절차가 도움이 될 것이다!
➡ _____

4. 첫째, 밖에 나가서 충분한 양의 햇볕을 쬐라.
➡ _____

5. 과학자들에 따르면 이것이 뇌 속에 특별한 화학물질을 만드는 데 도움을 주고, 이 화학물질은 당신을 행복하게 만든다고 한다.
➡ _____
 _____

6. 당신이 할 수 있는 또 다른 일은 운동이다.
➡ _____

7. 이것은 훨씬 더 많은 "행복 화학물질"을 만드는 데 도움을 준다.
➡ _____

8. 다음에 당신이 우울하다면 이 간단한 조언을 시도해 보라.
➡ _____

9. 화면 앞에 앉아 있는 대신, 밖에 나가 태양 아래에서 뛰어 다녀라!
➡ _____

MEMO

MEMO

MEMO

영어 기출 문제집

적중100

1학기

정답 및 해설

천재 | 이재영

중 3

적중100

영어 기출 문제집

1학기

정답 및 해설

천재 | 이재영

중 3

적중100

What Matters to You?

p.08

01 ④	02 ②	03 ①	04 ③
05 ⑤	06 ⑤	07 ③	
08 inventions			

01 "온종일 비가 내릴 거야."라는 말에 Really라는 반응은 놀라움을 나타낸다. 자신의 새 비옷을 입을 수 있어 기뻐한다는 것을 알 수 있다.

02 "You can say that again."은 상대의 말에 동의하는 표현이다.

03 "by trading"은 직업을 나타내는 것으로 직업을 통해서 가족을 "부양하다"라고 해야 한다.

04 goods: 상품, 제품

05 ① 동사 rain은 "비가 내리다"의 의미이다. ② "사람을 지루하게 하는"의 의미는 boring이다. ③ delicious는 "맛있는"이라는 뜻이다. ④ agree: 동의하다 ⑤ 동사 like는 "좋아하다"의 뜻이다.

06 chase A away A를 쫓아내다 / take good care of ~ ~을 잘 돌보다

07 "음식을 삼키기 전에 몇 번 물다"는 "음식을 씹다"에 해당한다.

08 many great의 수식을 받는 단어는 명사의 복수형이어야 한다. invent(발명하다)의 명사는 invention(발명, 발명품)이다.

p.09

01 (s)urprising	02 (a)llowance
03 (b)oring	04 (T)hanks to
05 (g)et over / (g)et over / (g)et over	
06 (p)uzzled	07 (p)resented	08 (g)ift
08 (1) subjects (2) hurry (3) mind	

01 주어진 단어는 동의어 관계이다. boring 지루한 dull 지루한, amazing 놀라운 surprising 놀라운

02 "규칙적이거나 특별한 목적을 위하여 주어지는 상당한 양의 돈"은 "용돈 = allowance"를 가리킨다.

03 주어진 단어는 반의어 관계이다. appear 나타나다, disappear 사라지다 exciting 흥미진진한 boring 지루한

04 paper를 가장 위대한 발명품이라고 생각하는 이유로 "종이 덕택에 우리가 책을 읽을 수 있고, 기록을 남길 수 있는 것"이므로

이유를 나타내는 "~ 덕택에, ~ 때문에"의 의미로 "Thanks to"가 적절하다.

05 • 스트레스를 극복하기 위하여 휴식 기간이 필요하다. • 혼자서 이 어려움을 극복하겠다. • 그가 너의 아픈 마음을 극복하도록 너를 도와 줄 것이다. get over = 극복하다

06 Antonio의 질문에 대하여 the queen이 다시 질문하는 것으로 보아 the queen은 아마 질문의 내용을 몰라서 "어리둥절해하는 =puzzled" 것이라고 할 수 있다.

07 하인이 가지고 온 상자를 "the queen이 Luigi에게 주었다"는 의미로 "present 주다"가 적절하다.

08 present는 "선물"이라는 뜻으로 다른 말로 gift라고 할 수 있다.

09 (1) 과목 = subject (2) 서두르다 = hurry (3) 염두에 두다 = have ~ in mind

교과서 Conversation

p.10~11

1 glad	2 (D) → (B) → (C) → (A)
3 (1) say (2) agree	4 (C) → (A) → (D) → (E) → (B)

04 (C) 감정 표현에 대한 동의, 상대에 대한 질문 → (A) 질문에 대한 대답 → (D) 고등학교 진학에 대한 고민 소개 → (E) 진학할 고등학교에 대한 질문 → (B) 대답으로 진학할 고등학교에 대한 생각 소개'의 순서가 자연스러운 배열이다.

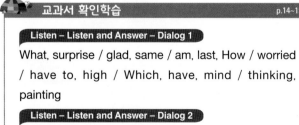

교과서 대화문 익히기

p.12

1 T 2 F 3 T 4 F 5 F

p.14~15

Listen – Listen and Answer – Dialog 1

What, surprise / glad, same / am, last, How / worried / have to, high / Which, have, mind / thinking, painting

Listen – Listen and Answer – Dialog 2

what, going, join / sure, about / join / heard, preparing / need, relax, need / get over / You can say / Why don't / for me, two left case looks / say that, as / wonder how much / Let, costs / expensive / agree, works as / buy / delighted, special / So am

weather report / going to rain / glad, wear / Good

boring, week / can say / don't think / agree, difficult subjects

(1) What, free, listen, greatest invention, live
(2) greatest invention, feel good, focus
(3) agree, Thanks to, read, write

serious, going / practicing / feel about / worried, make / sure, Break, leg

heard / What / won, prize / surprising, seems / walking

시험대비 기본평가   p.16

01 ①   **02** ①
03 You can say that again.   **04** ③

01 '비가 올 것이다'라는 말에 '새로운 레인코트'를 입을 수 있다는 것으로 보아 잘된 상황에서 할 수 있는 대답이 적절하다.

02 말하는 사람이 기쁘다고 감정을 드러내는 것을 보고, 그것에 대하여 '좋겠구나.'라고 말하는 것이 자연스럽다.

03 전적으로 동의해. = You can say that again.

04 (B) '연극에 대하여 어떻게 느끼느냐'는 질문에 (C) 실수할까 봐 걱정이라고 대답하고 (D) 위로가 되는 행운을 빌어준 다음 (A) 감사를 표시하는 순서가 자연스러운 배열이다.

시험대비 실력평가   p.17~18

01 ③   **02** ③   **03** ②   **04** Me
05 ③   **06** ②   **07** ①   **08** ②
09 ⑤   **10** (C) → (E) → (D) → (A) → (B)

01 대화의 내용으로 보아 소녀는 소년의 말에 동의하는 것으로 연결되는 것이 자연스럽다. "Me, neither."는 부정적인 내용에 동의하여 "나도 마찬가지야."라고 할 때 쓰는 말이다.

02 ③ red phone case가 너무 비싸다고 말한 것은 소년이다. ⑤ 마지막에 "So am I."를 보면 소년도 선물을 사게 된 것을 기뻐한다는 것을 알 수 있다.

---

03 두 사람의 대화를 보았을 때, 같은 반에 있게 된 것에 대하여 긍정적인 내용이 이어지는 것으로 보아 기뻐하는 것으로 생각할 수 있다.

04 상대방의 말에 대하여 동의하는 의미로 'Me, too.'가 적절하다.

05 상대의 걱정에 대하여 해결책을 주고, 위로하는 의미로 '너무 심각하게 여기지 마.'가 되도록 take가 적절하다.

06 상대의 걱정에 대하여 잘할 것이라고 위로하며 행운을 빌어주는 말은 'Break a leg.'이다.

07 일기예보를 들었는지 물어보는 질문에 (A) 대답하고, 하루 종일 비가 올 것이라고 알려준다. (C) 그 말을 듣고 새 레인코트를 입을 수 있다고 기뻐하는 것에 대하여 (B) 잘되었다고 대답하는 것이 자연스러운 순서이다.

08 학교 공부가 많아질 것에 대한 걱정에 (B) 동의하고 고등학교 진학에 대한 이야기를 한다. (A) 그 이야기를 듣고 어떤 고등학교를 갈 것인지 물어보고, (C) 그에 대하여 대답한다.

09 ⑤ 일기예보를 들었는지에 대한 질문을 받고 날씨를 이야기해주는 것으로 보아 일기예보를 들었다고 하는 것이 자연스러운 대화이다.

10 댄스 동아리 가입을 원한다는 말에 (C) 다른 준비를 한다는 것을 들었다는 놀라움을 표시하자 (E) 맞지만 휴식도 필요하다고 말한다. (D) 그 말에 동의하자 (A) 상대에게도 같이 하자는 권유를 하고, (B) 그것에 대한 거부를 표시하는 순서가 되어야 한다.

서술형 시험대비   p.19

01 time   **02** worried   **03** What
04 (m)istake   **05** Break a leg!   **06** won
07 He is a walking dictionary.
08 I don't really agree with you.

01 A의 말에 대하여 B가 반대하면서, 서둘러야 한다는 것으로 보아 빈칸에는 time이 적절하다.

02 학교 공부가 많아질 것이라는 내용을 원인으로 보았을 때 그 부담에 대한 걱정을 나타내는 말이 적절하다.

03 '무슨 일이 있느냐?'의 의미로 주어 역할을 할 수 있는 의문 대명사 What이 적절하다.

04 걱정을 한다는 내용에 이어지는 것으로 보아 그 이유가 연극에서 실수할까봐 걱정하는 것이라는 것을 알 수 있다.

05 leg를 포함하는 '행운을 빌어!'에 해당하는 표현은 'Break a leg!'이다.

06 대화의 내용으로 보아 Mr. Oh는 많은 것을 알고 있으므로 TV 퀴즈쇼에서 일등상을 수상했다는 것을 알 수 있다.

07 a walking dictionary: 박식한 사람, 만물박사

08 상대의 의견에 동의 여부를 나타낼 때는 agree를 사용한다.

3

Grammar

핵심 Check   p.20~21

1 (1) what   (2) what   (3) What   (4) that   (5) what

2 (1) draw   (2) set   (3) rising   (4) falling   (5) making
    (6) to go   (7) to take   (8) running   (9) falling   (10) fall

시험대비 기본평가   p.22

01 ③   02 ①

03 (1) He heard many people shout/shouting at the market.
    (2) Yuna saw them play/playing on the ground.

04 ③   05 ③

01 선행사를 포함한 관계대명사 what이 적절하다.

02 동사 ask, allow의 목적격보어는 to부정사이어야 하고, hear, see의 목적격보어는 to가 없는 원형부정사이어야 한다.

03 지각동사 hear, see의 목적격보어는 원형부정사를 쓴다. 진행의 의미를 강조할 때는 목적격보어로 현재분사를 쓸 수 있다.

04 동사 found의 목적어 역할을 하는 명사절로, 선행사가 포함된 관계대명사 what이 들어가야 한다.

05 지각동사 listen to의 목적격보어는 동사원형이나 현재분사가 되어야 한다.

시험대비 실력평가   p.23~25

01 ③   02 ③   03 ③   04 ③

05 ④   06 ①   07 ③

08 (1) that   (2) what   (3) What   (4) play   (5) running

09 (1) He didn't understand what I explained.
    (2) She didn't like what I had bought for her.
    (3) He showed me what he had painted.
    (4) I heard her cry in the room.
    (5) We expect him to come on time.

10 ③   11 ③, ④, ⑤   12 ③   13 ②

14 ②   15 ⑤   16 ③   17 ①, ③

18 We found what we could enjoy

19 ④   20 ①

01 ③ to meet은 목적을 나타내는 부사적 용법이고, 나머지는 모두 목적격보어로 쓰인 부정사이다.

02 목적격보어에 to부정사가 있는 것으로 보아 지각동사를 쓰기에는 어색하다.

03 동사 told, asked의 목적격보어는 to부정사이어야 하고, saw의 목적격보어는 원형부정사이다.

04 지각동사 hear의 목적격보어는 원형부정사이다.

05 ④ 'she wanted'의 목적어가 필요하므로 목적격 관계대명사이면서 선행사를 포함한 what이 들어가야 한다.

06 ① 지각동사는 목적격보어 자리에 동사원형, 현재분사가 올 수 있다.

07 ③ 지각동사 saw의 목적격보어는 원형부정사이어야 한다.

08 (1) 선행사 the gift가 있으므로 관계대명사 that (2), (3) 선행사가 없을 때는 관계대명사 what이 적절하다. (4), (5) 지각동사의 목적격보어는 원형부정사이다.바

09 (1) '내가 설명해 준 것'은 관계대명사 what을 사용하여 'what I explained'라고 한다. (2) '내가 그녀에게 사준 것'은 'what I had bought for her'이다. (3) 그가 그린 것 = what he had painted (4) 지각동사의 목적격보어는 원형부정사이다. (5) '기대하다 = expect'는 지각동사가 아니기 때문에 목적격보어로 to있는 부정사를 쓴다.

10 선행사 the building이 있을 때에는 관계대명사 that 또는 which를 쓴다. 선행사가 없을 때는 관계대명사 what을 쓴다.

11 ③ touches → touch[touching] ④ takes → take[taking] ⑤ to sing → sing[singing]

12 중요한 것 = What is important

13 지각동사 listened to의 목적격보어는 원형부정사 또는 현재분사를 쓰고, 일반동사 told의 목적격보어는 to부정사가 적절하다.

14 그가 말하는 것 = what he said

15 ⑤ 동사 order의 목적격보어는 to부정사가 되어야 한다.

16 ③ 선행사가 없는 명사절의 관계대명사는 what이다.

17 ①과 ③은 명사절로 선행사가 포함된 관계대명사 what이 적절하고, ②, ④, ⑤는 사물을 선행사로 하는 관계대명사 which 또는 that이 들어가야 한다.

18 우리가 즐길 수 있는 것 = what we could enjoy

19 지각동사 heard의 목적격보어는 원형부정사가 되어야 한다.

20 선행사를 포함하고 명사절을 유도하는 것은 관계대명사 what이다.

서술형 시험대비   p.26~27

01 (1) What surprised me was his rude answer.
    (2) He told me what he had heard at school.
    (3) You have to be responsible for what you are saying.
    (4) We saw him build/building the house last summer.
    (5) She asked me to open the door.
    (6) She heard us go out of the house.
    (7) We will give you what he brought to us.

02 (1) I heard him talk/talking on the phone.

(2) She felt the man pull/pulling her by the hand.

(3) They expected him to be quiet during the class

(4) What is important is to finish the work before dinner.

03 (1) ⓒ, She heard the child cry[crying].

(2) ⓔ, They saw him wearing that hat.

04 advised me to be satisfied with what I had

05 She watched them playing[play] soccer.

06 (1) drawing (2) what (3) that (4) to exercise

(5) walk[walking]

07 (1) I watched him stop at the traffic light.

(2) I saw him swimming in the pool

(3) My mother heard him laugh loudly at the table.

(4) I felt her push me on the back.

(5) I felt him pulling my hand.

08 (1) watched her brother cook

(2) eat what she cooked

(3) heard his mother open the window

(4) read what she had sent to me

09 what

---

01 (1) 나를 놀라게 한 것 = what surprised me (2) 그가 학교에서 들은 것 = what he had heard at school (3) 네가 말하는 것 = what you are saying (4), (6) 지각동사의 목적격보어는 원형부정사를 쓰고, (5) 동사 ask의 목적격보어는 to부정사를 써야 한다. (7) 그가 우리에게 가지고 온 것 = what he brought to us

02 (1), (2) 지각동사의 목적격보어는 원형부정사나 현재분사이어야 한다. (3) 동사 expect의 목적격보어는 to부정사가 되어야 한다. (4) 선행사를 포함하는 관계대명사는 what이다.

03 ⓒ 지각동사의 목적격보어는 원형부정사 또는 현재분사 ⓔ 지각동사의 인칭대명사 목적어는 목적격을 사용하여야 한다.

04 advise는 'advise+목적어+목적격보어(to부정사)'로 써서 '~에게 …하라고 조언하다'를 나타낸다. '~에 만족하다'는 be satisfied with이므로 to be satisfied with ~가 된다. '내가 가진 것'은 what을 사용하여 what I had라고 영작한다.

05 지각동사의 목적격보어는 동사원형 또는 현재분사가 되도록 한다.

06 (1) 지각동사의 목적격보어로 원형부정사나 현재분사 (2) 선행사를 포함하는 관계대명사는 what (3) the bag을 선행사로 하는 관계대명사는 that (4) 동사 advise의 목적격보어는 to부정사 (5) 지각동사 heard의 목적격보어는 원형부정사나 현재분사

07 (1), (2), (3), (4), (5) 지각동사의 목적격보어를 원형부정사나 현재분사로 하는 문장 형태를 만든다.

08 (1), (3) 지각동사의 목적격보어는 원형부정사가 되고 (2), (4)

명사절을 유도하는 관계대명사로 선행사를 포함하는 것은 what이다.

09 선행사를 포함하고 명사절을 유도하는 관계대명사는 what이다.

확인문제   p.28

1 T 2 F 3 T 4 F 5 T 6 F

확인문제   p.29

1 F 2 T 3 T 4 F 5 T 6 F

확인문제   p.30

1 T 2 F 3 F 4 T 5 T 6 F

교과서 확인학습 A   p.31~32

01 Priceless   02 an honest merchant

03 to support his family   04 filled, with

05 traded, for, for   06 Thanks to, what

07 had dinner with

08 was served, appeared, chased them away

09 greatly surprised   10 Are there no cats

11 looked puzzled   12 she asked

13 said to himself, What, not, but

14 brought, from, let them run

15 What, run   16 was filled with

17 Back, good fortune

18 the richest merchant, jealous

19 worthless   20 what

21 I'm sure   22 packed, with, works

23 took, to

24 a good friend of Antonio's

25 invited, to

26 sitting, presented, with, again and again

27 repay, with   28 whisper

29 excited, hopeful   30 more jewels than

31 presented, to   32 speechless

33 kitten   34 priceless

35 In return for, what is most valuable

36 far more than   37 look pleased

38 right thing to do   39 richer

40 a wiser one

1 A Priceless Gift

2 Long ago, an honest merchant lived in Genoa, Italy.

3 His name was Antonio, and he went to different places to support his family by trading.

4 One day, he filled his ship with goods and visited a faraway island.

5 There he traded tools for spices and books for nuts.

6 Thanks to Antonio, the islanders could get what they needed.

7 One night, Antonio had dinner with the island's queen at her palace.

8 When dinner was served, rats appeared, and some servants chased them away with sticks.

9 Antonio was greatly surprised that there were rats in the palace.

10 He asked, "Are there no cats on this island?"

11 The queen looked puzzled.

12 "What is a cat?" she asked.

13 The merchant said to himself, "What the islanders here need is not tools or books, but cats."

14 He brought two cats from his ship and let them run free.

15 "What amazing animals!" cried the queen when she saw all the rats run away.

16 She gave Antonio a chest that was filled with jewels.

17 Back in Italy, Antonio told his friends about his good fortune.

18 Luigi, the richest merchant in Genoa, heard the story and was jealous.

19 "Cats are worthless," Luigi thought.

20 "I'll bring the queen what is really valuable.

21 I'm sure that the queen will give me more jewels."

22 Luigi packed his ship with wonderful paintings and other works of art.

23 He took the gifts to the island.

24 To get a chance to meet the queen, he told the islanders a lie that he was a good friend of Antonio's.

25 When the queen heard about Luigi, she invited him to her palace for dinner.

26 Before sitting down at the table, Luigi presented the queen with all his gifts, and the queen thanked him again and again.

27 "I'll repay you with a priceless gift," said the queen.

28 Luigi watched the queen whisper in a servant's ear.

29 He became excited and hopeful.

30 He was sure that he would receive more jewels than Antonio.

31 After a while, the servant returned with a box, and the queen presented it to Luigi.

32 When Luigi opened the box, he was speechless.

33 There was a kitten in the box.

34 "Antonio gave us the priceless cats, and we now have some kittens," said the queen.

35 "In return for the wonderful gifts you gave us, we want to give you what is most valuable to us."

36 Luigi realized that, in the queen's mind, the kitten was worth far more than all the jewels in the world.

37 He tried to look pleased with the gift.

38 He knew that was the right thing to do.

39 Luigi did not return home a richer man.

40 But he was surely a wiser one.

01 ③	02 ①	03 ④	04 What
05 ④	06 ①	07 ⑤	

08 a good friend of Antonio's   09 ③

10 what is most valuable to us   11 ④

12 (A) what (B) other (C) Antonio's   13 ④

14 ③   15 ②

16 there was a kitten in the box

17 In spite of → In return for   18 one

19 (A) what (B) more (C) pleased   20 ②

21 was served   22 ④   23 rats

24 ③   25 ③ / ①, ④ / ②, ⑤

26 She gave Antonio a chest filled with jewels.

27 ④   28 ③   29 ②

01 ⓐ fill A with B: A를 B로 채우다, ⓑ trade A for B: A와 B를 교환하다

02 (A)와 ①은 부사적 용법, ②와 ⑤는 형용사적 용법, ③과 ④는 명사적 용법

03 Antonio가 여왕과 저녁식사를 한 장소는 '그의 배'가 아니라 '여왕의 궁전'이었다.

04 ⓐ에는 관계대명사 What, ⓑ에는 감탄문을 이끄는 What(단수 가산명사를 이끌 때에는 부정관사를 수반함)이 적절하다.

05 이 글은 '섬사람들이 필요로 하는 것은 고양이라고 생각하고,

Antonio가 고양이를 선물하는' 내용의 글이므로, 제목으로는 ④번 '그들이 정말 필요한 것은 고양이다!'가 적절하다.

06 ①의 his는 Luigi가 아니라 Antonio를 지칭한다.

07 ⓐ와 ⑤: 가치 없는, ① 대단히 귀중한, ②, ③, ④: 귀중한

08 한정사(관사/소유격/지시형용사)끼리 중복해서 쓸 수 없으므로 이중소유격(of+소유대명사/~'s)으로 쓰는 것이 적절하다.

09 present A to B: B에게 A를 주다

10 선행사를 포함하는 관계대명사 what을 써서 영작하면 된다

11 Antonio가 여왕에게 고양이를 몇 마리 줬는지는 알 수 없다. ① More jewels than Antonio received. ② A kitten. ③ He was speechless. ⑤ Because she wanted to give him what was most valuable to them in return for the wonderful gifts he gave them.

12 (A) '나는 여왕에게 정말로 귀중한 것을 가지고 갈 거야'라고 해야 하므로 선행사를 포함한 관계대명사 what이 적절하다. (B) another 뒤에는 단수 명사를 써야 하므로 other가 적절하다. (C) 한정사(관사/소유격/지시형용사)끼리 중복해서 쓸 수 없어서 이중소유격(of+소유대명사/~'s)으로 써야 하므로 Antonio's가 적절하다.

13 ④ invite: 초대하다, visit: 방문하다, ① envious: 부러워하는, 질투하는(= jealous), ② pack A with B: A를 B로 가득[빽빽히] 채우다, fill A with B: A를 B로 채우다, ③ opportunity: 기회, ⑤ again and again = over and over: 몇 번이고, 되풀이해서

14 Luigi는 Antonio의 친한 친구라고 거짓말을 했다.

15 뒤 문장에 '그는 Antonio보다 많은 보물을 받게 될 것이라고 확신했다'는 내용이 이어지므로 빈칸에는 '흥분된'과 '기대에 부푼'이 적절하다. ① nervous: 초조한, upset: 속상한, ③ hopeless: 가망 없는, 절망적인, ⑤ disappointed: 실망한

16 Antonio가 받았던 것보다 더 많은 보석 대신 '상자 안에 새끼 고양이가 들어 있었기' 때문이다.

17 '당신이 우리에게 준 멋진 선물에 보답하는 뜻에서'라고 해야 하므로, In spite of를 In return for로 고쳐야 한다. in spite of: ~에도 불구하고, in return for: ~의 답례로서

18 man을 대신하여 one을 쓰는 것이 적절하다. one은 앞에 이미 언급했거나 상대방이 알고 있는 사람이나 사물을 가리킬 때, 명사의 반복을 피하기 위해 쓸 수 있다.

19 (A) 관계대명사 앞에 선행사가 없으므로 what이 적절하다. (B) 여왕의 생각에는 세상의 온갖 보석보다 새끼 고양이가 훨씬 '더 가치 있다'고 해야 하므로 more가 적절하다. (C) 감정을 나타내는 동사는 사람을 수식할 때 보통 과거분사를 써야 하므로 pleased가 적절하다.

20 원치 않았던 선물을 받았지만 내색하지 않고 새끼 고양이를 선물로 준 여왕의 마음을 헤아린 것으로 보아 thoughtful(사려 깊

은)이 알맞다.

21 '식사가 나왔을 때'라고 해야 하므로, 수동태로 쓰는 것이 적절하다.

22 Antonio가 공구를 향신료와, 그리고 책을 견과류와 바꾸어 준 덕분에 섬사람들은 필요한 것을 얻을 수 있었다고 해야 하므로 ④번이 적절하다.

23 '쥐'를 가리킨다.

24 '여기 섬사람들이 필요로 한 것은 공구나 책이 아니라 고양이야'라고 하는 것이 적절하다. ① either A or B: A이거나 B인(A나 B 둘 중 하나), ② neither A nor B: A도 B도 아닌, ③ not A but B: A가 아니라 B, ④ both A and B: A와 B 둘 다, ⑤ at once A and B: A하기도 (하고) B하기도 하다(A이면서 동시에 B)

25 (A)와 ③은 의문대명사 What, (B)와 ①, ④는 관계대명사 What, (C)와 ②, ⑤는 감탄문을 이끄는 What(단수 가산명사를 이끌 때에는 부정관사를 수반함.)

26 주격 관계대명사 that과 be동사인 was를 생략할 수 있다.

27 ④ 'Luigi는 더 부유한 사람이 되어 집으로 돌아오지 않았다. 하지만 그는 분명히 더 현명한 사람이 되었다'고 해야 하므로, ⓐ에는 richer, ⓑ에는 wiser가 적절하다.

28 very는 원급을 강조하는 말이며, 비교급을 강조할 수 없다.

29 (B)와 ②, ⑤는 형용사적 용법, ①, ④는 부사적 용법, ③은 명사적 용법

🦉 서술형 시험대비

01 to get   02 were appeared → appeared

03 (A) spices   (B) nuts

04 ⓐ I'll bring what is really valuable to the queen.
   ⓑ the queen will give more jewels to me

05 he was a good friend of Antonio's

06 he sat   07 (A) greatly   (B) puzzled   (C) himself

08 What the islanders here need is not tools or books, but cats.

09 How   10 was full of   11 with it

12 worthless → priceless 또는 valuable   13 a kitten

14 (A) wonderful gifts[presents]   (B) most valuable

---

01 enable+목적어+to부정사: ~이 …할 수 있게 하다, 가능하게 하다, A+can+동사+thanks to B = B+enable+A+to부정사

02 appear는 자동사이므로 수동태로 쓸 수 없는 동사이다.

03 섬사람들은 Antonio와 '향신료'를 공구와 '견과류'를 책과 교환함으로써 그들이 필요로 하는 것을 얻을 수 있었다. trade A for

7

B: A와 B를 교환하다

04 bring과 give는 to를 사용하여 3형식으로 고친다.

05 '그는 Antonio의 친한 친구이다'라는 것을 가리킨다.

06 sitting을 '주어+동사'로 바꿔 쓸 수 있다.

07 (A) 형용사 'surprised'를 수식하므로 부사 greatly가 적절하다. (B) 감정을 나타내는 동사는 사람을 수식할 때 보통 과거분사를 써야 하므로 puzzled가 적절하다. (C) 주어와 목적어가 같을 때는 재귀대명사를 써야 하므로 himself가 적절하다.

08 관계대명사 'What'을 보충하여 등위 상관접속사 not A but B(A가 아니라 B)를 사용하여 배열하는 것이 적절하다.

09 What+(a/an)+형용사+명사+주어+동사! = How+형용사/부사+주어+동사!

10 be filled with = be full of: ~로 가득 차다

11 present+사물+to+사람 = present+사람+with+사물.

12 Antonio가 우리에게 '매우 귀한' 고양이들을 주었다고 해야 하므로 priceless 또는 valuable이 적절하다. priceless: 대단히 귀중한, worthless: 가치 없는

13 '새끼 고양이'를 가리킨다.

14 Luigi는 여왕에게 '멋진 선물'을 주고 Antonio보다 더 많은 보석을 받을 것이라고 확신했지만, 여왕은 새끼 고양이가 그들에게 '가장 값지기' 때문에 Luigi에게 보답으로 새끼 고양이를 주었다.

영역별 핵심문제 p.43~47

01 ②	02 ⑤	03 ⑤	04 ①
05 ①	06 ②	07 ①	08 ④
09 ①	10 So am I.	11 ④	12 ⑤
13 ③	14 ③	15 ④	16 ③
17 ③	18 (1) what (2) swimming (3) what		
(4) to take (5) study	19 ①		20 ④
21 ②, ④, ⑤	22 ②, ⑤	23 the things which[that]	
24 ①	25 ③, ⑤ / ①, ②, ④		26 ③
27 ②	28 ①, ②	29 aren't you	
30 (A)basketball shoes (B) a writer			31 ④

01 '무엇인가를 붙잡기 위하여 빠르게 따라가다'는 '추적하다 = chase'에 해당한다.

02 B가 애니메이션 고등학교를 생각 중이라고 대답하는 것으로 보아 "어떤 종류의 고등학교에 가기를 원하는지" 묻는 말로 '생각하다, 마음에 두다, 염두에 두다"의 의미로 "have in mind"가 적절하다.

03 상인은 물건을 사고파는 사람이므로 '거래하다 = trade'가 적절

하다.

04 'tell the time'은 '시간을 알다'의 의미이다.

05 월요일이 가장 지루한 요일이라는 주장에 대하여 목요일이 가장 지루한 요일이라고 하는 것으로 보아 동의하지 않는 의미가 되어야 한다.

06 일기예보를 들었는지 물어보는 말에 (B) 들어서 날씨를 알려 주고 (A) 비가 올 것이라는 내용을 듣고 기뻐하는 것에 대하여 (C) 좋겠다고 말하는 순서의 배열이 자연스럽다.

07 '살아있는 사전, 만물박사'의 의미는 'a walking dictionary'이다.

08 ④ 일기 예보에서 하루 종일 비가 올 것이라는 내용을 듣고 새로운 레인코트를 입을 기회를 가지게 된 것을 기뻐하는 내용이 자연스럽다.

09 가격에 대한 대답이 이어지는 것으로 보아 가격이 얼마인지 물어본다는 의미로 '궁금해 하다'의 의미인 wonder가 적절하다.

10 '나도 마찬가지야.'에 해당하는 세 단어는 'So am I.'이다.

11 그들의 어머니가 생일 선물로 무엇을 원하는지 알 수 없다.

12 그녀가 만든 것 = what she had made

13 선행사를 포함하는 관계대명사는 what이고, 지각동사의 목적격보어는 원형부정사를 쓰는 것이 적절하다.

14 관계대명사 what은 종속절에서 주어, 목적어 역할을 한다. ③ 'he had some time to rest'는 주어와 목적어가 있는 형태로 관계대명사 what을 쓸 수 없다.

15 ④ 지각동사 saw의 목적격보어는 to 없는 원형부정사가 와야 한다.

16 동사 listened to의 목적격보어는 원형부정사가 와야 한다.다.

17 동사 tell의 목적격보어는 to부정사가 적절하다.

18 (1), (3) 선행사가 없는 관계대명사는 what이고, (2), (5) 지각 동사의 목적격보어는 원형부정사 또는 현재분사이다. (4) 동사 ask의 목적격보어는 to부정사이다.

19 ① 지각동사 heard의 목적격보어는 원형부정사이다.

20 선행사가 없는 관계대명사로 '하는 것'의 의미를 가지는 것은 관계대명사 what이다.

21 ⓐ와 ②, ④, ⑤는 동명사, ①, ③은 현재분사

22 thanks to = because of = owing to = due to: ~ 때문에 ② instead of: ~ 대신에, ⑤ in spite of:~에도 불구하고

23 관계대명사 what은 the thing(s) which[that]으로 바꿔 쓸 수 있다. 지금은 교환하는 물건들이 여러 개이므로 선행사를 복수(the things)로 쓰는 것이 적절하다.

24 사역동사 let+목적어+원형부정사, 지각동사 saw+목적어+원형부정사(running도 가능함)

25 (A)와 ③, ⑤: 원인과 이유를 나타내는 부사절을 이끄는 접속사, (B)와 ①, ②, ④: 주격 관계대명사

26 '섬사람들이 공구나 책을 필요로 하지 않은 것'이 아니라, 'Antonio가 섬사람들이 필요로 하는 것은 공구나 책이 아니라 고양이라고' 혼잣말을 한 것이다.

27 ⓐ와 ②: (문학·예술 따위의) 작품, 저작물, 제작품, ① (기계의) 움직이는 부분, 장치, ③ 일하다, ④ 공장, 제작소, ⑤ (약 따위가) 작용하다, 듣다

28 ⓑ와 ①, ②는 형용사적 용법, ③, ⑤는 명사적 용법, ④는 부사적 용법

29 be동사가 있으므로, be동사를 사용하여 부가의문문을 만드는 것이 적절하다.

30 지훈이는 '농구 신발'이 농구 동아리에서 많은 친구들을 사귀도록 도와주었기 때문에, 그리고 그가 좋아하는 책이 '작가'가 되고 싶은 꿈을 그에게 주었기 때문에 그 두 가지를 타임캡슐에 넣었다.

31 (A)의 rats가 (C)의 rats를 가리키므로 (C) 다음에 (A)가 이어지고 (B)의 질문은 (A)의 마지막 질문에 대한 반문이므로 (A) 다음에 (B)가 와야 한다. 그러므로 (C)-(A)-(B)의 순서가 적절하다.

단원별 예상문제
p.48~51

01 ②	02 ④	03 (c)hest	04 (g)oods
05 ②	06 ①	07 (p)riceless	08 ⑤
09 ③	10 ④	11 Dancing is not for me.	
12 ①	13 ②	14 ⑤	15 ⑤
16 ②	17 ③	18 chased	19 ②
20 tools, books		21 ⑤	
22 two cats	23 (A) the rats　(B) jewels		
24 ③, ⑤	25 ②	26 ④	
27 because[as]		28 ④	

01 time capsule에는 원하는 물건을 담아서 보관하는 것이므로 '포함하다 = include'가 적절하다.

02 take good care of ~ = ~을 잘 돌보다

03 '물건을 옮기거나 보관하기 위하여 사용하는 크고 튼튼한 상자'는 chest이다.

04 '팔기 위하여 생산되는 물품'은 '상품=goods'이다.

05 '하루 종일 비가 올 것이다.'는 '일기예보를 듣고 대답하는 말이다.

06 'Don't take it so hard.'는 걱정할 때 위로하는 말이다.

07 delighted와 pleased는 비슷한 뜻이다. valuable과 유사한 의미로 priceless가 적절하다.

08 춤을 잘 추지 못해서 댄스 동아리에 가입하고 싶지 않다는 내용이 적절하다. have two left feet = 동작이 서툴다

09 Mr. Oh에 대하여 무슨 일이 있는지 묻는 질문에 (B) 퀴즈에서 상을 받았다는 소개를 하고, (C) 그가 많은 것을 알기 때문에 놀랄 일이 아니라는 말에 (A) 동의한다는 말을 하는 것이 자연스러운 배열이다.

10 상대방의 의견을 물어보거나 상대방에게 권하거나 제안하는 표현은 'How about ~?'이다.

11 '춤을 추는 것은 나와 어울리지 않아.'는 'Dancing is not for me.'이다.

12 ① 댄스 클럽에 가입하기를 원하는 사람은 소라이다.

13 지각동사 listen to의 목적격보어는 원형부정사 또는 현재분사이다.

14 선행사 the plan이 있는 경우 관계대명사는 that 또는 which이고, 선행사가 없는 경우의 관계대명사는 what이다.

15 지각동사 saw의 목적격보어는 동사원형이 되어야 한다.

16 전치사 with의 목적어 역할을 하는 명사절을 유도하며, 선행사가 없는 관계대명사 what이 들어가야 한다.

17 지각동사 saw의 목적격보어는 원형부정사이다.

18 chase: 쫓다, 쫓아내다, 어떤 것을 잡거나 닿기 위해 빨리 뒤쫓거나 따라가다, chase away: ~을 쫓아내다

19 fill A with B: A를 B로 채우다, pack A with B: A를 B로 가득[빽빽히] 채우다, ③ pick: 고르다, 선택하다, ④ gather: 모으다

20 '공구'와 '책'을 가리킨다.

21 전반부의 The queen looked puzzled.에서 'puzzled'를, 하반부의 What amazing animals!에서 'amazed'를 찾을 수 있다. ① bored: 지루한, ② nervous: 초조한, ③ confused: 혼란스러워 하는, ⑤ puzzled: 어리둥절해하는, amazed: 놀란

22 '고양이 두 마리'를 가리킨다.

23 Antonio가 배에서 가져온 고양이 두 마리가 자유롭게 돌아다니자 모든 '쥐들'이 도망치는 것을 여왕이 보았을 때, 그녀는 Antonio의 도움에 대해 보답하는 뜻으로 '보석'이 가득한 상자를 그에게 주었다. in return for: ~의 답례로서

24 지각동사 watched+목적어+원형부정사 또는 현재분사

25 이 글은 'Luigi가 많은 보석을 선물로 받을 것을 기대했다가 새끼 고양이를 선물로 받았다'는 내용의 글이므로, 제목으로는 '불쌍한 Luigi의 실현되지 못한 기대'가 적절하다.

26 Antonio가 언제 여왕에게 귀중한 고양이들을 주었는지는 대답할 수 없다. ① When he watched the queen whisper in a servant's ear. ② No. ③ No. ⑤ A kitten.

27 because of+명사구, because+주어+동사. because of일 때는 she drank가 수식하니까 dirty water 앞에 the를 붙였지만, because[as]로 고치면 수식하는 말이 없어지므로 dirty water

앞에 the를 생략하는 것이 적절하다.

28 Isabel은 그것을 어디나 가지고 다닌다.

서술형 실전문제
p.52~53

01 (1) left (2) support (3) Thanks (4) servants
02 (s)ervant
03 I'm a little worried that there'll[there will] be more schoolwork.
04 So am I
05 (1) I heard the rain fall[falling] on the window.
  (2) We saw him kicking the ball on the ground.
  (3) She couldn't understand what I told her.
06 (h)urry   07 certain, surely
08 to the queen
09 (A) merchant   (B) to support   (C) goods
10 Thanks to Antonio, the islanders could get what they needed.
11 chased away them → chased them away

01 (1) 동작이 서투르다 = have two left feet (2) 부양하다 = support (3) ~ 덕택에 = thanks to (4) 하인 = servant
02 '집을 청소하기, 요리하기, 손님맞이 등을 위하여 돈을 받는 사람'은 '하인 = servant'이다.
03 좀 = a little, 학교 공부가 더 많을 것이다. = there will be more schoolwork
04 Me, too.: 나도 그래.(=So am I.)
05 지각동사의 목적격보어는 원형부정사 또는 현재분사이고 선행사가 포함된 관계대명사는 what이다.
06 간식을 먹을 시간이 있다는 말에 동의하지 않는 것으로 보아 시간이 없어서 서둘러야 한다는 것을 알 수 있다.
07 I'm sure = It is certain = surely
08 present+사람+with+사물= present+사물+to+사람
09 (A) Antonio는 상품을 교역하는 사람이므로, '상인 (merchant)'이라고 하는 것이 적절하다. merchant: 상인, (특히) 무역상, consumer: 소비자, (B) 가족을 '부양하기 위해서'라고 해야 하므로 to support가 적절하다. (C) '상품'이라고 해야 하므로 goods가 적절하다. goods: 상품, 제품, good: 선(善); 좋은
10 thanks to: ~ 덕분에
11 이어동사에서 목적어가 인칭대명사일 때는 목적어를 동사와 부사 사이에 써야 하므로, chased them away로 고치는 것이 적절하다.

창의사고력 서술형 문제
p.54

|모범답안|
01 two cats, a chest filled with jewels, queen, presented a kitten to Luigi
02 (1) gimbap (2) To see[Seeing] movies
  (3) you told me
03 (A) a writer (B) basketball shoes
  (C) many friends (D) favorite book
  (E) a writer

01 Antonio는 여왕에게 고양이를 주고 보석 상자를 받았지만, Luigi는 비싼 선물을 주고 새끼 고양이를 받았다.

단원별 모의고사
p.55~58

01 (s)urprising   02 (e)xclude
03 (1) himself (2) (c)hest (3) (p)acked
04 ③   05 (m)erchant   06 ①
07 ③   08 ②   09 feet   10 ③
11 ⑤   12 So   13 ③   14 ①
15 ①   16 ④   17 ①   18 ③
19 (1) what (2) that (3) talk (4) taking   20 ②
21 ③   22 ③   23 chest
24 (A) worthless (B) valuable (C) priceless
25 ①, ④   26 ②, ⑤

01 주어진 단어는 유사한 의미를 가지는 단어로 amazing과 유사한 의미는 surprising이다.
02 두 단어의 관계는 반의어이다. delighted 기쁜, sorrowful 슬픈 include 포함하다 exclude 제외하다
03 (1) 혼잣말을 하다 = say to oneself (2) 상자 = chest, box (3) 채우다 = pack
04 'Don't take it so hard.'는 '너무 심각하게 여기지 마.'에 해당하는 의미이다.
05 '대량으로 물건을 사고파는 사람'은 '상인 = merchant'이다.
06 valuable 소중한 priceless 매우 가치 있는 valueless 가치 없는 worthless 가치 없는 expensive 비싼 terrible 지독한
07 '너무 비싸다'는 말에 (B) 동의하지 않는 내용과 새로운 기능을 언급하고 (C) 그렇다면 그것을 사자고 동의하고 (A) 거기에 동의하는 내용과 구입 결정의 순서가 자연스러운 배열이다.
08 쉬는 시간을 가지는 것은 스트레스를 극복하는 것이므로 '극복하다'의 의미로 'get over'가 되어야 한다.

10 정답 및 해설

09 '움직임이 서툴다'의 의미로 'have two left feet'이 적절하다.

10 소라의 질문에 "I'm not sure."라고 대답하는 것으로 보아 Oliver는 가입할 동아리를 정하지 못했다는 것을 알 수 있다.

11 이어지는 대화에서 가격에 대한 정보가 주어지는 것으로 보아 앞에서 가격에 대한 궁금증을 나타내는 표현이 있었음을 알 수 있다.

12 '~도 마찬가지이다.'의 의미로 동의를 나타낼 때는 'So+동사+주어.'의 표현이 된다.

13 ① Jimin은 전화기 케이스가 좋다고 동의한다. ② 싼 것을 구한다는 내용은 없다. ③ 소년의 말에 동의하지 않는 것으로 보아 소녀는 케이스가 너무 비싸다고 생각하지 않는다. ④, ⑤ 소년은 케이스 구입에 동의한다.

14 동사 told의 직접목적어가 되는 명사절을 유도하는 것은 관계대명사 what이다.

15 선행사 the picture가 있을 때 관계대명사는 that/which이다.

16 동사 expect의 목적격보어는 to부정사이다. arrive를 to arrive라고 해야 한다.

17 지각동사 heard의 목적격보어는 원형부정사가 되어야 한다.

18 ③ the letter라는 선행사가 있을 때는 관계대명사 that 또는 which를 써야 한다.

19 (1) 선행사를 포함하는 관계대명사는 what (2) the money를 선행사로 하는 관계대명사는 that (3), (4) 지각동사 heard, noticed의 목적격보어는 원형부정사

20 선행사를 포함하는 관계대명사 what이 이끄는 절이 '~하는 것'이라는 의미로 쓰여 문장에서 목적어 역할을 하고 있다.

21 Antonio가 머나먼 섬을 방문하는 데 얼마나 오래 걸렸는지는 대답할 수 없다. ① He lived in Genoa, Italy. ② He supported his family by trading. ④ He traded tools for spices and books for nuts. ⑤ They appeared when dinner was served.

22 ③번 다음 문장의 amazing animals에 주목한다. 주어진 문장의 two cats를 가리키므로 ③번이 적절하다.

23 chest: (보통 나무로 만든) 궤[상자], 물건을 보관하기 위해 사용되는 크고 무거운 상자

24 (A) 고양이는 '쓸모없다'고 해야 하므로 worthless가 적절하다. worthless: 가치 없는, priceless: 대단히 귀중한, (B) 나는 여왕에게 '값진' 것을 가져다 줄 것이라고 해야 하므로 valuable이 적절하다. valueless: 가치 없는, (C) '대단히 귀중한' 선물이라고 해야 하므로 priceless가 적절하다.

25 ⓐ와 ②, ③, ⑤는 부사적 용법, ① 명사적 용법, ④ 형용사적 용법

26 ⓑ와 ②, ⑤번: 동격의 접속사, ① 목적격 관계대명사, ③ 지시부사, ④ = the climate, [반복의 대명사로서] (…의) 그것

Animals, Big and Small

기는 집에서 흔히 보는 기계이다. 흔한: common

06 (1) keep an eye on 지켜보다 (2) have a long face 표정이 우울하다

07 내용상 '개는 사람보다 냄새에 예민하다'가 되어야 한다. 예민한 = sensitive

교과서
Conversation

핵심 Check p.64~65

1 (1) Which (2) prefer **2** (B) → (D) → (C) → (A)
3 tell / tell **4** (C) → (D) → (A) → (E) → (B)

04 (C) 새가 어려움을 겪는 것에 대하여 더 많은 설명을 요청한다. → (D) 새들이 어려움을 겪는 이유를 설명해 준다. → (A) 새들이 어려움을 겪는 것에 대한 설명을 듣고 상황을 이해하고 도움을 줄 방법을 묻는다. → (E) 새들에게 도움을 줄 방법을 설명해 준다. → (B) 도움을 줄 방법들에 대하여 칭찬한다.

교과서 대화문 익히기

Check(√) True or False p.66

1 F 2 T 3 T 4 F 5 F

교과서 확인학습 p.68~69

Listen – Listen and Answer – Dialog 1

how / great, having / Me, show, great / By, decide / yet, Which, think, better / hiking, see wild, insects / join, birds / heard, guide

Listen – Listen and Answer – Dialog 2

look, chestnut, woods / tell, how old / about / ten times / beehive up / guess, bees live / guess, big enough, hold / Unbelievable

Listen More - Listen and choose.

take, look / What, for / trying, choose, story / What's, about / tell, more about / endangered animals, Arctic / sounds / Which picture / showing, skinny

Speak – Talk in groups.

like better / like, friendly, How about / Me, much cleaner

시험대비 실력평가 p.62

01 ④ 02 ⑤ 03 ② 04 ①
05 ③ 06 ④ 07 ①
08 difference(s)

01 '꿀을 생산하기 위하여 벌이 길러지는 구조물'은 벌집이다.

02 '꿈에 대하여 말해 주겠니?'에 이어서 꿈에 대한 설명이 이어지는 것으로 보아 긍정적인 대답이 되도록 해야 한다.

03 'It's great.'에 이어지는 긍정적인 내용이 되어야 한다.

04 'Many of my friends have lost their homes.'를 통해서 서식지가 없어지는 파괴의 내용이 되어야 한다는 것을 알 수 있다.

05 'I was almost hit.'을 통해서 길을 건널 때 차량을 피하는 것이 어려움을 알 수 있다. 차량이 서둘러 지나가는 것을 나타내어 '서두르는'의 'in a hurry'가 되는 것이 적절하다.

06 ④ come out of nowhere: 느닷없이 나타나다

07 guess는 '추측하다'의 의미로 estimate와 비슷한 의미이다.

08 소유격에 이어지는 명사가 있어야 하므로 differ의 명사 difference가 적절하다.

서술형 시험대비 p.63

01 (r)egularly 02 (c)ontain
03 (A)rctic
04 (1) (t)errible (2) lost (3) (t)ell (4) (n)owhere
05 (1) (t)breathe (2) shy (3) after (4) common
06 (1) (k)eep, (e)ye, (o)n (2)(h)as, (l)ong, (f)ace
07 (s)ensitive

01 주어진 단어는 반의어의 관계이다. defend 방어하다 attack 공격하다 irregularly 불규칙적으로 regularly 규칙적으로

02 hold는 '수용하다'의 의미로 '포함하다, 담다'의 의미에 해당하는 contain이 적절하다.

03 '지구의 가장 북쪽과 관련이 있는'은 '북극의'에 해당하는 영어 설명이다.

04 (1) 끔찍한, 지독한 = terrible (2) 길을 잃다 = get lost (3) 분간하다 = tell (4) 느닷없이 나오다 = come out of nowhere

05 (1) 공기가 신선하여 등산하던 사람들이 천천히 숨을 쉬기 시작했다. 숨을 쉬다: breathe (2) 초등학교에 친구가 별로 없었던 이유는 내성적이어서였다. 내성적인: shy (3) 테레사 수녀는 가난한 사람을 돌보며 평생을 보냈다. 돌보다 look after (4) 세탁

대한 추가적인 설명을 해주고 (A) 마침내 무엇에 대한 설명인지 알아듣는 순서가 되어야 한다.

06 이어지는 대화를 보아 장기 자랑을 재미있어 하는 내용이 되도록 해야 한다. have a lot of fun = 매우 재미있게 보내다.

07 상대방의 말에 동의해서 '나도 그래.'라고 할 때는 'So+동사 + 주어.'를 사용한다. 앞에 나온 문장이 be동사를 사용하고 있어서 so 다음에는 be동사를 써야 한다.

08 그런데 = by the way, ~에 대하여 결정하다 = decide on, 오후 프로그램 = the afternoon program

09 "I'll join you."라고 한 것은 소년이었기 때문에 "소년이 소녀를 따라간다"라고 해야 한다.

10 소년이 수영하러 가는 것을 좋아하는 지는 나오지 않았다.

시험대비 기본평가　　　　　　　p.70

| 01 ④ | 02 ③ | 03 ① | 04 ② |

01 'Me, too.'라고 동의하는 대답을 했기 때문에 어젯밤의 장기 자랑에 대한 긍정적인 대답이 되도록 하여야 한다.

02 'It's about 150 years old.'라는 대답으로 보아 chestnut tree에 대한 설명 'This is the oldest tree in these woods.'에 대한 추가적인 내용을 묻는 질문이 되어야 한다.

03 상대방의 의견을 물어보는 표현이 되어야 한다.

04 'I like cats better.'에 대하여 동의하는 입장이기 때문에 고양이의 장점에 대한 설명이 이어지는 것이 적절하다.

시험대비 실력평가　　　　　　　p.71~72

| 01 ① | 02 ⑤ | 03 ② | 04 ⑤ |
| 05 ③ | 06 ② | 07 ③ | |

08 By the way, did you decide on the afternoon program?

| 09 ④ | 10 ⑤ |

01 이어지는 설명으로 보아 사진의 용도를 물어보는 표현이 되어야 한다. 용도를 물어볼 때는 'What ~ for?'라고 한다.

02 이어지는 고양이에 대한 긍정적인 설명으로 보아 고양이를 좋아한다는 말에 대한 동의의 표현이 적절하다.

03 (A) 음악의 구체적인 종류들이 나오기 때문에 사례를 나타내는 like가 적절하다. (B) 'like better'에 대한 대답이기 때문에 더 좋아한다는 내용이 어울린다. (C) 힙합을 더 좋아하기 때문에 그 이유가 될 만한 긍정적인 내용이 와야 한다.

04 (C) sunglasses가 무엇인지에 대한 질문을 하고 (B) 그 질문에 대하여 sunglasses가 무엇인지 설명을 하고, (A) 그에 대하여 추가적인 질문을 하는 순서가 자연스러운 배열이다.

05 (B) 앞에서 설명한 내용에 추가 설명을 요청하고 (C) 그 설명에

서술형 시험대비　　　　　　　p.73

01 wants to choose a picture for his story in the school newspaper

02 nature's future

03 I don't understand why people are in such a hurry.

04 What do you prefer, pizza or fried chicken? → Which do you prefer, pizza or fried chicken?

05 age

06 it's big enough to hold over 50,000 bees.

01 대화에 나온 "What are these for?"는 "이것들은 무엇을 위한 것이냐?"의 의미로 이유를 물어보는 질문이므로 그 대답에 해당하는 것을 써야 한다.

03 이해가 안 돼요 = I don't understand, 왜 사람들이 ~인지 = why people ~, 그토록 서두르다 = be in such a hurry

04 'A or B'처럼 범위가 정해진 것 중에서 어느 것인지를 물어볼 때는 what이 아니라 which로 물어본다.

05 나이를 물어본 질문에 이어지는 대화의 열 배는 자기의 나이를 기준으로 말한 것이다.

06 enough는 big 뒤에 써야 한다. 수용하다 = hold

교과서

Grammar

핵심 Check　　　　　　　p.74~75

1 (1) working　(2) sleeping　(3) walking　(4) is waiting
　(5) are　(6) broken　(7) discussed

2 (1) built　(2) written　(3) allowed　(4) climbing　(5) taken

3 (1) Since　(2) Though　(3) since　(4) Though　(5) though

13

01 ④	02 ④	03 ①	04 ④

05 (1) wearing　(2) since

01 '서 있는'의 의미를 가지는 현재분사를 써야 한다.

02 ④ 수식을 받는 food가 요리를 하는 것이 아니라 요리되는 것이기 때문에 과거분사를 써야 한다.

03 보기 문장의 밑줄 친 taken은 과거분사이다. 밑줄 친 부분 중 과거분사로 쓰인 것은 ①의 named이고 나머지는 모두 과거형이다.

04 주어진 의미에 맞도록 '날씨가 춥다'는 사실이 양보의 부사절이 되어야 하기 때문에 'it is cold'를 접속사 though가 유도해야 한다.

05 (1) 수식을 받는 the man이 셔츠를 입는 입장이기 때문에 현재분사 wearing이 되어야 한다. (2) 내용상 이유를 나타내기 때문에 since가 적절하다.

01 (1) The man running along the road was asking for help.
　(2) The boy eating lunch was sitting on the floor.
　(3) The man reading a book told us to be quiet.
　(4) The boys allowed to watch TV were eating snacks.

02 ③

03 (1) taken　(2) walking　(3) invited　(4) Since
　(5) Though

04 ⑤	05 ②	06 ③	07 ⑤
08 ④	09 ①		

10 (1) There was a boy playing on the beach.
　(2) I sat on the bench made of wood.
　(3) Since I am too young, I can't watch the film.

11 (1) made　(2) built　(3) painted　(4) moving
　(5) washed

12 ④	13 ④	14 ⑤	15 ④
16 ①	17 ④	18 ④	

01 (1) 현재분사 running ~이 명사 The man을 수식한다. (2) eating ~이 명사 The boy를 수식한다. (3) 현재분사 reading ~이 명사 The man을 수식한다. (4) 과거분사 allowed ~가 명사 The boys를 수식한다.

02 ③ 집에 머무르는 이유가 피곤하다고 느낀 것이므로 이유를 나타내는 접속사 since, because, as가 적절하다.

03 (1) 사진은 찍히기 때문에 과거분사 taken (2) 아이가 걷고 있는 것이므로 현재분사 walking (3) the man은 파티에 초대

를 받는 입장이기 때문에 invited (4) 이유를 나타내기 때문에 Since (5) 서로 대조적인 내용을 연결하기 때문에 양보의 접속사 Though가 적절하다.

04 ⑤ 주어진 내용은 이유를 나타내기 때문에 접속사를 Though가 아니라 Since, Because, As를 쓰는 것이 옳다.

05 동사는 look이고 sing은 현재분사가 되어서 the man을 수식하여야 한다.

06 ③의 found는 과거형 동사이고 나머지는 모두 과거분사이다.

07 ⑤ picture는 그려지는 것이기 때문에 수동의 의미를 나타내는 과거분사 painted가 되어야 한다.

08 내용상 원인과 결과의 관계가 성립하기 때문에 접속사 since가 적절하다.

09 그녀가 요리한 음식을 나타낼 때는 cook이 the food를 수식하는 과거분사가 되어서 'the food cooked ~'가 되어야 한다.

10 (1) 'There is/was ~'의 구문을 이용하고, '놀고 있는 아이'라는 뜻으로 'a boy playing ~'이라고 한다. (2) '나무로 만들어진 벤치'는 'bench made of wood'라고 한다. (3) 이유를 나타내는 접속사 since를 사용하여 문장을 연결한다.

11 (1) a cake는 만들어지는 것이므로 과거분사 made, (2) a castle은 지어지는 것이므로 과거분사 built (3) 벽은 칠해지는 입장이므로 과거분사 painted (4) the taxi driver는 가방을 운반하는 능동적인 입장이므로 현재분사 (5) a car는 세차되는 수동적인 입장이므로 과거분사가 적절하다.

12 ④ 문장의 주어는 An essay, 동사는 will receive이다. 동사 write는 essay를 수식하는 과거분사 written이 되어야 한다.

13 ④ 동사 enjoyed에 이어지는 talking은 동명사이고 나머지는 모두 현재분사이다.

14 ⑤ gift가 '주어진' 것이므로 수동의 의미를 지닌 과거분사 given이 되어야 한다.

15 수식을 받는 cold places가 Antarctica를 포함하기 때문에 현재분사형 전치사인 including이 적절하다.

16 서로 대조적인 내용의 절을 연결하는 접속사는 양보의 접속사 though, although이다.

17 ④의 since는 전치사로 쓰였고 나머지는 모두 접속사이다.

18 접속사 though를 기준으로 서로 대조되는 내용이 연결되도록 해야 한다.

01 (1) He didn't read the message sent to him.
　(2) The children playing basketball are my friends.
　(3) He was looking at the picture painted by my brother.

(4) Since the book was so interesting, I finished reading the book last night.

(5) Though I was hungry, I didn't eat the food.

02 Although

03 (1) sitting (2) lying (3) broken (4) showing
   (5) made

04 (1) Since (2) Though (3) Since (4) Though

05 a dog barking

06 The man walking his dogs is a famous singer.

07 becase[as, since]

08 (1) The church built 100 years ago has beautiful stained glass.

(2) The car rolling down the road made a loud noise.

(3) The woman cooking apple pies will give them to you.

(4) The photos taken by Ann show some wild birds.

(5) He was reading the message sent to him.

09 showing

10 (1) send → sent (2) sung → singing
   (3) eaten → eating

01 (1) message는 보내지는 수동의 입장이므로 sent로 수식한다. (2) '농구하고 있는 아이들'은 'children playing basketball' 이다. (3) '~에 의해서 그려진 그림'은 'a picture painted by ~'라고 한다. (4) '~해서'의 의미로 이유를 나타내는 접속사는 since이다. (5) 대조를 나타내는 접속사는 though이다.

02 대조를 나타내는 Though 대신에 쓸 수 있는 것은 Although 이다.

03 (1) The man은 앉아 있는 사람이기 때문에 현재분사 sitting (2) lie는 자동사로 '놓여 있는'이라고 할 때는 현재분사 lying (3) 문은 부서지는 것이므로 과거분사 broken (4) 사진이 보여 주고 있기 때문에 현재분사 (5) 수동의 의미이기 때문에 과거분사

04 (1), (3)은 이유를 나타내는 since, (2), (4)는 대조를 나타내는 though가 들어가야 한다.

05 "짖고 있는"이라는 의미로 명사 a dog를 꾸며주는 현재분사 "barking"을 쓰는 것이 적절하다.

06 walk는 '(동물을) 걷게 하다[산책시키다]'라는 뜻으로 현재분사 형태여야 한다.

07 이유를 나타내는 접속사 because[as, since]가 적절하다.

08 주어진 명사를 수식하는 분사구가 명사 뒤에 놓이도록 한다. 현재분사는 능동이나 진행의 의미로, 과거분사는 수동이나 완료의 의미로 사용한다.

09 '보여주는'에 해당하는 현재분사 showing이 적절하다.

10 (1) 신문이 보내진 것이므로 과거분사 sent (2) the actor는 노래를 부르기 때문에 현재분사 (3) 동물이 먹기 때문에 현재분사

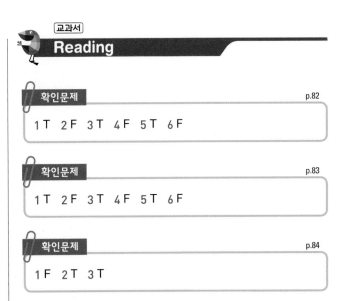

확인문제   p.82

1 T 2 F 3 T 4 F 5 T 6 F

확인문제   p.83

1 T 2 F 3 T 4 F 5 T 6 F

확인문제   p.84

1 F 2 T 3 T

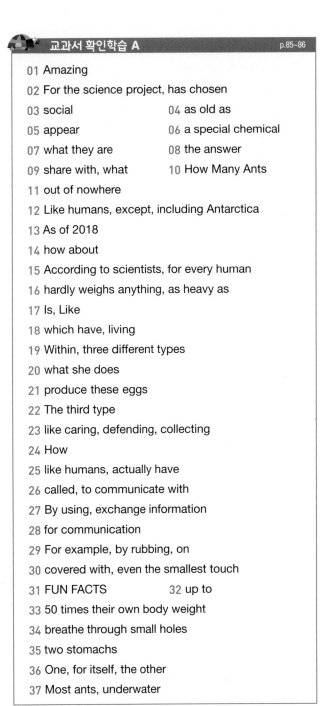

교과서 확인학습 A   p.85~86

01 Amazing

02 For the science project, has chosen

03 social   04 as old as

05 appear   06 a special chemical

07 what they are   08 the answer

09 share with, what   10 How Many Ants

11 out of nowhere

12 Like humans, except, including Antarctica

13 As of 2018

14 how about

15 According to scientists, for every human

16 hardly weighs anything, as heavy as

17 Is, Like

18 which have, living

19 Within, three different types

20 what she does

21 produce these eggs

22 The third type

23 like caring, defending, collecting

24 How

25 like humans, actually have

26 called, to communicate with

27 By using, exchange information

28 for communication

29 For example, by rubbing, on

30 covered with, even the smallest touch

31 FUN FACTS   32 up to

33 50 times their own body weight

34 breathe through small holes

35 two stomachs

36 One, for itself, the other

37 Most ants, underwater

15

1 The Amazing Ants

2 For the science project, our group has chosen very special insects.

3 They are very social.

4 They are as old as the T-Rex.

5 They appear in Aesop's stories.

6 They use a special chemical to communicate.

7 Can you guess what they are?

8 Yes, the answer is ants.

9 We want to share with you what we have learned about these insects.

10 How Many Ants Are on Earth?

11 We often see ants come out of nowhere.

12 Like humans, they live almost everywhere in the world, except a few extremely cold places including Antarctica.

13 As of 2018, there were over 7 billion people on Earth.

14 Then, how about ants?

15 According to scientists, there are about one million ants for every human in the world.

16 Though each ant hardly weighs anything, one million ants are as heavy as a human being weighing about 62 kilograms.

17 What Is the Ant Society Like?

18 Ants live in colonies which have lots of residents living together.

19 Within a colony, there are usually three different types of ants.

20 There is the queen, and what she does her entire life is lay eggs.

21 The second type of ant is the male that helps the queen produce these eggs.

22 The third type of ant is the worker.

23 Worker ants are all female and do very important jobs, like caring for eggs, defending the colony, and collecting food.

24 How Do Ants Communicate?

25 Though ants do not speak like humans, they actually have a "language."

26 Ants produce a chemical called a pheromone to communicate with one another.

27 By using the chemical, they can exchange information about food or danger.

28 Ants also use touch for communication.

29 For example, if an ant finds food, it passes on the good news by rubbing its body on its neighbor.

30 Since an ant has legs covered with very sensitive hairs, it can sense even the smallest touch.

31 FUN FACTS ABOUT ANTS

32 01 Some Queen ants live up to 30 years.

33 02 Some ants can carry things that are 50 times their own body weight.

34 03 Ants do not have lungs but breathe through small holes in their bodies.

35 04 An ant has two stomachs.

36 One stomach holds food for itself, and the other holds food to share with others.

37 05 Most ants can swim and live 24 hours underwater.

01 ③	02 ②	03 ⑤	04 ①, ④
05 has → have		06 colony	07 ②
08 ②, ③, ⑤	09 ①	10 ②	11 ①
12 먹이를 발견한 것		13 weighing	14 ②, ③
15 ④	16 (A) which	(B) produce	(C) third
17 ②, ③	18 ①, ④	19 ③	
20 (A) times	(B) the other	(C) others	21 ②
22 ②	23 ②	24 ③	25 ③

26 that are 50 times their own body weight

27 개미는 폐가 없지만, 몸에 있는 작은 구멍을 통해 호흡한다.

28 하나의 위에는 자신의 먹이를 저장하고 다른 하나의 위에는 다른 개미들과 함께 나눌 먹이를 저장한다.

01 개미가 등장한다고 했으므로, Aesop's stories는 인간 이외의 동물 또는 식물에 인간의 생활 감정을 부여하여 사람과 꼭 같이 행동하게 함으로써 그들의 행동 속에 교훈을 나타내려고 하는 '우화'에 속한다고 할 수 있다. ① 시, ② 수필, ③ 우화, ④ 희곡, ⑤ 시나리오

02 ⓑ와 ①, ③, ④: 부사적 용법, ②와 ⑤: 명사적 용법

03 '저희들은 이 곤충에 관해 알게 된 것을 여러분과 함께 나누고 싶습니다.'라고 했으므로, ⑤번이 적절하다.

04 그녀가 평생 하는 일은 '알을 낳는 것'이다. lay eggs는 문장의 보어로서, be동사 뒤에서 to부정사가 보어로 쓰일 때 to가 종종 생략된다. 이 경우 주어가 what이나 the only 등이고 do[does] 동사를 포함해야 한다.

05 which가 이끄는 주격 관계대명사절의 선행사가 colonies이므로 동사를 have로 고쳐야 한다.

06 colony: (동일 지역에 서식하는 동·식물의) 군집, 함께 살거나 자라는 같은 유형의 생물 집단

07 ⓐ 인간처럼 개미도 남극을 포함한 일부 극도로 추운 곳을 '제

외한' 전 세계 거의 모든 곳에 살고 있다고 해야 하므로, except 가 적절하다. except: ~ 제외하고는[외에는], ⓑ for: [each, every, 수사 등의 앞에 쓰여] …마다, …에 대하여

08 ⓒ와 ②, ③, ⑤: 현재분사, ①, ④: 동명사

09 개미는 소수의 아주 추운 곳에서는 살지 않는다고 언급되었다. ③ 개미들의 숫자가 인간들의 숫자보다 약 백만 배 더 많다.

10 (A)의 also에 주목한다. 개미들의 의사소통 방법을 설명한 (B) 에 이어서 또 다른 의사소통 방법을 설명하는 것이므로 (B) 다 음에 (A)가 이어지고 (C)의 touch가 (A)의 첫 부분에 나오는 touch에 이어지므로 (A) 다음에 (C)가 와야 한다. 그러므로 (B)-(A)-(C)의 순서가 적절하다.

11 이 글은 '개미들의 의사소통 방법'에 대한 글이므로, 주제로는 ①번이 적절하다.

12 좋은 소식은 '먹이를 발견한 것'을 가리킨다.

13 a human being을 수식하는 현재분사 weighing이 적절하다.

14 ① In spite of+명사구, ④ Despite+명사구, ⑤ As though: 마치 ~인 것처럼

15 위 글은 개미의 숫자에 관한 글이므로, 제목으로는 '지구상에는 얼마나 많은 개미가 있을까?'가 적절하다.

16 (A) 뒤에 불완전한 절이 이어지므로 관계대명사 which를 쓰는 것이 적절하다. (B) help는 준사역동사로 목적보어로 원형부 정사나 to부정사를 쓰는 것이 적절하다. (C) '세 번째' 종류라고 해야 하므로 서수 third가 옳다.

17 ⓐ와 ②, ③: 선행사 포함하는 관계대명사(~하는 것), ①, ⑤ 의문대명사(무엇) ④ 의문형용사(감탄문에서)

18 ⓑ와 ①, ④: ~을 돌보다, ② take after: ~을 닮다, ③ make sure: ~을 확실히 하다, ⑤ look for: ~을 찾다

19 ⓐ와 ③: (특정한 수)까지, ① (육체적·정신적으로) ~할 수 있 는, ② (특히 나쁜 짓을) 하고 있는, ④ ~의 의무[책임]인, ⑤ (특정한 기준)만큼

20 (A) 자기 몸무게의 '50배'라고 해야 하므로 times가 옳다. times: ~배, hours: ~ 시간, (B) 둘 중 하나는 one, 다른 하나 는 the other로 나타내므로 the other가 옳다. (C) '다른 개미 들'이라고 해야 하므로 others가 옳다.

21 '개미의 몸무게'는 알 수 없다. ① 30년. ③ 몸에 있는 작은 구멍 을 통해 호흡한다. ④ 두 개. ⑤ 24시간 동안 살 수 있다.

22 앞의 내용의 예가 나오고 있으므로 For example이 가장 적절 하다.

23 (A)와 ②, ③, ⑤: 동명사, ①, ④: 현재분사

24 ⓐ to: 한계, 범위, 기간의 끝을 나타냄, ⓑ feed on: ~을 먹다 [먹고 살다]

25 ③ 암컷이 수컷보다 더 오래 살 수 있는 이유는 대답할 수 없다. ① In places with still water. ② For about five to seven days. ④ No. ⑤ Up to 300 eggs.

26 50 times: 50배

27 03번의 내용을 쓰면 된다.

28 04번의 내용을 쓰면 된다.

01 what   02 in order / so as / in order that, may[can] / so that, may[can]

03 Can you guess what they are?

04 ⓐ out of nowhere   ⓑ As of 2018

05 how many ants

06 Since → Though[Although]

07 who[that] live

08 the queen, the male, the worker

09 such as

10 (A) called   (B) exchange   (C) covered

11 but   12 (A) chemical   (B) touch

01 뒤에 불완전한 절이 이어지므로 관계대명사를 써야 하는데, 선행사가 없으므로 what을 쓰는 것이 적절하다. 관계대명사 what은 선행사를 포함하여 '~하는 것'이라고 해석한다.

02 목적을 나타내는 to부정사는 in order to = so as to = in order that[so that] ~ may[can]로 고칠 수 있다.

03 이 문장은 Yes나 No로 대답할 수 있으므로, '동사가 guess일 때 간접의문문에서 의문사를 맨 앞으로 보내는 경우'에 해당하 지 않는다. what they are가 동사 guess의 목적어 역할을 하 는 간접의문문으로, '의문사+주어+동사'의 어순으로 쓰는 것이 적절하다.

04 ⓐ out of nowhere: 어디선지 모르게, 느닷없이 ⓑ as of: ~ 현재, ~일자로

05 바로 뒤 문장에 'According to scientists, there are about one million ants for every human in the world.'라는 말 이 나오므로, 'how about ants?(개미는 어떨까?)'는 '지구상에 얼마나 많은 개미가 있을까?'라는 의미임을 알 수 있다.

06 개미 한 마리는 거의 무게가 '나가지 않지만' 백만 마리의 개미 는 체중이 약 62kg인 사람 한 명과 무게가 같다고 해야 하므로 Since를 Though(Although)로 고치는 것이 적절하다.

07 living together는 lots of residents를 수식하는 분사구이며, who(that) live together로 바꾸어 쓸 수 있다.

08 '여왕개미', '수개미', '일개미'를 가리킨다.

09 like = such as: …와 같은

10 (A) 페로몬이라고 '불리는' 화학물질이라고 해야 하므로 called 가 옳다. (B) 정보를 '교환할 수 있다'고 해야 하므로 exchange 가 옳다. exchange: 교환하다, change: 변하다, 바꾸다, (C) 털로 '덮인' 다리라고 해야 하므로 covered가 옳다.

11 Though 대신 but을 쓸 수 있다.

12 개미는 페로몬이라고 불리는 '화학물질'과 '접촉'을 사용하여 의 사소통을 할 수 있다.

01 ①	02 ④	03 ③	04 ⑤
05 ①	06 ②	07 ③	08 ②
09 ⑤			

10 it's time to get serious about protecting birds.

11 ②	12 ④	13 ②	14 ③
15 ①	16 ③		

17 (1) I like every song sung by the singer.

    (2) He tried not to wake up the baby sleeping on the bed.

18 ②   19 endangering → endangered

20 ⑤   21 ②

22 (1) He is carrying a basket filled with cherries.

    (2) Since it is cold, I want to drink something hot.

    (3) I am tired though I slept enough last night.

23 ③	24 ⑤	25 ②	26 ④
27 ①, ④	28 ⑤	29 where → which[that]	

30 (A) honey   (B) hundreds of trips

01 '정확한지 확실하지 않을 때 질문에 답하거나 의견을 형성하려고 하다'는 '추측하다'에 해당한다.

02 '장기 자랑이 재미있었어.'에 동의하는 입장을 나타낼 수 있는 말이 되어야 한다.

03 'too bright'와 대조적인 의미로 'dark 어두운'가 적절하다.

04 ⑤ 동사 like는 '좋아하다'의 의미이다.

05 사진을 살펴보라는 말에 대하여 사진의 용도를 물어보았기 때문에 사진의 용도를 나타낼 수 있는 말이 되어야 한다.

06 이어지는 'Me, too.'에 따라오는 고양이의 장점을 보았을 때 고양이에 대한 긍정적인 언급이 있었다는 것을 알 수 있다.

07 (B) 앞에 나온 질문에 대답하고 선호를 묻는다. (C) 그 질문에 대하여 hiking이라고 대답하고 이유를 말한다. (D) 그 이유를 듣고 함께 가겠다고 하니까 (A) 잘 되었다고 대답한다.

08 ② 이어지는 설명에 '길을 잃어버린다.'는 내용을 보면 새가 겪는 어려움에 대한 언급이 있었음을 알 수 있다.

09 이어지는 새들에게 도움이 되는 일을 해야 한다는 언급을 보면 새들의 어려움에 안타까움을 나타내는 말이 적절하다.

10 ~할 시간이다 = it's time to ~ 진지해지다 = get serious 조류를 보호하다 = protect birds

11 새들이 길을 잃는 것은 밤에 너무 밝은 도시 때문이다.

12 child를 수식하는 현재분사가 와야 한다.

13 나이가 어리다는 것이 이유이므로 'I am young'을 접속사 since가 유도하여야 한다.

14 ③ 동사 mind는 동명사를 목적어로 가진다. your brother는 의미상의 주어이고, talking은 동명사이다. 나머지는 모두 현재분사이다.

15 서로 대조적인 내용을 연결하는 접속사 though가 적절하다.

16 수동의 의미이므로 과거분사가 적절하다.

18 제시된 문장과 ②의 밑줄 친 부분은 현재분사이고 나머지는 모두 동명사이다.

19 '멸종위기에 처한'이라는 의미는 endangered이다.

20 "매우 조심스럽게 일하는 여자"는 'the woman working very carefully'라고 한다.

21 ② 문맥상 이유를 나타내므로 since, because, as를 쓴다.

22 (1) '~로 가득 찬'이라고 할 때는 과거분사 filled (2) 문맥상 이유를 나타내므로 since, as, because가 알맞다. (3) 서로 대조되는 내용의 연결에서는 접속사 though

23 ③번 다음 문장의 내용에 주목한다. 주어진 문장(개미는 어떨까? 즉, 지구상에 얼마나 많은 개미가 있을까?)의 대답에 해당하므로 ③번이 적절하다.

24 ⓐ와 ⑤ ~처럼(전치사), ① ~와 비슷한(전치사), ② 좋아하다(동사), ③ ~과 같은(such as)(전치사), ④ 비슷한(형용사)

25 백만 마리의 개미는 체중이 약 62kg인 사람 한 명과 무게가 같다고 했으므로, 백만 마리의 개미의 무게는 약 62kg이다. ③ less 원급 than: ~보다 덜 …한, ④ not so 원급 as: ~만큼 …하지 않은

26 화학물질과 접촉을 사용한 개미의 의사소통 방법을 설명하는 글이므로, 개미들은 실제로 '언어'를 가지고 있다고 하는 것이 적절하다. ① 문자, ② 규칙, ③ 상징(물), ⑤ 문화

27 ⓑ와 ①, ④: [이유를 나타내어] …이므로, ②, ③, ⑤ …부터 [이후]

28 ⑤ 개미들은 아주 미세한 접촉도 감지할 수 있다.

29 where 뒤에 절의 주어가 없기 때문에, where를 관계대명사 which[that]로 고쳐야 한다.

30 적은 양의 '꿀'을 만들기 위해 일벌은 '수백 번의 이동'을 하고, 그렇게 하면서 식물이 수분(受粉)하는 것을 돕는다.

01 (p)rovide	02 endangered	03 ①	
04 ④	05 ③	06 ③	07 ②
08 ③	09 ②	10 ④	11 ④
12 ①	13 ④	14 covered	15 ②
16 ③	17 ②	18 ④	

19 ⓐ caring   ⓑ defending   ⓒ collecting

20 ③	21 ⑤	22 ①, ③	23 an ant
24 legs	25 ②		

26 (A) 개미는 항상 바쁘고 전혀 휴식을 취하지 않는 것처럼 보이는 것

    (B) 일개미는 하루에 약 250번의 짧은 잠을 자며 휴식을 취하고, 이 잠은 불과 1분 정도 이어진다는 것

    (C) 여왕개미는 하루에 90번 잠을 자고, 한 번에 약 6분 동안 잠을 자는 것

01 주어진 단어는 비슷한 말의 관계이다. offer 제공하다 provide 제공하다

02 북극에 있는 동물들이 '멸종 위기에 처했다.'는 의미로 '멸종 위기에 처한 = endangered'가 적절하다.

03 unbelievable 믿을 수 없는 – incredible 믿을 수 없는

04 'like better'에 대한 대답이기 때문에 '더 좋아하다'에 해당하는 의미가 되어야 한다.

05 communication은 소식을 전하는 것을 나타낸다. give up 포기하다 get over 극복하다 pass on 전달하다 look after 돌보다 wait for 기다리다

06 '여러 가지 중에서 어느 것을 원하는지 결정하다'는 '선택하다'에 해당한다.

07 동식물이 무리를 이루어 살고 있는 집단을 'colony 군집, 군락'이라고 한다.

08 코끼리 무리에서 새끼를 돌보는 것은 암컷이다.

09 문맥상 캠프가 재미있다는 말에 동의하는 내용이기 때문에 "The talent show last night was good."이 적절하다.

10 오후 프로그램으로 hiking을 선택했기 때문에 수영에 관해서는 위 대화를 통해서 알 수 없다.

11 빈칸 뒤에 이어지는 내용으로 보아 빈칸에는 상대방의 말에 동의하는 표현이 들어가야 한다. 'Me, too.'나 'So do I.'가 적절하다.

12 빈칸 앞에 추가 설명을 요청하는 표현이 주어진 것으로 보아 앞에서 설명한 대상에 대한 추가적인 정보를 제공하는 말이 적절하다.

13 제시된 문장과 ④는 현재분사이고 나머지는 동명사이다.

14 legs는 hairs로 덮이는 수동의 입장이기 때문에 과거분사 covered가 적절하다.

15 ② language는 말해지는 수동의 입장이므로 과거분사 spoken이 되어야 한다.

16 소설은 Albert Camus에 의해서 쓰여진 것이기 때문에 과거분사 written이 되어야 한다.

17 '~ 때문에'에 해당하는 since가 적절하다.

18 (A) 서로 대조되는 내용을 연결하는 접속사 (B) 이유를 나타내는 접속사

19 전치사 like 뒤에 동명사 caring, defending, collecting이 병렬로 연결되는 것이 적절하다.

20 (A)와 ②, ③, ⑤: 관계대명사, ①, ④: 지시대명사

21 일개미는 모두 '암컷'이다.

22 ⓐ와 ①, ③: 부사적 용법, ②, ⑤: 명사적 용법, ④: 형용사적 용법

23 '개미'를 가리킨다.

24 개미는 (자극에) 매우 민감한 털로 덮인 '다리' 덕분에, 아주 미세한 접촉도 감지할 수 있다.

25 ⓐ 일개미가 하루에 4시간 정도 잠을 자는 반면에, 여왕개미는 하루에 90번 잠을 잔다고 해야 하므로 On the other hand가 적절하다. ⓑ 앞 문장에서 개미들의 수면 시간을 설명하고 있으므로, '즉', 방식이 다르기는 하지만 개미도 우리처럼 잠을 자

고 휴식을 취한다고 하는 것이 적절하다. In short = In brief: 즉, 간단히 말해서, ① Thus: 이렇게 하여; 이와 같이, To sum up: 요컨대, 요약해서 말하면, ③ As a result: 그 결과

26 각각 앞문장의 내용을 가리킨다.

서술형 실전문제   p.106~107

01 insect   02 (s)elect
03 (1) decide   (2) hold
04 (1) Ants   (2) language   (3) chemical   (4) information
05 better   06 (1) painting   (2) made   (3) invited
07 (T)hough   08 (A) out of   (B) almost   (C) people
09 Though[Although] each ant hardly weighs anything
10 There are about one million ants.
11 ⓐ using   ⓑ rubbing
12 (A) which[that] is   (C) which[that] are
13 먹이를 발견할 경우 개미는 자기 몸을 이웃의 개미에게 문질러서 좋은 소식을 전달한다.

01 여섯 개의 다리와 때로는 날개를 가진 파리나 개미 같은 작은 생물은 '곤충'이다.

02 '선택하다' choose의 비슷한 말은 select이다.

03 (1) 결정하다 = decide (2) 수용하다 = hold

04 (1) 군집을 이루는 것은 보기에서 개미이다. (2) 소통을 하기 위한 언어가 적절하다. (3) 페르몬이라 불리는 것은 화학물질이다. (4) 화학물질을 통해서 정보를 주고받는다.

05 빈칸 앞에서 더 좋아하는 것을 소개하고 상대방의 경우에는 어떤지 물어 본 것이기 때문에 빈칸에는 더 좋아하는 것에 대한 대답이 되도록 한다.

06 (1) 명사 the man을 꾸며주는 분사가 명사와 능동의 관계이므로 현재분사 (2) 명사 the pizza를 꾸며주는 분사가 명사와 수동의 관계이므로 과거분사 (3) 명사 The people을 꾸며주는 분사가 명사와 수동의 관계이므로 과거분사가 적절하다.

07 '비록 ~해도, ~할지라도'의 의미는 대조를 나타내는 접속사 though가 되어야 한다.

08 (A) '난데없이 나타나는' 개미들이라고 해야 하므로 out of가 옳다. out of nowhere 어디선가 모르게. 느닷없이, into: ~ 안으로, (B) '거의' 모든 곳이라고 해야 하므로 almost가 옳다. almost: 거의, most: 대부분의, (C) 70억이 넘는 '인구(사람들)'라고 해야 하므로 people이 옳다. people: 사람들, peoples: 민족들

09 '비록 ~이지만'이라는 뜻의 양보를 나타내는 접속사 Though[Although]를 사용하는 것이 적절하다.

10 세상에는 사람 한 명당 약 백만 마리의 개미가 있다.

11 전치사 by 다음에 동명사로 쓰는 것이 적절하다.

12 주격 관계대명사와 be동사가 생략되어 있다.

13 For example 다음의 내용을 쓰는 것이 적절하다.

19

창의사고력 서술형 문제 p.108

|모범답안|

01 (1) keep an eye on (2) has a long face
   (3) was all ears (4) turn my nose up at
   (5) learn by heart (6) cost an arm and a leg

02 (1) Since (2) since (3) Though (4) though

03 (A) warm places (B) five years
   (C) about seven weeks (D) to collect food
   (E) hundreds of trips (F) grow

01 (1) keep an eye on: ~을 지켜보다 (2) has a long face: 표정이 우울하다 (3) be all ears: 경청하다 (4) turn one's nose up at: ~을 거절하다 (5) learn by heart: ~을 암기하다 (6) cost an arm and a leg: 비싼 값을 치르다

01 (1) 비가 심하게 내려서 축구 경기가 취소되었다. (2) 함께 이야기할 사람이 없기 때문에 나는 파티에 가기를 원하지 않는다. (3) 비록 그가 웃고 있어도, 그는 그리 행복해 보이지 않는다. (4) 비록 추워도 날씨는 맑았다.

단원별 모의고사 p.109~112

01 (f)emale 02 (s)elect 03 ① 04 ④
05 ③ 06 (1) weighs (2) colonies
   (3) exchange (4) sensitive
07 ⑤ 08 ①
09 Is there anything we can do to help them?
10 ⑤ 11 ① 12 ③ 13 ②
14 ② 15 ④ 16 ③ 17 ④
18 ⑤ 19 ③ 20 ②, ⑤
21 (A) billion (B) how about (C) hardly 22 ②
23 여왕개미: 평생 알을 낳는다.
   수개미: 여왕이 알을 낳는 것을 돕는다.
   일개미: 알을 돌보고, 군집을 방어하며, 먹이를 모으는 것과 같은 매우 중요한 일을 한다.
24 a pheromone 25 sensible → sensitive

01 주어진 단어의 관계가 반의어이므로 'male 수컷 : female 암컷'이 되어야 한다.

02 주어진 단어의 관계가 비슷한 말이므로 'choose 선택하다 : select 선택하다'의 관계가 되어야 한다.

03 '사람들이 원하는 것을 제공하다' offer 제공하다, 제안하다

04 질문이 선호하는 것이기 때문에 대답도 선호하는 것이 되어야 한다. prefer = like better

05 곤충, 식물, 동물의 집단을 '군집, 군락 = colony'이라고 한다.

06 (1) 무게가 나가다 weigh (2) 군집 colony (3) 교환하다 exchange (4) 예민한 sensitive

07 ⑤의 chemical은 명사로 쓰여서 '화학물질'이라는 뜻이다.

08 hold는 '수용하다'는 뜻으로 '담다 = contain'이 적절하다.

09 ~가 있니? = Is there ~?, 우리가 할 수 있는 어떤 일 = anything (that) we can do, 그들을 돕기 위하여 = to help them

10 새들이 밝은 밤하늘에서 길을 찾는 데 어려움이 있으므로 새들을 돕기 위하여 밤에 불필요한 불은 꺼야 한다. catch on 유행하다 turn around 돌아가다 get over 극복하다 care for 좋아하다 turn off 끄다

11 ① 새들이 어려움에 처해 있는 것은 밤에 길을 찾는 것이다.

12 (B) 앞에 나온 질문에 대답을 하고 벌이 몇 마리 사는지 다시 질문한 것에 (C) 500이라고 대답한다. 그리고 (A) 그 대답에 대한 추가 설명이 이어지는 순서가 자연스러운 배열이다.

13 ② 자신이 선호하는 것을 말하고, 상대방은 어떤지 물어보았기 때문에 선호하는 것에 대한 대답이 나와야 한다.

14 어젯밤 장기 자랑에 대한 이야기에서 다른 화제로 전환할 때는 'by the way = 그런데'가 적절하다.

15 ④ 내용상 함께 하이킹을 가기로 하는 내용이므로 '함께 할게.'에 해당하는 말이 들어가야 한다.

16 ③ 'G: I'll go hiking because we can see wild birds and insects in the woods.'를 보면 소녀는 오후 프로그램을 정했다는 것을 알 수 있다.

17 ④ 동사 enjoy는 동명사를 목적어로 가지기 때문에 jogging은 동명사이고 나머지는 분사이다.

18 ⑤ 대조되는 내용을 연결하는 접속사는 though이다. '시간이 별로 없지만 = Though I don't have much time'

19 ③ 원인을 유도하는 접속사는 since가 적절하다. though는 서로 대조적인 내용을 나타내기 때문에 이 문장에서는 적절하지 않다.

20 '지각동사(see)+목적어+목적보어' 구문으로, 목적보어 자리에 동사원형이나 현재분사가 적절하다.

21 (A) 앞에 숫자가 있을 때는 billion에 s를 붙이지 않는다. (B) '그렇다면. 개미는 어떨까?'라고 해야 하므로 how about이 옳다. (C) 개미 한 마리는 '거의 무게가 나가지 않지만'이라고 해야 하므로 hardly가 옳다. hardly: 거의 ~ 아니다[없다]

22 위 글은 개미 사회에 대한 글이므로, 제목으로는 '개미 사회는 어떠한가?'가 적절하다.

23 ⓐ 뒤에 이어지는 문장들의 내용을 쓰면 된다.

24 '페로몬'을 가리킨다.

25 개미는 (자극에) 매우 '민감한' 털로 덮인 다리가 있기 때문에, 아주 미세한 접촉도 감지할 수 있다고 하는 것이 적절하다. sensitive: 예민한, 민감한, sensible: 분별[양식] 있는

The Full Jar

교과서
Reading

📎 **확인문제**   p.116

1 T   2 F   3 T   4 F   5 T   6 F

📎 **확인문제**   p.117

1 T   2 F   3 T   4 F   5 T   6 F

교과서 확인학습 A   p.118~119

01 Full	02 before his class
03 a large jar	04 fill, with, from the bag
05 Is the jar full	06 They all
07 out of the bag, poured them	
08 a little, rolled into	
09 the same question, the same answer	
10 took out, poured, into	11 fill, once more
12 replied	13 out of the bag
14 fill the spaces	15 is just like
16 what is most important	17 is lost
18 valued	19 all the small things
20 there's no room for	21 The same goes for
22 spend, on, what is really important	
23 Take care of, matter	24 sitting, raised
25 you asked	26 seem full, room for

교과서 확인학습 B   p.120~121

1 The Full Jar

2 Mr. Jenkins stood before his class.

3 He had a large jar and a big bag on the teacher's desk.

4 When the class began, he picked up the jar and started to fill it with golf balls from the bag.

5 He asked the students, "Is the jar full?"

6 They all said, "Yes."

7 The teacher took a box of small stones out of the bag and poured them into the jar.

8 He shook the jar a little, and the stones rolled into the open areas between the golf balls.

9 He asked the same question and got the same answer from his students.

10 Next, the teacher took out a bottle of sand and poured it into the jar.

11 After he watched the sand fill the spaces between the stones, he asked once more, "Is the jar full?"

12 All the students replied, "Yes."

13 Suddenly Mr. Jenkins took a can of apple juice out of the bag.

14 He poured the apple juice into the jar, and his students watched it fill the spaces in the sand.

15 "Now," the teacher said, "I want you to understand that your life is just like the jar.

16 The golf balls are what is most important in life: your family, your friends, your health, and your dreams.

17 Even when everything else is lost, your life can still be full.

18 The stones are the other things valued by people, like your job, your house, and your car.

19 The sand is all the small things."

20 "If you put the sand into the jar first," he said, "there's no room for the stones or the golf balls.

21 The same goes for life.

22 If you spend all your time and energy on the small things, you will never have room for what is really important to you.

23 Take care of the balls first — the things that really matter."

24 One student sitting in the back raised her hand and asked, "What does the apple juice mean?"

25 Mr. Jenkins smiled, "I'm glad you asked.

26 It just shows that though your life may seem full, there's always room for a cool drink with a friend."

서술형 실전문제   p.122~124

01 taking / taking   02 value

03 (1) same   (2) suddenly   (3) full

04 (s)pace   05 ⓒto build → build(또는 building)

06 (1) raised   (2) (r)eply

07 (1) They've already poured a lot of time and money into this project.

(2) The air was filled with the scent of roses.

(3) It does not matter how you do it

08 (1) I can play the piano a little

(2) I often watch him play[playing] tennis.

(3) The symbols stand for what we all want: beauty, fame, and wealth.

(4) Can you make yourself understood in French?

(5) She is not the one wearing sunglasses indoors to avoid eye contact.

09 (1) Herold is the boy dancing to the music.

(2) There were many soldiers injured in the war.

(3) We had a special dish made with milk and ice.

10 (1) She is talking with a girl wearing glasses.

(2) She heard him open[opening] the window.

11 (1) Robert watched a thief steal[stealing] a lady's bag.

(2) Theresa heard her dog barking loudly.

12 small stones → golf balls / golf balls → small stones

13 ⓐ Is the jar full? ⓑ Yes.

14 roll into, the golf balls

15 what   16 such as

17 (1) 인생에서 가장 중요한 것: 여러분의 가족, 친구, 건강, 꿈

(2) 사람들이 소중하게 여기는 다른 것들: 여러분의 직업, 집, 자동차

(3) 온갖 사소한 것들

18 ⓐ the small things

ⓑ what is really important to you 또는 the things that really matter

19 병에 모래를 먼저 채우면 돌이나 골프공을 채울 공간이 없어지는 것처럼, 사소한 것에 여러분의 시간과 에너지를 모두 허비한다면, 여러분에게 진정으로 중요한 것을 채울 공간은 절대로 없을 것이다.

20 a room → room

01 take care of ~: ~을 돌보다, ~에 신경을 쓰다 / 네가 떠나 있는 동안에 누가 개를 돌봐주니? take out: ~을 꺼내다 / 그 공무원은 그녀의 공책을 꺼내기 시작했다.

02 우리가 그 문헌을 더 많이 연구하면 할수록 저자들의 지혜를 더욱더 높이 평가하게 된다. value: ~을 높이 평가하다, 중시하다 appreciate: ~을 높이 평가하다

03 (1) same: 같은 / 그는 매일 밤 같은 의자에 앉는다. (2) suddenly: 갑자기 / 나를 따라오는 사람이 있다는 것을 갑자기 깨달았다. (3) full: 가득 찬 / 입에 음식을 가득 넣은 채로 말을 하지 마라.

04 space: (비어 있는) 공간 / 비어 있는 공간.

05 watch+목적어+동사원형[현재분사]: 목적어가 ~하는 것을 보다

06 (1) raise: ~을 들다 (2) reply: 대답하다

07 (1) pour A into B: A를 B에 붓다 (2) scent: 향기 fill A with B: A(그릇·장소 등)를 B(물건·사람)로 채우다 (3) matter: 중요하다

08 (1) a little: 조금(은), 다소는, 좀 a few: 조금[약간]은 있는, 조금의, 여기서 little은 부사로 쓰이고 있으나 few에는 부사로서의 용법이 없다. (2) '지각동사(watch)+목적어+원형부정사[현재분사]'이므로 play나 playing이 적절하다. (3) for와 want의 목적어 역할을 할 수 있도록 that을 what으로 고쳐야 한다. (4) yourself가 남에게 이해되는 것이므로 수동의 의미를 나타내는 과거분사가 적절하다. (5) is라는 본동사가 있으므로 wears를 the one을 수식하는 현재분사 wearing으로 고치는 것이 적절하다.

09 분사에 다른 수식어구가 함께 있는 경우 명사를 뒤에서 수식하며 이때 '관계대명사+be동사'를 생략한 형태로 볼 수 있다.

10 (1) 안경을 끼고 있는 것이므로 현재분사가 수식하도록 한다. (2) 지각동사의 목적어가 목적격보어의 행위의 주체이므로 목적격보어로 원형부정사나 현재분사를 쓴다.

11 (1), (2) 지각동사의 목적어가 목적격보어의 행위의 주체이므로 목적격보어로 원형부정사나 현재분사를 쓸 수 있고 진행형의 문장이면 목적격보어로 현재분사가 더 적절하다.

12 Mr. Jenkins는 병에 '골프공'을 먼저 넣고, 그 다음에 '작은 돌들'을 넣었다.

13 ⓐ '병이 가득 찼나요?' ⓑ '네'를 가리킨다.

14 '골프공' 사이의 틈새로 돌이 '굴러 들어가도록' 하기 위해서이다. let+목적어+원형부정사

15 관계대명사 what이 적절하다.

16 like = such as: ~와 같은

17 각각 이어지는 설명을 쓰면 된다.

18 ⓐ는 '사소한 것들'을, ⓑ는 '당신에게 정말 중요한 것' 또는 '정말 중요한 것들'을 상징한다.

19 The same goes for: ~도 마찬가지이다

20 room이 '공간', '여지'의 뜻일 때는 셀 수 없는 명사로 쓰인다.

단원별 예상문제   p.125~128

01 ②   02 ③   03 ③   04 space

05 (1) a bottle of (2) lose (3) (o)pen (4) (T)hough

06 ②

07 (1) He quickly gets bored with his toys and wants them replaced with new ones.

(2) The ball went over the fence and they looked at it fly through the air.

(3) I cannot find the book that I just put on the table.

(4) He addressed himself to her though[although] he was shy.

08 ④   **09** ③

10 (1) The pen is what I wanted to buy.

(2) The student who[that] was sitting in the back raised her hand.

11 (A) the jar   (B) small stones   **12** ⑤

13 ④   **14** (A) full   (B) room

15 ⓐ the sand   ⓑ the apple juice   **16** valued

17 ④   **18** ②

19 The same goes for life.   **20** ②, ⑤

21 are, important

22 (A) sitting   (B) shows   (C) full   **23** ③

24 친구와 시원한 음료를 나눌 여유

01 ②번은 spends가 어울리며 이외의 보기들은 matter가 어울린다. ①, ④ 문제(명사) ② spend: 소비하다, 쓰다 ③, ⑤ 중요하다(동사)

02 (A) fill A with B: A(그릇·장소 등)를 B(물건·사람)로 채우다 / 우리는 카운터에 서서 그릇을 샐러드로 채웠다. (B) spend A on B: A를 B하는 데 소비하다, 쓰다 / 그들은 매주 꽤 많은 돈을 외식하는 데 쓴다.

03 take care of ~: ~을 보살피다 / 당신이나 누군가가 확실히 안전하고, 건강하도록 하게 하다; 당신 자신이나 다른 사람을 돌보다

04 space: (비어 있는) 공간 room: 공간 / 내 여행가방이 너무 가득 차서 다른 것을 위한 공간을 가지고 있지 않다.

05 (1) a bottle of ~: ~ 한 병 (2) lose: 잃어버리다 (3) open: 비어 있는 (4) though: 비록 ~일지라도, ~이지만

06 How you play the game is what really counts.

07 (1) 장난감을 교체하는 것이 아니라 교체되는 것이므로 '수동'의 의미를 갖는 replaced가 되어야 한다. (2) 지각동사 다음에 동사원형이나 현재분사가 나와야 한다. (3) the book이 선행사로 나왔으므로 what이 아니라 which나 that을 써야 한다. (4) 뒤에 절이 나오고 있으므로 despite가 아니라 though[although]를 써야 한다.

08 ④번은 목적격보어로 to부정사가 나와야 하며 나머지는 모두 지각동사나 사역동사의 목적격보어로 동사원형이 나와야 한다.

09 ① The golf balls are what is most important in life. ② There's no room for the stones or the golf balls. ④ They were seated on each side of the upper platform. ⑤ Though summer is a fun season, I can't stand the heat!

10 (1) something that = what (2) 명사를 뒤에서 수식하는 분사는 '관계대명사+be동사'가 생략된 것으로 볼 수 있다.

11 (A)는 '병'을, (B)는 '작은 돌들'을 가리킨다.

12 ⓐ 가방에서 작은 돌 한 상자를 끄집어냈다. ⓑ 작은 돌들이 골프공 사이의 '틈새로' '굴러 들어갔다'.

13 Jenkins 선생님은 작은 돌들을 병에 부었다.

14 겉보기에는 병이 꽉 차 보였지만, 모래와 사과 주스가 들어갈 공간이 있었다.

15 ⓐ는 '모래를', ⓑ는 '사과 주스'를 가리킨다.

16 사람들에 의해 '소중하게 여겨지는'이라고 해야 하므로 과거분사로 써야 한다. which[that] are valued에서 주격 관계대명사와 be동사를 생략한 것이다.

17 (A)와 ④: …와 비슷한(전치사), ①, ③: 좋아하다(동사), ② 비슷한(형용사: 명사 앞에만 씀), ⑤ …처럼(전치사)

18 셋 중에서 크기가 가장 큰 골프공은 '인생에서 가장 중요한 것'을 상징하는 것이다.

19 The same goes for: ~도 마찬가지이다

20 ⓑ와 ②, ⑤: 공간, 여지, ①, ③, ④: 방

21 matter = be important: 중요하다

22 (A) '앉아 있는' 학생이라고 해야 하므로 sitting이 적절하다. One student to sit: 앉을 학생, (B) '보여 준다'고 해야 하므로 shows가 적절하다. see: 보다, (C) '여러분의 인생이 '가득 차' 보일지라도'라고 해야 하므로 full이 적절하다.

23 ⓐ와 ③: 들어올리다, ① (안건·문제 등을) 제기[언급]하다, ② (아이·어린 동물을) 키우다[기르다], ④ (자금·사람 등을) 모으다, ⑤ (양·가격·요금·임금 따위)를 끌어올리다

24 room for a cool drink with a friend

Be Positive, Be Happy

시험대비 실력평가
p.132

01 (a)rtificial 02 (n)ervous 03 ①   04 ⑤
05 ⑤   06 ①   07 ②

01 주어진 단어는 반의어 관계이다. cause 원인 effect 결과
artificial 인공적인 natural 자연적인

02 주어진 단어는 반의어 관계이다. patient 참을성이 있는
impatient 조바심을 내는 nervous 불안한 calm 차분한

03 '종종 화를 내면서 말로 다른 사람과 의견을 달리하다'는 '주장하
다'에 해당한다.

04 'used to+동사원형'에서 used to는 조동사로 '~하곤 했다'의
의미이다.

05 인공조명 불빛으로 인해서 생기는 문제는 밤에 잠을 자는 것과
관련된 문제이다.

06 put on: ~을 입다 deal with:~을 다루다

07 ① bother 성가시게 하다 ② nothing/something ③ scary
무서운 ④ spend 보내다, 쓰다 ⑤ gloomy 우울한

서술형 시험대비
p.133

01 out   02 (c)ommon   03 stressed
04 (1) decide   (2) artificial   (3) sleepy
05 (a)rtificial   06 with
07 (1) relax   (2) deep   (3) counting   (4) drinking
   (5) happy

01 stress out 지치게 하다 take some time out 잠시 동안 시간
을 내다

02 "드문, 희귀한"이라는 뜻의 "rare"와 의미상 반대가 되는 단어
는 "common 흔한"이다.

03 '스트레스를 주다'에 해당하는 동사의 과거분사 형용사를 써서
'스트레스를 받은'이라는 의미가 되도록 해야 한다.

05 '진짜처럼 보이도록 만들어졌지만 진짜가 아니거나 자연적인 것
으로 만들어지지 않은'은 '인공적인'에 해당하는 의미이다.

06 deal with 처리하다, 해결하다 spend time with ~와 시간을
보내다

07 (1) 기분이 상했을 때 긴장을 가라앉히는 방법 (2) 깊은 숨을 쉬
다 (3) 열까지 세기 (4) 차가운 물 마시기 (5) 행복한 생각하기'
의 의미가 자연스럽다.

Conversation
교과서

핵심 Check
p.134~135

1 (1) talk   (2) let's, Because, sense
2 (A) out   (B) used   (C) What   (D) focus

02 (A) 스트레스로 지치게 하다 = stress out (B) ~하곤 했
다. ~했었다 = used to (C) ~에 집중하다 = focus, concentrate

교과서 대화문 익히기

Check(√) True or False
p.136

1 T   2 T   3 T   4 F

교과서 확인학습
p.138~139

Listen and Answer – Dialog 1
talk, about, What, feel, stressed, About, answered, As,
see, common cause, Over, stresses, Problems, took ,
with, Next, worries, get stressed, appearance

Listen and Answer – Dialog 2
What / studying for, Grades / used to, way / know /
stress, helpful / What / got stressed, at, focus / help
/ improve

Listen More – Listen and choose.
talk, decide / Let, designs / choose, short / say /
Because, wear / makes sense, about / cute /
expensive

Speak – Talk in groups.
talk, One, well-known

Speak – Talk in pairs.
spend / makes / make / makes

My Speaking Portfolio Step 3
like, relax, upset, take deep, counting, drinking, Lastly

Wrap Up – Listening & Speaking 1
talked, foods, are good, like to, healthy eating, slowly,
eating

Wrap Up – Listening & Speaking 2
don't, make / make / basketball / say / we need

시험대비 기본평가
p.140

01 ④   02 ②   03 ②   04 ③

01 주제를 소개할 때는 'I'd like to talk about ~'라고 한다.

02 이유를 물어보는 말로 'What makes you say that?'이라고 한다.

03 talk about: ~에 대하여 말하다

04 ③ 'different foods that are good for your health.'는 지난번 소개한 주제이기 때문에 지금부터 소개할 내용은 아니다.

시험대비 실력평가 p.141~142

01 성적 때문에 스트레스를 받는 것
02 What makes you say that?   03 ③
04 ③   05 ③   06 ⑤   07 ①
08 ①   09 ②   10 (B) → (A) → (D) → (C)

01 that way는 앞 문장의 내용을 받는다.

02 "What makes you ~?"는 이유를 묻는 표현이다.

03 약간의 스트레스가 도움이 된다는 엄마의 말에 왜 그런지를 묻는 것으로 보아 Oliver는 그 사실을 모르고 있었다.

04 ③ 스트레스의 가장 흔한 원인은 학교 공부이다.

05 소셜 미디어에 시간을 많이 쓰겠다는 생각을 소개하고 (C) 거기에 대하여 이유를 물어보고, (A) 그 이유에 대한 질문에 대답하는 순서가 자연스러운 배열이다.

06 내용의 흐름상 동의하는 내용이 적절하다. ①~④는 동의하는 의미이고, ⑤는 동의하지 않을 때 쓰는 말이다.

07 소녀가 스포츠 클럽을 만들자는 제안에 대하여 소년은 야구 클럽을 만들고 싶어 하지만, 소녀는 농구가 더 낫다고 서로 다른 의견을 말하고 있다.

08 시험을 앞두고 수학 공부를 할 때 느낄 수 있는 스트레스에 대한 이야기가 적절하다.

09 'Did stress help you in other ways?'를 보면 스트레스가 도움이 되었다는 설명에 이어 또 다른 도움이 된 사실에 대한 설명이라는 것을 파악할 수 있다.

10 (B) 화면에 보여준 티셔츠 중에서 자신이 좋아하는 것을 고른다. (A) 거기에 대하여 이유를 묻는 질문을 하고, 그 뒤에는 그 대답이 이어진다. (D) 또 다른 것에 대한 제안을 하고 그것을 들은 B2는 거기에 대해서 긍정적인 대답을 한다. (C) 앞에 선택된 것에 대한 긍정적인 언급에 이어 또 다른 긍정적인 면에 대한 언급이 이어진다.

서술형 시험대비 p.143

01 What makes you feel the most stressed?
02 Next came family and worries about the future.
03 schoolwork
04 Oliver의 어머니도 스트레스를 느꼈다는 것   05 at
06 it's good to take deep breaths

01 의문대명사 what을 주어로 시작한다.

02 부사 Next로 시작하면 문장은 "부사+동사+주어"의 순서가 되도록 한다.

03 'As you can see, schoolwork was the most common cause of stress.'를 보면 십대의 가장 큰 스트레스 원인은 schoolwork이라는 것을 알 수 있다.

05 at the same time: 동시에

06 심호흡을 하다 = take deep breaths

교과서

Grammar

핵심 Check p.144~145

1 (1) looking   (2) writing   (3) living
2 (1) have been waiting   (2) has been reading
3 (1) so   (2) such
4 (1) so cold that we didn't
   (2) so expensive that he didn't
   (3) so strong that they stopped

시험대비 기본평가 p.146

01 ⑤   02 ⑤
03 has been teaching English at this middle school
   for 20 years
04 so, that   05 ①

01 태어난 이후로 현재까지 살았고 지금도 살고 있다는 의미로 현재완료진행이 되어서 'have been living'이 되어야 한다.

02 ⑤ that절에서 eat의 목적어가 필요하다. eat → eat them

04 문맥상 'so ~ that' 구문이 되도록 한다.

05 동사 was의 보어로 형용사가 들어가야 한다.

시험대비 실력평가 p.147~149

01 (1) She has been sitting on the bench for an hour.
   (2) She has been working at the store since 2010.
   (3) Tom has been cleaning the room since this
       morning.
02 ②   03 ③
04 I've been writing 'Me Time' on my calendar for
   two months.
05 ②   06 ④   07 ④

08 (1) She was so tired that she went to bed early.

(2) The cake looked so delicious that he decided to buy it.

(3) The story was so interesting that he read it in a day.

09 that　　　10 ③　　　11 ①

12 (1) been　(2) cleaning　(3) so　(4) so　　13 ③

14 ②　　　15 ①　　　16 ①　　　17 ⑤

18 has been watching

01 과거에 시작하여 현재에도 계속하고 있는 행위는 현재완료진행으로 나타내고, 형태는 'have/has been –ing'이다.

02 ② 과거형 수동태이므로 was가 들어가야 한다. 나머지는 모두 been이 들어간다.

03 현재완료진행의 동사 형태는 'have/has been –ing'이다.

04 'I've'에 이어지는 것은 과거분사이고 과거분사 been에 이어질 수 있는 것은 –ing 형태인 writing이다. writing의 목적어는 'Me Time'이고 거기에 이어서 장소와 시간의 부사구가 따라온다.

05 ⓒ 'It was such fine that we went outside.'는 'It was so fine that we went outside.'가 되어야 한다. ⓔ 'She has been living here for 5 years.'가 되어야 한다.

06 ④의 that은 관계대명사이고 나머지는 모두 부사절을 유도하는 접속사이다.

07 ④ 문장의 주어는 부정사나 동명사가 되어야 하기 때문에 Drinking이 되어야 한다.

08 '매우 ~해서 …하다'의 의미를 나타낼 때는 'so ~that' 구문을 이용한다. so와 that 사이에 형용사나 부사를 쓴다.

09 '너무 ~해서 …하다'는 내용을 'so ~ that' 구문으로 나타낸 표현이어서 빈칸에는 that이 들어간다.

10 '한 시간 동안 ~하고 있다'는 'have/has been –ing'의 형태로 현재완료진행형을 사용한다. was → has

11 ① so 뒤에는 형용사나 부사를 쓴다. 'a+형용사+명사' 앞에는 such를 쓴다.

12 (1), (2) 현재완료진행 시제는 'have/has been –ing' 형태가 되어야 하고 (3), (4)는 'so 형용사 that'의 구문이다.

13 ③ 현재완료시제와 함께 사용하는 시간의 표현에서 기간을 나타내어 '~ 동안'이라고 할 때는 전치사 for를 사용한다.

14 '너무 고통스러워 ~할 수 없었다'는 'so painful that ~ couldn't ...'이다.

15 ① 현재완료 시제에서 '~ 동안'은 전치사 for, '~ 이래로'는 since를 사용하여 나타낸다.

16 '너무 ~해서 ~할 수 없다'는 'so+형용사/부사+that ~'이나 'such a+형용사+명사+that ~'의 형태로 나타낸다.

17 ⑤ 현재완료는 과거의 시간 표시와 함께 쓸 수 없다.

18 5시간 전부터 텔레비전을 보기 시작해서 지금도 보고 있으므로 현재완료진행형을 써서 나타낸다.

01 (1) She has been teaching English at this school for 10 years.

(2) It has been raining since last night.

(3) He drove the car so fast that his father told him to drive slowly. .

02 a high mountain

03 (1) Has Mike been doing

(2) Jack hasn't been playing

04 (1) talking　(2) been

05 has been playing tennis for two hours

06 so rich

07 She is so kind[nice] that everybody likes her.

08 Ann and I have been studying Chinese since last week.

09 (1) so tired　(2) heavy that

(3) that they wanted more

10 has been using

11 Some people spend time with friends when they feel low.

12 (1) She is so hungry that she can't swim any more.

(2) The car was so old that it couldn't run fast.

(3) It was so cold that he put on his coat.

01 전부터 지금까지 하고 있는 일은 현재완료진행 시제로 나타내고, '너무 ~해서 …하다.'는 'so ~ that' 구문으로 나타낸다.

02 '너무 ~해서 ~할 수 없다'는 'such a+형용사+명사+that ~'의 형태로 나타낼 수 있다.

03 (1) 현재완료진행형(have[has] been -ing)의 의문문은 'Have+주어+been –ing ~?'의 어순이다. (2) 현재완료진행형의 부정문은 'have[has] not been -ing'이다.

04 (1), (2) 현재완료진행 시제는 'have[has] been –ing'이다.

05 두 시간 전부터 현재까지 테니스를 치고 있다는 내용의 현재완료진행형(has been playing)을 사용한다.

06 "so ~ that 주어 can" 너무 ~해서 …할 수 있다

07 '매우 ~해서 …하다'는 so ~ that 구문을 이용한다.

08 지난주부터 현재까지 공부하고 있다는 내용은 과거부터 현재까지의 진행을 포함하는 현재완료진행형(have been studying)을 사용한다.

09 '너무 ~해서 …하다'의 의미는 'so 형용사/부사 that'의 구문으로 나타낸다.

10 두 시간 전부터 현재까지 컴퓨터를 사용하고 있다는 내용의 현재완료진행형(has been using)을 사용한다.

11 Some people에 이어지는 동사 spend를 쓰고 종속절은 접속사 when으로 이어지도록 한다.

12 "너무 ~해서 …하다."의 의미로 "so 형용사/부사 that ~"의 구문으로 바꾼다.

Reading

확인문제   p.152

1 T   2 F   3 T   4 F

확인문제   p.153

1 T   2 F   3 F   4 T   5 T   6 F

교과서 확인학습 A   p.154~155

01 Goodbye	02 feel low
03 Others, to feel better	04 Still others
05 deal with	
06 suggest different ways	
07 saying, breaking, arguing	
08 When this happens	09 so, that
10 at the top of my lungs	
11 thanks to, what bothers me	
12 I've been using, works	13 graduated from
14 he's been looking for	
15 he's stressed out, by going fishing	
16 gets upset	
17 so, that, can leave, behind	
18 Besides, to be	19 focusing on, forget
20 second-year, free from	
21 seems to like, for a good reason	
22 number-one way	23 so, that
24 feel like, relieving	
25 looks tidy, looks brighter	26 what
27 all the things she has to do	28 she's under stress
29 takes some time out	
30 reads, watches,talks	
31 matter, as long as	32 I've been writing
33 work for you	
34 to say goodbye to stress	

교과서 확인학습 B   p.156~157

1 Say Goodbye to Stress

2 Some people spend time with friends when they feel low.

3 Others eat special foods to feel better.

4 Still others simply sleep for a while.

5 How do you deal with stress?

6 Here are some stories about people who suggest different ways.

7 Sometimes my friends give me stress by saying bad things about me, breaking promises, or arguing over small things.

8 When this happens, I watch horror movies!

9 Good horror movies are so scary that I scream a lot.

10 I guess that screaming at the top of my lungs helps me feel better.

11 Also, thanks to scary scenes and sound effects, I can forget about what bothers me.

12 I've been using this method for the past several months, and it really works.

13 My uncle graduated from college two years ago.

14 He lives with my family, and he's been looking for a job for some time.

15 I know that he's stressed out, but he always tries to be positive by going fishing.

16 He never gets upset when he doesn't catch any fish.

17 He says, "While I fish, I'm so focused that I can leave all my worries behind.

18 Besides, it teaches me to be patient."

19 I'm sure that focusing on one thing helps us forget about something else.

20 My sister, a second-year student in high school, has a wonderful way to stay free from stress.

21 She feels a lot of stress from schoolwork, but my mother seems to like the situation for a good reason.

22 It is because cleaning is my sister's number-one way to make life better!

23 When she's so stressed that her life looks gloomy, she cleans her room.

24 She says, "As I clean my room, I feel like I'm also relieving stress.

25 When my room looks tidy, my life looks brighter."

26 Let me tell you what my mother does about her stress.

27 She feels stressed by all the things she has to do at work and at home.

28 When she's under stress, she writes "Me Time" on her calendar.

29 This means she takes some time out for herself.

30 She reads a book, watches a movie, or talks with her friends.

31 She says, "It doesn't really matter what I do, as long as it's something I like.

32 I've been writing 'Me Time' on my calendar for two months, and I feel much better."

33 Which methods will work for you?

34 Try some of these ideas yourself, and find your best way to say goodbye to stress.

시험대비 실력평가
p.158~161

01 ⑤   02 ②   03 ③   04 ②
05 ③   06 ②, ⑤   07 tidy
08 she cleans her room
09 (A) because (B) looks (C) relieving
10 ③   11 what I do   12 ②   13 ④
14 ①   15 screaming at the top of my lungs
16 ③, ④   17 ③   18 fishing   19 ②
20 (A) a job (B) going fishing (C) gets upset
21 ④   22 ①, ③
23 (A) cleans her room (B) make life better
24 ③, ⑤   25 hello → goodbye

01 ⑤는 현재분사, 나머지는 동명사

02 ⓐ와 ② 효과가 있다, ① 일하다, ③ (문학·예술 따위의) 작품, ④ 토목공사, ⑤ (기계장치 등이) 작동되다

03 ③ too ~ to: 너무 ~해서 …할 수 없다, Good horror movies are scary enough to make Mina scream a lot. 으로 고치는 것이 적절하다.

04 ⓐ graduate from: ~을 졸업하다, ⓑ focus on: ~에 집중하다, 초점을 맞추다

05 ③ 낙관적인, 낙천적인, 준호의 삼촌은 스트레스를 받고 있지만 낚시를 다니며 긍정적으로 지내려고 항상 노력한다고 했으므로, '낙천적인' 성격이라고 할 수 있다. ① 수동적인, 소극적인, ② 짜증난[안달하는], ④ 후한, 관대한, ⑤ 부정적인

06 (A)와 ②, ⑤: 계속 용법, ①, ④: 경험 용법, ③ 완료 용법

07 정돈되고, 조직적인 방식으로 배열된, tidy: 깔끔한, 잘 정돈된

08 '그녀가 방을 청소하는 것'을 가리킨다.

09 (A) 뒤에 '이유'를 설명하는 말이 이어지므로 because가 적절하다. why 뒤에는 앞에서 말하고 있는 내용의 '결과'에 해당하는 말이 이어진다. (B) 뒤에 형용사가 나오므로 looks가 적절하다. look+형용사, look like+명사: ~처럼 보이다 (C) 스트레스도 해소되는 것 같다고 해야 하므로 relieving이 적절하다. relieve: (불쾌감·고통 등을) 없애[덜어] 주다

10 (b)와 ③: ~할 때, ① …와 같이; …대로, ② …와 같은 정도로 (as ... as ~에서, 앞의 as는 지시부사, 뒤의 as는 접속사), ④

[이유] …이기 때문에, ⑤ …으로서(전치사)

11 ⓐ '내가 무엇을 하는지' ⓑ '내가 하는 것'

12 이 글은 '스트레스를 다루는 Yulia의 엄마의 방법'에 관한 글이므로, 제목으로는 ②번이 적절하다.

13 ④ 'Yulia의 어머니가 얼마나 자주 "Me Time"을 가지는지' 는 대답할 수 없다. ① By all the things she has to do at work and at home. ② She writes "Me Time" on her calendar. ③ It means she takes some time out for herself. ⑤ For two months.

14 주어진 문장의 this에 주목한다. ①번 앞 문장의 내용을 받고 있으므로 ①번이 적절하다.

15 scream at the top of one's lungs: 있는 힘껏 소리를 지르다

16 ⓑ와 ③, ④: 관계대명사, ① 의문형용사, ②, ⑤ 의문대명사, ② be in debt: 빚이 있다

17 이 글은 '스트레스를 다루는 방법'에 관한 글이므로, 주제로는 ③번이 적절하다. ④ benefit: 이익, 혜택

18 go -ing: ~하러 가다

19 빈칸 앞 문장들에서 '물고기를 한 마리도 잡지 못했을 때에도 삼촌은 절대 속상해 하지 않는다.'고 하면서, '낚시하는 동안, 나는 아주 몰입해서 모든 걱정을 잊을 수 있어.'라고 했고, 빈칸 뒤의 문장에서 낚시는 나에게 인내를 가르쳐 준다.'고 했으므로, 주로 무엇에 대한 또 다른 이유나 주장을 제시할 때 쓰이는 Besides(게다가)가 적절하다. teach+목적어+to부정사: ~하는 법을 가르치다 ① 대신에, ⑤ 그에 반해서, 그와 대조적으로

20 준호의 삼촌은 얼마 전부터 '직장'을 구하고 있다. 그는 스트레스를 받고 있지만 '낚시를 다니며' 긍정적으로 지내려고 항상 노력하고, 물고기를 한 마리도 잡지 못했을 때에도 삼촌은 절대 '속상해 하지' 않는다.

21 ⓐ와 ②: 형용사적 용법, ①, ⑤: 부사적 용법, ③, ④: 명사적 용법

22 뒤에 셀 수 없는 명사가 나오므로, many와 a number of는 바꿔 쓸 수 없다. a lot of와 lots of는 수와 양이 많은 경우에 다 쓸 수 있다.

23 청소가 도빈이 누나의 '삶을 향상하는' 최고의 방법이라서, 스트레스를 너무 많이 받아서 인생이 우울해 보일 때 그녀가 '방을 청소하기' 때문이다.

24 ⓐ와 ③, ⑤: (원하는) 효과가 나다[있다], (계획 따위가) 잘 되어 가다, ① (해야 할) 일(명사), ② (기계나 장치 등을) 작동시키다, ④ 직장(명사)

25 '스트레스와 이별하는 방법'이라고 해야 하므로, hello를 goodbye로 고쳐야 한다. say hello to: ~에게 안부를 전하다, say goodbye to: ~에게 작별인사를 하다

01 ⓐ saying   ⓑ breaking   ⓒ arguing

02 Good horror movies are so scary that I scream a lot.

03 (A) horror movies   (B) her lungs

04 (A) for   (B) positive   (C) so

05 being → to be

06 no difficulty → difficulty   07 what

08 so long as   09 two months, writing

10 without

11 도빈이의 누나가 학업 때문에 많은 스트레스를 받는 상황

12 (A) schoolwork   (B) cleaning her room

13 (A) tell   (B) under   (C) herself

14 자신을 위해 잠깐 시간을 내는 것

15 even, still, far, a lot 중에서 두 개를 쓰면 된다.

01 전치사 by 다음에 동명사를 쓰는 것이 적절하다.

02 so+형용사/부사+that절: 너무 ~해서 …하다

03 미나는 스트레스를 느낄 때 '공포영화'를 보면서 '있는 힘껏' 소리를 지른다.

04 (A) '얼마 동안'이라고 해야 하므로 for가 적절하다. for: ~ 동안, since: ~ 이후로, (B) '긍정적'으로 지내려고 한다고 해야 하므로 positive가 적절하다. positive: 긍정적인, negative: 부정적인, (C) 뒤에 명사는 없고 형용사만 나오므로 so가 적절하다. so+형용사/부사+that절: 너무 ~해서 …하다, such+a+형용사+명사+that절

05 teach+목적어+to부정사: ~에게 …하기를 가르치다

06 '준호의 삼촌은 얼마 전부터 직장을 구하고 있다'고 했으므로, 일자리를 찾는 데 어려움을 '겪고 있다'로 고치는 것이 적절하다. have difficulty ~ing: ~하는 데 어려움을 겪다

07 ⓐ에는 관계대명사 what, ⓑ에는 의문대명사 what이 적절하다.

08 as long as = so long as: ~이기만[하기만] 하면

09 '두 달째 달력에 '나만의 시간'을 적어 왔다'는 것은 '두 달' 전에 달력에 '나만의 시간'을 쓰기 시작해서 지금도 여전히 '쓰고 있는 중'이라는 뜻이다.

10 free from = without: ~이 없는

11 바로 앞의 내용을 가리킨다.

12 (A) 도빈이 누나의 스트레스의 원인: 학교 공부, (B) 스트레스를 해소하는 도빈이 누나의 방법: 그녀의 방을 청소하는 것

13 (A) '사역동사 let+목적어+동사원형'을 써야 하므로 tell이 적절하다. (B) '스트레스를 받고 있다'고 해야 하므로 under가 적절하다. be under stress: 스트레스를 받고 있다, (C) 주어와 목적어가 같을 때는 재귀대명사를 써야 하므로 herself가 적절

14 뒤 문장(This means she takes some time out for herself.)의 내용을 쓰면 된다.

15 much는 비교급을 강조하는 말이며, '훨씬'으로 해석한다.

01 ①   02 (a)rtificial   03 ②   04 ①

05 ②   06 ①   07 (m)akes   08 ③

09 ②   10 ①   11 help   12 ④

13 I guess that screaming at the top of my lungs helps me feel better.

14 tell you what my mother does about her stress

15 ①   16 ④   17 ①   18 ②

19 (1) Little → A little   (2) improving → (to) improve

20 ②   21 ③   22 ⑤

23 ⓐ Some   ⓑ Still   ⓒ who[that]   24 ①, ④

25 What → How   26 ②

27 focusing on one thing helps us forget about something else

28 ③   29 ①

30 When my room looks tidy, my life looks brighter

31 ⓐ Mouth   ⓑ Nose   32 ①

01 '다른 사람에게 보여지는 방식'은 '겉모습, 외모'라는 뜻이다.

02 주어진 단어는 반의의 관계이다. agree 동의하다 disagree 동의하지 않다 artificial 인공적인 natural 자연적인

03 소셜 미디어에 시간을 많이 보내는 이유는 친구를 사귈 수 있다는 장점 때문이다.

04 'cheerless'는 '활기 없는'이라는 뜻으로 gloomy에 해당한다.

05 (B) 상대의 말에 다른 의견을 제시하고 (A) 이에 대한 이유를 묻고 (C) 거기에 대하여 설명하는 순서가 자연스럽다.

06 ① "I'd like to talk about some good ways to relax when you get upset."를 통해서 여기서 소개하는 것은 화를 푸는 방법이라는 것을 알 수 있다.

07 'make sense'는 '의미가 통하다, 말이 되다'의 뜻으로 상대의 말에 동의하는 의미이다.

08 ⓒ 짧은 소매가 좋다는 것으로 보아 여름에 입을 것이라고 생각할 수 있다.

09 시험 공부를 하면서 스트레스를 받는 것으로 보아 성적이 스트레스의 원인이라는 것을 알 수 있다.

10 ① '무엇 때문에 그렇게 말하나요?'는 '무엇 때문에 그렇게 생각하나요?'로 바꿀 수 있다.

11 대답을 통해서 스트레스가 주는 유익함에 대한 질문임을 알 수 있다.

29

12 '너무 ~해서 …하다'의 의미를 나타내는 'so ~ that …'의 구문이다.

13 '있는 힘껏 소리를 지르는 것이 기분 좋게 느끼도록 도와준다고 생각해'의 의미로 'I guess'를 주절로 하고 종속절의 주어는 'screaming at the top of my lungs'가 되도록 한다.

14 'Let me'에 이어지는 동사원형 tell을 쓰고 직접목적어는 what이 이끄는 명사절이 되도록 한다.

15 ⓓ 명백한 과거를 나타내는 'when she was a child'는 현재완료진행형과 함께 쓸 수 없다.

16 '~ 이후로'의 의미일 때는 since를 쓴다.

17 ① '너무 ~해서 …하다'는 'so 형용사/부사 that ~'의 구문으로 나타낸다.

18 '너무 ~해서 …하다'는 'so 형용사/부사 that ~'의 구문으로 나타낸다.

19 (1) 문맥상 '약간의'라는 긍정의 의미가 되어야 한다. (2) 동사 help의 목적어는 to부정사나 원형부정사이다.

20 ② 부사 Next로 시작하는 문장은 주어와 동사를 도치하도록 한다.

21 ③ makes의 주어가 되어야 하므로 why 대신 what이 와야 한다.

22 '그녀는 아주 정직해서 거짓말을 할 수 없었다.'의 의미인데, ⑤ '그녀는 거짓말을 했지만 '아주 정직했다'라는 뜻이다.

23 Some, Others, Still others: 몇몇은, 다른 사람들은, 또 다른 사람들은, ⓒ 관계대명사 who[that]가 적절하다.

24 (A)와 ①, ④는 부사적 용법, ② 형용사적 용법, ③, ⑤는 명사적 용법

25 What 뒤에 완전한 문장이 이어지므로, What을 부사인 How로 고치는 것이 적절하다.

26 '여기에 다른 방법을 제안하는 사람들에 대한 몇 가지 이야기들이 있다.'고 했으므로, ②번이 적절하다.

27 on을 보충하면 된다. focus on: ~에 집중하다, 초점을 맞추다

28 준호의 삼촌은 스트레스를 받고 있지만 낚시를 다니며 '긍정적'으로 지내려고 항상 노력한다고 했으므로, '부정적인' 태도를 가지고 있다고 한 ③번이 옳지 않다.

29 free from: ~이 없는

30 look+형용사: ~하게 보이다

31 ⓐ '약간의 차를 마셔라.'라고 했으므로, Mouth가 적절하다. ⓑ '신선한 꽃 냄새를 맡아라.'라고 했으므로, Nose가 적절하다.

32 ① 야외에 있을 때는 '하늘'을 보라고 했다.

단원별 예상문제
p.170~173

01 (b)oring	02 ①	03 ④	04 ②
05 ②	06 ⑤	07 (m)essy	08 ①

---

09 ①	10 (1) free (2) reason (3) gloomy		
11 ①	12 ②	13 ⑤	14 ④
15 ⑤	16 ③	17 ③	

18 친구들이 미나에 관해 나쁜 말을 하거나, 약속을 어기거나, 혹은 사소한 일을 두고 언쟁을 하며 미나에게 스트레스를 주는 것

19 using

20 ① scary scenes ② sound effects

21 (A) graduated from (B) upset (C) patient

22 ①, ②

23 her → herself

24 important

25 (A) all the things she has to do (B) Me Time

26 ②

27 (A) going outdoors and getting plenty of sunlight (B) Exercise

---

01 주어진 단어는 동의어 관계이다. boring 지루한 dull 지루한

02 '사람이 약간 걱정되거나 속상하게 만들다'는 '성가시게 하다, 괴롭히다'의 의미이다.

03 decide on: ~을 결정하다 thanks to: ~ 덕택에

04 ① graduated 졸업했다 ② '그가 지쳤다'의 의미로 stressed가 들어가는 것이 적절하다. ③ positive 긍정적인 ④ focused 집중한 ⑤ forget 잊어버리다

05 공포영화를 설명할 수 있는 단어는 ② 'scary 무서운'이다.

06 '있는 힘껏'이라는 뜻으로 'at the top of my lungs'가 되어야 한다.

07 주어진 단어는 반의어 관계이다. cause 원인 effect 결과 tidy 깔끔한 messy 어질러진

08 ① 여기에 사용된 grade는 '성적'이라는 뜻이다.

09 '화내지 않고 어려움을 받아들이거나 긴 시간 차분하게 기다릴 수 있는'은 'patient 인내하는'에 해당하는 의미이다.

10 (1) '~가 없는'의 뜻으로 'free from'이 적절하다. (2) ~한 이유로 = for a ~ reason (3) 우울한, 침울한 = gloomy

11 ② 소녀는 스포츠 클럽 만드는 것에 동의한다. ③ 소녀는 농구 클럽을 원한다. ④ 소녀는 야구 클럽을 만들고자 하는 소년과 의견이 다르다. ⑤ 소녀가 야구를 좋아하는지는 알 수 없다.

12 with: ~이 있는, ~을 가지고 있는

13 내용상 앞에서 선택한 것에 대한 장점이 언급되어 있는 것이 적절하다.

14 대화의 내용으로 보아 그들은 티셔츠를 여름에 입을 것이다.

15 현재완료진행시제는 'have/has been –ing'가 되어야 한다.

16 ③ 현재완료진행시제와 함께 사용하는 시간 표현에서 '~동안'은 전치사 for를 쓴다.

17 ⓒ that절에서 buy의 목적어인 it(= the bag)이 필요하다. ⓓ '너무 ~해서 …하다'는 'so 형용사 that'이다. ⓔ since this morning과 함께 쓰는 문장은 현재완료나 현재완료진행시제를 쓴다.

18 앞 문장의 내용을 가리킨다.

19 과거에 시작한 행동을 지금까지 계속하는 것을 강조할 때에는 현재완료진행형(have been -ing)으로 나타낸다.

20 공포영화의 '무서운 장면들'과 '음향 효과' 덕분에 그녀를 괴롭히는 것들을 잊을 수 있다.

21 (A) 대학을 '졸업했다'고 해야 하므로 graduated from이 적절하다. graduate from: ~을 졸업하다, (B) 물고기를 한 마리도 잡지 못했을 때에도 삼촌은 '속상해 하지' 않는다.고 해야 하므로 upset이 적절하다. relaxed: 느긋한, 여유 있는, (C) 낚시는 나에게 '인내'를 가르쳐 준다고 해야 하므로 patient가 적절하다. impatient: 짜증난, 참을성 없는

22 ⓐ와 ③, ④, ⑤: 게다가, 더욱이, ① 그러므로, ② In addition to 뒤에는 목적어가 와야 한다. ⓐ의 경우, In addition과는 바꿔 쓸 수 있다.

23 for 뒤의 목적어가 주어 자신이므로 재귀대명사 herself를 써야 한다.

24 matter = be important: 중요하다

25 (A) Yulia의 어머니의 스트레스의 원인: 직장과 집에서 해야 하는 온갖 일, (B) 스트레스를 해소하는 Yulia의 어머니의 방법: "나만의 시간"을 가지는 것

26 화면 앞에 앉아 있는 '대신' 밖에 나가 태양 아래에서 뛰어다녀라고 해야 하므로 ②번이 적절하다. Instead of: ~ 대신에, ①, ⑤: 게다가, ③ ~에 덧붙여, ④ ~에도 불구하고

27 (A)는 '밖에 나가서 충분한 양의 햇볕을 쐬는 것', (B)는 '운동'을 가리킨다.

서술형 실전문제   p.174~175

01 (r)eason   02 (w)orried   03 (e)ffect
04 stressed   05 helpful   06 makes
07 무엇이 여러분이 가장 스트레스를 느끼도록 만드는가?
08 appearance
09 My mother has been cooking dinner since 6:00.
10 so, that   11 ⓐ so   ⓑ that
12 (A) happens   (B) helps   (C) what
13 this method   14 ago, is, looking
15 enough to   16 (A) fishing   (B) positive

01 주어진 단어는 동의어 관계이다. bother 성가시게 하다 – disturb 방해하다 cause 원인 – reason 이유

02 주어진 단어는 반의어 관계이다. cheap 싼 expensive 비싼 – relieved 안심이 되는 worried 걱정되는

03 '어떤 사건이나 행동에 의해서 초래된 변화'는 '결과, 영향'이라는 뜻이다.

04 that way는 '그렇게'의 뜻으로 stressed를 받는다.

05 was의 보어가 되는 형용사로 고친다.

---

06 이유를 물어보는 말로 'What makes you say that?'이 되어야 한다.

07 this question은 앞 문장을 받는다.

08 appear의 명사형으로 고친다.

09 6시 이후부터 현재까지 요리를 하고 있다는 내용의 현재완료진행형(has been cooking)시제를 사용한다.

10 '너무 ~해서 …하다'의 의미로 'so ~ that …'이 되어야 한다.

11 so+형용사/부사+that절: 너무 ~해서 …하다

12 (A) happen은 자동사로서 수동태로 쓸 수 없으므로 happens가 적절하다. (B) 주어가 동명사 screaming이므로 helps가 적절하다. (C) 뒤에 불완전한 절이 이어지고 선행사가 없으므로 관계대명사 what이 적절하다.

13 '이 방법'을 가리킨다.

14 준호의 삼촌이 '얼마 전부터 직장을 구하고 있다'는 것은 얼마 '전에' 직장을 구하기 시작해서 지금도 여전히 '구하고 있는 중'이라는 뜻이다.

15 so ~ that S can ... = ~ enough to 동사원형

16 준호의 삼촌은 낚시를 하러 다니는 덕분에, 직장을 구하는 데 어려움을 겪고 있어도 긍정적인 태도를 가지고 있다.

창의사고력 서술형 문제   p.176

|모범답안|

01 working, change, fish stresses, worry
02 have been living in this city / I have been living in this city since I was ten. I have been hanging out with my best friend since I was ten. I have been learning English since I was ten. I have been playing the guitar since I was ten. I have been using this computer since I was ten.
03 (A) Eye   (B) Mouth   (C) Hand   (D) Nose (E) Ear

단원별 모의고사   p.177~180

01 ②   02 ④   03 ⑤   04 ②
05 stress → stressed   06 ②   07 ③
08 My father has been repairing his car since this morning.
09 ①   10 so hot that
11 (1) like to talk about some good ways to relax when you get upset
(2) fish, I'm so focused that I can leave all my worries behind

12 ①	13 ③	14 keeping → breaking
15 the thing which[that]	16 ①, ④	17 fishing
18 from	19 ②	20 This → It
21 ①	22 ②	

01 주어진 단어는 동의어 관계이다. tidy 깔끔한 neat 깨끗한 – scream 소리를 지르다 shout 소리치다

02 '더 좋게 만들다 또는 더 좋아지다'의 의미는 improve 이다.

03 patient 참을성이 있는 impatient 조바심이 나는

04 (B) 상대의 말에 이유를 묻고 (A) 그 질문에 대한 이유를 설명하고 (C) 거기에 대하여 동의하는 순서가 자연스럽다.

05 ⑤ '스트레스를 받다'는 'get stressed'로 'get+과거분사'의 형태로 수동의 의미를 나타낸다.

06 'Let me show you some designs on the screen'을 보면 티셔츠 디자인을 화면을 보고 결정할 것이라는 것을 알 수 있다.

07 ③ 'such a+형용사+명사'의 순서가 된다.

08 오늘 아침 이후부터 지금까지 차를 수리하고 있다는 뜻으로 현재완료진행형(has been repairing)을 사용한다.

09 현재완료진행시제와 함께 쓰인 시간 표현에서 '~ 동안'의 의미일 때 전치사 for를 쓴다.

10 '너무 ~하기 때문에 …하다'는 so ~ that ...'으로 바꾸어 쓸 수 있다.

11 (1) ~하고 싶다 = would like to ~ ~하는 좋은 몇 가지 방법 = some good ways to ~ (2) 낚시하는 동안 = While I fish

12 ① 현재완료진행과 함께 쓰인 시간 표현에서 '~ 동안'이라는 의미일 때는 전치사 for로 나타낸다.

13 ⓑ, ⓔ '너무 ~해서 …하다'는 'so ~ that ...'이다. ⓕ 현재완료진행시제는 /have/has been –ing' 형태이다.

14 친구들이 약속을 어김으로써 미나에게 스트레스를 준다고 해야 하므로, keeping을 breaking으로 고쳐야 한다. keep promises: 약속을 지키다, break promises: 약속을 어기다

15 동사가 bothers이므로 선행사를 단수인 the thing으로 쓰는 것이 적절하다.

16 ⓐ와 ①, ④: …하고 있는 동안에(접속사), ② 동안, 시간(명사), ③, ⑤: [주절 뒤에서 반대·비교·대조를 나타내어] 그런데, 한편(으로는)

17 '낚시'를 가리킨다.

18 ⓐ free from: ~이 없는, ⓑ from schoolwork: 학업 때문에

19 도빈이의 어머니는 그 상황을 좋아하는 것 같다고 했다.

20 진주어에 해당하는 간접의문문 what I do를 받은 것이기 때문

에, 가주어 It으로 고쳐야 한다.

21 ⓑ와 ④: 계속 용법, ① 경험 용법, ② 결과 용법, ③, ⑤: 완료 용법

22 ② Yulia의 어머니 직업이 무엇인지는 위 글에서 알 수 없다.

교과서 파헤치기

Lesson 1

1 kitten, 새끼 고양이   2 priceless, 소중한
3 palace, 궁전   4 include, 포함하다   5 merchant, 상인
6 repay, 갚다   7 jewel, 보석   8 pack, 짐을 꾸리다
9 chase, 추적하다   10 allowance, 용돈
11 whisper, 속삭이다   12 animation, 만화 영화
13 chest, 상자   14 servant, 하인   15 tool, 도구, 연장
16 chew, 씹다

단어 TEST Step 1   p.02

01 짐을 꾸리다, 가득 채우다	02 나타나다
03 소중한	04 추적하다 05 깨닫다
06 준비하다	07 씹다 08 음식을 날라 주다
09 질투하는	10 쉬다 11 갚다
12 서두르다	13 상자, 가슴 14 용돈
15 포함하다	16 말문이 막힌 17 궁전
18 발명, 발명품	19 멀리 떨어진 20 가치 없는
21 하인	22 주다, 선사하다 23 상인
24 과목	25 도구, 연장 26 기쁜
27 향료	28 당황스러운
29 무역하다, 교역하다	30 소중한
31 속삭이다	32 기쁜 33 새끼 고양이
34 놀라워하다	35 잠시 후에 36 ~ 덕택에
37 A를 쫓아내다	38 ~을 돌보다 39 극복하다
40 하루 종일	41 동작이 어색하다, 몸치이다
42 ~을 심각하게 받아들이다	43 ~을 확신하다

단어 TEST Step 2   p.03

01 chase	02 delighted[pleased]	
03 raincoat	04 goods	05 hurry
06 appear	07 speechless	08 servant
09 allowance	10 faraway	11 kitten
12 tool	13 jewel	14 trade
15 repay	16 merchant	17 pack
18 chest	19 spice	20 relax
21 palace	22 present	23 whisper
24 include	25 priceless	26 puzzled
27 chew	28 realize	29 prepare
30 invention	31 jealous	32 serve
33 worthless	34 valuable	35 get over
36 all day long	37 take care of ~	
38 have two left feet		39 Break a leg!
40 thanks to ~	41 chase A away	42 be sure that ~
43 tell the time		

대화문 TEST Step 1   p.05~06

Listen – Listen and Answer – Dialog 1

What, surprise / glad, same class / am, too, last year, How, feel / a little worried / have to, high / Which kind, have, mind / thinking, painting

Listen – Listen and Answer – Dialog 2

what club, going, join / sure, How about / to join / heard, preparing for / need, to relax, need, to get over / You can say / Why don't / thanks, for me, two left feet

Listen More – Listen and say

case looks nice / say that, as, birthday present / wonder how much, costs / Let, see, costs / expensive / agree, works as, too / let's buy / delighted to buy, special / So am

Speak – Talk in pairs.

hear, weather report / going to rain, long / glad, wear, raincoat / Good for

Speak – Talk in groups.

the most boring, week / can say, again / don't think, most boring / agree, difficult subjects

My Speaking Portfolio.

1. What, free, listen, greatest invention, live without
2. greatest invention, feel good, focus better
3. agree, Thanks to, read, write, down

Wrap Up - Listening & Speaking ❺

look, serious, going on / practicing / How, feel about / worried, make, mistake / sure, Break, leg

Wrap Up - Listening & Speaking ❻

Have, heard / What about / won, prize / surprising, seems to / walking dictionary

대화문 TEST Step 2   p.07~08

Listen – Listen and Answer – Dialog 1

G: Hey, Minjun. What a surprise!
B: Hi, Sora. I'm glad we're in the same class.

G: I am, too. We're now in our last year in middle school. How do you feel?

B: I'm a little worried that there'll be more schoolwork.

G: Me, too. We also have to think about our high school.

B: Which kind of school do you have in mind?

G: I'm thinking of an animation high school. I love painting.

Listen – Listen and Answer – Dialog 2

G: Oliver, what club are you going to join?

B: I'm not sure. How about you, Sora?

G: I want to join the school dance club.

B: Really? But I heard you're preparing for an animation high school.

G: Right, but I need some time to relax. We all need to do something to get over stress.

B: You can say that again.

G: Why don't you join me? It'll be fun.

B: No, thanks. Dancing is not for me. I have two left feet.

Listen More – Listen and say

B: Jimin, look! That red phone case looks nice!

G: You can say that again! Mom would love it as a birthday present.

B: I wonder how much it costs.

G: Let me see. It costs 40,000 won.

B: Really? That's so expensive.

G: I don't agree. Look! It works as a wallet, too.

B: Oh, I didn't see that. Then let's buy it for Mom.

G: Okay. I'm delighted to buy something special for Mom.

B: So am I.

Speak – Talk in pairs.

A: Did you hear the weather report?

B: Yes. It's going to rain all day long.

A: Really? I'm glad I can wear my new raincoat.

B: Good for you.

Speak – Talk in groups.

A: I think the most boring day of the week is Monday.

B: You can say that again.

C: I don't think so. Thursday is the most boring.

D: I agree. We have all the difficult subjects on Thursday.

My Speaking Portfolio.

1. B1: What do you do in your free time? I listen to music. I think it's the greatest invention. I can't live without it.

2. G: I think chocolate is the greatest invention. It makes me feel good. It also helps me focus better when I study.

3. B2: Many people will agree that paper is the greatest invention. Thanks to paper, we all can read books and write things down.

Wrap Up - Listening & Speaking ❺

B: You look so serious. What's going on?

G: Oh, I'm just practicing for the school play tomorrow.

B: How do you feel about it?

G: I'm worried I may make a mistake.

B: I'm sure you'll do well. Break a leg!

G: Thanks.

Wrap Up - Listening & Speaking ❻

G: Have you heard about Mr. Oh?

B: No. What about him?

G: He won first prize in the TV quiz show.

B: It's not surprising. He seems to know about everything.

G: You can say that again! He's a walking dictionary.

본문 TEST Step 1   p.09~11

01 Priceless Gift

02 ago, honest merchant, in

03 places, support, by trading

04 filled, with goods, faraway

05 traded, spices, for nuts

06 Thanks to, what, needed

07 dinner with, queen, palace

08 served, appeared, chased, away

09 greatly surprised, there, palace

10 Are there no cats   11 looked puzzled

12 cat, she asked   13 said, himself, not, but

14 brought, from, let, run   15 What, when, run away

16 chest, filled with jewels

17 Back, told, good fortune

18 richest merchant, heard, jealous

19 are worthless, thought   20 bring, what, valuable

21 sure, queen, me, jewels

22 packed, with, other works

23 took, gifts, island

24 chance, islanders, lie, good

25 heard, invited, palace, dinner

26 sitting, presented, with, again

27 repay, with, priceless   28 watched, whisper, ear

29 became excited, hopeful

30 receive more jewels than

31 while, returned, presented, to

32 When, opened, speechless

33 There, kitten, box

34 gave, priceless, kittens, queen

35 return, what, most valuable

36 realized, mind, worth far

37 tried, look pleased   38 right thing to do

39 return home, richer man

40 surely, wiser one

01 Priceless Gift

02 an honest merchant lived

03 to support his family by trading

04 filled, with, faraway island

05 traded, for, for

06 Thanks to, what, needed

07 had dinner with

08 was served, appeared, chased them away with sticks

09 greatly surprised, there were

10 Are there no cats

11 looked puzzled   12 she asked

13 said to himself, What, not, but

14 brought, from, let them run free

15 What amazing, run away

16 was filled with   17 Back in, good fortune

18 the richest merchant, heard, jealous

19 worthless, thought   20 what, valuable

21 I'm sure, more jewels

22 packed, with, works of art

23 took, to

24 To get, a good friend of Antonio's

25 heard about, invited, to

26 sitting, presented, with, thanked, again and again

27 repay, with, priceless   28 watched, whisper

29 excited, hopeful

30 was sure, more jewels than

31 After a while, presented, to

32 opened, speechless   33 kitten

34 priceless

35 In return for, what is most valuable

36 realized, mind, worth far more than

37 look pleased with   38 right thing to do

39 return home, richer

40 surely a wiser one

1 소중한 선물

2 먼 옛날 이탈리아 제노바에 정직한 상인 한 명이 살았다.

3 그의 이름은 Antonio로, 그는 교역으로 가족을 부양하기 위해 여러 곳을 다녔다.

4 어느 날 그는 배에 상품을 가득 싣고 머나먼 섬으로 갔다.

5 거기서 그는 공구를 향신료와 바꾸었고, 책을 견과류와 바꾸었다.

6 Antonio 덕에 섬사람들은 필요한 것을 얻을 수 있었다.

7 어느 날 밤, Antonio는 궁전에서 그 섬의 여왕과 저녁 식사를 했다.

8 식사가 나왔을 때 쥐들이 나타났고, 하인 몇 명이 막대기로 쥐를 쫓아내었다.

9 Antonio는 궁전에 쥐가 있다는 사실에 무척 놀랐다.

10 그는 "이 섬에는 고양이가 없습니까?"라고 물었다.

11 여왕은 어리둥절한 것처럼 보였다.

12 "고양이가 뭔가요?"라고 그녀가 물었다.

13 상인은 "여기 섬사람들이 필요로 하는 것은 공구나 책이 아니라 고양이야."라고 혼자 중얼거렸다.

14 그는 배에서 고양이 두 마리를 데리고 와서, 자유롭게 돌아다니도록 풀어놓았다.

15 "정말 놀라운 동물이네요!" 쥐가 모두 도망가는 것을 보자 여왕이 감탄하였다.

16 그녀는 Antonio에게 보석이 가득한 상자를 주었다.

17 이탈리아로 돌아와서, Antonio는 자신에게 일어난 행운을 친구들에게 이야기했다.

18 제노바에서 가장 부유한 상인인 Luigi는 그 이야기를 듣고 시샘이 일었다.

19 "고양이는 쓸모없어." Luigi가 생각했다.

20 "난 여왕에게 정말로 귀중한 것을 가지고 갈 거야.

21 틀림없이 여왕이 내게 더 많은 보석을 줄 거야."

22 Luigi는 멋진 그림들과 다른 예술 작품을 배에 실었다.

23 그는 선물을 섬으로 가지고 갔다.

24 여왕을 만날 기회를 얻기 위해서, 그는 자신이 Antonio의 친한 친구라고 섬사람들에게 거짓말을 했다.

25 Luigi에 관해 듣고, 여왕은 그를 궁전으로 저녁 식사에 초대했다.

26 식탁에 앉기 전에 Luigi는 여왕에게 자신이 가져온 온갖 선물을 전했고, 여왕은 그에게 여러 차례 감사하다고 했다.

27 "당신께 값진 선물로 보답하겠습니다."라고 여왕이 말했다.

28 Luigi는 여왕이 하인의 귀에 대고 속삭이는 것을 지켜보았다.

29 그는 흥분되고 기대에 부풀었다.

30 그는 Antonio보다 많은 보석을 받게 될 거라고 확신했다.

31 잠시 후에 하인이 상자 하나를 가지고 돌아왔고, 여왕은 그것을 Luigi에게 주었다.

32 상자를 열어본 Luigi는 말문이 막혔다.

33 상자 안에는 새끼 고양이 한 마리가 들어 있었다.

34 "Antonio가 우리에게 매우 귀한 고양이들을 줬는데, 이제

새끼 고양이 몇 마리가 생겼어요."라고 여왕이 말했다.

35 "당신이 우리에게 준 멋진 선물에 보답하는 뜻에서, 우리에게 가장 값진 것을 당신에게 드리고 싶어요."

36 여왕의 생각에는 세상의 온갖 보석보다 새끼 고양이가 훨씬 더 가치 있다는 것을 Luigi는 깨달았다.

37 그는 선물에 대해 기뻐하는 표정을 지으려고 애썼다.

38 그게 올바른 행동이라는 것을 그는 알았다.

39 Luigi는 더 부유한 사람이 되어 집으로 돌아오지는 않았다.

40 하지만 그는 분명히 더 현명한 사람이 되었다.

본문 TEST Step 4-Step 5 p.18~23

1 A Priceless Gift

2 Long ago, an honest merchant lived in Genoa, Italy.

3 His name was Antonio, and he went to different places to support his family by trading.

4 One day, he filled his ship with goods and visited a faraway island.

5 There he traded tools for spices and books for nuts.

6 Thanks to Antonio, the islanders could get what they needed.

7 One night, Antonio had dinner with the island's queen at her palace.

8 When dinner was served, rats appeared, and some servants chased them away with sticks.

9 Antonio was greatly surprised that there were rats in the palace.

10 He asked, "Are there no cats on this island?"

11 The queen looked puzzled.

12 "What is a cat?" she asked.

13 The merchant said to himself, "What the islanders here need is not tools or books, but cats."

14 He brought two cats from his ship and let them run free.

15 "What amazing animals!" cried the queen when she saw all the rats run away.

16 She gave Antonio a chest that was filled with jewels.

17 Back in Italy, Antonio told his friends about his good fortune.

18 Luigi, the richest merchant in Genoa, heard the story and was jealous.

19 "Cats are worthless," Luigi thought.

20 "I'll bring the queen what is really valuable.

21 I'm sure that the queen will give me more jewels."

22 Luigi packed his ship with wonderful paintings and other works of art.

23 He took the gifts to the island.

24 To get a chance to meet the queen, he told the islanders a lie that he was a good friend of Antonio's.

25 When the queen heard about Luigi, she invited him to her palace for dinner.

26 Before sitting down at the table, Luigi presented the queen with all his gifts, and the queen thanked him again and again.

27 "I'll repay you with a priceless gift," said the queen.

28 Luigi watched the queen whisper in a servant's ear.

29 He became excited and hopeful.

30 He was sure that he would receive more jewels than Antonio.

31 After a while, the servant returned with a box, and the queen presented it to Luigi.

32 When Luigi opened the box, he was speechless.

33 There was a kitten in the box.

34 "Antonio gave us the priceless cats, and we now have some kittens," said the queen.

35 "In return for the wonderful gifts you gave us, we want to give you what is most valuable to us."

36 Luigi realized that, in the queen's mind, the kitten was worth far more than all the jewels in the world.

37 He tried to look pleased with the gift.

38 He knew that was the right thing to do.

39 Luigi did not return home a richer man.

40 But he was surely a wiser one.

구석구석지문 TEST Step 1 p.24

My Speaking Portfolio

1. the greatest invention
2. I'd say, tell the time
3. don't, agree with, the greatest invention
4. say that again

All Ears

1. don't agree with, on that issue / didn't know, didn't like
2. glad, go to the zoo
3. going to, Good for
4. think, time to eat
5. don't agree, hurry to go back

구석구석지문 TEST Step 2   p.25

My Speaking Portfolio

1. A: What is the greatest invention in history?
2. B: I'd say the clock. We can't tell the time without it.
3. C: I don't really agree with you. I think the cell phone is the greatest invention.
4. D: You can say that again.

All Ears

1. M: 1. I don't agree with you on that issue.
   2. I didn't know you didn't like the plan.
2. A: I'm glad I can go to the zoo.
3. B: You're going to the zoo? Good for you.
4. A: I think I have time to eat a snack.
5. B: I don't agree. You must hurry to go back.

Wrap Up - Reading

1. Isabel lives in a small village near Kakamega, Kenya.
2. In the past, she had to walk a long distance every day to get clean water.
3. She sometimes got sick because of the dirty water she drank.
4. Three months ago, she received a valuable gift from a volunteer worker.
5. It looks like a thick straw.
6. Dirty water goes into the straw, and clean water comes out of it.
7. Isabel carries the straw everywhere.
8. Now, she does not get sick anymore.
9. She can go to school every day.
10. So, the straw is what is most valuable to Isabel.

Lesson **2**

단어 TEST Step 1   p.26

01 문지르다, 비비다	02 방어하다	03 밤
04 벌집	05 수용하다, 지니다	06 믿을 수 없는
07 위험에 처한, 멸종 위기의		08 북극의
09 여윈, 두께가 얇은	10 줄무늬	11 제공하다
12 전체의	13 남성의, 수컷의	14 교환하다
15 살, 고기	16 ~에 민감한, 예민한	
17 멀리 떨어진	18 폐	19 호흡하다
20 수중의, 물속의	21 낮잠	22 보호하다
23 여성의, 암컷의	24 사회적인, 사교적인	
25 나타나다, (글 속에) 나오다		26 화학물질
27 ~을 제외하고	28 극심하게	29 ~을 포함하여
30 십억	31 거의 ~않다	32 무게가 나가다
33 군락, 군집	34 거주자	35 전달하다
36 어려움을 겪다	37 암기하다	
38 어디선지 모르게, 느닷없이		39 비싼 값을 치르다
40 서로	41 ~을 지켜보다, ~을 감시하다	
42 표정이 우울하다	43 경청하다	

단어 TEST Step 2   p.27

01 stripe	02 Arctic	03 skinny
04 sensitive	05 beehive	06 appear
07 chemical	08 hold	09 unbelievable
10 flesh	11 nap	12 resident
13 faraway	14 chestnut	15 except
16 protect	17 extremely	18 including
19 endangered	20 billion	21 hardly
22 weigh	23 colony	24 entire
25 male	26 defend	27 rub
28 female	29 lung	30 breathe
31 underwater	32 produce	33 exchange
34 million	35 lay eggs	
36 out of nowhere		37 one another
38 keep an eye on		39 learn by heart
40 have a hard time		41 look after
42 be all ears	43 have a long face	

단어 TEST Step 3   p.28

1 weigh, 무게가 나가다 2 defend, 방어하다
3 Arctic, 북극의 4 beehive, 벌집 5 nap, 낮잠
6 skinny, 여윈 7 breathe, 호흡하다 8 stripe, 줄무늬

9 choose, 고르다　10 resident, 거주자

11 prefer, 선호하다　12 watermelon, 수박

13 insect, 곤충　14 colony, 군락, 군집

15 exchange, 교환　16 endangered, 위험에 처한

대화문 TEST Step 1　p.29~30

Listen – Listen and Answer – Dialog 1

how, like / great, having a lot of / Me, show, great / By the way, decide / yet, Which, think, better, swimming / hiking, see wild, insects / join, birds, insects / heard, guide

Listen – Listen and Answer – Dialog 2

look, chestnut, the oldest, woods / tell, how old it is / about / ten times, age / beehive up / guess, bees live / guess, big enough, hold over / Unbelievable

Listen More - Listen and choose.

take, look at / What, for / trying, choose, story / What's, about / future / tell, more about / endangered animals, Arctic areas / sounds / Which picture, think, better / showing, skinny

Speak – Talk in groups.

Which, like better / like, better, friendly, How about / like, better / Me, much cleaner

Speak – Talk in pairs.

are, drawing / elephant / animal / tell me more about / big, that has

My Speaking Portfolio Step 1

1. come, woods, destroy, lost, where

2. scared whenever, cross, almost hit, understand why, in such a hurry

3. terrible stomachache, ate something strange, what, threw into

4. get lost, too dark, too bright, which way to fly

Wrap Up - Listening & Speaking ❺

do, free time / listen to, like / Which, like better / prefer / sounds more exciting

---

대화문 TEST Step 2　p.31~32

Listen – Listen and Answer – Dialog 1

B: Amber, how do you like the camp?

G: It's great. I'm having a lot of fun.

B: Me, too. The talent show last night was really great.

G: Yeah. By the way, did you decide on the afternoon program?

B: No, I haven't yet. Which do you think is better, hiking or swimming?

G: I'll go hiking because we can see wild birds and insects in the woods.

B: I'll join you. I like birds and insects.

G: Great. I heard we'll have a hiking guide.

B: Sounds good.

Listen – Listen and Answer – Dialog 2

W: Everyone, look at this chestnut tree. This is the oldest tree in these woods.

B: Can you tell me how old it is?

W: It's about 150 years old.

B: Wow! It's ten times my age.

G: Ms. Oh, is that a beehive up in the tree?

W: Yes. Can you guess how many bees live there?

G: 500 bees?

W: Good guess, but it's big enough to hold over 50,000 bees.

B, G: Unbelievable!

Listen More - Listen and choose.

B: Sora, can you take a look at these pictures?

G: What are these for?

B: I'm trying to choose a picture for my story in the school newspaper.

G: What's your story about?

B: Nature's future.

G: Can you tell me more about it?

B: It's about endangered animals in the Arctic areas.

G: That sounds interesting.

B: Which picture do you think is better?

G: I like the one showing a skinny polar bear.

Speak – Talk in groups.

A: Which do like better, dogs or cats?

B: I like dogs better. They are more friendly. How about you?

C: I like cats better.

D: Me, too. Cats are much cleaner than dogs.

Speak – Talk in pairs.

A: What are you drawing?

B: An elephant.

A: What's an elephant?

B: It's an animal.

A: Can you tell me more about it?

B: It's a big animal that has a long nose and big ears.

My Speaking Portfolio Step 1

1. People come to the woods and destroy the forest. Many of my friends have lost their homes. I don't know where to go.

2. I get scared whenever I have to cross a big street. This morning I was almost hit. I don't understand why people are in such a hurry.

3. I have a terrible stomachache. I ate something strange. I think it's what someone threw into the sea.

4. Sometimes I get lost not because it's too dark but because it's too bright. When lights are too bright, I can't tell which way to fly.

Wrap Up - Listening & Speaking ❺

G: What do you do in your free time?

B: I listen to music like EDM or hip-hop.

G: Which do you like better?

B: I prefer hip-hop.

G: Why?

B: Well, it sounds more exciting.

본문 TEST Step 1 — p.33~34

01 Amazing Ants
02 project, has chosen, insects
03 very social   04 as old
05 appear, stories
06 use, chemical, communicate
07 guess what, are   08 answer, ants
09 share with, what, learned
10 How Many, on   11 out of nowhere
12 Like, except, extremely, including
13 As of, over, billion   14 how about
15 According to, about, every
16 hardly, anything, heavy, weighing
17 Is, Like
18 colonies, lots, residents living
19 Within, three different types
20 what, entire, lay
21 type, male, produce
22 third type, worker
23 like caring, defending, collecting
24 How Communicate
25 Though, like humans, actually
26 called, communicate with, another
27 By using, exchange information
28 touch for communication
29 For, by rubbing, on
30 Since, covered with, smallest
31 FUN FACTS, ANTS   32 live up to
33 carry, times, body weight
34 lungs, breathe through   35 ant, stomachs

36 One, itself, other, with
37 Most ants, live, underwater

본문 TEST Step 2 — p.35~36

01 Amazing Ants
02 For the science project, has chosen, special insects
03 social   04 as old as
05 appear, Aesop's stories
06 a special chemical, communicate
07 guess what they are   08 the answer, ants
09 share with, what, have learned
10 How Many Ants, on
11 out of nowhere
12 Like humans, except, extremely, including Antarctica
13 As of 2018, over, billion people
14 how about
15 According to scientists, for every human
16 hardly weighs anything, as heavy as, being weighing
17 Is, Like
18 which have, residents living
19 Within, colony, three different types
20 what she does, lay eggs
21 second type, male, produce these eggs
22 The third type, worker
23 like caring for, defending, collecting
24 How, Communicate
25 Though, like humans, actually have
26 called, to communicate with one another
27 By using, exchange information, danger
28 touch for communication
29 For example, by rubbing, on its neighbor
30 covered with, even the smallest touch
31 FUN FACTS   32 live up to
33 carry things, 50 times their own body weight
34 breathe through small holes
35 two stomachs
36 One, for itself, the other, share with
37 Most ants, underwater

p.37~38

1 놀라운 개미

2 과학 프로젝트를 위해, 우리 모둠은 매우 특별한 곤충을 선택했습니다.

3 그들은 매우 사회적입니다.

4 그들은 티라노사우루스만큼 오래되었습니다.

5 그들은 이솝 이야기에 등장합니다.

6 그들은 의사소통하기 위해 특별한 화학물질을 사용합니다.

7 그들이 어떤 곤충인지 추측할 수 있나요?

8 네. 정답은 개미입니다.

9 저희들은 이 곤충에 관해 알게 된 것을 여러분과 함께 나누고 싶습니다.

10 지구상에는 얼마나 많은 개미가 있을까?

11 우리는 종종 난데없이 나타나는 개미들을 본다.

12 인간처럼, 개미도 남극을 포함한 일부 극도로 추운 곳을 제외한 전 세계 거의 모든 곳에 살고 있다.

13 2018년 현재, 지구상에 70억이 넘는 인구가 있었다.

14 그렇다면, 개미는 어떨까?

15 과학자들에 의하면, 세상에는 사람 한 명당 약 백만 마리의 개미가 있다.

16 개미 한 마리는 거의 무게가 나가지 않지만 백만 마리의 개미는 체중이 약 62kg인 사람 한 명과 무게가 같다.

17 개미 사회는 어떠할까?

18 개미는 많은 거주자가 함께 사는 군집을 이루어 산다.

19 군집 안에는 보통 세 가지 다른 종류의 개미가 있다.

20 여왕개미가 있고, 그녀가 평생 하는 일은 알을 낳는 것이다.

21 두 번째 종류는 여왕이 알을 낳는 것을 돕는 수개미이다.

22 세 번째 종류는 일개미이다.

23 일개미는 모두 암컷인데, 알을 돌보고, 군집을 방어하며, 먹이를 모으는 것과 같은 매우 중요한 일을 한다.

24 개미는 어떻게 의사소통할까?

25 개미들이 인간처럼 말을 하는 것은 아니지만, 그들은 실제로 '언어'를 가지고 있다.

26 개미는 서로 소통하기 위해 '페로몬'이라고 불리는 화학물질을 분비한다.

27 그 화학물질을 사용하여 그들은 먹이나 위험에 관한 정보를 교환할 수 있다.

28 개미는 또한 의사소통을 위해 접촉을 이용한다.

29 예를 들어, 먹이를 발견할 경우 개미는 자기 몸을 이웃의 개미에게 문질러서 좋은 소식을 전달한다.

30 개미는 (자극에) 매우 민감한 털로 덮인 다리가 있기 때문에, 아주 미세한 접촉도 감지할 수 있다.

31 개미에 관한 재미있는 사실

32 01 어떤 여왕개미는 30년까지 살 수 있다.

33 02 어떤 개미들은 자기 몸무게의 50배에 달하는 것을 들 수 있다.

34 03 개미는 폐가 없지만, 몸에 있는 작은 구멍을 통해 호흡한다.

35 04 개미는 위가 두 개 있다.

36 하나에는 자신의 먹이를 저장하고 다른 하나에는 다른 개미들과 함께 나눌 먹이를 저장한다.

37 05 대부분의 개미는 수영할 수 있고 물속에서 24시간 동안 살 수 있다.

p.39~43

1 The Amazing Ants

2 For the science project, our group has chosen very special insects.

3 They are very social.

4 They are as old as the T-Rex.

5 They appear in Aesop's stories.

6 They use a special chemical to communicate.

7 Can you guess what they are?

8 Yes, the answer is ants.

9 We want to share with you what we have learned about these insects.

10 How Many Ants Are on Earth?

11 We often see ants come out of nowhere.

12 Like humans, they live almost everywhere in the world, except a few extremely cold places including Antarctica.

13 As of 2018, there were over 7 billion people on Earth.

14 Then, how about ants?

15 According to scientists, there are about one million ants for every human in the world.

16 Though each ant hardly weighs anything, one million ants are as heavy as a human being weighing about 62 kilograms.

17 What Is the Ant Society Like?

18 Ants live in colonies which have lots of residents living together.

19 Within a colony, there are usually three different types of ants.

20 There is the queen, and what she does her entire life is lay eggs.

21 The second type of ant is the male that helps the queen produce these eggs.

22 The third type of ant is the worker.

23 Worker ants are all female and do very important jobs, like caring for eggs, defending the colony, and collecting food.

24 How Do Ants Communicate?

25 Though ants do not speak like humans, they actually have a "language."

26 Ants produce a chemical called a pheromone to

communicate with one another.

27 By using the chemical, they can exchange information about food or danger.

28 Ants also use touch for communication.

29 For example, if an ant finds food, it passes on the good news by rubbing its body on its neighbor.

30 Since an ant has legs covered with very sensitive hairs, it can sense even the smallest touch.

31 FUN FACTS ABOUT ANTS

32 01 Some Queen ants live up to 30 years.

33 02 Some ants can carry things that are 50 times their own body weight.

34 03 Ants do not have lungs but breathe through small holes in their bodies.

35 04 An ant has two stomachs.

36 One stomach holds food for itself, and the other holds food to share with others.

37 05 Most ants can swim and live 24 hours underwater.

구석구석지문 TEST Step 1 p.44

Communicate: Speak

1. Which, prefer

2. choose the toppings I like, How about

3. like, better

4. Me, too, meat lover

My Speaking Portfolio

1. are easily found, have many plants

2. lives up to, only live for

3. from, to, to collect food

4. hundreds of, a small amount of

5. By moving around, help, grow

Wrap Up - Reading

1. seem to, all the time

2. not true

3. rest by taking, about, a day

4. Each of, lasts, about a minute

5. for about four hours each day

6. On the other hand, fall asleep, at a time

7. that, for about nine hours each day

8. In short, like, though, in a different way

구석구석지문 TEST Step 2 p.45

Communicate: Speak

1. A: Which do you prefer, pizza or fried chicken?

2. B: I like pizza better. I can choose the toppings I like. How about you?

3. A: I like fried chicken better.

4. C: Me, too. I'm a meat lover.

My Speaking Portfolio

1. M: Honeybees are easily found in warm places which have many plants and flowers.

2. A queen lives up to five years, but worker bees only live for about seven weeks.

3. Honeybees go from flower to flower to collect food.

4. A worker bee makes hundreds of trips to produce a small amount of honey.

5. By moving around, honeybees help plants grow.

Wrap Up - Reading

1. Ants seem to be busy all the time and never rest.

2. But this is not true.

3. Worker ants rest by taking very short naps about 250 times a day.

4. Each of these naps lasts only about a minute.

5. This means that the worker ants sleep for about four hours each day.

6. On the other hand, queen ants fall asleep 90 times a day, and they sleep for about six minutes at a time.

7. This means that they sleep for about nine hours each day.

8. In short, ants sleep and rest just like us though they do so in a different way.

Lesson S

단어 TEST Step 1
p.46

01 ~을 들어 올리다	02 골프공	03 같은
04 건강	05 대답하다	06 중요하다
07 채우다, 메우다	08 굴러가다	
09 열려 있는, 막혀 있지 않은		10 (비어 있는) 공간
11 병, 항아리	12 잃어버리다	13 서 있다
14 가득 찬	15 붓다, 따르다	
16 ~으로 보이다, ~(인 것) 같다, ~(인 것으)로 생각되다		
17 공간, 여지	18 흔들다	
19 비록 ~일지라도, ~이지만		
20 ~을 높이 평가하다, 중시하다		21 소비하다, 쓰다
22 갑자기	23 ~을 꺼내다	24 ~을 집어올리다
25 ~ 한 병	26 ~ 밖으로, ~로부터	
27 ~에 신경을 쓰다, ~을 돌보다		28 A를 B에 붓다
29 A를 B하는 데 소비하다[쓰다]		
30 목적어가 ~하는 것을 보다		31 B로 A를 채우다

단어 TEST Step 2
p.47

01 golf ball	02 health	03 matter
04 open	05 raise	06 fill
07 shake	08 pour	09 full
10 space	11 reply	12 value
13 same	14 stand	15 jar
16 seem	17 lose	18 though
19 suddenly	20 roll	21 spend
22 room	23 out of	24 pick up
25 a bottle of ~	26 take out	27 pour A into B
28 watch+목적어+동사원형(ing)		29 spend A on B
30 take care of ~	31 fill A with B	

단어 TEST Step 3
p.48

1 matter, 중요하다   2 space, (비어 있는) 공간

3 fill, 채우다, 메우다   4 suddenly, 갑자기   5 full, 가득 찬

6 spend, 소비하다   7 reply, 대답하다   8 shake, 흔들다

9 jar, 병, 항아리   10 lose, 잃어버리다

11 value, ~을 높이 평가하다, 중시하다

12 take care of ~, ~을 돌보다, ~에 신경을 쓰다

본문 TEST Step 1
p.49~50

01 Full Jar	02 stood before, class
03 jar, on, desk	04 picked up, fill, with
05 asked, jar full	06 They all said
07 out of, poured, into	
08 little, rolled into, between	
09 same question, answer, from	
10 took out, poured, into	11 fill, once more, full
12 All the, replied	
13 Suddenly, took, out of	
14 poured, watched, fill, spaces	
15 understand that, just like	
16 what is most important	17 Even, is lost, full
18 stones, other, valued, like	
19 all the small things	
20 there's no room for	21 same goes for
22 spend, on, room, what	
23 Take care, things, matter	
24 sitting, raised, mean	
25 smiled, you asked	26 seem full, room for

본문 TEST Step 2
p.51~52

01 Full Jar	02 before his class
03 a large jar, teacher's desk	
04 picked up, fill, with, from the bag	
05 Is the jar full	06 They all
07 a box of, out of the bag, poured them into	
08 a little, rolled into, open areas	
09 the same question, the same answer	
10 took out, poured, into	
11 watched, fill, once more, full	
12 All the students replied	
13 Suddenly, out of the bag	
14 poured, into, fill the spaces	
15 want, understand, is just like	
16 what is most important, health, dreams	
17 Even when, is lost	18 valued, like
19 all the small things	
20 put, into, there's no room for	
21 The same goes for	
22 spend, on, room, what is really important	
23 Take care of, matter	
24 sitting, raised, What, mean	
25 smiled, you asked	26 seem full, room for

1 가득 찬 병

2 Jenkins 선생님이 교실 앞에 섰다.

3 교탁 위에는 큰 병과 커다란 가방이 놓여 있었다.

4 수업이 시작하자, 선생님은 병을 집어 들고 가방에서 꺼낸 골프공으로 채우기 시작했다.

5 그는 학생들에게 "병이 가득 찼나요?"라고 질문했다.

6 학생들은 모두 "예."라고 대답했다.

7 선생님은 가방에서 작은 돌 한 상자를 끄집어내어 병 안에 부었다.

8 그가 병을 살짝 흔들자, 돌들이 골프공 사이의 틈새로 굴러 들어갔다.

9 그는 같은 질문을 했고 학생들에게서 같은 대답을 들었다.

10 그런 다음, 선생님은 모래 병을 꺼내 병 안에 부었다.

11 모래가 돌 사이의 공간을 채우는 것을 지켜보고 나서 그는 "이 병이 가득 찼나요?"라고 한 번 더 물었다.

12 모든 학생들이 "예."라고 답했다.

13 갑자기 Jenkins 선생님은 가방에서 사과 주스 한 캔을 꺼냈다.

14 그는 사과 주스를 병 안에 부었고, 학생들은 주스가 모래 사이의 빈틈을 채우는 것을 지켜보았다.

15 "자, 이제," 선생님이 말했다. "여러분의 인생이 병과 같다는 것을 이해하기 바랍니다.

16 골프공은 여러분의 가족, 친구, 건강, 꿈과 같이 인생에서 가장 중요한 것이랍니다.

17 다른 모든 것을 잃게 될 때라도 여러분의 인생은 여전히 가득 차 있을 수 있습니다.

18 돌은 여러분의 직업, 집, 자동차처럼 사람들이 소중하게 여기는 다른 것들에 해당합니다.

19 모래는 온갖 사소한 것들이랍니다."

20 "만약 병에 모래를 먼저 채우면, 돌이나 골프공을 채울 공간이 없게 됩니다.

21 인생도 똑같습니다.

22 여러분의 시간과 에너지를 사소한 것에 모두 허비한다면 여러분에게 진정으로 중요한 것을 채울 공간은 절대로 없을 겁니다.

23 골프공, 즉 정말로 중요한 것들을 먼저 챙기기 바랍니다."라고 선생님이 말했다.

24 뒤에 앉아 있던 학생 하나가 손을 들고 질문했다. "사과 주스는 무슨 뜻입니까?"

25 Jenkins 선생님은 미소 지었다. "질문을 해줘서 기뻐요.

26 그것은, 여러분의 인생이 가득 차 보일지라도 친구와 시원한 음료수를 나눌 여유는 늘 있다는 점을 보여 줍니다."

1 The Full Jar

2 Mr. Jenkins stood before his class.

3 He had a large jar and a big bag on the teacher's desk.

4 When the class began, he picked up the jar and started to fill it with golf balls from the bag.

5 He asked the students, "Is the jar full?"

6 They all said, "Yes."

7 The teacher took a box of small stones out of the bag and poured them into the jar.

8 He shook the jar a little, and the stones rolled into the open areas between the golf balls.

9 He asked the same question and got the same answer from his students.

10 Next, the teacher took out a bottle of sand and poured it into the jar.

11 After he watched the sand fill the spaces between the stones, he asked once more, "Is the jar full?"

12 All the students replied, "Yes."

13 Suddenly Mr. Jenkins took a can of apple juice out of the bag.

14 He poured the apple juice into the jar, and his students watched it fill the spaces in the sand.

15 "Now," the teacher said, "I want you to understand that your life is just like the jar.

16 The golf balls are what is most important in life: your family, your friends, your health, and your dreams.

17 Even when everything else is lost, your life can still be full.

18 The stones are the other things valued by people, like your job, your house, and your car.

19 The sand is all the small things."

20 "If you put the sand into the jar first," he said, "there's no room for the stones or the golf balls.

21 The same goes for life.

22 If you spend all your time and energy on the small things, you will never have room for what is really important to you.

23 Take care of the balls first — the things that really matter."

24 One student sitting in the back raised her hand and asked, "What does the apple juice mean?"

25 Mr. Jenkins smiled, "I'm glad you asked.

26 It just shows that though your life may seem full, there's always room for a cool drink with a friend."

Lesson 3

단어 TEST Step 1 · p.59

01 인공적인	02 성가시게 하다	03 원인
04 안심이 되는	05 우울한	06 우정
07 도움이 되는	08 긍정적인	09 스트레스 받은
10 개선하다	11 외모	12 소리를 지르다
13 유명한	14 덜다	15 주장하다
16 인내하는	17 화학물질	18 그 외에도
19 방법	20 흔한	21 불안한
22 지루한	23 문제가 되다, 중요하다	
24 무서운	25 생산하다	26 효과
27 집중하다	28 짠	29 졸리는
30 깔끔한	31 효과가 있다	32 학교 공부
33 매체	34 남겨두다	35 ~하곤 했다
36 ~ 덕택에	37 동시에	38 우울하게 느끼다
39 ~에 따르면	40 의미가 통하다	
41 ~을 다루다, 처리하다		42 ~하는 한
43 ~에 어려움이 있다		

단어 TEST Step 2 · p.60

01 media	02 relieved	03 produce
04 argue	05 helpful	06 sleepy
07 besides	08 focus	09 improve
10 scream	11 appearance	12 matter
13 chemical	14 scary	15 common
16 leave	17 nervous	18 stressed
19 patient	20 method	21 well-known
22 relieve	23 boring	24 salty
25 tidy	26 work	27 gloomy
28 artificial	29 bother	30 cause
31 positive	32 effect	33 schoolwork
34 friendship	35 according to	36 in other ways
37 as long as	38 forget to	
39 at the same time		40 instead of
41 deal with	42 break a promise	
43 used to		

단어 TEST Step 3 · p.61

1 friendship, 우정   2 method, 방법
3 well-known, 유명한   4 artificial, 인공적인
5 cause, 원인   6 effect, 효과   7 gloomy, 우울한
8 improve, 개선하다   9 positive, 긍정적인

10 argue, 주장하다   11 tidy, 깔끔한
12 common, 흔한   13 appearance, 외모
14 bother, 성가시게 하다   15 scream, 소리를 지르다
16 focus, 집중하다

대화문 TEST Step 1 · p.62~63

Listen and Answer – Dialog 1
talk, about, What makes, feel, stressed, About, answered, As, see, common cause, Over half of, stresses, Problems, took, with, Next, worries, get stressed because of, appearance

Listen and Answer – Dialog 2
What, doing / studying for, Grades / used to, way, too / know / a little stress, helpful / What makes, say / got stressed, at the same time, focus, try harder / help, in other ways / improve, memory

Listen More – Listen and choose.
talk, have to decide / Let, show, designs / choose, short sleeves / What makes, say / Because, wear / makes sense, about / cute / expensive, best one

Speak – Talk in groups.
like to talk, One, most well-known paintings

Speak – Talk in pairs.
spend / makes, say / make, around the world / makes sense

My Speaking Portfolio Step 3
like, good ways to relax, upset, take deep breaths, counting, drinking, Lastly, thinking, thoughts

Wrap Up – Listening & Speaking 1
talked, foods, are good, like to, healthy eating, slowly, to stop eating, full

Wrap Up – Listening & Speaking 2
don't, make / make / basketball, better idea / makes, say / we need

대화문 TEST Step 2 · p.64~65

Listen and Answer – Dialog 1
W: Today, I'd like to talk to you about teen stress. What makes you feel the most stressed? About 9,000 teens answered this question. As you can see, schoolwork was the most common cause of stress. Over half of the students said schoolwork stresses them the most. Problems with friends took second place with 15.3%. Next came family and worries about the future. 8.2% of the

students said they get stressed because of their appearance.

W: What are you doing, Oliver?

B: I'm studying for the math test, Mom. Grades stress me out.

W: I understand. I used to feel that way, too.

B: Really? I didn't know that.

W: Yeah, but a little stress was helpful for me.

B: What makes you say that?

W: I got stressed when I had an exam, but at the same time it made me focus and try harder.

B: I see. Did stress help you in other ways?

W: Yes, it helped improve my memory.

B1: Today, let's talk about the class T-shirt. We have to decide on the design.

G: Let me show you some designs on the screen.

B2: We have to choose a T-shirt with short sleeves.

B1: What makes you say that?

B2: Because we'll wear the T-shirt on Sports Day. It's in June.

G: That makes sense. What about this green one?

B2: I like it. The bee on the T-shirt is so cute.

G: And it's not expensive.

B1: Yes. I think it's the best one.

Hi. Today, I'd like to talk about Frida Kahlo. She was a Mexican painter. One of her most well-known paintings is *Viva la Vida*.

A: I want to spend more time on social media.

B: What makes you say that?

A: I can make more friends from around the world.

B: That makes sense.

I'd like to talk about some good ways to relax when you get upset. First, it's good to take deep breaths. Second, counting to ten is a great idea. Also, drinking cold water helps. Lastly, thinking happy thoughts can help.

W: Hello, teens. I'm Dr. Broccoli. Last time, I talked about different foods that are good for your health. Today, I'd like to talk about healthy eating habits. First, try to eat slowly. Second, it's important to stop eating when you're full.

G: Why don't we make a sport club?

B: Sounds good. Let's make a baseball club.

G: Well, I think a basketball club is a better idea.

B: What makes you say that?

G: All we need is a ball to play basketball.

---

01 Goodbye, Stress

02 spend, with, feel low

03 Others, feel better

04 Still others, while   05 How, deal with

06 Here, suggest different ways

07 by saying, breaking, arguing

08 When, happens, horror   09 so, that, lot

10 screaming, top, lungs, feel

11 thanks, scenes, effects, bothers

12 been using, method, works

13 graduated from, ago

14 with, been looking for

15 stressed out, going fishing

16 gets upset, catch, fish

17 While, so, that, behind

18 Besides, be patient

19 sure, focusing on, forget

20 second-year, way, free from

21 seems, like, for, reason

22 because, number-one way, better

23 so, that, looks glommy

24 As, feel like, relieving

25 When, tidy, looks brighter   26 Let, tell, what

27 stressed, things, has, work

28 under stress, writes, calendar

29 takes, out, herself

30 reads, watches, talks

31 matter, as long as   32 been writing, on

33 Which methods, work for

34 Try, yourself, way, stress

---

01 Say Goodbye

02 spend time with, feel low

03 Others, to feel better

04 Still others, for a while   05 deal with

06 suggest different ways

07 saying, breaking, arguing over

08 When this happens   09 so, that

---

10 at the top of my lungs helps, feel

11 thanks to, scenes, effects, what bothers me

12 I've been using, several months, works

13 graduated from, ago

14 he's been looking for

15 he's stressed out, always tries, by going fishing

16 gets upset

17 so, that, can leave, worries behind

18 Besides, to be patient

19 focusing on, forget something else

20 second-year, to stay free from

21 seems to like, for a good reason

22 number-one way to make

23 so, that, looks gloomy

24 As, feel like, relieving

25 looks tidy, looks brighter   26 Let, what

27 all the things she has to do at work

28 she's under stress

29 takes some time out

30 reads, watches, talks

31 matter what, as long as

32 I've been writing, feel much better

33 Which, work for you

34 to say goodbye to stress

---

1 스트레스와 이별하라

2 어떤 사람들은 울적할 때 친구들과 시간을 보낸다.

3 다른 사람들은 기분이 좋아지도록 특별한 음식을 먹는다.

4 또 다른 사람들은 그저 잠시 잠을 자기도 한다.

5 여러분은 스트레스를 어떻게 다루는가?

6 여기 다양한 방법을 제안하는 사람들의 이야기가 있다.

7 때때로 내 친구들은 나에 관해 나쁜 말을 하거나, 약속을 어기거나, 혹은 사소한 일을 두고 언쟁을 하며 내게 스트레스를 준다.

8 이럴 때, 나는 공포 영화를 본다!

9 훌륭한 공포 영화는 너무 무서워서 나는 소리를 많이 지르게 된다.

10 있는 힘껏 소리 지르는 것은 내 기분이 나아지는 데 도움이 된다고 생각한다.

11 또한, 무서운 장면과 음향 효과 덕분에 나를 괴롭히는 것들을 잊을 수 있다.

12 나는 지난 몇 달간 이 방법을 써 오고 있는데, 효과가 아주 좋다.

13 우리 삼촌은 2년 전에 대학을 졸업했다.

14 삼촌은 우리 가족과 함께 살고 있고, 얼마 전부터 직장을 구하고 있다.

15 나는 삼촌이 스트레스를 받고 있지만 낚시를 다니며 긍정적으로 지내려고 항상 노력한다는 것을 안다.

16 물고기를 한 마리도 잡지 못했을 때에도 삼촌은 절대 속상해하지 않는다.

17 삼촌은 "낚시하는 동안, 나는 아주 몰입해서 모든 걱정을 잊을 수 있어.

18 게다가 낚시는 나에게 인내를 가르쳐 준단다."라고 말한다.

19 한 가지 일에 집중하는 것이 다른 무언가를 잊는 데 도움이 된다고 나는 확신한다.

20 고등학교 2학년인 우리 누나에게는 스트레스에서 벗어나는 훌륭한 방법이 있다.

21 누나가 학업 때문에 많은 스트레스를 받지만, 그럴 만한 이유로 우리 어머니는 그 상황을 좋아하시는 것 같다.

22 그것은 바로, 청소가 누나의 삶을 향상하는 최고의 방법이기 때문이다.

23 스트레스를 너무 많이 받아서 인생이 우울해 보일 때, 누나는 방을 청소한다.

24 누나는 "방을 청소하면서 스트레스도 해소되는 것 같아.

25 내 방이 깔끔해 보이면 내 삶도 더 밝아 보여."라고 말한다.

26 우리 어머니께서 스트레스를 어떻게 다루시는지 소개하려고 한다.

27 어머니는 직장과 집에서 해야 하는 온갖 일로 인해 스트레스를 받으신다.

28 스트레스를 받을 때면 어머니는 달력에 '나만의 시간'이라고 적으신다.

29 이것은 어머니 자신을 위해 잠깐 시간을 낸다는 의미이다.

30 어머니는 책을 읽거나, 영화를 보거나, 친구들과 이야기를 나누신다.

31 어머니는 "내가 좋아하는 것이라면, 무엇을 하는지는 별로 중요하지 않아.

32 나는 두 달째 달력에 '나만의 시간'을 적어 왔고, 기분이 훨씬 좋아졌어."라고 말씀하신다.

33 어떤 방법이 여러분에게 효과가 있을까?

34 이 아이디어 중 몇 개를 직접 해 보고, 스트레스와 이별하는 자신만의 최고의 방법을 찾아라.

---

1 Say Goodbye to Stress

2 Some people spend time with friends when they feel low.

3 Others eat special foods to feel better.

4 Still others simply sleep for a while.

5 How do you deal with stress?

6 Here are some stories about people who suggest different ways.

7 Sometimes my friends give me stress by saying bad things about me, breaking promises, or

arguing over small things.

8 When this happens, I watch horror movies!

9 Good horror movies are so scary that I scream a lot.

10 I guess that screaming at the top of my lungs helps me feel better.

11 Also, thanks to scary scenes and sound effects, I can forget about what bothers me.

12 I've been using this method for the past several months, and it really works.

13 My uncle graduated from college two years ago.

14 He lives with my family, and he's been looking for a job for some time.

15 I know that he's stressed out, but he always tries to be positive by going fishing.

16 He never gets upset when he doesn't catch any fish.

17 He says, "While I fish, I'm so focused that I can leave all my worries behind.

18 Besides, it teaches me to be patient."

19 I'm sure that focusing on one thing helps us forget about something else.

20 My sister, a second-year student in high school, has a wonderful way to stay free from stress.

21 She feels a lot of stress from schoolwork, but my mother seems to like the situation for a good reason.

22 It is because cleaning is my sister's number-one way to make life better!

23 When she's so stressed that her life looks gloomy, she cleans her room.

24 She says, "As I clean my room, I feel like I'm also relieving stress.

25 When my room looks tidy, my life looks brighter."

26 Let me tell you what my mother does about her stress.

27 She feels stressed by all the things she has to do at work and at home.

28 When she's under stress, she writes "Me Time" on her calendar.

29 This means she takes some time out for herself.

30 She reads a book, watches a movie, or talks with her friends.

31 She says, "It doesn't really matter what I do, as long as it's something I like.

32 I've been writing 'Me Time' on my calendar for two months, and I feel much better."

33 Which methods will work for you?

34 Try some of these ideas yourself, and find your best way to say goodbye to stress.

Words in Action

1. stress, out, me more stress
2. Worry less, never helps
3. a lot of work to do
4. change, change my hairstyle
5. caught, a few, to fish

Speak – Get ready.

1. spend, less time
2. Working on, can be, helpful
3. watching, better
4. Having, part-time job, bad

Wrap Up - Reading

1. stressed, feeling low
2. some good news
3. A few, steps, help
4. outdoors, plenty of
5. According to, produce, in your brain, makes you feel
6. Another thing you can do
7. produce even more, happiness chemical
8. Try, simple tips, feel low
9. Instead of sitting, front, run around

Words in Action

1. Tests stress me out. Grades give me more stress.
2. Worry less, smile more. Worry never helps.
3. I work hard. I have a lot of work to do.
4. I need a change. I will change my hairstyle.
5. I caught just a few fish. I want to fish some more.

Speak – Get ready.

1. I want to spend more/less time on social media.
2. Working on a team can be difficult/helpful.
3. I like watching/playing sports better.
4. Having a part-time job as a teen can be good/bad.

Wrap Up - Reading

1. Are you stressed or feeling low?
2. Then here is some good news for you.
3. A few simple steps can help you!
4. First, go outdoors and get plenty of sunlight.
5. According to scientists, this helps produce a special chemical in your brain, and the chemical makes you feel happy!
6. Another thing you can do is exercise.
7. This helps produce even more of the "happiness chemical."
8. Try these simple tips the next time you feel low.
9. Instead of sitting in front of a screen, go outdoors and run around in the sun!

MEMO

적중100

영어 기출 문제집

정답 및 해설

천재 | 이재영